THE VISION OF THE FIRM

ITS GOVERNANCE, OBLIGATIONS, AND ASPIRATIONS:

A TEXTBOOK ON THE ETHICS OF ORGANIZATIONS

TIMOTHY L. FORT, PhD, JD

Eveleigh Professor of Business Ethics
The Kelley School of Business
Indiana University

MAT# 41379421

© 2014 LEG, Inc. d/b/a West Academic
444 Cedar Street, Suite 700
St. Paul, MN 55101
1-877-888-1330
West, West Academic Publishing, and West Academic
are trademarks of West Publishing Corporation, used under license.
Printed in the United States of America

ISBN: 978-0-314-28649-9

DEDICATION

To my students whose studies have allowed me to be a teacher

———————

*To my mentors whose wisdom, generosity and belief in me
allowed me to be more than I knew I could be*

———————

*To my family who showed me what being a teacher looked like
from the time of my birth to this very day*

———————

And

———————

*To the Spirit(s) of this universe who so plainly
put this profession in my face that even someone
as dumb as me couldn't possibly miss it*

TABLE OF CONTENTS

THE VISION OF THE FIRM

ITS GOVERNANCE, OBLIGATIONS, AND ASPIRATIONS: A TEXTBOOK ON THE ETHICS OF ORGANIZATIONS

INTRODUCTION

I N TWENTY-SEVEN YEARS of teaching business ethics and corporate responsibility courses in business schools, I have often noted the wonderful number of excellent textbooks on the subject. I have used many of them in my classes. The natural question, then, is: why do we need another? I think we might for four reasons.

First, while I hope that philosophers keep a strong hand in the teaching and researching of this subject, my sense is that because of their success, along with some events in popular and business culture, the topic has become much more mainstream. That lends itself to a course being taught by those who do not have a normative background. Those fresh perspectives will help the field grow and the topic develop, but I do believe it would be a mistake to lose a normative core to an ethics course. At its heart, ethics is not only about describing what people do, but offering insights as to what they should do and what they can do.

At the same time, it is not so easy to jump into teaching Kant and Aristotle, and so, I want to offer a book that bridges more mainstream approaches with the foundational philosophical paradigms that established the field in business schools to begin with. Thus, I ground this book in three, influential normative frameworks from the field of business ethics itself: Shareholder Theory, Stakeholder Theory, and Virtue Ethics. I propose a way of applying these theories through a decision-making framework attentive to issues pertaining to cognitive biases in making ethical evaluations.

And then, rather than simply trying to resolve ethical issues or arguing about intractable dilemma, I also want to provide a model of how to create the ethical corporate cultures that make good decisions habitual rather than occasional. Indeed, while talking about dilemmas is a good way to get conversations started in classrooms, they are self-defeating strategies if not complemented by a wider set of considerations.

That's because dilemmas are dilemmas because there is no clear answer to them. If there were clear answers to them, they wouldn't be called dilemmas. If we spend most of our time in an ethics course talking about dilemmas, we will have great discussions but those discussions won't really get anywhere.

If the first reason seeks to connect a core of philosophical ethics to a more mainstream approach, the second reason is to add to the literature more materials that grounds business ethics from in the daily life of corporations: the Law. When I started my first tenure track position at the University of Michigan in 1994, I did a short survey to determine who taught ethics courses in the top twenty-five MBA programs in the United States. Lawyers taught the course more than anyone followed by philosophers and then others. While I think experts in Management and Strategy, as well as other disciplines, have increased their numbers teaching these courses, I also am pretty sure that there are a significant number of lawyers who still teach this course.

I also am very sure that legal requirements drive a good number of ethics initiatives in corporations today. A central reason why companies have ethics codes, mission statements, training programs, and other similar initiatives is because of court cases (such as the U.S. Supreme Court case, *Burlington Industries v. Ellerth*[1] that strongly incents sexual harassment awareness and internal processes to reduce the likelihood of harassment) or legislation such as the Federal Sentencing Guidelines that provide significant incentives for companies to adopt various kinds of compliance program that aim both toward legal performance as well as building ethical cultures. Sometimes, it is a direct requirement of a Deferred Prosecution Agreement.[2] In short, when the time comes for a company to develop an ethics initiative, the law often is lurking as an incentive for action

Businesspeople need to know the law. Many issues that the public calls "ethics" are legally prescribed rules concerning things such as conflicts of interests, or campaign disclosure, or other attempts to separate personal and official business duties. We can't pretend to do ethics for business without some attention to what business people think of when they hear the word ethics. At the same time, law and ethics are not coterminous. That is, we don't always meet our ethical obligations by complying with the law. If ignoring the law is one mistake, making the law coterminous with ethics makes the opposite mistake. Law is integral and will always be integral to understanding corporate responsibility, and it serves as motivation for companies to get serious about compliance and about ethics. Sometimes, the law does lag behind moral changes in a society. At times—such as with Civil Rights issues—the law has driven social change while other social institutions lag.

The third reason is to offer a book that tries to integrate many approaches to ethics today. Law and philosophy, of course, begin that effort, but these disciplines also need sciences such as psychology and biology. Our physical nature does inform and limit what we are capable of doing. We need to pay attention to that. As someone who tends to lean toward Aristotelian insights, I have often noticed that the term "community" is tossed around quite easily. The idea is that if we have a sense of how we are in community with each other—how we are connected with each other—we will care more about how we treat each other. I wholeheartedly agree, but our physical nature—in this case, our neurobiology—provides some limits to how many relationship we can process to understand that we are in community with each other. Those limitations are at the heart of what I

---

1   524 U.S. 742 (1998).

2   A deferred prosecution agreement is a voluntary alternative to a full judicial proceeding in which a prosecutor grants amnesty for a given offense in exchange for the defendant fulfilling certain requirements, which can take the form of fines, community service, victim reconciliation programs, therapeutic programs, or even a simple apology.

have called a mediating institutions approach to ethics: recognizing that it's pretty hard to be in a community with 100,000 other employees or six billion inhabitants of the earth. This book will try to account—undoubtedly, inadequately—for these limitations.

Finally, I want to offer a more sustained inquiry as to what we want corporations to be in the future. To achieve this, I include papers drawn primarily from a conference I hosted in 2010 on "The Vision of the Firm and Its Governance." These presentations offer ways to think about where business ethics is going and, I believe, is unique to current textbooks.

This approach to business ethics aims to clarify values, to create ethical awareness, to provide a decision-making model, and to address how to build ethical business cultures. I believe we owe it to students to be this aggressive. Consideration of ethical issues in business schools is now well-established. We need to be bold in how we challenge our students. I hope this current volume is one that challenges teachers and students alike.

PART I:

ETHICAL AWARENESS AND VALUE CLARIFICATIONS

SHORT, SIMPLE, STORIES AND SCENARIOS TO START

CHAPTER ONE

Story-Telling, Values Clarification, and Values Sharing

THE MOST NATURAL WAY for people to talk about ethics is to tell stories. Philosophical principles, legal rules, and evidence of social scientific bias are all good to know about and helpful in making decisions, but the way people tend to think and talk about ethics is to tell stories. Integral to telling stories, not surprisingly, is speaking. We learn much about ourselves when we speak about what is important to us and, of course, as we talk about our values with others. I'd like to start this book with two exercises in line with this view.

Exercise One: Your Story

Write a story about something that you saw in business that you thought was ethical. Make the story about someone you personally know (as a friend, relative or even yourself). Why was it ethical? Part I is about what happened. Part II is about why you think the event or action was ethical. Part II has three subparts.

a) Everyone agrees with your idea of the good.[3] So your idea can be evaluated, you must define your notion of the good and articulate it to another person. Feel free to draw upon your own experiences, religion, or study of philosophy in defining the good.

b) Someone reject your theory? Moreover, *be very careful to analyze the good you are defending and not the alternatives to the particular action.*

c) After considering a strong objection to your vision of the good, why is your theory still compelling?

One of the purposes of this assignment is to show you that there are a great number of ethical things occurring in life, including business, so that a person interested in being ethical is "not alone." Occasionally, I have had students who prepared a paper based on this assignment who wonder whether they have ever seen an ethical act in business! If you have that reaction, I encourage you to think through the matter again because I think you will be able to come up with something. Businesses depend on people keeping their promises; that itself has ethical content.

Another purpose of the paper is for students to really try to identify what the good is. The story and analysis doesn't have to be a terrific dilemma. Aristotle said that we

---

3   There are philosophical differences between "ethical" and "good" but at this point, I am not very concerned with them.

don't even think about most of our ethics actions; they're so much a part of our habits that we simply do them almost without thinking.

When I'm explaining this in class, I stop at this point and I say, you know, I've been talking here for 15 minutes or so, and no one yet has thrown something at me. And my guess is that most students haven't sat there agonizing over the decision of whether this is the point where I hurl that tomato at Fort or not. It's just something that you don't do. It is a habit of expected behavior. There is ethics in that. And so, the personal action does not have to be a grand dilemma. It can be a simple way of how human beings treat the other person.

As an example, let me tell you the story I presented during my freshman year of college when I received a variation of the assignment from Professor Stanley Hauer was. Please note that when I was assigned this paper, it was not for a business ethics class. Instead it was for a theological ethics class. Thus, while there is a business reference, it is not an example of a story about a business situation. But I do think it is easy to adapt the assignment to a business example.

My father was an attorney in a very small town (population 800) in western Illinois from 1949 until his death in 1998. When I was in high school, his secretary looked out onto the street on a bitterly cold afternoon (wind-chill more than forty degrees below zero) at the end of the workday to see a late middle-aged man wandering the streets without a coat. The man's parents, with whom he lived, had very recently passed away and he was now living alone. The man had done very little business with my father's law firm. Dad's secretary brought him over to the office and my father, after calling my mother, brought him out to the house for dinner.

The man was very depressed and frightened. He stayed overnight with us, never looking at my mother or me. He was afraid to return to his house because he thought that someone would kill him.

The next day, my father took him out to the house with an unloaded (unknown to our guest) German luger pistol smuggled out of World War II by one of my father's clients and given to Dad as a gift. Together Dad and this frightened man searched every room of the farm house and its outlying buildings. Finally, convinced that it was safe, the man agreed to stay.

Dad knew that that the previous twenty-four hours were just the tip of the iceberg. The deeper problem was that this man did not know how to navigate life. He didn't have friends. He didn't have anybody to talk to. Dad decided to take it upon himself to call the guy every day to check on him and to try to be a friend, to help him make friends, and to bring him into the community where he can make more friends.

So at 7:00 every morning, Dad would give him a call. How did last night go? Did you watch the game? How did you sleep? What are you going to do during the day? He called him every day for five years! For five years, my father picked up the phone at 7:00 AM and called this fellow and gradually brought him into the town, first for lunch and then to introduce him to some of the fellows at the restaurant who would have watched the game on TV the night before. The man never became a social butterfly but he grew to have friends, and he had a pretty happy rest of his life all because my father took the time to make those phone calls.

I very proudly handed my story in to my professor, who was a rigorous taskmaster. I got the assignment back from him about a week later, and at the bottom of the paper was a bad grade and the words, "what's so good about that" scrawled at the bottom. I was dumbfounded. What do you mean what's so good about that, I thought? It's obvious what's so good about that. But my lack of explanation was the point. You will likely write a moving story that is going to touch you in a way that writing about my father touched me. But, as my professor wanted me to do, then explain why your story demonstrates a good action.

With a few decades of retrospection, I would say now that it is a good thing for a person to help a vulnerable individual, as long as in doing so they do not make others vulnerable. For instance, if my father had put my mother and myself in a threatening situation, bringing the fellow home to spend the night with us may not have been a good thing. Absent that, helping the vulnerable would be a principle of the good.

What would be an objection to that principle? Let me tell you what it wouldn't be. An objection would not be that my father should have called a psychiatrist or a social worker so that this fellow could have some therapy. That may have been a reasonable alternative, but it *is* an alternative. It is not an objection to helping a vulnerable person. So an objection could be that we're in a Darwinian world where it's survival of the fittest (a term, by the way, that Darwin never used). Life is a survival of the fittest and we can't spend our time worrying about the vulnerable. We need to spend our time competing, and improving, and sometimes that means that people are going to have to fall by the wayside. I don't believe that statement, but that would be an objection to my principle. That's part 2-B.

Part 2-C then is why is your vision of the good still compelling? I would argue that evolutionary theory shows that species often survive by taking time to help and protect the vulnerable. This is one example of how to take a story that's going to personally resonate with you and then to provide a principled description of why it was good, an objection to the principle, and then why it's still compelling.

Exercise Two: Your Virtues

The second exercise is a bit harder to coordinate, but equally enlightening. Assume you and your classmates will form a for-profit company. Each of you will be an owner-operator, so there will be no differentiation between owner and employee. Then each person should nominate the values they would like to see that organization operate by. Or to put it another way, each person should state what virtues they think are important for the group. Or, to put it one more way, each person should nominate the characteristics they have seen in others that they admire. Philosophically, these three formulations of the exercise are not the same thing, but they are close enough for where we begin this text so as not to matter much. If everyone in your group does this, they will find out a few things.

First, the total number of different virtues will be about the same number as people nominating them, and perhaps a bit more. So if seventy people are nominating the virtues, you'll end up with seventy virtues, suggesting a tremendous variety of virtues that are important to individuals. Second, there will be strong agreement on five or six of the values. So, while there will be diversity, there will also be commonality.

I have run this exercise hundreds of times and the above paragraph replicates itself consistently. For that matter, the same core virtues tend to appear time and again, suggesting that there are some kinds of universal values that glue human beings together. This should give us some confidence that, as different as we are, there are still some common virtues that bind us together. But let me add three additional points that arise from this exercise.

One of those points is that I or any professor teaching an ethics course could come into the class and simply announce that, based on their research and education, they are able to identify the core virtues for humanity. If a professor does that, the reaction of the students, at least in their mind, is likely to be to give the middle finger to the professor. Just who the hell is s/he to tell me what my values are! I can decide them for myself, thank you very much. And this reaction is likely to be true *even if the students agree with the professor's statement of the core virtues.*

There is something to be learned here. It's likely to be true in business as well. When they set up their mission statements and values statements, companies can fall prey to the temptation to simply tell their employees what the company's values are. And sometimes they should so that employees can understand the company's history and culture. But I often tell executives in companies that they should ask the employees what they believe is important. Of course, there will be some idiosyncratic things—maybe that there should be annual 500% pay raises every year—but the core values aren't going to be that different. Moreover, there will be greater buy-in from employees—as with students—if they get to voice their beliefs rather than being told to accept and obey an authority's statement of virtues.

A second thing to be learned is that, most of the time, students don't have a lot of time to debate the virtue list. They either just nominate the virtues and their nominations are tabulated or an initial list of nominations is created and then the students vote on the top virtues. The results in my classes have been the same either way, but there will be overlaps among the various virtues. Are creativity and innovation the same thing? The meaning of these terms cries out for greater dialogue and yet, the opportunity to examine the matter is rarely presented. Companies will also state company values without a lot of discussion. But bringing these values to life requires that people talk about them. When they do, they tend to learn and inculcate them as well, which helps to build ethical culture. Here is an example of the importance of defining what a virtue really might mean.

"Honesty" tends to do very well in these surveys. But what is honesty? Suppose that one drove an old, beat-up car with well over 100,000 miles on it. After one had started the car up and gone for a drive, it started to jerk occasionally. Not every time, but often, and only after the car had been driven for a couple of hours. The time comes when you are ready to trade the car in for a new one. Assuming the car dealer doesn't ask you if there are any problems with the car, would you volunteer that there *might* be a problem with the car after driving if for a couple of hours? Some people might, but many would say that car dealers are big boys and girls with their own mechanics and can take care of themselves quite well. If they don't ask, I don't tell.

Now suppose that the person whom that car owner was selling the car to was not a car dealer, but your eighteen year-old nephew. There is a huge jump in the requirements of honesty because of the importance of the long-term quality of the relationship. The more one is in a relationship, the more that many virtues become even more important. Indeed, one could say that ethics are the rules and principles that sustain relationships, whether between a husband and a wife, an employer and an employee, or two nation-states. One must abide by certain principles in order to sustain the relationship; if one violates those principles, the relationship ends.

There is one final teaching that arises from this virtue exercise. Several virtues may conflict. Aristotle had a term for addressing this. He called it *phronesis*. It means judgment or wisdom. It looks at what virtue is particularly appropriate for a given situation.

Suppose a woman is dying a slow, painful death from an infection that had resulted from a malfunction of her dialysis equipment. The woman also loved Christmas and decorated her house from top to bottom, loving everything about the holiday, especially the music of the season since she was a church organist. A bit more than two weeks before Christmas found the woman on her deathbed and in an uncomfortable and slightly agitated state.

Her doctor entered the room and she asked the doctor if she would be able to go home for Christmas. Perhaps she was asking about going to a great beyond—some death-and-dying books translate a dying person's reference to "home" as that—but those with her thought she was asking to go back to her house. The doctor paused and said yes, the woman might well go home for Christmas. And for the first time in quite a while, the woman relaxed and rested.

Every person in the room knew the doctor had lied, but it may be the case that as good a virtue as honesty is, the most important one at that moment was compassion. That's *phronesis*. Without giving a green light to lie whenever convenient, there are, simply and complexly, times when each virtue gives way to the other. Figuring out when and why and how requires wisdom. It is an acquired skill. Skills are developed through practice, which suggests that becoming ethical is not simply an innate attribute of either "you are a good person or you are not," but instead, is the result of talking, discussing, and practicing.

These two, introductory exercises help us to become more aware of our own values, to clarify them, and to see that core values are often shared by others. The next chapter looks at how we can be blinded by our own biases in making ethical judgments.

———————————

Chapter 2

Cognitive Limitations in Awareness

A. Optics: How and What We See

MANY OF OUR MORAL DISAGREEMENTS arise from our seeing things differently[4]. If two people can't learn to describe what they see and to be able to understand what another person is seeing, then the only thing that will change in their debate will be the decibel level. Take a look at the following optical illusions and write down what you see and also look to see if you can understand what another person might be seeing as well.

---

4   *Rubin's Vase,* illustration based on the work of Danish Psychologist Edgar Rubin, in his two-volume work *Synsoplevede Figurer ("Visual Figures"). http://en.wikipedia.org/wiki/Rubin_vase.*

"My Wife and My Mother-in-Law"   *"Face in the Trees"*

These illusions are fun to play with[5]. When I first saw the Young Lady-Old Lady picture, I saw the young lady immediately and found it very difficult to adjust my perspective to see the old lady. But then I moved away from this illusion for a few years; when I came back to it, I could see the old lady clearly but had difficulty seeing the young lady. Maybe it is just because I grew older myself! But it is not unusual for us to clearly see one thing and struggle to see the other.

This may be fun, but it has ethical implications as well. If you see an old lady and another person sees a young lady, your argument as to who is right will get nowhere. You will just get louder and more frustrated in your disagreement unless one (or both) of you start to describe what s/he sees and then takes the time to try to see things from another's point of view.

For example, I know someone who was raised on a farm and who has always been sympathetic to the plight of farmers. For decades small farmers in particular found it very difficult to survive because the market prices of their products equaled or were lower than their production costs. Only government subsidies, themselves resented, kept many a farmer from going bankrupt. Many went bankrupt anyway.

---

5   "My Wife and My Mother-in-Law", a famous optical illusion. Appears in *Puck*, v. 78, no. 2018 (1915 Nov. 6), p. 11; 06 November 1915. "Face in the Trees", www.Face-in-trees-illusion_maniacworld_com.jpeg.

So when ethanol emerged as an alternative fuel to oil, the woman was enthused. She recognized that ethanol has its own environmental issues and receives its own subsidies that themselves are not sustainable. But to see market prices for corn and soybeans skyrocket felt like justice a long time in coming. That's the way she saw it.

She was startled, though, when an elderly in-law, raised in the city and who lived through the Great Depression and who has strong views about not wasting food, plopped an issue of a news magazine showing an ear of corn with a hose fueling a car and said "That's immoral." This relative was a very quiet, humble person, not prone to such declarations. For him, using food to fuel a car was simply awful. He saw the same thing she saw but in starkly different terms.

They could have both argued that each was right in their perspectives, but that just doesn't get very far in trying to understand each other or in coming to any kind of moral resolution. In these situations, the problem is that we have cognitive limitations that "prove" to us, rightly, that we are indeed right. Thus, one step of ethics is simply learning to describe what we see—akin to values clarification—and then learning to articulate to others what we are seeing and stopping to listen to what the other person is seeing.

B. Two Vignettes on "Seeing"

So, let's take this lesson in "seeing" and apply to actual legal/ethical situations. The first comes from the work of Lawrence Kohlberg, *The Story of Heinz*.[6]

> "A woman was near death from cancer. One drug might save her, a form of radiation a druggist in the same town had recently discovered. The druggist was charging $2,000.00, ten times what the drug cost him to make. The sick woman's husband, Heinz, went to everyone he knew to borrow the money, but he could only get together about half of what it cost. He told the druggist that his wife was dying and asked him to sell it cheaper or let him pay later. But the druggist said "no." The husband got desperate and broke into the man's store to steal the drug for his wife. Should the husband have done that? .... Why do you think so?"

Did Heinz do the right thing? How do you know what the right thing to do is? Should Heinz have used another way to get the drug? What would that have been? Was the druggist unethical? Did the druggist do anything illegal, that you can think of? Should laws require a pharmacist to provide drugs in situations like these? What would such a law look like?

---

6   Lawrence Kohlberg, page 19 (1981). San Francisco, CA: Harper & Row.

The Heinz case is a classic moral dilemma. There are at least two ways of seeing the issues in the case and once one is locked into just one of them, it becomes hard to see the other side. The following case is another dilemma, a real one drawn from a famous court case, *Mays v. Twigg*.

> ...The respondents, Ernest and Regina Twigg, have alleged that some ten years ago staff personnel at Hardee Memorial Hospital, Wauchula, switched their healthy newborn daughter with one born on approximately the same date to Robert Mays' late wife, Barbara, and that both couples went on to raise children not actually their own natural offspring. The child raised by the Twiggs, Arlena Beatrice, later died from a congenital heart condition. Shortly before Arlena's death the Twiggs learned, based on the child's blood type, that neither of them could have been her biological parent. Kimberly Mays was the only other white female in occupancy at Hardee Memorial Hospital at the time of Arlena's birth.

> Respondents began the underlying litigation by filing a "Petition for Order Compelling Blood Test to Confirm Paternity of Female Child," later substituting a complaint for declaratory relief. The amended complaint demands a declaration that Kimberly Mays is the Twiggs' natural biological child...

> Assuming that both the Twiggs and Mr. Mays are good parents, who should parent Kimberly? How someone "sees" this case is crucial to deciding it. If the mental viewing frame is about "parental rights," then it is likely the decision will hinge on the perception that this is a case of frustrated parental rights (the Twiggs). If one sees this case as one of rights associated with being a parent, then Kimberly should be raised by the Twiggs who had their daughter taken from them through no fault of their own. She is, officially, their daughter. But is seeing this through the lens of the rights of parents the best way to look at it? If someone "sees" the moral issue as focused on the best interests of the child, a different decision is likely. Doesn't parenting a child for ten years count for something as well? How would you resolve this case? How would you get each side to see the other's point of view? If you can do that—get each side to see the other point of view—does that provide any additional possible ways to resolve the case?

C. Cognitive Ethical Theories: Biases

Continuing with the theme that we all have limitations because of our human nature, many ethicists utilize psychology to identify cognitive limitations that create danger zones for us. Perhaps our desire to conform to the ways other see things puts our ethical judgments on the backburner. After all, human beings are social creatures—a point that will be re-visited throughout this book—and so we want to get along with those close to us, to fit in, to get along. And so we conform.

Or perhaps we separate our personal from our professional lives. We may believe that we should be compassionate and even altruistic when it comes to our friends, families, and neighbors, but when it comes to business, well, that's a different story. Athletes are a great example of this. The headhunting baseball pitcher or the fiercest middle linebacker may be a terror on the field, putting the health and well-being of an opponent in real jeopardy, but be a gentle, cuddly fellow off the field. There is a role to play that pushes to the side day-to-day moral sentiments.

Just as with conformity, there is a rationale for this. There is business to be done and rules to be followed while playing that game. The issues with role morality is how far one goes with it and just how much the role requires the jettisoning of common-sense ethics. Does being a baseball pitcher who throws brush back pitches require moving the hitter back off the plate or, perhaps, evening plunking him in the ribs, or does it mean aiming a 100 MPH fastball at the hitter's temple? Being a middle linebacker does require hard-hitting; does it require twisting a running back's ankle in a pile-up? Sometimes, people use role morality to go too far and in businesses less extreme that sports, one might hear a worker say that business-is-business not so much because the role really requires the exclusion of moral issues, but simply as an excuse not to factor them in. Laziness rather than role morality is really the issue.

These are two examples of how cognitive limitations can reduce the scope of our actions. The following article provides a much more in-depth assessment of common cognitive limitations that impact business decision-making.

Avoiding Ethical Danger Zones[7]

David Messick, Max Bazerman, & Lisa Stewart

Introduction

Today's business leaders face a number of complex ethical challenges that impact themselves, their businesses, and other stakeholders. Often unconsciously, decisions are made using underlying principles that predispose decision makers to biases and errors in judgment. By recognizing these challenges, business decision makers can learn to avoid ethical danger zones and become more effective leaders within their organizations.

---

7   Business Roundtable Institute for Corporate Ethics, Bridge Paper[TM] *http://www.corporate-ethics.org/pdf/danger_zones.pdf*

We can learn to make improved ethical decisions by employing the same learning tools that we use to improve general decision making. Working toward this end, the Business Roundtable Institute for Corporate Ethics brings together leaders from business and academia to fulfill its mission to renew and enhance the link between ethical behavior and business practice.

To develop a framework to improve their ethical decision making, managers can focus on three key areas: quality, breadth, and honesty.

Quality

To better the quality of decisions that executives make they must collect and consider all potentially meaningful facts regarding a decision's consequences. This process requires recognizing potential risks, making accurate judgments of the risks associated with our strategies, and being aware of the psychological biases of decision making. Managers must not ignore or suppress information to make the decision making process more manageable. A few underlying principles impacting the quality of a decision include ethnocentrism, stereotypes and faulty perceptions of causes.

Ethnocentrism and Stereotypes

With globalization managers are increasingly exposed to a growing variety of peoples and cultures. Given this global context, it is more important than ever that managers be tolerant of differences in custom, practice, and style. Like many other countries, the United States prohibits discrimination in employment with regard to social or personal information such as religion, race, gender, and age. Managers face many opportunities with the increased diversity of the business environment, which, in turn, presents greater opportunity for inappropriate behavior related to personal differences. Incorrect beliefs about social groups markedly increase these dangers. Managers, like other individuals, are likely to hold flawed assumptions about other groups.[8]

Ethnocentrism is the view that "our" ways of doing things are ordinary and better and that other approaches are in some way inferior. One's own group or society seems normal, while another might seem peculiar. The implicit notion here is that what is normal for us is preferable in general and what is unfamiliar is less good. In an ethnocentric view, our group's views and values become the bar against which others are measured. The same actions by one's own group and by another group might be described using language that is descriptively comparable, yet, nevertheless, implies a negative bias toward the other. We describe ourselves as being devoted, diligent, and proud; others we may describe as being cliquish, unwavering, and egotistical.

---

8   For additional information on these issues, consult: S. Worcheland and W.G. Austin, *Psychology of Intergroup Relations* (Chicago: Nelson-Hill, 1986).

A manager's ethnocentrism amplifies differences between groups and cultures, increasing the risk that a manager will fail to make decisions that are ethically sound. Ethnocentrism is as much about giving special assistance to "us," or "in-group favoritism," as it is about treating other groups negatively.[9] For example, in mortgage lending, more minority than white applicants are turned down for loans, even after accounting for income differences, job stability, credit records, and other creditworthiness indicators. Mortgage lenders, however, claim to be equitable across racial groups. In-group favoritism suggests that the variance may not be due to cases involving the denial of qualified minority applications, so much as in the approval of loans to questionably qualified white applicants. Thus, for lenders seeking to ensure equitable treatment, a review of minority loan applications that had been rejected would not detect the problem because the pool of qualified minorities whose applications are rejected is not the site of discrimination. Instead, the lender must review questionably qualified white applications to see if in-group favoritism exists. If it does, this will be indicated by a greater percentage of questionably qualified white applicants receiving loans than their minority counterparts with similar qualifications. Managers would improve the quality of decision-making by using this example to consider potentially faulty assumptions in their own organizations and industries.

Besides the idea that "our" group is superior to others, people often have unconscious prejudices, or stereotypes, about people who differ from us with regard to sex, nationality, race, and occupation. Managers who depend on stereotypes instead of facts about individuals are more likely to make decisions that are less fair, less correct, and perhaps less in line with the law. As with ethnocentrism, managers are unconsciously influenced by stereotypes, which has the added danger of convincing them that their prejudices regarding other groups are factual. Sometimes managers will point to experience as evidence of these beliefs; forgetting that they might be misled by experience. For example, when asked to think about effective leaders and to identify traits they associate with these leaders, many people will identify masculine qualities. These results are conditioned more by a paternalist cultural history than by individual abilities or qualities. Here, our history may in part blind us to viewing women as effective leaders.

> As with ethnocentrism, managers are unconsciously influenced by stereotypes, which has the added danger of convincing them that their prejudices regarding other groups are factual.

---

9   M.B. Brewer, "In-Group Bias in the Minimal Intergroup Situation: A Cognitive-Motivational Analysis," *Psychological Bulletin* 86 (1979): 307-324.

Executives make many important personnel decisions such as promoting, hiring, and terminating employees. In situations where the criteria for assessment and the qualifications are somewhat murky, executives need to consciously avoid bringing improper views about others groups into the process. Here clear sets of guidelines can be helpful. If company policy dictates that the individual with the leading sales record is the one promoted, the impact of any ethnocentric or stereotypical views will be limited. Having clear and quantified criteria keeps stereotyping out of the process to a much greater extent than imprecise qualifications like leadership ability.

Our biases have a greater impact on our actions when our decisions are made on intuitive or subjective grounds instead of being rooted in concrete, objective information. Some managers prefer a more vague, qualitative process of assessment that relies more on their own judgment, but this method has some inherent dangers. By using a quantitative process, managers can better avoid areas where improper beliefs might impact their decisions. In most cases, the quantitative approach will have the same result as the qualitative one—but, the quantitative approach will be less subjective and is likely to be deemed more fair by all parties due to its objective criteria.

Companies need to embrace proactive strategies and policies for keeping biases out of the decision-making process, such as reiterating to employees that such biases are not tolerated within the organization, and approving equal opportunity principles that are enforced. Leading companies in this area look beyond compliance measures and have figured out the value proposition of how increased workforce diversity leads to competitive advantages.

Perception of Causes

[handwritten: What goes into causing the Boat to sink? A number of factors like shown.]

Managers' beliefs concerning what causes events to occur or not occur may be flawed, which can also affect a decision's quality. We all have opinions regarding why businesses succeed and fail. Managers must often look beyond the obvious causes and collect relevant data to determine the roots of a problem or situation. Our understanding of causality in part determines how we assess moral responsibility and whom we blame or laud—an individual, an organization or a policy—for a particular result. We often forget, however, even under the most transparent circumstances, causation is multifaceted and difficult to determine. When the result is an unpleasant one, any consequent disputes typically revolve around different interpretations of causation: who is responsible; who should be blamed; and what is just punishment.

Several years ago, more than 180 people drowned off the coast of Belgium when the ferry *Herald of Free Enterprise* (the *Herald*), which took cars from the

> We need to recognize that systems and environments can either limit or multiply human error which is bound to occur.

Belgian port of Zeebrugge to Dover,England, sank in calm conditions shortly after departing from Zeebrugge. The *Herald* went down because water flowed into the bow doors through which cars were loaded onto the ship. Tragically,these doors had been left open and the assistant bosun—the crew member responsible for shutting them—was asleep when the ship left port.

The *Herald* did not have an automated system to alert other crew members when the bow doors were open or closed, even though the captain had recommended that the ship line install such a system. Since the first mate was charged with monitoring the bow doors closing, the company felt such a system was not required. In this instance, however, the first mate was covering other duties related to a staff shortage, and he did not check to make sure that the doors were closed. Also, there was a "negative"check system—from an electrical switch that was "off" when the bow gate was down—so when he did not get a signal,the captain assumed this meant that everything was in order for the *Herald*'s launch. In reality, the bulb was burned out so, although there was no signal, it was due to a completely different and unanticipated reason. The *Herald* was 20 minutes behind schedule when it left Zeebrugge and to make up the time,the captain decided not to pump out additional ballast the ship had taken on in order to load cars on its upper deck. This extra ballast caused the *Herald* to create a bow wave as it moved out of the harbor, allowing water to flow into the open bow doors, which would have been several meters above sea level without the added weight.

Focus on People

In determining the cause of the accident,whom should we blame? The list of potential culprits includes the captain,the sleeping assistant bosun, the first mate, the executive who thought warning lights unnecessary, the individual who designed the negative check system, or the owners who did not properly staff the *Herald.*

In assessing blame, most people tend to blame a person. Even when intricate technologies are involved (as is the case with the *Herald*), we find it simpler to blame individuals since, with hindsight,we can easily imagine how they could have acted differently to prevent a given disaster. We can easily imagine an assistant bosun who stayed awake, a first mate who made sure the bow doors were closed, and a captain who pumped out the extra ballast even though it would make it difficult for the ship to stay on schedule.

We have a harder time imagining the *Herald* being equipped with different systems and protocols and are less likely to see these as having caused the ship's sinking. If the *Herald* had warning lights to indicate the bow doors were open, it would not have left Zeebrugge until they were closed. If a positive check system had been in place—where there would be a signal needed to inform the captain that the doors had been closed—the captain would have known that the doors were open. Human error arises within systems that differ greatly with regard to how proactive they are for preventing errors from being made. While we tend to view human beings as causal agents,we need to recognize that systems and environments can either limit or multiply human error which is bound to occur. From a strategic perspective, what is the simpler change to make – adding warning lights or increasing employee alertness? To counteract the tendency to simply blame a person, managers should thoughtfully consider all possibilities—including systems, procedures and environments—to diagnose a situation and make decisions.

Sins of Omission

It makes sense to hold the assistant bosun partially responsible for the tragic sinking of the *Herald*, since he failed to complete the task assigned to him. Sometimes, however, we are tempted to use another's failure to act to blind ourselves and others to our own responsibility. This is especially true if respective duties and expectations are vaguely defined. If an executive neglects to report an incompetent colleague, does he bear some responsibility for any damage this person causes the firm? If a CEO refuses to terminate a manager who ignores ethical regulations, how responsible is she for this manager's impact on the firm? Many of us would tend to point to the moral failing of the colleague and manager as the sites of blame, perhaps ignoring culpability on the parts of the executive and CEO. The executive and the CEO are logically as culpable as the assistant bosun, however, since like him, they had ability to prevent damage to the firm if they had acted. Evil prevails when good people fail to act, as the adage goes, but too seldom do we hold the "good" people who failed to act accountable.

Breadth

While quality entails assessing a decision's full range of consequences, breadth requires that we account for the potential effects on all stakeholders. Using moral imagination[10] to look beyond the direct and obvious impact of a specific decision, managers should make an effort to imagine other possible moral implications for additional stakeholders. Managers should maintain openness to things they may not have considered. The psychological tendency to simplify consequences might affect the breadth of a decision.

To make decisions that are ethical requires that we have realistic views on the world. This means, at the least, that we must explore the full range of results that a decision may have for various stakeholders. Our biases act like blind spots when we try to envision this range of potential outcomes.

Simplifying Consequences

Executives must often judge the risks associated with particular strategies, outlining and assessing the range of likely outcomes. In order to make this process simpler to manage, executives often curtail the range of possible outcomes that they consider.

---

10   Patricia H. Werhane, *Moral Imagination and Management Decision Making*, Oxford University Press, 1999.

Ignoring some potential outcomes, however, can lead to various biases including ignoring low-probability events, ignoring the possibility that the public will "find out," and discounting the future.

Ignoring Low-Probability Events

Sometimes we avoid facing the possibility of troubling risks, if we believe there is a potential for a significant gain. For example, managers might ignore or underestimate the potential impact of a flaw in a hot new product which is expected to have a dramatic impact on the firm's profits. In March 2005, a 21-year-old Minnesota college student died when his heart defibrillator failed to work properly. The *New York Times* reported in May 2005 that for three years Guidant Corporation had knowingly withheld information from doctors about a malfunction affecting a small number of their defibrillator products. Although the malfunctioning defibrillator had a reported failure incidence rate of only 0.07 percent, as Dr. Barry J. Maron of Abbott Northwestern Hospital in Minneapolis stated, "it is a statistical argument that has little to do with real people.[11]" The importance of this information was insufficiently appreciated. The point for managers is certainly not that low-probability events should drive decision-making, but rather that such events should be appropriately considered in the process.

imp. ★ Low-Prob can still occur ★

Ignoring That the Public May "Find Out"

Managers and executives are well-served to always consider society in general as a stakeholder. Managers should consider what would be the public's reaction to a decision and to the reasons for it. If they are concerned about this reaction, managers should question the decision. An added risk to a decision that requires secrecy is that the information might come to light. With today's level of information technology, the likelihood of maintaining these secrets has become increasingly diminished. Additionally, damage to the respect of both the organization and the individuals involved in the deception should be considered. An often ignored risk is the need to continue the pattern of deceit. Besides hiding the original issue, the deception itself must also be concealed.

> To avoid using psychological techniques for simplifying consequences, first, develop a list of the stakeholders.

Often managers' decisions involve confidential or proprietary information which cannot be disclosed. Transparency does not mean that managers must reveal sensitive information. It is appropriate and ethical to maintain the secrecy of certain information. When the executive's motivation in maintaining secrecy is that they fear public reaction, then it is inappropriate. A manager can ask herself if she feels the need to conceal

---

11   Barry Meier, "Maker of Heart Device Kept Flaw From Doctors," *The New York Times,* 24 May 2005.

information about certain aspects of the project from the public. If the answer is yes, she may need to reconsider whether or not it is an ethical undertaking.

Discounting the Future *More emphasis on short-term accurences than longterm.*

We often give shorter shrift to issues that will face us in the future than we do to those with more immediate consequences, often neglecting the fact that the impact of our decisions tends to grow over time. Managers who do not deal with the issue of the distribution of consequences over time will not understand why they have not been more successful, and they may face accusations that they exploited the present at the expense of the future. The bias toward discounting the future is of relevance to the United States budget deficit, decaying urban centers, and global climate change.

An example of an executive taking a leadership position in considering future consequences is the case of Ray Anderson, founder, chairman and CEO of Interface, Inc. According to a May 1999 *Fortune* magazine article, Anderson decided to change his industry-leading flooring company into a sustainable business, one that didn't cause any harm to the environment. "For the first 21 years of the company's existence, I never gave one thought to what we were taking from the earth or doing to it, except to be sure we were in compliance and keeping ourselves 'clean' in a regulatory sense,"Anderson explained. Based on his view of how his company, the industry, and business in general had been operating,Anderson predicted that "In the future,people like me will go to jail." Anderson held future generations and the impact of his industry in the forefront of his business decision making.

To avoid using psychological techniques for simplifying consequences,first, develop a list of the stakeholders. One way to identify these groups is to develop a transparent decision-making process that invites stakeholder participation, including potential critics. Access to public information will differ according to stakeholder group, so a manager using this technique risks overlooking key stakeholders.

Another possible approach is to invite select stakeholder representatives to be a part of the decision-making team. It is important for managers to think broadly when identifying these representatives. Potential critics may read openness as a sign that your firm has nothing to hide,nor to fear. In the past, for example, Nike was widely criticized on "sweatshop labor" issues. In 2005, Nike adopted a stakeholder transparency approach by releasing a comprehensive company social performance report with detailed information about their factories and suppliers from around the world. *link solution*

Once stakeholders have been identified, the next task is to assess and judge the potential impact of a decision from the stakeholders' perspectives. Executives who make socially responsible decisions tend to view their firm in the wider community context, recognizing that the firm impacts this group. If the community opposes a company practice,it is a much better strategy to deal with this transparently, rather than being publicly ambushed by the other party at a later date. Information technology has empowered small groups to quickly muster strong opposition toward a corporate policy or decision in ways that were previously not possible.

Finally, executives must recognize that their decisions impact the future as well the present. Executives need to protect vital social and natural resources for future generations, while managing their firms. Executives should forgo the appeal of privileging their own generations over future generations. Current generations should try to leave future generations with a better situation than what they inherited and not with the bill for their own activities. *Imp*

Breadth is a critical component of making ethical decisions—it is both ethically appropriate and strategically valuable. Recognizing breadth is both the right thing to do and the smart thing to do. Not only is intentionally excluding stakeholders' interests or contributions a poor ethical decision, it is also strategically unsound since it invites opposition and resentment where there could be common ground.

Honesty

Known by many different names—integrity, one's North Star, moral compass — honesty must be central in all aspects of business, including decision making. Biases such as overconfidence can unknowingly affect the integrity of a decision.

Overconfidence *We tend to make decisions based on incorrect data that we discount because of overconfidence*

Managers not only need to be truthful with other people, they must also be critical of and honest with themselves. Managers may not be conscious of how they have developed judgments and beliefs. People perceive their own memories to be accurate, but there is solid research that indicates otherwise. People believe they understand why they judge others in a certain way, but research reveals different reasons. Our views of ourselves are often partially inaccurate for a range of reasons.[12]

Confidence, intelligence, and moral strength allow managers to make hard decisions that may not be popular with others. Often these decisions are required and expected of managers, however, ethical problems can arise if a manager's views about herself are distorted. A manager's self-perception may not include sufficient openness, modesty and self-criticism with regard to her abilities, thus allowing the overconfidence bias to cloud her judgment.

Managers must guard against overconfidence and potentially irrational, unethical decisions. People can learn to question their own judgment, to habituate themselves to calculate risk, and to test their intentions in assessing others. As a manager, ask yourself: "Am I using reliable data or stereotypes to evaluate subordinates?" Managers might be unconsciously biased to favor their own views or those held by their firms. Getting external input may not be sufficient to eradicate or decrease these biases because we are

---

12   For example, see: S.E. Taylor, *Positive Illusions* (New York: Basic Books, 1989).

inclined to notice and cling to information that supports our beliefs, which can prevent us from learning from our experience.

Most executives are overly certain of their knowledge. Academic surveys that ask people to respond to fact-based questions and then ask respondents to predict whether their answers are true, show that peoples' judgments of their accuracy far exceed the actual number of questions they answer correctly.[13] People who answer a sizeable set of two-option questions—and claim a 75 percent accuracy rate—tend to give the correct response only 60 percent of the time.[14] When respondents predict 100 percent accuracy, commonly they tend to have the correct answer in 85 percent of the cases.

Overconfidence, coupled with other biases, is a harmful blind spot to making decisions that are rational and ethical. Overconfidence is dangerous when executives base decisions or policies on information that is not accurate.

These policies may prove harmful to the executives making the decision and to others whom the decision affects. People who are overconfident in their own knowledge and understanding of a state of affairs will forgo a search for more and better information. Overconfidence may cause a manager to avoid gathering additional information about an issue before making a critical decision.

> *Overconfidence may cause a manager to avoid gathering additional information about an issue before making a critical decision.*

Even managers who recognize that more or better information is needed may seek that information in a way that is slanted toward affirming their existing beliefs.[15] A series of studies tasked subjects with determining the rule of which the number sequence, 2-4-6, is an instance. Subjects were permitted to pose other three number sequences to an experimenter who would then state whether the sequences followed the rule that defined the set. Participants could decide when they had sufficient information to determine the rule.

---

13   S. Lichtenstein, B. Fischhoff, and L.D. Phillips, "Calibration of Probabilities," in D. Kahneman, P. Slovic, and A. Tversky, eds., *Judgement under Uncertainty: Heuristics and Biases* (Cambridge: Cambridge University Press, 1982), pp. 306-334.

14   B. Fischoff, P. Slovic, and S. Lichtenstein, "Knowing with Certainty: The Appropriateness of Extreme Confidence," *Journal of Experimental Psychology: Human Perception and Performance* 3 (1977): 552-564.

15   P.C. Wason, "On the Failure to Eliminate Hypotheses in a Conceptual Task," *Quarterly Journal of Experimental Psychology* 12 (1960): 129-140

Commonly, subjects assumed the rule to be: the second number is larger than the first number by the same amount as the third number is larger than the second number. The actual rule is: any three ascending numbers. When subjects tested confirming sequences such as 4-5-6, 20-25-30, or 310-317-324, they received positive feedback which increased their belief in the initial, erroneous rule. In order to learn that their initial guess was errant, participants had to check their hypothesis by recommending sequences that did not fit their hypothesis. The lesson for managers here is that, in seeking unbiased information, they need to ask questions that would disconfirm their assumption if answered positively. Acquiring information in this way is less comfortable, in part because it can make it look like we are less confident.

In light of this, consider the case of a manager who is interviewing an engineer regarding a tool grip's safety. The manager is overconfident in his belief that the grip is safe and unconsciously may want to confirm this idea. A question's phrasing can bias how it will be interpreted and answered. If the manager asks "This grip is completely safe, right?" or "Our grip complies with all of the standards for this type of tool, doesn't it?" the manager unknowingly influences the engineer's response. The manager is showing a confirmation bias by asking questions he expects to be answered "yes." Also, unintentionally, he is taking advantage of social politeness, because people are more likely to agree than to disagree. In framing his questions in this way, the manager hurts his chances of learning if the engineer has real reservations regarding the product's design features. Flipped so that the answer "yes" would either disprove the manager's idea or not display any confirmation bias, better questions to ask might be "Are there any features with this design we might need to be concerned about?" or "What are the advantages and disadvantages of the grip?"

Erroneous views of the self such as overconfidence are most problematic when managers see themselves as above the normal rules, codes, and obligations. If a successful manager or executive holds himself above conventional ethics, he may only follow self-imposed rules that others might view as self-serving. He may see his valuable contribution to the firm as a valid excuse for inflating an expense account or using company resources for personal benefit. He might justify deceiving shareholders or employees by altering financial reports to achieve important financial gains on their behalf. Finally, he may do something immoral or illegal, convinced that he will never be caught.

To counteract overconfidence, managers can use their conscience to test whether or not a decision is ethical. If it cannot withstand public scrutiny, then the idea may be ethically managers try to envision how they would react if their actions appeared on the front page of a major newspaper. One executive from a recent Institute seminar offered the following guidance for determining ethicality: "If there is a doubt, there is no doubt."

The biases that lead managers to self-deception and overconfidence can also allow them to trick themselves into justifying false answers to hypothetical tests. Managers should, therefore, imagine whether their stakeholders would accept their ideas or decisions. In particular, they should ask whether the people with the most to lose would accept the reasons for their actions. If not, they may be approaching an ethical danger zone. To combat overconfidence,for instance, managers should consider ways in which their decision or assumption might be wrong. Another overconfidence filter for managers is assigning someone to scrutinize a decision for false assumptions and optimistic projections.

Human memory is unreliable, which can threaten rational and ethical decision making. Managers must acknowledge and compensate for flawed memory with improved, detailed record keeping. Record keeping and benchmarking are critical for objectively measuring process performance. Erroneous views and biases threaten ethical leadership.

To avoid decision making traps,managers can use three pillars—quality, breadth and honesty—to develop a framework for business decision-making. The right thing to do is not always a clear choice for the decision maker, and is often not the opposite of the wrong thing. Unethical behavior in organizations is commonly affected by psychological tendencies that create undesirable biased behavior. When they identify and confront these biases, managers make more rational and ethical business decisions and increase the likelihood of success for the organizations they lead.

D. Self-Interest?

Philosophers rightly caution us to avoid committing the "naturalistic fallacy." This means that one should not confuse what is with what ought to be. One version of the naturalistic fallacy is to take note of the fact that a lot of unethical behavior takes place and to say, well, that's the way things are. In other words, this is the way things work in *the real world*. In the midst of discussions, a student will often provide an example of a business person who did something bad and got away with it to make the point that while an ethics class talks about how companies ought to act, in the real world things are different. The person offering the comment may be exactly right, but they are not providing an ethics example as much as they are describing a certain kind of behavior and its apparent outcome. Simply because some people act badly and seemingly get good results for themselves doesn't mean that that is the way we *should* behave. It's a fallacy to claim that because things are the way they are that this is how they should be.

Another version of the naturalistic fallacy is to use science to document aspects of human nature and to therefore conclude that human nature precludes us from acting in different ways. For example, high testosterone levels may incline men (in particular) toward violence. That may be scientifically true and it may constitute an "is." But an "is" doesn't not lead to an "ought." We should simply accept violence (and, as a scientific matter, human beings—yes, even men—do have pacific aspects of their nature as well) even if testosterone levels incline us to be violent.

While avoiding the naturalistic fallacy, there is also room, though, for a well-grounded understanding of what our biological, neurological, and other capabilities are, so that we can best formulate improvements on how we might act that takes into account our limitations (such as the next chapter's insights into our cognitive capabilities). As a start, it is worth looking historically into some arguments of whether or not human beings even have a sense of the ethical or whether acting well is simply drawn from a fear of being caught.

1. Plato's Ring of Gyges[16]

The following vignette comes from Plato, but the notion of a magic ring is one that should be familiar to readers of J.R.R. Tolkien's and his "Hobbit" trilogy:

> Now that those who practise justice do so involuntarily and because they have not the power to be unjust will best appear if we imagine something of this kind: having given both to the just and the unjust power to do what they will, let us watch and see whither desire will lead them; then we shall discover in the very act the just and unjust man to be proceeding along the same road, following their interest, which all natures deem to be their good, and are only diverted into the path of justice by the force of law. The liberty which we are supposing may be most completely given to them in the form of such a power as is said to have been possessed by Gyges the ancestor of Croesus the Lydian. According to the tradition, Gyges was a shepherd in the service of the king of Lydia; there was a great storm, and an earthquake made an opening in the earth at the place where he was feeding his flock. Amazed at the sight, he descended into the opening, where, among other marvels, he beheld a hollow brazen horse, having doors, at which he stooping and looking in saw a dead body of stature, as appeared to him, more than human, and having nothing on but a gold ring; this he took from the finger of the dead and reascended. Now the shepherds met together, according to custom, that they might send their monthly report about the flocks to the king; into their assembly he came having the ring on his finger, and as he was sitting among them he chanced to turn the collet of the ring inside his hand, when instantly he became invisible to the rest of the company and they began to speak of him as if he were no longer present. He was astonished at this, and again

---

16   This translation is available at *http://classics/mit.edu/Plato/Republic.3.ii.html*

touching the ring he turned the collet outwards and reappeared; he made several trials of the ring, and always with the same result-when he turned the collet inwards he became invisible, when outwards he reappeared. Whereupon he contrived to be chosen one of the messengers who were sent to the court; where as soon as he arrived he seduced the queen, and with her help conspired against the king and slew him, and took the kingdom. Suppose now that there were two such magic rings, and the just put on one of them and the unjust the other; no man can be imagined to be of such an iron nature that he would stand fast in justice. No man would keep his hands off what was not his own when he could safely take what he liked out of the market, or go into houses and lie with any one at his pleasure, or kill or release from prison whom he would, and in all respects be like a God among men. Then the actions of the just would be as the actions of the unjust; they would both come at last to the same point. And this we may truly affirm to be a great proof that a man is just, not willingly or because he thinks that justice is any good to him individually, but of necessity, for wherever any one thinks that he can safely be unjust, there he is unjust. For all men believe in their hearts that injustice is far more profitable to the individual than justice, and he who argues as I have been supposing, will say that they are right. If you could imagine any one obtaining this power of becoming invisible, and never doing any wrong or touching what was another's, he would be thought by the lookers-on to be a most wretched idiot, although they would praise him to one another's faces, and keep up appearances with one another from a fear that they too might suffer injustice. Enough of this.

Now, if we are to form a real judgment of the life of the just and unjust, we must isolate them; there is no other way; and how is the isolation to be effected? I answer: Let the unjust man be entirely unjust, and the just man entirely just; nothing is to be taken away from either of them, and both are to be perfectly furnished for the work of their respective lives. First, let the unjust be like other distinguished masters of craft; like the skilful pilot or physician, who knows intuitively his own powers and keeps within their limits, and who, if he fails at any point, is able to recover himself. So let the unjust make his unjust attempts in the right way, and lie hidden if he means to be great in his injustice (he who is found out is nobody): for the highest reach of injustice is: to be deemed just when you are not. Therefore I say that in the perfectly unjust man we must assume the most perfect injustice; there is to be no deduction, but we must allow him, while doing the most unjust acts, to have acquired the greatest reputation for justice. If he have taken a false step he must be able to recover himself; he must be one who can speak with effect, if any of his deeds come to light, and who can force his way where force is required his courage and strength, and command of money and friends. And at his side let us place the just man in his nobleness and simplicity, wishing, as Aeschylus says, to be and not to seem good. There must be no seeming, for if he seem to be just he will be honoured and rewarded, and then we shall not know whether he is just for the sake of justice or for the sake of honours and rewards; therefore, let him be clothed in justice only, and have no other covering; and he must be imagined in a state of life the opposite of the former. Let him be the best of men, and let him be thought the worst; then he will have been put to the proof; and we shall see whether he will be affected by the fear of infamy and its consequences. And let him continue thus to the hour of death; being just and seeming to be unjust. When both have reached the uttermost extreme, the one of justice and the other of injustice, let judgment be given which of them is the happier of the two.

Socrates: Heavens! my dear Glaucon, I said, how energetically you polish them up for the decision, first one and then the other, as if they were two statues.

What is your view? Do people have a noble nature, as Socrates believed, that inspires them to do good for the sake of the good? Or do people attend to ethics only out of a fear of being caught? As you can see from this vignette, the debate on this issue goes back a long way. But it remains relevant today. Indeed, it serves as a major issue in how one develops corporate culture. If people only do the right thing because they are afraid of being caught, then a company will need to set up many oversight checks of employees because they really can't trust them. On the other hand, if human beings have a desire, also, to do good, then one might have a culture designed to take advantage of that trait, which would call for reduced looking over the shoulder.

2. The Nature of Self-Interest

Another example of what human beings' human nature—and self interest—compel us to do comes from a famous 1974 vignette from Garrett Hardin. Hardin uses this vignette to talk about issues of imbalances between rich and poor, but pare back his example and just think of it in term of the basic story he relates of a shipwreck at sea with 150 people in the water and a lifeboat that holds only fifty. Assume the water is warm (so that people don't freeze to death as with the victims of the Titanic disaster), that sharks are not circling those in the water, and that land is not immediately in sight. How do people resolve this situation? With these stipulations in mind, read the case and then think through how people confronted with this situation would handle it.[17]

Lifeboat Ethics: The Case Against Helping the Poor[18]
by Garrett Hardin

Environmentalists use the metaphor of the earth as a "spaceship" in trying to persuade countries, industries and people to stop wasting and polluting our natural resources. Since we all share life on this planet, they argue, no single person or institution has the right to destroy, waste, or use more than a fair share of its resources.

But does everyone on earth have an equal right to an equal share of its resources? The spaceship metaphor can be dangerous when used by misguided idealists to justify suicidal policies for sharing our resources through uncontrolled immigration and foreign aid. In their enthusiastic but unrealistic generosity, they confuse the ethics of a spaceship with those of a lifeboat.

A true spaceship would have to be under the control of a captain, since no ship could possibly survive if its course were determined by committee. Spaceship Earth certainly has no captain; the United Nations is merely a toothless tiger, with little power to enforce any policy upon its bickering members.

If we divide the world crudely into rich nations and poor nations, two thirds of them are desperately poor, and only one third comparatively rich, with the United States the wealthiest of all. Metaphorically each rich nation can be seen as a lifeboat full of comparatively rich people. In the ocean outside each lifeboat swim the poor of the world, who would like to get in, or at least to share some of the wealth. What should the lifeboat passengers do?

---

17   I am grateful to LaRue Hosmer for teaching me this use of the case.

18   Garrett Hardin, "Lifeboat Ethics: The Case Against Helping the Poor," *Psychology Today* (Sep. 1974), available at *http://www.garretthardinsociety.org/articles/art_lifeboat_ethics_case_against_helping_poor.html.*

First, we must recognize the limited capacity of any lifeboat. For example, a nation's land has a limited capacity to support a population and as the current energy crisis has shown us, in some ways we have already exceeded the carrying capacity of our land.

Adrift in a Moral Sea

So here we sit, say 50 people in our lifeboat. To be generous, let us assume it has room for 10 more, making a total capacity of 60. Suppose the 50 of us in the lifeboat see 100 others swimming in the water outside, begging for admission to our boat or for hand-outs. We have several options: we may be tempted to try to live by the Christian ideal of being "our brother's keeper," or by the Marxist ideal of "to each according to his needs." Since the needs of all in the water are the same, and since they can all be seen as "our brothers," we could take them all into our boat, making a total of 150 in a boat designed for 60. The boat swamps, everyone drowns. Complete justice, complete catastrophe.

Since the boat has an unused excess capacity of 10 more passengers, we could admit just 10 more to it. But which 10 do we let in? How do we choose? Do we pick the best 10, "first come, first served"? And what do we say to the 90 we exclude? If we do let an extra 10 into our lifeboat, we will have lost our "safety factor," an engineering principle of critical importance. For example, if we don't leave room for excess capacity as a safety factor in our country's agriculture, a new plant disease or a bad change in the weather could have disastrous consequences.

Suppose we decide to preserve our small safety factor and admit no more to the lifeboat. Our survival is then possible although we shall have to be constantly on guard against boarding parties.

While this last solution clearly offers the only means of our survival, it is morally abhorrent to many people. Some say they feel guilty about their good luck. My reply is simple: "Get out and yield your place to others." This may solve the problem of the guilt-ridden person's conscience, but it does not change the ethics of the lifeboat. The needy person to whom the guilt-ridden person yields his place will not himself feel guilty about his good luck. If he did, he would not climb aboard. The net result of conscience-stricken people giving up their unjustly held seats is the elimination of that sort of conscience from the lifeboat.

How would people react in this situation? In some old legal cases, it appears that some on the boat would kill and eat the others, so this situation may become grim. But there are also times when individuals will give up their seats, as Hardin recognizes, for someone else. That might be particularly true if they give up their seats for a loved one, but sometimes it might even happen for a stranger. But Hardin also has a response for this: If the test of conscience is to give up one's seat, then by definition, the group that survives will have the least amount of moral sentiment possible (because those with such sentiments will have exited). And, in corporate life, this is true as well. It may seem that getting out of a bad situation is the best possible solution, but then it may be that a company with a conscience may contribute the most by staying in a difficult situation and contributing. Or to put it another way, if only those with a conscience leave the company when tough ethical choices are made, the remaining members of the company will have less conscience to contribute with difficult decisions need to be made.

There are other options too, such as rowing away quickly or clubbing those in the water over the head so they don't get on the lifeboat. But, as Professor Hosmer points out, these are short term solutions. Neither will engender any degree of cooperation from those in the water who may just have the power to get angry and overturn the boat, in which case everyone will lose. Indeed, what may be in the long-term *self-interest*, Professor Hosmer says, is to work out an arrangement where those in the water hang on to the side of the boat, buoyant in the sea, as everyone tries to figure out a solution. In short, Hosmer says, what seems to be in the short-term self-interest of those on the boat (row away or crack people over the head with an oar) and what is in the long-term self-interest (working together with a wider group of affected people) may be in contradiction. He applies this insight to short-term vs. long-term shareholder theory as well. What is in the short-term interests of the company and what is in the long-term interests may be two very different things.

E. Theories of Moral Development

Theories of moral development attempt to integrate the realities of human nature and self-interest with an awareness of our biases and also normative aims. That is a tall task but before looking at more philosophical efforts to articulate how to be ethical in business, it is worth looking at psychological issues. The following, edited article provides a helpful summary of some of the leading efforts in this area.

Moral Development and Moral Education: An Overview[19]

Larry Nucci, Prof Emeritus; University of Illinois at Chicago

Moral education is becoming an increasingly popular topic in the fields of psychology and education. Media reports of increased violent juvenile crime, teen pregnancy, and suicide have caused many to declare a moral crisis in our nation.

---

19 *Moral Development and Moral Education: An Overview*, UIC.COM (last visited July 29, 2013), *http://tigger. uic.edu/~lnucci/MoralEd/overviewtext.html.*

While not all of these social concerns are moral in nature, and most have complex origins, there is a growing trend towards linking the solutions to these and related social problems to the teaching of moral and social values in our public schools. However, considerations of the role schools can and should play in the moral development of youth are themselves the subject of controversy. All too often debate on this topic is reduced to posturing reflecting personal views rather than informed opinion. Fortunately, systematic research and scholarship on moral development has been going on for most of this century, and educators wishing to attend to issues of moral development and education may make use of what has been learned through that work. The following overview provides an introduction to the main perspectives guiding current work on moral development and education.

* * *

Piaget's Theory

Jean Piaget is among the first psychologists whose work remains directly relevant to contemporary theories of moral development. In his early writing, he focused specifically on the moral lives of children, studying the way children play games in order to learn more about children's beliefs about right and wrong (1932/65). According to Piaget, all development emerges from action; that is to say, individuals construct and reconstruct their knowledge of the world as a result of interactions with the environment. Based on his observations of children's application of rules when playing, Piaget determined that morality, too, can be considered a developmental process. For example, Ben, a ten year old studied by Piaget, provided the following critique of a rule made-up by a child playing marbles: "it isn't a rule!

JEAN PAIGET

Photo: Wikicommons

It's a wrong rule because it's outside of the rules. A fair rule is one that is in the game." Ben believed in the absolute and intrinsic truth of the rules, characteristic of early moral reasoning. In contrast, Vua, aged thirteen, illustrates an understanding of the reasoning behind the application of rules, characteristic of later moral thinking. When asked to consider the fairness of a made-up rule compared to a traditional rule, Vua replied "It is just as fair because the marbles are far apart" (making the game equally difficult).

In addition to examining children's understanding of rules about games, Piaget interviewed children regarding acts such as stealing and lying. When asked what a lie is, younger children consistently answered that they are "naughty words". When asked why they should not lie, younger children could rarely explain beyond the forbidden nature of the act: "because it is a naughty word". However, older children were able to explain "because it isn't right", and "it wasn't true". Even older children indicated an awareness of intention as relevant to the meaning of an act: "A lie is when you deceive someone else. To make a mistake is when you make a mistake". From his observations, Piaget concluded that children begin in a "heteronomous" stage of moral reasoning, characterized by a strict adherence to rules and duties, and obedience to authority.

This heteronomy results from two factors. The first factor is the young child's cognitive structure. According to Piaget, the thinking of young children is characterized by egocentrism. That is to say that young children are unable to simultaneously take into account their own view of things with the perspective of someone else. This egocentrism leads children to project their own thoughts and wishes onto others. It is also associated with the uni-directional view of rules and power associated with heteronomous moral thought, and various forms of "moral realism." Moral realism is associated with "objective responsibility", which is valuing the letter of the law above the purpose of the law. This is why young children are more concerned about the outcomes of actions rather than the intentions of the person doing the act. Moral realism is also associated with the young child's belief in "immanent justice." This is the expectation that punishments automatically follow acts of wrong-doing. One of the most famous cases of such childhood thinking was that of the young boy who believed that his hitting a power pole with his baseball bat caused a major power blackout in the New York city area.

The second major contributor to heteronomous moral thinking in young children, is their relative social relationship with adults. In the natural authority relationship between adults and children, power is handed down from above. The relative powerlessness of young children, coupled with childhood egocentrism feeds into a heteronomous moral orientation.

However, through interactions with other children in which the group seeks a to play together in a way all find fair, children find this strict heteronomous adherence to rules sometimes problematic. As children consider these situations, they develop towards an "autonomous" stage of moral reasoning, characterized by the ability to consider rules critically, and selectively apply these rules based on a goal of mutual respect and cooperation. The ability to act from a sense of reciprocity and mutual respect is associated with a shift in the child's cognitive structure from egocentrism to perspective taking. Coordinating one's own perspective with that of others means that what is right needs to be based on solutions that meet the requirements of fair reciprocity. Thus, Piaget viewed moral development as the result of interpersonal interactions through which individuals work out resolutions which all deem fair. Paradoxically, this autonomous view of morality as fairness is more compelling and leads to more consistent behavior than the heteronomous orientation held by younger children.

* * *

Kohlberg's Theory of Moral Development and Education

Moral Development

Lawrence Kohlberg (shown here in 1969) modified and elaborated Piaget's work, and laid the groundwork for the current debate within psychology on moral development. Consistent with Piaget, he proposed that children form ways of thinking through their experiences which include understandings of moral concepts such as justice, rights, equality and human welfare. Kohlberg followed the development of moral judgment beyond the ages studied by Piaget, and determined that the process of attaining moral maturity took longer and was more gradual than Piaget had proposed.

LAWRENCE KOHLBERG

Photo: Harvard University Archives.

On the basis of his research, Kohlberg identified six stages of moral reasoning grouped into three major levels. Each level represented a fundamental shift in the social-moral perspective of the individual. At the first level, the preconventional level, a person's moral judgments are characterized by a concrete, individual perspective. Within this level, a Stage 1 heteronomous orientation focuses on avoiding breaking rules that are backed by punishment, obedience for its own sake and avoiding the physical consequences of an action to persons and property. As in Piaget's framework, the reasoning of Stage 1 is characterized by egocentrism and the inability to consider the perspectives of others. At Stage 2 there is the early emergence of moral reciprocity. The Stage 2 orientation focuses on the instrumental, pragmatic value of an action. Reciprocity is of the form, "you scratch my back and I'll scratch yours." The Golden Rule becomes, "If someone hits you, you hit them back." At Stage 2 one follows the rules only when it is to someone's immediate interests. What is right is what's fair in the sense of an equal exchange, a deal, an agreement. At Stage 2 there is an understanding that everybody has his(her) own interest to pursue and these conflict, so that right is relative (in the concrete individualist sense).

Individuals at the conventional level of reasoning, however, have a basic understanding of conventional morality, and reason with an understanding that norms and conventions are necessary to uphold society. They tend to be self-identified with these rules, and uphold them consistently, viewing morality as acting in accordance with what society defines as right. Within this level, individuals at Stage 3 are aware of shared feelings, agreements, and expectations which take primacy over individual interests. Persons at Stage 3 define what is right in terms of what is expected by people close to one self, and in terms of the stereotypic roles that define being good - e.g., a good brother, mother, teacher. Being good means keeping mutual relationships, such as trust, loyalty, respect, and gratitude. The perspective is that of the local community or family. There is not as yet a consideration of the generalized social system. Stage 4 marks the shift from defining what is right in terms of local norms and role expectations to defining right in terms of the laws and norms established by the larger social system. This is the "member of society" perspective in which one is moral by fulfilling the actual duties defining one's social responsibilities. One must obey the law except in extreme cases in which the law comes into conflict with other prescribed social duties. Obeying the law is seen as necessary in order to maintain the system of laws which protect everyone.

Finally, the post conventional level is characterized by reasoning based on principles, using a "prior to society" perspective. These individuals reason based on the principles which underlie rules and norms, but reject a uniform application of a rule or norm. While two stages have been presented within the theory, only one, Stage 5, has received substantial empirical support. Stage 6 remains as a theoretical endpoint which rationally follows from the preceding 5 stages. In essence this last level of moral judgment entails reasoning rooted in the ethical fairness principles from which moral laws would be devised. Laws are evaluated in terms of their coherence with basic principles of fairness rather than upheld simply on the basis of their place within an existing social order. Thus, there is an understanding that elements of morality such as regard for life and human welfare transcend particular cultures and societies and are to be upheld irrespective of other conventions or normative obligations. These stages (1-5) have been empirically supported by findings from longitudinal and cross-cultural research (Power et al., 1989).

* * *

Domain Theory: Distinguishing Morality and Convention

In the early 1970s, longitudinal studies conducted by the Kohlberg research group began to reveal anomalies in the stage sequence. Researchers committed to the basic Kohlberg framework attempted to resolve those anomalies through adjustments in the stage descriptions (see the Power, Higgins, & Kohlberg, 1989 reference for an account of those changes). Other theorists, however, found that a comprehensive resolution to the anomalous data required substantial adjustments in the theory itself. One of the most productive lines of research to come out of that period has been the domain theory advanced by Elliot Turiel and his colleagues.

Within domain theory a distinction is drawn between the child's developing concepts of morality, and other domains of social knowledge, such as social convention. According to domain theory, the child's concepts of morality and social convention emerge out of the child's attempts to account for qualitatively differing forms of social experience associated with these two classes of social events. Actions within the moral domain, such as unprovoked hitting of someone, have intrinsic effects (i.e., the harm that is caused) on the welfare of another person. Such intrinsic effects occur irregardless of the nature of social rules that may or may not be in place regarding the action. Because of this, the core features of moral cognition are centered around considerations of the effects which actions have upon the well-being of persons. Morality is structured by concepts of harm, welfare, and fairness.

ELLIOT TURIEL

Photo: University of California, Berkeley.

In contrast, actions that are matters of social convention have no intrinsic interpersonal consequences. For example, there is nothing intrinsic to the forms of address we employ that makes calling a college teacher "professor" better or worse than calling the person Mr. or Ms., or simply using their given names. What makes one form of address better than another is the existence of socially agreed upon rules. These conventions, while arbitrary in the sense that they have no intrinsic status, are nonetheless important to the smooth functioning of any social group. Conventions provide a way for members of the group to coordinate their social exchanges through a set of agreed upon and predictable modes of conduct. Concepts of convention then, are structured by the child's understandings of social organization.

These hypothesized distinctions have been sustained through studies over the past 20 years. These studies have included interviews with children, adolescents and adults; observations of child-child and adult-child social interactions; cross-cultural studies; and longitudinal studies examining the changes in children's thinking as they grow older. An example of the distinction between morality and convention is given in the following excerpt from an interview with a four-year-old girl regarding her perceptions of spontaneously occurring transgressions at her preschool.

MORAL ISSUE: Did you see what happened? Yes. They were playing and John hit him too hard. Is that something you are supposed to do or not supposed to do? Not so hard to hurt. Is there a rule about that? Yes. What is the rule? You're not to hit hard. What if there were no rule about hitting hard, would it be all right to do then? No. Why not? Because he could get hurt and start to cry.

CONVENTIONAL ISSUE: Did you see what just happened? Yes. They were noisy. Is that something you are supposed to or not supposed to do? Not do. Is there a rule about that? Yes. We have to be quiet. What if there were no rule, would it be all right to do then? Yes. Why? Because there is no rule.

Morality and convention, then, are distinct, parallel developmental frameworks, rather than a single system as thought of by Kohlberg. However, because all social events, including moral ones, take place within the context of the larger society, a person's reasoning about the right course of action in any given social situation may require the person to access and coordinate their understandings from more than one of these two social cognitive frameworks. For, example, whether people line up to buy movie theater tickets is largely a matter of social convention. Anyone who has traveled outside of Northern Europe or North America can attest to the fact that lining up is not a shared social norm across cultures. Within the United States or England, for example, lining up is the conventional way in which turn-taking is established. The act of turn-taking has a moral consequence. It establishes a mechanism for sharing - an aspect of distributive justice. The act of breaking in line within the American or British context is more than merely a violation of convention. It is a violation of a basic set of rules that people hold to maintain fairness. How people coordinate the possible interactions that may arise between issues of morality and convention is a function of several factors including: the salience of the features of the act (what seems most important - the moral or conventional elements); and the developmental level of the person (adolescents for example view conventions as unimportant and arbitrary norms established by adult authority).

It was Turiel's insight to recognize that what Kohlberg's theory attempts to account for within a single developmental framework is in fact the set of age-related efforts people make at different points in development to coordinate their social normative understandings from several different domains. Thus, domain theory posits a great deal more inconsistency in the judgments of individuals across contexts, and allows for a great deal more likelihood of morally (fairness and welfare) based decisions from younger and less developed people than would be expected from within the traditional Kohlberg paradigm.

* * *

Carol Gilligan and the Morality of Care

A second major critique of Kohlberg's work was put forth by Carol Gilligan, in her popular book, "In a Different Voice: Psychological Theory and Women's Development" (1982). She suggested that Kohlberg's theories were biased against women, as only males were used in his studies. By listening to women's experiences, Gilligan offered that a morality of care can serve in the place of the morality of justice and rights espoused by Kohlberg. In her view, the morality of caring and responsibility is premised in nonviolence, while the morality of justice and rights is based on equality. Another way to look at these differences is to view these two moralities as providing two distinct injunctions - the injunction not to treat others unfairly (justice) and the injunction not to turn away from someone in need (care). She presents these moralities as distinct, although potentially connected.

CAROL GILLIGAN

Photo: Creative Commons.

In her initial work, Gilligan emphasized the gender differences thought to be associated with these two orientations. The morality of care emphasizes interconnectedness and presumably emerges to a greater degree in girls owing to their early connection in identity formation with their mothers. The morality of justice, on the other hand, is said to emerge within the context of coordinating the interactions of autonomous individuals. A moral orientation based on justice was proposed as more prevalent among boys because their attachment relations with the mother, and subsequent masculine identity formation entailed that boys separate from that relationship and individuate from the mother. For boys, this separation also heightens their awareness of the difference in power relations between themselves and the adult, and hence engenders an intense set of concerns over inequalities. Girls, however, because of their continued attachment to their mothers, are not as keenly aware of such inequalities, and are, hence, less concerned with fairness as an issue. Further research has suggested, however, that moral reasoning does not follow the distinct gender lines which Gilligan originally reported. The preponderance of evidence is that both males and females reason based on justice and care. While this gender debate is unsettled, Gilligan's work has contributed to an increased awareness that care is an integral component of moral reasoning.[20]

* * *

20   Gilligan, C. (1982). *In A Different Voice: Psychological Theory and Women's Development.* Harvard University Press: Cambridge.

Kohlberg, L. & Turiel, E. (1971). *Moral development and Moral Education.* In G. Lesser, ed. *Psychology and Educational Practice.* Scott Foresman.

Piaget, J. (1965). *The Moral Judgment of the Child.* The Free Press: New York. Power, F. C., Higgins, A., & Kohlberg, L. (1989). "Lawrence Kohlberg's Approach to Moral Education." New York: Columbia University Press.

Smetana, J. G. (1996, in press). "Parenting and the Development of Social Knowledge Reconceptualized: A Social Domain Analysis." To appear in J.E. Grusec & L. Kuczynski (Eds.), *Handbook of Parenting and the Transmission of Values.* New York: Wiley.

Turiel, E. (1983). "The Development of Social Knowledge: Morality & Convention." New York: Cambridge University Press.

The contrast between Kohlberg's and Gilligan's model frequently resonates on a gender basis on a variety of issues. Are ethics about rules or are they about relationships? Under Kohlberg's analysis, ethical reasoning that centers on relationships means that the person is stuck in the middle of his moral development model. Yet, if one takes Gilligan's approach, an emphasis on relationships speaks to a higher moral value. On specific dilemmas, this can make a difference. Think, for instance, of the example of the woman dying and asking her doctor if she will be able to go home for Christmas. A strict rule that says that we should be honest at all times would require the doctor to tell the dying patient that she wouldn't be able to go home for Christmas. And, with certain patients, perhaps complete honesty would have been exactly the right thing to do. But in that situation, the doctor had a very deep sense of the patient and her family and knew what the patient needed at that moment was some rest. And in speaking to a patient whose mental awareness was compromised, the answer, "Yes, I think you will get to go home for Christmas" was a compassionate act that supported the patient and her family.

One can, of course, imagine that relationships can ask too much. What if your best friend was embezzling money from the company? Is your ethical duty to preserve your friendship and keep quiet to protect your friend or is it to proactively, honestly reveal the wrong-doing? This is where the hard part of ethics comes in. What is the mix or balance between different virtues? What is the balance between friendship and honesty? In fact, one could reframe the embezzling friend dilemma in these terms: what is the relationship that has priority? Should the primary concern be to protect the relationship of two individuals or to protect a relationship with a larger community that will suffer if embezzlement is permitted?

Though edited out of the article, Piaget rejected Emile Durkheim's emphasis on community. Piaget focused on individual decision-making, whereas Durkheim emphasized communal norms and identity. This contrast too provokes debate. Should ethics be about individual decision-making or should it see the individual in relationship with a community in which she lives and works? This tension will be a dynamic throughout this book and, frankly, in nearly every businessperson's experience. Part II of this book focuses more on making reasoned decisions by an individual faced with a dilemma. Part III of the book focuses on building ethical corporate cultures. Both are important, and they reflect many of the issues of moral development just presented.

Moreover, Turiel's domain model of innate moral values associated with harm, welfare, and fairness will coincide with the notions of Hard, Real and Good Trust which will be a primary organizing principle for Part III. Differences of norms of social construction play directly into this model, which when applied proactively, assists in the creation of corporate culture. Applied retroactively to a dilemma that has already occurred, the model taps into contemporary, philosophical categories of business ethics.

A final aspect is worth considering. These theories attend to moral development in children, but their principles are quite relevant to businesspeople today in the sense of the tug-of-war between individual and community and between rules and relationships. But they also bring to mind what moral character corporations themselves have. Corporations have been described in the law as "persons," but where would they fit on any of these development scales? One might think that, to use Kohlberg as an example, corporations might be akin to a two year-old who grasps what he can as long as he doesn't get caught. Can companies gain a higher level of moral development or are such things merely for individuals? Discussion of these kinds of issues becomes increasingly important for Part IV of this book.

CHAPTER 3

Making the Case for Ethics

E D FREEMAN, a seminal figure in the field of business ethics, established the Business Roundtables Institute for Corporate Ethics. One of the important contributions made by the Institute is a series of "Bridge Papers." These are papers where academics apply scholarship to business practices as a way o enhance both. In the previous chapter, we saw one of these in the writing of David Messick, Max Bazerman and Lisa Stewart. The following paper is another in the series. This one is written by James Walsh, Joshua Margolis, and Dean Krehmeyer. They provide a compelling rationale for the study and the practice of business ethics.

As long as ethics has been a topic in business schools, the question has been posted: Why be ethical? One philosophical response to that question is that human being should be, well, as they should be and so we should all aim to be ethical. Like Socrates in Plato's *Ring of Gyges*, being just is a noble end unto itself.

Another, more practical response is that ethics pays. Especially in the long-term, business concepts like goodwill, reputation, and social capital have economic value. In the aftermath of the Enron and Arthur Anderson controversies, Federal Reserve Chair Alan Greenspan testified on Capitol Hill that in today's economy, reputation is what firms bring to the market and if that reputation is undermined, so is the company. Placing a value on goodwill for tomorrow's decision of how to book revenue, of course, is considerably harder, but there are many empirical studies suggesting that "ethics pays" or that "corporate social performance and corporate financial performance" are linked.

Then there is the leadership argument. This more inspirational approach suggests that leaders lead through their values and leaders can choose to set new standards of how to run businesses that attract followers.

In the following article, these highly regarded academic leaders provide some very pragmatic reasons for business leaders to lead ethically.

Building the Business Case for Ethics

by James Walsh, Joshua Margolis, and Dean Krehmeyer

I n the Business Roundtable Institute for Corporate Ethics' seminars with chief executive officers and their senior executive teams, an introductory module poses the question "Does Ethics Pay?" During this interactive session we explore the business case for whether or not corporations should care about ethics. We have found that in our Institute's seminars, the answer from these influential attendees is a clear "yes."This is apparent most importantly from the depth of discussion, but we also recognize the fact that these leaders take a full day of their busy schedules to participate in the seminars –through their attendance they do indeed "vote with their feet" their belief that "ethics pays."

While we are reassured by the seminar participants' anecdotal evidence, we also analyze the research that has explored the relationship between the ethical foundations of companies and their financial performance. Managers and executives today are expected to build the "business case" for all corporate initiatives, including programs and activities that encompass social or ethical performance. Beyond searching only for the link between social (or ethical) and financial performance is a more fundamental question: Why are companies called upon to engage in social initiatives in the first place?

There appear to be two related responses to the question: (1) Social trends result in continuing reevaluation of the roles and responsibilities of firms, changing the expectations of companies, and (2) Firms find themselves in situations that demand response, independent of any systematic consideration of a firm's purpose. The most prominent recent examples are the natural disasters of the Asian Tsunami and Hurricane Katrina. Companies were expected to respond and they collectively answered the call by providing hundreds of millions of dollars worth of aid. Perhaps more valuable than the dollars provided is the extent to which businesses responded with their "core competencies"– logistics infrastructure for moving goods quickly to those in need, medical supplies for the injured, mobile telecommunications systems, and many other essential goods and services. These "competencies" represent the products, services, and skills that are quite simply among the best developed in the world, and they could not have been quickly achieved through traditional monetary aid. A *Fortune* magazine cover trumpeted "Government Broke Down. Business Stepped Up." in its post-disaster coverage of Hurricane Katrina to recognize the contributions of the corporate community. (*Fortune*, October 3, 2005)

For many of the forces drawing firms into social performance initiatives, the logic rests on the conviction that companies, as the engines of economic growth, might be able to expand what they do to help humanity beyond merely their contributions to economic growth. This may even be viewed by certain interest groups as a moral imperative. However, from the viewpoint of executives, managers, and shareholders, this logic of targeting firms for moral and social appeals doesn't speak to the impact that such activities have on the firm itself. Business cases that can document financial gains from social and ethical performance may hasten efforts to rally corporate involvement, allay fears about costs to the company, and provide value in communications and branding for the company and its executives. In designing such a business case for corporate social performance, an important first step is to analyze the research studies. One of the most complete compendiums of research in this area—"People and Profits? The Search for a

Link Between a Company's Social and Financial Performance" by Joshua Margolis and James Walsh—provides this initial analysis.[21]

This compendium analysis of 95 studies covering over 30 years of research indicates a positive relationship between social performance and financial performance. For today's business leaders, a more focused analysis in their own organizations will hopefully not only support the general conclusion of a positive relationship between social performance and financial performance, but will also contribute to more effective identification, support, and management of corporate social and ethical initiatives. If these initiatives can be shown to contribute to improved financial performance, then companies benefit from adopting practices that provide value to a variety of stakeholders.

It is first worth noting that the collective research reviewed in *People and Profits* utilizes an exceptionally broad definition of social performance. Falling under the definitional umbrella of social performance are organizational programs,charitable contributions, community investment, environmental practices, human rights, human relations, quality of services/products, and all-encompassing omnibus measures such as the *Fortune* Most Admired rankings. Indeed, the social performance measures evaluated may be cumulatively understood to represent the interests of a broad range of a corporation's stakeholders, including employees, customers, communities, and the like. A more contemporary version of the question addressed by *People and Profits* is to ascertain the relationship between the social, or stakeholder, performance of companies and their financial performance. Can a firm effectively attend to both people and profits in conducting its business?

Research Results

The research studies in *People and Profits* look at corporate social performance as both an independent and dependent variable. Put another way, whether corporate social performance contributes to, or is a product of, corporate financial performance. In the 80 studies evaluating whether corporate social performance contributes to corporate financial performance, 53% of them point to a positive relationship. No relationship is identified in 24% of the studies, 4% find a negative relationship, and the remaining 19% of the studies yield mixed exploring this question, 68% of those results. The conclusion often drawn from identify a positive relationship, with these cumulative results is that social 16% showing no relationship, and 16% initiatives contribute to the bottom line–companies do well by doing good.

21 Margolis, Joshua D., and James P. Walsh. *People and Profits? The Search for a Link Between a Company's Social and Financial Performance.* Mahwah, N.J.: Lawrence Erlbaum Associates, 2001.

When evaluating corporate social performance as an outcome of financial performance, again the studies support the correlation. With only 19 studies exploring this question, 68% of those identify a positive relationship, with 16% showing no relationship, and 16% providing mixed results. A common conclusion from these studies is that companies which are profitable have the ability to support social initiatives. Exhibits 1 and 2 provide a summary of all of the study results.

Exhibit 1. Summary Results of 95 Research Studies

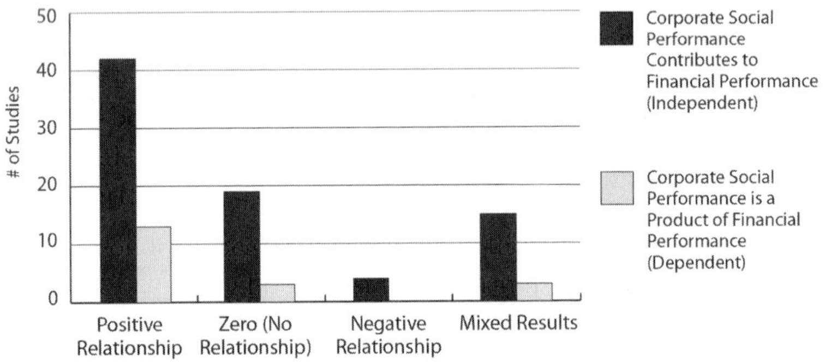

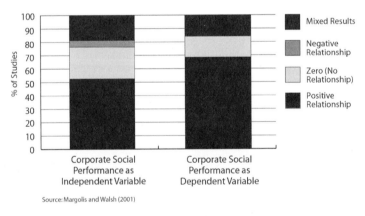

Source: Margolis and Walsh (2001)

Exhibit 2. Summary Percentage Results of 95 Research Studies

Source: Margolis and Walsh (2001)

Evolution of "Measuring" Corporate Social Performance

While a definition of corporate social performance has been gradually refined over the course of 30 years, its measurement continues to evolve. Overall, the 95 studies reviewed utilize 27 different data sources in assessing social performance and cover 11 different forms of social performance, such as organizational programs, disclosures, charitable contributions, and others. However, in general, the definition of corporate social performance has evolved from one-issue evaluations toward more broad, multi-faceted analyses, supported by the increased ability of researchers to utilize more reliable and available data. Some of the earliest corporate social responsibility studies from the 1970s reflected the most visible and publicized social issues of that time, such as pollution and withdrawal from South Africa, and broad conclusions were drawn on the study of those single issues. Moreover, the availability and transparency of information at the time resulted in measurement methods that would seem to fall short against the mechanisms used in today's age of increased availability of corporate information. In a 1978 study, for instance, a researcher reviewed annual reports and then coded companies as "mention" or "none" depending on the percentage of total lines of text dedicated to corporate social responsibility topics.[22] Clearly for a number of reasons, managers would be hard-pressed to build a business case today on "mentions" in an annual report.

While a firm's environmental practices are the most commonly measured assessment of social responsibility, omnibus measures, including *Fortune* reputation rankings, represent the second most frequent measure and have also become a more common measurement in several of the most current individual research studies. Two examples of omnibus measures illustrate the expanse of what constitutes corporate social performance, both in practice and in research. In 1975, Milton Moskowitz, an advocate for corporate social responsibility, listed the following criteria for evaluating social performance:

> "Pollution control, equal employment opportunity, minority and female representation on the board of directors, support of minority enterprise, responsible and irresponsible advertising, charitable contributions, community relations, product quality, plant safety, illegal politicking, disclosure of information, employee benefits, respect for privacy, support for cultural programs, responsiveness to consumer complaints, fair dealings with customers."[23]

The Kinder, Lydenberg, Domini (KLD) index is a second omnibus assessment widely utilized in the research. The KLD index evaluates companies against a scale for the following five criteria: community, diversity, employee relations, natural environment, and This variety is seen as capturing the product safety and quality.

---

22 Margolis and Walsh. p. 51

23 Margolis and Walsh. p. 9

Most recently, the *Fortune* Most Admired measure, in which executives, outside directors, and corporate analysts annually evaluate companies along eight attributes, is utilized in 16% (15 of 95) of the research studies reviewed. Certainly, some scholars applaud the multiple methods, measures, and data sources that have been utilized in assessing corporate social performance. This variety is seen as capturing the diversity of corporate practices that constitute social performance. Critics see it in the opposite way, as an indication that corporate social performance is an incoherent jumble of practices. Exhibits 3 and 4 provide research results by domain of investigation for corporate social performance as an independent variable.

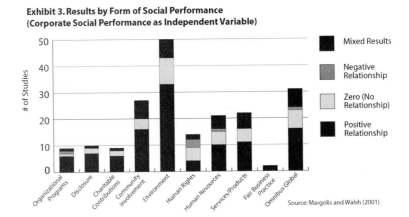

Exhibit 3. Results by Form of Social Performance
(Corporate Social Performance as Independent Variable)

Source: Margolis and Walsh (2001)

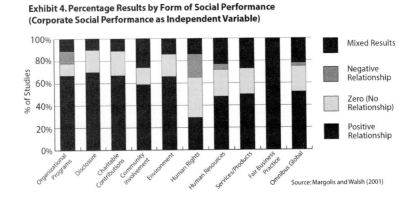

Exhibit 4. Percentage Results by Form of Social Performance
(Corporate Social Performance as Independent Variable)

Source: Margolis and Walsh (2001)

Breadth of Measuring Financial Performance

For the 95 research studies covered, 70 different metrics are used to measure financial performance. The two dominant methods of financial performance are accounting measures (e.g., ROE, ROA, ROS, ratios, etc.), which are taken to be indicators of historical performance, and market measures (e.g., annual return, total return, Alpha, Beta, etc.), which are taken to reflect future performance. Exhibit 5 provides the five most common accounting and market measures of financial performance utilized in the research studies.

Exhibit 5. Financial Performance Indicators

Accounting Measures		Market Measures	
...indicators of past performance...		...indicators of future performance...	
Measure	# of Studies where used	Measure	# of Studies where used
Return of Equity (ROE)	31	Alpha	8
Return on Assets (ROA)	28	Beta	8
Return on Sales (ROS)	13	Cumulative Annual Returns	7
Debt/Equity (e.g., Risk)	6	P/E Ratio	7
Current Ratio (e.g., Risk)	4	Total Returns	6

Source: Margolis and Walsh (2001)

Implications and Takeaways For Managers

TAKEAWAY #1: *A positive relationship exists between social (ethical) performance and financial performance.*

The signal from the 95 studies and 30 years of research reviewed is that a positive relationship exists between social (ethical) performance and financial performance. Paying attention to ethics issues and initiatives does not destroy financial value and does not distract managers from creating value for the company's stakeholders. There are nonetheless lingering questions for further research, particularly about the validity and diversity of measures used to assess social performance.

TAKEAWAY #2: *Evaluating ethical performance solely on financial performance risks ignoring other benefits and beneficiaries*

Numerous great organizations undertake ethical initiatives even in the face of financial reasons not to do so. Why? The positive financial performance supports the initiatives, but it does not mandate such actions. Organizations and their leaders should ultimately engage in ethical initiatives and actions because they see a more expansive definition of "return" and "value creation"—including elements such as employee morale, benefit to the community and society, innovation, and reputation, among other considerations. All of these considerations ultimately tie in to the organization's mission, principles, and values.

TAKEAWAY #3: *It's time to move beyond the question of "Does Ethics Pay?" and toward the action-driven inquiry, "How can managers be equipped to meet rising financial and ethical expectations?"*

Moving beyond the question of "Does Ethics Pay?" requires companies to focus instead on other questions such as:

1. What are our organization's objectives, duties and concerns? In other words, what do we stand for and want to accomplish?

2. How is our organization best able to accomplish its ethical and financial objectives?

3. How should our organization respond and act (toward social/ethical issues) when the two sets of objectives are in tension?

Ethics and Economics

It is worth remembering that Adam Smith was a moral philosopher. The use of Smith's writing, especially, *Wealth of Nations,* frequently lies in his comments about the baker and butcher seeking their self-interest and how by doing that, an invisible hand creates a greater overall good. Yet, the framework Smith proposes is one that is based on a foundation of moral action among a community where certain actions are off the table exactly because they are unethical and undermine both a sense of moral and political community and also because they undermine market functions.

Ethicists point out these problems all the time, but the issue has captured the attention of economists as well. Some, such as F.A. Hayek, who we will see later in this book, have been more explicit in connecting issues of ethics and the market. But contemporary ethicists today see this quite clearly as well. As an example of this, the following interview with economist David Rose will show this more clearly. Rose has shown that the market functions best when it rests on a foundation of morality. For him, that morality is one based on restraint: there are certain things we should not do and the fact that we feel guilty about doing them efficiently precludes them from happening, which reduces the kinds of opportunistic behavior that can undermine the market. Rather than reprinting a portion of his book, the following interview helpfully and conversationally spells out his main points.

Rose shows that this interaction between ethics and the market is deep and the market, indeed, depends on some levels of ethics in order to flourish. Rose focuses more on duty; at the end of Part III, we will see a similar argument from Spanish economist, Javier Aranzadi, who focuses more on virtue and aspiration.

David Rose on the Moral Foundations of Ethical Behavior[24]

Hosted by Russ Roberts

D avid Rose of the University of Missouri, St. Louis and the author of *The Moral Foundation of Economic Behavior* talks with EconTalk host Russ Roberts about the book and the role morality plays in prosperity. Rose argues that morality plays a crucial role in prosperity and economic development. Knowing that the people you trade with have a principled aversion to exploiting opportunities for cheating in dealing with others allows economic actors to trust one another. That in turn allows for the widespread specialization and interaction through markets with strangers that creates prosperity. In this conversation, Rose explores the nature of the principles that work best to engender trust. The conversation closes with a discussion of the current trend in morality in America and the implications for trust and prosperity.

Russ: Let's go back to the moral issue now, which is: What's necessary to create behavior on the part of individuals basically to turn down, reject, and resist the chances to be opportunistic when nobody is watching? What do we need? There are a couple of things that you need.

Guest: Number one, the person's predilection to be trustworthy cannot be merely an exercise in incentive compatibility. Which is what most economists want to do. They want to model trust behavior and trustworthiness as an exercise in incentive compatibility.

---

24   Interview of David Rose by Russ Roberts, Jan. 23, 2012, available at *http://www.econtalk.org/archives/2012/01/ david_rose_on_t.html.*

Russ: Explain what you mean by incentive compatibility.

Guest: It's the idea that it's an exercise in enlightened self-interest because it's in your own best interest to behave in a trustworthy manner. The most common example is to say: Markets breed honesty and honesty breeds markets. Suppose you've got a guy and he's a car mechanic. If he behaves in an untrustworthy way it gets back to the customers; he has less business. If he behaves in a trustworthy way, he gets rewarded for that by virtue of having more business. And so on and so forth. So, that's an example of the kind of argument that most economists like to make about trust. Which is: It's no big deal, it's easy to explain. It's in your own best interest to be trustworthy anyway. That's all well and good but the problem is if that's all there is to trust then trust is going to fall down exactly where the word is most meaningful. This is such an empty approach that Toshiyo Yamagishi, who is a pretty famous social capital theorist, sociologist in Japan, says this isn't even trust at all. We should call it assurance; that's all it is.

Russ: I agree. I don't trust you. I just know you are going to act *as if* you were trustworthy. Not the same thing.

Guest: And Oliver Williamson is very dismissive of a great deal of the trust literature; and he would say that this is what he would call calculative trust, which is a contradiction in terms anyway. So, for a situation in which there is a genuine golden opportunity is possible.

Russ: Explain that again.

Guest: A golden opportunity is a situation in which the person who may or may not behave in an opportunistic way believes there is zero probability of being caught. In any way, shape, or form. They can do it and they can get away with it, perfectly.

Russ: And this terminology comes from Robert Frank.

Guest: Yes, Bob Frank first introduced that phrase I believe in 1988 in the book *Passions Within Reason*. That's the first place I ever saw it. You've got to be able to deal with that. And so, Frank's argument, and I think he was absolutely right although he was kind of dismissed at the time, was that the only way to bust out of that is for trustworthiness to be based on moral taste. If it's in any way an exercise in rational behavior, it's not going to work for a golden opportunity. So, the thing that's producing the trustworthiness has to be in a sense pre-rational, antecedent to the rational calculation problem. So, he said it had to be moral taste. It was a heretical thing to say when he said it and people have largely dismissed it. And I think that's been a huge mistake.

Russ: They dismissed it because economists generally don't like arguments based on taste. They prefer to use arguments based on prices, incentives, etc., institutions as we talked about. But this is basically saying you'd better have a taste for being good. Or not doing a bad thing. It had better be part of your makeup, to solve that. And that is an unappealing argument methodologically. It could be true—which is the problem—but it's unappealing methodologically partly because you don't want to be in a position to say: Well, the way we'll make the world a better place is we'll get people to be better people. That obviously—most economists are uncomfortable with that kind of logic. But that doesn't mean it's not true.

Guest: This one's also uncomfortable with it. I don't like arguments that are grounded in taste, but nature doesn't care what we like. The explanation just is what it is. If it is indeed the case that tastes carry the day, then it's incumbent upon us to move forward with that as our working theory. Turns out things are not quite as bad as people think, and we can circle back to this later when we talk about culture. But anyway, you were asking what do we need: Well, first of all it needs to be taste. That's where Bob left it. He just said it's got to be taste. I pushed the ball down the field by saying if it's got to be taste, then what kind of moral taste? And then I worked through the thought experiment to discover that first and foremost, if the reason why you think something is wrong is because of the harm it does to other people, which is by the way what I would call harm-based moral restraint, and that is kind of the foundation for why most of us are reluctant to be opportunists. But if that's the only reason why you won't behave opportunistically is because of the harm that's done, then the problem is, if you are in a situation where you think nobody is going to be harmed by your opportunism, you'll still be opportunistic. And just think about it for a minute. That is not a big problem in very small group society, where you live in hunter-gatherer bands or small tribes. The number of people involved is fairly small, so even if we don't get caught, we do know that our actions might measurably harm someone that we care about, or maybe we don't care about him but we don't want to be feeling like we hurt somebody.

Russ: By the way, we should mention: guilt is a lot of what we are talking about here. Talk about that for a second.

Guest: Guilt is the mechanism through which all of this works; and the question is how do you put guilt to work? You put guilt to work by having moral values that actuate it. The point of my book is that moral values are important also, but even more important is how they are structured, because otherwise you are not going to get guilt triggered in the right sort of way.

Russ: And this point about small versus large, I found very interesting, because basically what you are saying is that guilt is going to be triggered by empathy. When I realize that I'm harming someone I'm going to feel bad about that, which is I think a universal truth. We may differ in how bad we feel about harming others and differ dramatically in how we emotionally react knowing we've hurt someone; but the insight you have which I really like is: you might be wrong, but if you don't believe you are hurting anyone, either because you don't perceive it or it's so small—the harm is spread out across many people, as it would be in a large group—the guilt is going to be very small. And you give the example, which I thought was very good, of a false insurance claim. Explain how that would work.

Guest: The basic idea is usually when we do something in a small group to behave opportunistically, somebody gets hurt and we feel guilty about it. But the greater the number of people in the group over which the cost of that harm is divided, the more likely it is that there will not be a single human being who is harmed and who we can therefore empathize with and therefore sympathize with and therefore feel guilty about having harmed.

Russ: Or, if they are harmed, it's by such a small amount they might not even perceive it.

Guest: At some point we don't even have to make that qualification. If I exaggerated my income tax deduction, if I got $1000 more dollars back from the government than otherwise, there is not a single person on the planet who is harmed. There isn't. We don't even need to quibble. We are talking about way less than a penny per person in the United States. People can't even perceive that. It's not even there. Noise swamps it by orders of magnitude. So, no one is harmed. And that's why many people who seem to be nice guys and seem like they would never do anything to hurt you or your family or anybody, very generous, good people, might cheat on their taxes.

Russ: Or inflate their expense account at work.

Guest: Exactly. And that's a fundamental problem. It's a problem everywhere, but it's an especially big problem in countries outside the West. Outside the West, if people feel like they are not hurting anybody, they really feel like they can just do whatever they want as long as they don't get caught. So, you are only left with incentives to combat opportunistic behavior. So, the point of that is that harm-based moral restraint is not enough to deal with the empathy problem; and the empathy problem is fundamental because it's a problem that gets worse the larger the group size is. And you are going to be an impoverished society if you can't sustain very large institutions, large markets, large firms. Bigness is the key. Smith is right, and getting big means that our hardwired sense of moral restraint is going to fall down on the job.

Russ: Because that's a small group thing.

Guest: Right. Because we are a small-group species.

* * *

Russ: Let's move away from the morality. Let's talk about the implications for growth, development, and our standard of living. If this is correct, and much of it seems correct to me, there are two implications. One is: Societies, cultures, that have successfully inculcated the view that stealing is just wrong, don't do it, you never want to perceive yourself as a thief—and that's either done through religion or other cultural means—those societies find it easier to specialize and grow. Societies that don't inculcate that or haven't—again there's no thing called society that tries to, but societies with individuals who have not adopted those beliefs are going to find it much more difficult to grow and be successful, because specialization and exchange in large groups is going to be much more difficult. Two questions. Number one: What's the evidence that this is true? It has an appealing casual truth to it. Might there be some specific evidence that it's true. And the second question I would have is: It seems to me, and we've talked about this informally in the last few minutes, that there's been an erosion of that moral imperative in the United States at least over the last 30-40 years. Do you think that's true and do you see any signs that it might make a difference in how we behave towards each other?

Guest: Well, as far as evidence, we do have empirical work on measured trust across the world, and measured levels of trust do co-vary well with economic performance and general quality of life in societies. That suggests that however it is they are able to achieve this trust, if they can, it does pay off. And so that doesn't cinch the argument, but it's certainly consistent with the kind of evidence that we would need to see.

Russ: Aren't there people who have done experiments—this reminds me of these experiments where you take a wallet, you leave the wallet in the middle of the street, and in some cultures, you find a wallet that isn't yours, you stuff it in your pocket as quickly as you can and hope nobody is looking or notices and nobody says: Hey, what have you got there? You just take the wallet and you get home and take the money and dump the rest in the garbage. But there are other cultures, and we know this happens, where people find that wallet and they return it to a stranger with the money in it.

Guest: And if a person was asked to come up with a list of societies where they think most people would act the latter way, they'd probably be right. Their preconceived notions are basically right. And most of those societies are well-developed and prosperous societies. But my point gets behind that point. My point is that in order to get to that condition, moral beliefs have to have a particular kind of structure. If they don't have that kind of structure, you won't have the unconditional trustworthiness and you therefore won't have an environment of trust. Because it will be unsustainable. People will not extend trust if they are continuously punished for doing so. If it's not rational to extend trust, you don't.

Russ: Like a sucker, and after a while you'd rather not be a sucker.

Guest: Right.

Russ: The second question was: Do you sense an erosion in these attitudes in civilization, in Western society. And one thing you might talk about is: where do those views come from? Do they come from folk wisdom? Religion? Does it matter? And where are we headed.

Guest: Robert Putnam has documented a pretty-much across-the-board reduction in measured levels of trust. He's focused on social capital, but he does measure trust directly. Eric Uslaner has also done this. From 1950 until the present, it's pretty grim.

In the United States, the downward slope is clear. Measured level of trust and trustworthiness are both going down through time.

* * *

PART II:

ETHICAL DECISION MAKING

ETHICAL DECISION-MAKING

ETHICS IS SUBJECTIVE but it is not only subjective. A sound decision-making process overcomes the biases we have to allow decisions that are less idiosyncratic. By setting out the steps of a decision and by applying leading scholarship to decisions, we can make it less likely that we will make decisions blinded by our biases. Learning a six-step decision making process in which one applies three leading, contemporary business ethics frameworks is the aim of this part of the book.

As we saw in the previous chapter, David Messick has argued that empirical studies demonstrate that we value our own self-interest over the well-being of others. There is nothing too surprising about that finding, but it is one that does create issues for the decisions we make. The more we are biased toward our own self-interest, the more we are likely to rationalize any decision we make and often demonize another person's actions if they annoy us.

Thus, an aim of a decision-making process is to make better, more objective decisions. The model I follow tracks heavily with that of Professor LaRue Hosmer, now emeritus at the University of Michigan. There are other models, but they tend to aim toward the same objective and pose similar questions and steps.

In this Part II, I will outline the six steps. Step Five is where the three, contemporary business ethics frameworks are introduced, and they will take some additional space to explain. Separate chapters will be devoted to Shareholder Theory, Stakeholder Theory and Virtue Theory. Each of these three chapters will begin with a case or two that sets out issues relevant to these frameworks followed by a brief explanation for the framework itself..

Perhaps it is due to my legal training, but I have found that law cases provide good examples of ethical issues. Sometimes, the law settles the issue, which itself instructively connects ethics to the power of the law; only a foolish business person would ignore that enforcement of ethical values that can cost companies dearly. But even when the law doesn't resolve the case—or it does so controversially—the issues raised often are independently interesting ethics cases.

CHAPTER 4

Hosmer's Six Step Decision Making Process

T HE FOLLOWING CASE was prepared by Alex Caine, who was a student of mine at George Washington University in 2013. To introduce Hosmer's decision-making process, read Caine's case. Then, we will work through Hosmer's process with the answers Caine and her co-author Jorge Riera, provided in the paper they submitted for the class.

★ Students wrote this ★

Crossing the Invisible Line of Ethical Boundaries

Alex Caine & Jorge Rivera

"Each person owes a duty to the Company to act with integrity. Integrity requires, among other things, being honest, fair and candid. Deceit, dishonestly and subordination of principle are all inconsistent with integrity."

—Form of Code of Ethics, American Apparel, Section 2: Honest, Ethical and Fair Conduct

A merican Apparel is a vertically integrated clothing manufacturer, wholesaler and retailer that was founded by Dov Charney in 1989. Their clothing line attracts young, "hipsters" looking for basic knit and cotton pieces that range from t-shirts, cardigans and leggings to vintage shoes and accessories. Currently, the company has 260 stores in 19 countries worldwide[1]. The company's main competitors are other retail stores such as Urban Outfitters, Abercrombie and Fitch and the Gap. In 2009, American Apparel just avoided bankruptcy by receiving an $80 million loan. Again, in 2011, the company announced that it might have to pursue bankruptcy until it was loaned another $80 million. American Apparel has not been profitable since 2010. In the first quarter of 2013, the company had approximately $138 million in sales, up 4% since the first quarter of 2012.[2]

---

1   https://www.americanapparel.net/aboutus/global/

2   http://investors.americanapparel.net/secfiling.cfm?filingID=1336545-13-18

Sweatshop Free and Environmental Innovations

In an industry where sweatshops are rampant, American Apparel is a "sweatshop free" manufacturer. Most retail manufacturing is outsourced to factories in developing countries where laborers working in poor conditions are overworked and underpaid. Unlike the majority of the industry, American Apparel's primary apparel manufacturing operation is in downtown Los Angeles where laborers are provided ample benefits and an opportunity to earn a fair wage. "The average sewer with experience at American Apparel is making about $25,000 per year... almost twice the federal minimum."[3] Benefits of working for the company include affordable health care for the employee and their family, subsidized transportation, subsidized meals, free massages, and a bike-lending program. Additionally, they offer free English language classes to their predominantly immigrant labor force. Domestic production is also an effective way to stimulate the local economy through employee purchasing power and taxes.[4] The CEO of American Apparel has stated that providing a sweatshop free environment is not an advertising ruse "criticizing other business models"[5] but a way of "taking care of the people who take care of the company."[6] American Apparel's entire business model is an anomaly in the clothing industry. Unlike other clothing manufacturers who use laborers to cut costs, American Apparel treats their laborers like human beings and respects their human needs.

In addition to their progressive labor model, American Apparel has multiple environmental initiatives that further differentiate them from industry competitors. The company's manufacturing process is aimed at minimizing their ecological footprint. Their L.A. factory is powered by a "state-of-the-art solar panel... [that] generates 150 kilowatts of clean, renewable power, contributing 15% of"[7] the energy needed. American Apparel also efficiently recycles and creatively reuses leftover fabric scraps. Scraps are either reused for new garments or they are donated to Trash for Teaching (T4T). T4T is a Los Angeles based non-profit aimed at minimizing waste by creating projects for students that recycle and reuse materials that would otherwise be trash. American Apparel also uses 100% recycled paper for their catalogues and sustainable fabrics in their product line.

American Apparel's sustainable edition is arguably one of the "greenest" clothing lines on the market. The line offers select styles made with 100% certified organic cotton and produced to minimize environmental harm. "The cultivation of organic cotton works with natural systems to help protect the health of people and wildlife while not

---

3   http://www.americanapparel.net/aboutus/verticalint/workers/

4   http://www.americanapparel.net/aboutus/verticalint/usa/

5   http://www.americanapparel.net/aboutus/verticalint/workers/

6   Dov Charney (2007). YouTube American Apparel—Don Charney Interview. CBS News, @3:28

7   http://www.americanapparel.net/aboutus/corpresp/environment/

contaminating the environment."[8] They also use a low-impact dyeing process that reduces the amount of water and chemical waste as well as provides environmental and health benefits when compared to similar processes. Finally, American Apparel is a member of the clean cotton campaign, which aims at incorporating cleaner cotton into clothing product lines. The campaign does so by providing cotton farmers with "profitable strategies for reducing chemical use."[9] From the selection of raw materials to the production process to even their marketing techniques, American Apparel is an extremely progressive company but unfortunately not all of their progressive practices are as valued.

Provocative Advertising, Provocative Culture, Provocative CEO

While most 21st century clothing advertisements display retouched, tall, thin models with perfectly symmetrical faces, American Apparel takes an entirely different approach. Advertisements are designed and created in house by the CEO and his associates, none of which are professional photographers. Their model selection process also differs significantly from other clothing retailers. Few models are selected through professional photographs as Charney picks many of the models up in stores or off the streets. The advertisements are rarely retouched and display aesthetic imperfections such as blemishes, sweat marks and tan lines. "The ads are also highly suggestive… showcasing underwear or clingy knits. They depict young men and women in bed or the shower; if they are casually lounging on a sofa or sitting on the floor their legs happen to be spread… and a couple of the young women appear to be in a heightened state of pleasure."[10] The women in the ads are frequently over-exposed with their nipples visible under lace body suits. Their advertisements are not only sexually explicit but have at times been offensive, taking advantage of human tragedy to generate sales.

In November of 2012, hurricane Sandy struck the Northeastern United States. It was a category 2 storm that caused billions of dollars in damage, left millions without power and directly caused 147 deaths.[11] American Apparel, realizing the impact the storm would have on in-store sales, decided to use the hurricane as an advertising ploy. The clothing retailer issued a 20% off everything ad targeted specifically at those affected by the hurricane. Many customers were outraged by the controversial ad and took to social media to express their discontent. Some even expressed intent to boycott the store and never shop there again. Summer Luu posted via twitter "another tasteless marketing campaign by American Apparel. Why am I not surprised."[12] The spokesperson for American Apparel, Ryan Holiday, responded by saying that the company was not trying "to

---

8   http://www.americanapparel.net/aboutus/corpresp/organic/

9   http://www.americanapparel.net/aboutus/corpresp/organic/

10   http://www.nytimes.com/2006/04/23/magazine/23apparel.html?pagewanted=2

11   http://www.nhc.noaa.gov/data/tcr/AL182012_Sandy.pdf

12   http://abcnews.go.com/blogs/business/2012/10/hurricane-sandy-sales-good-business-or-bad-taste/

offend anyone or capitalize on a natural disaster"[13], in fact, the company is committed to disaster relief per their credo. Holiday also stated "people forget how expensive it is to run a Made in USA brand like American Apparel... Retail stores are the lifeline of a brand like ours so when they are closed we need to come up with ways to make up for that lost revenue... to keep the machine going—for the sake of our employees and stakeholders."[14] The company ran the ad as a mechanism to maintain short-term profits because the closures would significantly affect the revenue for the retail stores in the area. While the ad may have achieved its' short-term objective, it hurt the reputation of the brand and supported the public issue with American Apparel's "no shame" advertising. Despite the public reaction to the insensitivity of the ad, the CEO and spokesperson did not show any remorse. Charney said that he would not lose sleep over the Hurricane Sandy ad, arguing that the brand is the largest US made brand and that business cannot stop because of a storm.

American Apparel

Charney's provocative nature extends from the company's advertising to the day-to-day workplace. In 2008, Charney publicly called Ken Cieply, the CFO of American Apparel, a complete loser. A few weeks later Cieply resigned and American Apparels stock price plummeted. Charney is also known for his "belief that sexual relationships in the workplace are appropriate; 'I think it's a First Amendment right to pursue one's affection for another human being.'"[15] He has also been accused of "using crude languages and gestures, conducting job interviews in his underwear, ordering the hiring of women in whom he had sexual interest and giving one of the employees a vibrator."[16] In 2004 he masturbated in front of a reporter, Claudine Ko, who was writing a profile for Jane magazine about American Apparel's founder. Charney has also had many sexual harassment suits filed against him; by March of 2011 five former employees had filed suits against him.

---

13   http://www.huffingtonpost.com/2012/11/01/american-apparel-hurricane-sandy-marketing-dov-charney_n_2056410.html

14   http://www.huffingtonpost.com/2012/11/01/american-apparel-hurricane-sandy-marketing-dov-charney_n_2056410.html

15   http://theweekinethics.wordpress.com/2011/03/13american-apparel-and-the-ethics-of-a-sexually-charged-workplace/

16   http://hbr.org/product/american-apparel-unwrapping-ethics/an/W12134-HCB-ENG

Abercrombie and Fitch is one of American Apparel's competitors that has long been criticized for their racy ads and use of sex in advertising. In 2003, they had to recall their holiday catalogue in response to negative reactions from advocacy groups claiming the catalogue "promotes sexual promiscuity."[17] The company has also had many lawsuits against them for sexual assault, namely models being forced to masturbate during photo shoots. Recently, Mike Jeffries, the CEO of Abercrombie stated, "a lot of people don't belong [in our clothes], and they can't belong. Are we exclusionary? Absolutely... Those companies that are in trouble are trying to target everybody: young, old, fat, skinny."[18] Similar to American Apparel, Abercrombie uses racy, sex-driven advertisements to attract a certain clientele. Arguably, a sex-driven corporate culture is a marketing ploy necessary to attract a certain clientele in the clothing industry and the drives the use of provocative advertising.

American Apparel is a company that has long had a disconnect between its "socially progressive labor policies and uses of significant environmental advances in their manufacturing, mixed with a highly sexualized nature of the companies advertising."[19] The company has used their devotion to American nationalism to justify insensitive advertisements. Arguably, to capture the value of their corporate culture, American Apparel should extend their progressivity from production to advertisements. On the other hand, perhaps progressive production processes and a sex-driven culture are mutually exclusive. Is there a moral issue here? If so, what is it? Or are these approaches by American Apparel simply separate parts of the company's strategy and marketing that can be sustained over the long-term?

Decision-making processes attempt to mute biases that we have so that we can make decisions more rationally and to defend our reasoning more clearly. Ethics is not unique in this. In a Strategy or Marketing class, it is not enough to simply say that your gut feeling tells you to adopt a certain new marketing effort or corporate strategy. Gut feelings are important, but a company goes through a process to determine best strategies, marketing and human resources approaches. They do this so that they make better decisions. Once they are made, a process allows others to better understand why they are made rather than simply being told that the decision came from the CEO's gut instincts (though that does happen sometimes).

It is a bit strange, then, when people say that ethics can't be taught or that they are simply subjective intuitions or traits of personal character that either one has or

---

17   http://money.cnn.com/2003/12/09/news/companies/abercrombie/

18   http://www.cbc.ca/news/business/story/2013/05/08/business-abercrombie-plus-size.html

19   http://hbr.org/product/american-apparel-unwrapping-ethics/an/W12134-HCB-ENG

one doesn't have. Of course, there are intuitions in ethics, just as there are intuitions in strategy. Of course, some people have traits that lend themselves well to making ethical decisions in marketing. But decisions can be made better and are better explained when one tries to apply a reasoning process to dilemmas. That is as true of ethics as it is of anything else.

There is another anomaly about ethics: it is personal and it is private. Well, yes, sort of, and so what? Ethics are personal. They comprise decisions about who we are as human beings, what we value, what we stand for, and how we are identified to the world. There certainly is a personal dimension to ethics, which is why in Part I, this textbook opened with a request that you share a personal story about something that moved you.

Is ethics private? In one sense, it is absurd to think that it is. Ethics are about how we treat other people, so how could interacting with other people be considered private? Ethics are always about some degree of public interaction where we ask how others should be treated. Ethics cannot be purely private. A follow up response, however, requires us to consider how big of a circle we are thinking of when talking about ethics. Ethical conduct is crucial to a relationship with a significant other. There is privacy in that relationship, but it is not purely private. The wider we draw the circle—to friends, to community, to a business, to a nation, to the human race, to the ecosystem—the more questions are raised of just how private or public our decisions are. As we draw those circles, some things are indeed private. But they are never purely private.

So what? What if they are personal and what if they are a mix of private and public? Even if that is true, we human beings don't simply sit around and let other people do whatever they want to do. Or, when we do see such inaction, we can get pretty disgusted. None of us would say, well, Adolf Hitler had his moral views and they are personal and private to him and so we should not do anything as he kills six million Jews. That would be an absurd moral position. When we see such things, we react. We do not allow anyone to do whatever they please when such actions negatively impact others. So even if there are degrees of personal conduct and of private conduct, there are limits too. Defining what those limits are is tough stuff. But I want to be certain to disabuse you of some of these dismissive—and frankly, thoughtless—rules of thumb that some will toss out to argue that ethics is so different from any other subject in a business or law school that it cannot be taught. *Imp*

With this in mind, let's look at the decision-making model. The six steps of Hosmer's Moral Reasoning Process ("HMRP") are as follows:

1. Identify the Moral Issue

2. Identify Additional Facts Helpful to Making a Decision

3. Identify the Alternatives Available to Apply to the Problem

4. Identify the Personal Impacts to the Decision Maker

5. Apply Three Leading Contemporary Theories of Business Ethics: Shareholder, Stakeholder, and Virtue

6. Conclude With a Decision

HMRP Step One: *Identify the Moral Problem*

A quick and dirty way of identifying the moral issue is asking who has been harmed and whether they have been harmed in a significant way. Of course, people are harmed all the time. People lose all the time. It's one thing to lose; it's another thing to create an ethical dilemma. Just because your favorite team loses a game, or you lose a job or another company or another individual wins a bid does not mean that there is an ethical dilemma. In a capitalist society, there are winners and losers. Fair or not, the free market system is the one we find ourselves in, and this decision-making framework assumes that to be the case.

Professor LaRue Hosmer

In identifying a moral issue, one is looking at a situation where there has been harm to a vulnerable party who has been unable to protect him or herself particularly well. For instance, we will see a case in the next chapter where there was a depletion of well water for an agricultural plant to operate in Mexico. Residents had previously been able to get clean drinking water by drilling sixty feet deep, but with the depletion, one had to drill 450 feet deep. As a result, children now drink sewage with human waste in it. And so when a five-year old asks, "Daddy, can I have a drink of water?" the father will have to give him human waste to drink. That constitutes a moral dilemma.

In another famous case, orphaned street children sniffed glue in Central America. It may be true that their parents have the primary responsibility to make sure their kids aren't sniffing glue. It is also probably true that the government and the society has a responsibility to make sure that those kids are cared for and not just left on the street where they end up sniffing the glue in order to relieve hunger pangs and to make them high and to give a bit of relief in an otherwise pretty dreary existence. But this does not preclude a tertiary responsibility, a third level of responsibility held by companies doing business in the area, whose product is what the children sniff. The only thing standing between the children sniffing glue and sniffing his or her brains out and potentially dying is what the company chooses to do.

The moral issue can be stated in a sentence or two. There could be twenty moral harms in a given case. Picking one doesn't mean that that's necessarily the only one that has been brought up in a particular case, but this step provides a focus for an evaluation.

Recalling the short case on American Apparel, here is how the students framed the moral issue:

> American Apparel is a company that has long had a disconnect between its socially progressive labor policies and uses of significant environmental advances in their manufacturing, mixed with a highly sexualized nature of the companies advertising. The company pushes some ethical boundaries, justifying them by the company's ethical devotion to American nationalism. Considering the financial difficulties of the company, it is relevant to consider whether this disconnect is sustainable or whether the highly sexualized nature of the company and its advertisements should be changed. American Apparel has some alternatives to address their moral dilemma. They can do nothing; maintain their business practices in a highly sexualized culture. They can completely change the culture; use trendy fashion to sell their brand rather than sex. Or they can do something in between. In order to determine the best alternative for American Apparel, it is relevant to consider four basic ethical theories; stakeholder theory, shareholder theory, virtue theory and total integrity management (*Internal citations omitted*).

HMRP Step Two: *Additional Facts*

Business students and businesspeople tend to do quite well in finding many additional facts and identifying questions that they want to have answers to before they make a conclusion. That's healthy. One of the best things you can do in making an ethical analysis is to find additional facts so that you're not gossiping. This step thus becomes the opportunity to recognize the additional facts that would be helpful to know. One still must often make a decision based on insufficient information; life tends to require that. But this is an opportunity to identify three or four additional facts that would be helpful to know in making a moral decision. Of course, these facts need to be relevant. One can come up with many different facts that are of some kind of interest, but might there be, for instance in the American Apparel case, any empirical studies that demonstrate a relationship between racy apparel ads and anti-social conduct. Another relevant fact might be whether there is evidence of objections customers have raised concerning the ads or not. Additional facts need not be determinative, but they do need to be germane.

HMRP Step Three: *Available Alternatives*

Step three looks at additional alternatives. Sometimes, we may think of an ethical issue as an either-or choice. You must either do the saintly thing or risk selling your soul. Frequently there are a lot of options in between. When H.B. Fuller was faced with street children sniffing its shoe-repair glue in Honduras, the company could have book-end choices: get out of the market or continue to sell the product as is. Yet, there were many alternatives Fuller could pursue. It could fund social service agencies to help the kids, place better warning labels so the kids recognize the danger of the product even if they even they were illiterate, or conduct additional research and development to have a safer product. Thus, between the bookends, one finds alternatives.

What alternatives might American Apparel have in this case that would link its commitment to integrity while also having effective marketing?

HDMP Step Four: *Identify Personal Impacts*

Personal impacts are not the impacts on the various human beings that are affected by a corporate decision. That's what stakeholder theory is about. Personal impacts apply to the following: Assume that you are in the position of being the decision-maker or a person who's making a recommendation to the decision-maker. In that position, what are the consequences to you as a person and what are the consequences to your career resulting from the decision you make? Recognize that from a career standpoint, it can cut both ways. If the company thinks that you spend too much money in order to head off an ethical problem, you may be viewed as a profligate spender who has no business in the tough world of being a manager and therefore lose your career track or be fired.

On the other hand, if you ignore the problem, things could go the opposite way: you could become the scapegoat. One can imagine an executive saying, "You know, if Tim had told me there was a problem, I would have done something about it. He stayed quiet, he's to blame." So recognize that in many situations, the personal impacts could go in a couple of different directions.

In addition to this career issue, there are personal impacts that relate to your conscience and well-being. These personal impacts have become clichés. The problem with a cliché is that it has enough truth in it to bear repeating, which is why it gets repeated, which is how it becomes a cliché. While I prefer not to perpetuate clichés, let me repeat them one more time.

The first one is the newspaper approach. Are you comfortable with having your proposed action being reported in a newspaper of wide circulation: *Washington Post, New York Times, Wall Street Journal, Le Monde,* or whatever the paper of importance is to you? A variation of this test is the loved one test. There is a wonderful book that was written several years ago by Yale Law Professor Amy Chua, entitled *World on Fire.* Professor Chua interviewed many executives around the world. One executive told Professor Chua that he would never tell his family what he did during the day. Well, if you can't tell your family what you're doing during the day because you're embarrassed by what you do, maybe there's a problem with what you're doing.

The final variation is the tombstone test. What would you like to have said about you on your tombstone or your gravestone? As what kind of a person will you be remembered?

HMDP Step Five: *Apply Three Moral Frameworks*

Professor Hosmer's Step Five applies ten ethical principles drawn from thousands of years of philosophy. The modification I have made is to reduce these to three leading, contemporary business ethics frameworks which capture the historical philosophies and place them into a business application. Each of the three frameworks has its own chapters and so the details of each can be saved for those full treatments. But one preparatory comment is in order. One learns the most about making ethical decisions by applying those frameworks as you think their expositor would. How would they have tried to solve the problem given the situation they faced? You will learn much from each of them even if you conclude that philosophers Tom Donaldson or Pat Werhane belong on Pluto. I happen to think that they do not belong on Pluto; I think that they have much wisdom to share, but if you ultimately disagree with them, there is a place for you to say so.

Returning to the American Apparel case, here is how the students applied these frameworks. *(Please note that a significant portion of Part II of this book will explain each of these frameworks in more detail.—Ed.)*

Stakeholder Theory

In order to apply stakeholder theory to a company, it is first important to consider the relevant stakeholders. A stakeholder is any individual who has a stake in the company and is affected by the success or failure of the organization. In the case of American Apparel, the relevant stakeholders are the employees, the shareholders, the environment and the customers. Stakeholder theory is multi-faceted. The first facet considers basic versus non-basic rights. American Apparel does not violate the basic rights to life, water, food, shelter, or health of any of their stakeholders. In fact, by providing subsidized health care and meals, American Apparel enhances the basic rights of their employees. The company also enhances the basic right of health for the environment their innovative tactics. One could argue that sexual assault violates the basic right to freedom from torture. Based on the cases against American Apparel, none of the allegations against Charney appear to be on the level of torture. Thus, the company does not violate any basic rights, although they do violate two competing non-basic rights.

In the case of American Apparel, two non-basic rights can include the right to work in an environment free of sexual discrimination and assault and freedom of expression. Both of these non-basic rights are in conflict with each other. Charney creates a culture that allows for freedom of expression, even if the expression it is sexual in nature. The sexual explicitness of the company, as seen through the company's advertisements and Charney's actions, fosters an environment where instances of sexual assault can be underrated. In the case of two conflicting non-basic rights, a compromise between them is essential. The most sensible compromise is to provide a work environment free of sexual assault and allow freedom of expression within limits whereby sexual discrimination and harassment are not permitted under freedom of expression.

One could argue in favor of freedom of expression by saying that it is a part of American Apparel's corporate culture and brand but this would raise the question of whether a company can sell sex without promoting instances of sexual assault. Abercrombie and Fitch is a company that has long been criticized for their use of sex in advertising. In 2003, they even had to recall their holiday catalogue in response to negative reactions from advocacy groups claiming the catalogue promotes sexual promiscuity. Similarly to American Apparel, Abercrombie uses sex to sell their clothing line, and also has lawsuits against them for sexual assault, namely models being forced to masturbate during photo shoots. Thus, it seems that a sex-driven corporate culture and sexual assault instances are linked and perhaps cannot be separated. In other words, it appears that a company that uses sex in advertising is unable to prevent sexual assault in the work place.

The justice portion of stakeholder theory emphasizes the importance of equity in the workplace. Workers should be compensated equally for equal work. Based on the justice aspect of stakeholder theory, American Apparel offers more than equal treatment to their workers. They offer significantly better treatment to their employees relative to the rest of the industry. Justice is also about protecting the vulnerable. In a similar case, *Dornhecker vs. Malibu Grand Prix*, Mr. Rockefeller has similar conduct to that of Charney. "Rockefeller put his hands on her hips in an airport ticket line and dropped his pants in front of passengers while waiting to board the airplane. He touched her breasts." While the sexual lawsuits filed against American Apparel were either thrown out or sent to arbitration, and the case against Rockefeller was overturned, it does not make the conduct acceptable. Evidently, Charney's sexual nature, discrimination and acts of assault are taking advantage of the vulnerable. "The irony of sexual freedom in the workplace is that it is about power, not romance. If often ends up exploiting those most vulnerable."Under the justice component of stakeholder theory, it appears that sexually explicit acts in a business setting can be deemed unjust as they take advantage of the weak (*internal citations omitted*).

Utilitarianism focuses on providing the greatest amount of utility to the greatest number of stakeholders. Under a utilitarian view, if American Apparel had to choose between their two biggest ethical stances, certainly providing sweatshop free labor would win. It provides 7,500 jobs in Los Angeles at a higher than minimum rate. But, a culture free of sexual assault and sweatshop free labor are not mutually exclusive; that is to say a company does not have to pick one or the other. The greatest utility to the greatest number of stakeholders would be provided if American Apparel kept the sweatshop free labor, progressive environmental habits and stopped using sex as a component of their corporate culture. This would be the most satisfactory outcome for all the employees.

Evidently, American Apparel is a company with competing moral drivers. In some instances they are industry innovators, creating a better environment for their stakeholders, whereas in other instances they are using their corporate culture as an excuse for the promiscuity of their CEO. The major flaw that American Apparels has is the conflict between two non-basic rights: freedom of expression and sexual assault in the workplace. Disregarding any other theories, stakeholder theory would state that the company should stop using sex as a corporate driver continue the labor and environmental practices. Whether the sex driven culture drives profits will be further considered under shareholder theory but considering rights, equality and maximum utility the culture should be changed.

Shareholder Theory

While traditionally shareholder theory is aimed at maximizing shareholder profitability, recently it has been adjusted to include non-economic lawful directives as well as lawful directives. While American Apparel has a duty to maximize profit and distribute the wealth to its investors, it also has a duty to enhance the reputation of the firm and take interest in the public good. Shareholder theory is one of the few theories in which the sweatshop free factory in Los Angeles can be appeared as a negative. While it is right and just to provide those employees with fair employment, the rest of the industry does not, so why should American Apparel? Those other companies are also earning a higher profit margin enabling them to redistribute more wealth to their shareholders. On the other hand, the sweatshop free factory creates a precedent for American Apparel. Customers appreciate the brand more knowing that the garments are produced in a fair manner. It is still important to consider whether sweatshop free factories provide American Apparel with longevity and a sustainable business plan. Having been close to bankruptcy twice in the past 5 years indicates that perhaps a change in the structure may be necessary. When Nike was accused of using child labor to manufacture their clothing, their sales and stock price dropped significantly. This was only temporary as eventually sales and the price rose back up. Despite a short run plummet in profits, American Apparel may be able to use sweatshops in the long run but doing so would completely defy one of the biggest non-economic lawful directives and branding labels of the company—being sweatshop free. American Apparel's advertising, on the other hand, may seem to have short-term benefits at huge long-term costs.

The ad that American Apparel ran during Hurricane Sandy was considered to be a marketing ploy in order to prevent the loss of an excess of funds due to the storm. "People forget how expensive it is to run a Made in USA brand like American Apparel and if we made a mistake here it came from the good place of trying to keep the machine going—for the sake of our employees and stakeholders." The company's short term thought process on the importance of maintaining a profit seemed to overlook the long-term importance of branding and reputation. Many individuals took to Twitter offended by the sale and indicating that they were going to boycott American Apparel and never shop there again. While the company claims they were trying to fulfill what can be seen as an economic lawful directive, to generate a profit for stakeholders and maintain jobs for employees, the ad was insensitive to those who lost their homes and extremely insensitive to those who lost their lives. Furthermore, the reaction of the spokesperson and CEO were appalling. Neither showed any remorse for those who were offended by the ad and the CEO said that he would not lose sleep over the Hurricane Sandy ad that the company ran. In the short term, the ad boosted revenue though in the long term it hurt the reputation of the brand and furthered public issue with American Apparel's no-shame advertising *(internal citations omitted)*.

Virtue Theory

Virtue theory focuses on the fact that human beings are social beings and thus by definition have to practice ethics. The first relevant virtue under virtue theory is integrity. American Apparel discusses integrity in its credo; "each person owes a duty to the Company to act with integrity. Integrity requires, among other things, being honest, fair and candid. Deceit, dishonesty and subordination of principle are all inconsistent with integrity." American Apparel does not act with sexual integrity despite its importance being clearly stated in their credo. While their definition of integrity is clear, sexual integrity can be defined as being modest and humble when it comes to one's personal life. This requires some separation of work and sex, something that is not at all present at American Apparel *(internal citations omitted)*.

Another relevant virtue for American Apparel is innovation. Whether it is its progressive labor or environmental practices, American Apparel is a leader within the industry. They continually innovate to find more environmentally friendly ways of recycling and producing their materials. They are also industry leaders on their sweatshop-free labor practices. A third relevant virtue to American Apparel is efficiency-profitability. Taken independently of other virtues, American Apparel does not necessarily value this virtue. Their labor practices make their costs significantly higher than those of other companies in the same industry. Furthermore, there are more efficient locations and processes that the company could use although they would not be as environmentally friendly. Disregarding the profitability of long-term reputation, in raw dollars the company's practices do not transform efficiency into profit.

HMDP Step Six: *Conclusion*

You can say this person belongs on Pluto and no one should never listen to them again in step six. Step six calls for a conclusion. This could be to choose the Justice approach in the Stakeholder Theory. It could be to choose maximizing profitability in the short term. It could be a mix of a variety of the frameworks. For example, one would design a solution based on respecting rights and protecting the vulnerable because in the long term, such attention is going to create the greatest good for the greatest number, which will also equate with long-term shareholder value.

Returning to the American Apparel case, here is how the students concluded:

Shares, Stakes, Virtues and Integrity

American Apparel is a company that has a significant disconnect between some of its ethical practices, being innovative and avant-garde for the industry, and its advertising ploys that are offensive and create a negative corporate culture. It appears that the ethical and unethical aspects of the company do not go hand in hand, that is one can be let go without harming the other. American Apparel has established a do-good reputation from its labor practices and does not need racy advertising ploys to be a recognized. In fact, according to virtually all the frameworks above, the company can completely remove sex from its corporation. American Apparel ought to stop using sex to sell their clothing and stop creating a sexually explicit corporate culture. The company may be unable to do so under the rule of the current CEO in which case he should be replaced. Nothing is more personal than providing services to people that they cannot provide for themselves. This is exactly what businesses do and in doing so, businesses ought to act in the best interest of the people. American Apparel needs to align their labor employees with their other employees and provide the same environment for both. That would make American Apparel a truly ethical company.

Every year, studies report that a large percentage of people think that they themselves are highly ethical, while they also think that a large percentage of the rest of the world is not.[20] It's hard to square those two observations except to note, as we saw in Part I, that we are biased and we deceive ourselves. We need something to keep ourselves honest. A framework such as Hosmer's helps us do just that and will help us to make better ethical decisions in business.

---

20   Ann E. Tenbrusnel et al., *The Ethical Mirage: A Temporal Explanation as to Why We Aren't as Ethical as We Think We Are* (2007).

CHAPTER 5

Contemporary Ethical Theory in Business: Legal Compliance/Shareholder Theory

SCHOOLS OF MANAGEMENT and Law tend to emphasize the duty of mangers to the shareholders of the firm. They emphasize it so much, they often oversimplify it so that much of its richness—and its complexity—is lost. This chapter tries to mess things up a bit and present a wider range of materials and perspectives on what the law requires of managers.

Charles Darwin did not find corporations as an example of evolutionary development. Nor did Moses bring the idea of managerial responsibility to shareholders down the mountain nor, as far as we can tell, was it part of the Buddha's spiritual enlightenment. Tom Donaldson and Tom Dunfee, whose work we will see later on this chapter, have called corporations "artifactual."[21] They are creations of society not principles of nature or divine order. Societies have prescribed different kinds of relationships between shareholders and managers over time and even today. That history and nuance is frequently lost in the emphasis on managers maximizing shareholder value, a value that is typically measured in the short-term. Contradicting that ideological assertion—which is not to say that the ideology is bad, but simply that it is an ideology—can seem to place one outside of mainstream thinking. In one post-Enron book, an employee of Enron noted that any raising of ethical issues in his the Accounting, Marketing, or Finance courses of his University's MBA Program was ridiculed.[22] While maximizing shareholder value has its place, this Chapter's aim is to show how the law prescribes a considerably more sophisticated set of rules regarding a manager's responsibility. Thus, the chapter will examine two law cases that seemingly contradict each other, but because they are still good law, also provide a window into the complexity to which I refer. Then the chapter provides a theoretical description of key elements of shareholder theory based on the law. The following chapter will examine specific laws that have a major impact on business.

---

21   Thomas Donaldson and Thomas W. Dunfee , *Toward a Unified Conception of Business Ethics: Integrative Social Contracts Theory*, 19(2) Acad. Management Rev. 252, 258 (1994).

22   Brian Cruver, *The Anatomy of Greed* (2006)

A. Two Case Studies: *Dodge v. Ford* and *Wrigley v. Shlensky*

Dodge v. Ford Motor Co.

170 N.W. 668 (Mich. 1919)

OSTRANDER, CJ.

* * *

Mr. Henry Ford is the dominant force in the business of the Ford Motor Company. No plan of operations could be adopted unless he consented, and no board of directors can be elected whom he does not favor. One of the directors of the company has no stock. One share was assigned to him to qualify him for the position, but it is not claimed that he owns it. A business, one of the largest in the world, and one of the most profitable, has been built up. It employs many men, at good pay.

'My ambition,' said Mr. Ford, 'is to employ still more men, to spread the benefits of this industrial system to the greatest possible number, to help them build up their lives and their homes. To do this we are putting the greatest share of our profits back in the business.'

'With regard to dividends, the company paid sixty per cent. on its capitalization of two million dollars, or $1,200,000, leaving $58,000,000 to reinvest for the growth of the company. This is Mr. Ford's policy at present, and it is understood that the other stockholders cheerfully accede to this plan.'

He had made up his mind in the summer of 1916 that no dividends other than the regular dividends should be paid, 'for the present.'

> 'Q. For how long? Had you fixed in your mind any time in the future, when you were going to pay—
>
> 'A. No.
>
> 'Q. That was indefinite in the future?
>
> A. That was indefinite; yes, sir.'

The record, and especially the testimony of Mr. Ford, convinces that he has to some extent the attitude towards shareholders of one who has dispensed and distributed to them large gains and that they should be content to take what he chooses to give. His testimony creates the impression, also, that he thinks the Ford Motor Company has made too much money, has had too large profits, and that, although large profits might be still earned, a sharing of them with the public, by reducing the price of the output of the company, ought to be undertaken. We have no doubt that certain sentiments, philanthropic and altruistic, creditable to Mr. Ford, had large influence in determining the policy to be pursued by the Ford Motor Company—the policy which has been herein referred to.

It is said by his counsel that—

> 'Although a manufacturing corporation cannot engage in human-itarian works as its principal business, the fact that it is organized for profit does not prevent the existence of implied powers to carry on with humanitarian motives such charitable works as are incidental to the main business of the corporation.'

And again:

> 'As the expenditures complained of are being made in an expan-sion of the business which the company is organized to carry on, and for purposes within the powers of the corporation as hereinbefore shown, the question is as to whether such expenditures are rendered illegal because influenced to some extent by humanitarian motives and pur-poses on the part of the members of the board of directors.'

Let's stop here for a moment. With the facts of this case set out, who do you think won this case? Who do you think should have won this case? The first question is a descriptive one: As a matter of prediction, what do you think the Court decided? The second question in an ethical one: Regardless of what the Court actually decided, what do you think the Court should have decided? Think about this for a few moments and then proceed on to see the results.

The difference between an incidental humanitarian expenditure of corporate funds for the benefit of the employees, like the building of a hospital for their use and the employment of agencies for the betterment of their condition, and a general purpose and plan to benefit mankind at the expense of others, is obvious. There should be no confusion (of which there is evidence) of the duties which Mr. Ford conceives that he and the stockholders owe to the general public and the duties which in law he and his co-directors owe to protesting, minority stockholders. A business corporation is organized and carried on primarily for the profit of the stockholders. The powers of the directors are to be employed for that end. The discretion of directors is to be exercised in the choice of means to attain that end, and does not extend to a change in the end itself, to the reduction of profits, or to the nondistribution of profits among stockholders in order to devote them to other purposes.

There is committed to the discretion of directors, a discretion to be exercised in good faith, the infinite details of business, including the wages which shall be paid to employees, the number of hours they shall work, the conditions under which labor shall be carried on, and the price for which products shall be offered to the public.

* * *

Assuming the general plan and policy of expansion and the details of it to have been sufficiently, formally, approved at the October and November, 1917, meetings of directors, and assuming further that the plan and policy and the details agreed upon were for the best ultimate interest of the company and therefore of its shareholders, what does it amount to in justification of a refusal to declare and pay a special dividend or dividends? The Ford Motor Company was able to estimate with nicety its income and profit. It could sell more cars than it could make. Having ascertained what it would cost to produce a car and to sell it, the profit upon each car depended upon the selling price. That being fixed, the yearly income and profit was determinable, and, within slight variations, was certain.

Henry Ford, top; John and Horace Dodge, bottom.

Defendants say, and it is true, that a considerable cash balance must be at all times carried by such a concern. But, as has been stated, there was a large daily, weekly, monthly receipt of cash. The output was practically continuous and was continuously, and within a few days, turned into cash. Moreover, the contemplated expenditures were not to be immediately made. The large sum appropriated for the smelter plant was payable over a considerable period of time. So that, without going further, it would appear that, accepting and approving the plan of the directors, it was their duty to distribute on or near the 1st of August, 1916, a very large sum of money to stockholders.

In reaching this conclusion, we do not ignore, but recognize, the validity of the proposition that plaintiffs have from the beginning profited by, if they have not lately, officially, participated in, the general policy of expansion pursued by this corporation. We do not lose sight of the fact that it had been, upon an occasion, agreeable to the plaintiffs to increase the capital stock to $100,000,000 by a stock dividend of $98,000,000. These things go only to answer other contentions now made by plaintiffs, and do not and cannot operate to estop them to demand proper dividends upon the stock they own. It is obvious that an annual dividend of 60 per cent. upon $2,000,000, or $1,200,000, is the equivalent of a very small dividend upon $100,000,000, or more.

The decree of the court below fixing and determining the specific amount to be distributed to stockholders is affirmed.

Does the result of this case surprise you or confirm the prediction you made at the midpoint of its presentation above? In my 25-plus years of teaching this case, slightly more than half of the students reading this case expected Ford to win. Henry Ford, after all, was the majority shareholder and the CEO of the company. If he decided to do something, it would be done. Students also argue that Ford's philosophy seems fairly contemporary and wise. He is executing an approach that will result in more market share (or as the auto industry was in its infancy, assure that Ford's large market share would be maintained). Paying employees more also played into another Ford policy of paying his workers enough to be able to purchase the product they produced. So slightly more than half of my students have been very surprised with the result.

Those who weren't surprised advanced two reasons. The first was a rationale based on reverse engineering: there is a Dodge Motor Company so they probably got the dividend to help fund their own company. The second was more philosophical: shareholders rule.

What was your reaction to the way the case came out, both as a matter of prediction—i.e. who won the case—and do you think the Court made the right decision?

Dodge v. Ford's emphasis on the duty of managers to its shareholders has been a staple of shareholder advocates for decades. Indeed, it would be a foolish executive who would ignore his/her obligations to the shareholders. But just when one would think that shareholder theory is a simple, straight-forward set of duties from management to shareholders to maximize shareholder value, along comes the Chicago Cubs to confuse things.

Shlensky v. Wrigley

237 N.E.2d 776 (Ill. App. 1968)

SULLIVAN J.

* * *

Plaintiff is a minority stockholder of defendant corporation, Chicago National League Ball Club (Inc.), a Delaware corporation with its principal place of business in Chicago, Illinois. Defendant corporation owns and operates the major league professional baseball team known as the Chicago Cubs. The corporation also engages in the operation of Wrigley Field, the Cubs' home park, the concessionaire sales during Cubs' home games, television and radio broadcasts of Cubs' home games, the leasing of the field for football games and other events and receives its share, as visiting team, of admission moneys from games played in other National League stadia. The individual defendants are directors of the Cubs and have served for varying periods of years. Defendant Philip K. Wrigley is also president of the corporation and owner of approximately 80% of the stock therein.

Plaintiff alleges that since night baseball was first played in 1935 nineteen of the twenty major league teams have scheduled night games. In 1966, out of a total of 1620 games in the major leagues, 932 were played at night. Plaintiff alleges that every member of the major leagues, other than the Cubs, scheduled substantially all of its home games in 1966 at night, exclusive of opening days, Saturdays, Sundays, holidays and days prohibited by league rules. Allegedly this has been done for the specific purpose of maximizing attendance and thereby maximizing revenue and income.

The Cubs, in the years 1961–65, sustained operating losses from its direct baseball operations. Plaintiff attributes those losses to inadequate attendance at Cubs' home games. He concludes that if the directors continue to refuse to install lights at Wrigley Field and schedule night baseball games, the Cubs will continue to sustain comparable losses and its financial condition will continue to deteriorate.

Plaintiff alleges that, except for the year 1963, attendance at Cubs' home games has been substantially below that at their road games, many of which were played at night.

Plaintiff compares attendance at Cubs' games with that of the Chicago White Sox, an American League club, whose weekday games were generally played at night. The weekend attendance figures for the two teams was similar; however, the White Sox week-night games drew many more patrons than did the Cubs' weekday games.

Plaintiff alleges that the funds for the installation of lights can be readily obtained through financing and the cost of installation would be far more than offset and recaptured by increased revenues and incomes resulting from the increased attendance.

Plaintiff further alleges that defendant Wrigley has refused to install lights, not because of interest in the welfare of the corporation but because of his personal opinions 'that baseball is a 'daytime sport' and that the installation of lights and night baseball games will have a deteriorating effect upon the surrounding neighborhood.' It is alleged that he has admitted that he is not interested in whether the Cubs would benefit financially from such action because of his concern for the neighborhood, and that he would be willing for the team to play night games if a new stadium were built in Chicago.

Plaintiff alleges that the other defendant directors, with full knowledge of the foregoing matters, have acquiesced in the policy laid down by Wrigley and have permitted him to dominate the board of directors in matters involving the installation of lights and scheduling of night games, even though they knew he was not motivated by a good faith concern as to the best interests of defendant corporation, but solely by his personal views set forth above. It is charged that the directors are acting for a reason or reasons contrary and wholly unrelated to the business interests of the corporation; that such arbitrary and capricious acts constitute mismanagement and waste of corporate assets, and that the directors have been negligent in failing to exercise reasonable care and prudence in the management of the corporate affairs.

————————————

Let's stop here again as we did with the *Dodge v. Ford* case with the same two questions. Who do you think won the case? Who do you think should have won the case? Take a moment to think about those questions and then continue on with the case.

————————————

* * *

Plaintiff argues that the allegations of his amended complaint are sufficient to set forth a cause of action under the principles set out in *Dodge v. Ford Motor Co.*, 170 N.W. 668 (Mich.). In that case plaintiff, owner of about 10% Of the outstanding stock, brought suit against the directors seeking payment of additional dividends and the enjoining of further business expansion. In ruling on the request for dividends the court indicated that the motives of Ford in keeping so much money in the corporation for expansion and security were to benefit the public generally and spread the profits out by means of more jobs, etc. The court felt that these were not only far from related to the good of the stockholders, but amounted to a change in the ends of the corporation and that this was not a purpose contemplated or allowed by the corporate charter.

* * *

Plaintiff in the instant case argues that the directors are acting for reasons unrelated to the financial interest and welfare of the Cubs. However, we are not satisfied that the motives assigned to Philip K. Wrigley, and through him to the other directors, are contrary to the best interests of the corporation and the stockholders. For example, it appears to us that the effect on the surrounding neighborhood might well be considered by a director who was considering the patrons who would or would not attend the games if the park were in a poor neighborhood.

* * *

There is no allegation that the night games played by the other nineteen teams enhanced their financial position or that the profits, if any, of those teams were directly related to the number of night games scheduled. There is an allegation that the installation of lights and scheduling of night games in Wrigley Field would have resulted in large amounts of additional revenues and incomes from increased attendance and related sources of income. Further, the cost of installation of lights, funds for which are allegedly readily available by financing, would be more than offset and recaptured by increased revenues. However, no allegation is made that there will be a net benefit to the corporation from such action, considering all increased costs.

Plaintiff claims that the losses of defendant corporation are due to poor attendance at home games. However, it appears from the amended complaint, taken as a whole, that factors other than attendance affect the net earnings or losses. For example, in 1962, attendance at home and road games decreased appreciably as compared with 1961, and yet the loss from direct baseball operation and of the whole corporation was considerably less.

The record shows that plaintiff did not feel he could allege that the increased revenues would be sufficient to cure the corporate deficit. The only cost plaintiff was at all concerned with was that of installation of lights. No mention was made of operation and maintenance of the lights or other possible increases in operating costs of night games and we cannot speculate as to what other factors might influence the increase or decrease of profits if the Cubs were to play night home games.

[P]laintiff's allegation that the minority stockholders and the corporation have been seriously and irreparably damaged by the wrongful conduct of the defendant directors is a mere conclusion and not based on well pleaded facts in the amended complaint.

Finally, we do not agree with plaintiff's contention that failure to follow the example of the other major league clubs in scheduling night games constituted negligence. Plaintiff made no allegation that these teams' night schedules were profitable or that the purpose for which night baseball had been undertaken was fulfilled. Furthermore, it cannot be said that directors, even those of corporations that are losing money, must follow the lead of the other corporations in the field. Directors are elected for their business capabilities and judgment and the courts cannot require them to forego their judgment because of the decisions of directors of other companies. Courts may not decide these questions in the absence of a clear showing of dereliction of duty on the part of the specific directors and mere failure to 'follow the crowd' is not such a dereliction.

For the foregoing reasons the order of dismissal entered by the trial court is affirmed.

As a child growing up in rural Illinois at the time of this case, I listened to hundreds of Cubs' games during the day. Mr. Wrigley's commitment to day baseball went even further than reported in this case. He once claimed that God made baseball to be played under the sun. In court, however, what emerged was a long-term strategy to be a unique family and business venue. Indeed, though the Cubs have not won the World Series since 1907 and have not even been in the World Series since 1945, they regularly draw three million fans a year these days, suggesting the wisdom of playing baseball during the day.[23] The Cubs embraced a wider range of stakeholders in deciding to play all (or now most) of their games during the day and in the process became very profitable.

23

This is an essential dimension of the long-term version of shareholder theory because the reputation of the company is held by those outside of the company, yet counts as a company asset and is valued and valuable over the long-term. In fact, many studies show connections between economic success and ethics/social responsibility as measure over the long term.[24] The Cubs saw that a commitment to non-economic directives can pay off; this is an important reason why shareholder theory is more complex than simply maximizing shareholder value.

B. An Overview of Shareholder Theory/Legal Compliance

The proper way to state shareholder theory from a legal perspective, at least in the United States—and in many other countries, its meaning is even more expansive—is that managers have a duty to carry out the lawful directives of the shareholders. One of those lawful directives is undoubtedly going to be to maximize profitability or at least to make a profit. Companies have to stay in business. Even nonprofits have to match revenues and expenses; if they don't pay attention to that, they won't stay in existence.

But it's important to remember that there can be noneconomic, lawful directives. Three different kinds of companies could have a different sense of what shareholder theory looks like. For instance, in a family or a closely-held business where the number of shareholders may be 10, 15, maybe even 30, it's quite conceivable that you can have a meeting of all of those 30 shareholders where they would decide on various noneconomic directives that they want to pursue. The shareholders may decide that they're going to devote 10 to 15 percent of their profits to a local community charity or that they're only going to hire people with disabilities. There's not necessarily anything illegal about such policies even if it costs the shareholders money. Thus, with a small business there may exist the ability to define quite precisely those noneconomic objectives.

On the other end of the spectrum would be a big publicly-held company with a million shareholders. The common denominator may only be making money. Even here, though, things are more complicated. As we just saw, in *Wrigley v. Shlensky*, a publicly-held company found a significant amount of wiggle room to pursue long-term objectives that may not have an immediate economic component or where the economic component may be harder to specify.

The market may not be so forgiving. Through the New York Stock Exchange or NASDAQ, the shareholders may say, what's your profit in the next quarter? If we don't like your profitability, we'll sell your stock or fire your president. *Dodge v. Ford*, after all, is still good law. So is *Wrigley v. Shlensky*.

---

24 *See, e.g.*, James Wash, Joshua Margolis, and Dean Krehemeyer, *Building the Business Case for Ethics* (2006), *available at* http://www.corporate-ethics.org/pdf/business_case.pdf.

Then, there are companies in the middle that were family-owned, and at the time they did their initial public offering, said to the world, "this is the way that we play the game. If you want to invest in us, realize that this is where our priorities lie." For instance, Johnson & Johnson has its famous corporate credo, which was articulated in the 1940s at the time the company did its public offering. The Credo lists the stakeholders to whom they have responsibilities. It starts with doctors, nurses, and parents, and then it addresses employees, the suppliers, the community, and the government. Finally, the Credo says if we have met the objectives for all these stakeholders, our shareholders will get a fair return on their profit on their investment. As a matter of property law, shareholders could overturn the corporate credo, but it does serve as a kind of contract between investors, potential investors, and management: if you want to invest in us, this is the way that we play the game.

Milton Friedman.

Portrait courtesy of The Friedman Foundation for Educational Choice, via Wikimedia Commons

In applying shareholder theory, one should first ask about the laws that apply to the business? That's part of legal compliance; complying with whatever regulations are applicable to the company's business. Another part of legal compliance is to live up to the objectives of the shareholders, whatever those objectives may be provided they are lawful.

Another aspect of shareholder theory is the difference between long-term and short-term versions of shareholder value.. In the long term, things like reputation, good will, brand name, and social capital have a real value. The difficulty is that one has to get through the short term in order to get to the long term and in the short term, measuring the economic value of reputation and goodwill is notoriously difficult. Thus, there is a balancing act between short-term and long-term versions of shareholder theory. These nuances make shareholder theory a more complex framework.

Milton Friedman wrote that if a manager uses shareholder money for his/her own personal viewpoint of what is good, the manager is essentially committing theft. It's not the executive's money. It's the shareholders' money. If the managers want to make a philanthropic donation of their own money, that's fine. A manager, then, should, according to Friedman, maximize profitability and distribute the resources or the profits to the shareholders, so the shareholders can then make their choices and their decisions of what they think is appropriate.[25]

Taken to an extreme, that would mean on September 12, 2001 if somebody came into your company and said we're starting a relief fund for victims of the disaster yesterday, you would respond, "It's not my money. I shouldn't contribute any corporate

---

25   Milton Friedman, "The Social Responsibility of a Company Is to Maximize its Profits," *New York Times Magazine* (Sep. 13, 1970), available at http://highered.mcgraw-hill.com/sites/dl/free/0073524697/910345/Appendices.pdf.

funds. Go ask the shareholders to contribute individually to your charity." Even Friedman would say that such a response would be a mistake because Friedman would also acknowledge that if a charitable contribution or a socially responsible activity is going to enhance the reputation of the firm, and therefore its economic value, that is a reason to contribute to the charity from corporate funds.

Sometimes people cite Friedman's famous *New York Times Magazine* article, "The Social Responsibility of a Company Is to Maximize Its Profits," as precluding any corporate engagement with society. Friedman is more nuanced than that. He states that one should comply with the law, one should stay within the fair rules of competition, and one should consider the long-term reputation and goodwill of the company. Frankly, his argument could justify the *Dodge v. Ford* case as well as the *Wrigley v. Shlensky* case.

Do you think Friedman's argument would or would not support the positions taken in these cases and, if so, in what ways?

Friedman comes from the Chicago school of economics. There is another famous free-market school of economics, the Austrian school, that is more explicit about the place of the business behaviors within society (though it still takes a dim view of corporate social responsibility per se). In a very fine book, Spanish economist Javier Aranzadi has detailed the common and differing features of the two schools and particularly notes the moral foundation of economics, especially within the Austrian School.[26]

Friedrich Hayek, a Nobel Prize-winning economist from Austria, argues that trade thrives when individuals and companies adhere to ethical virtues such as truth-telling, promise-keeping and production of high-quality goods and services. Such virtues engender trust, which lubricates trade, which allows for more trade and economic growth much better than would occur simply by having a government acting as watchdog. In other words, it is not efficient to attempt to police behavior. Trade works best when individuals and organizations can trust each other sufficiently to reliably exchange goods and services without excessive oversight. That much is in line with much of free-trade thinking, but Hayek is more explicit that the reliable exchange of goods without excessive oversight implies that people and businesses are acting in a trustworthy manner (otherwise, they would need oversight and policing). Acting in a trustworthy matter places ethical business conduct directly into the affairs of economics and trade.

Indeed, Hayek argues that this dynamic relationship between trade and ethics could even lead to international peace. The more we can trust each other, the more we can trade. The more we can trade, the wider our relationships can extend, again, as long as we can trust each other. The more trade there is and the more trust there is, the less likely it will be that individuals and countries will need to resort to violence to settle disputes.

---

26 *Liberalism Against Liberalism*

In making these arguments, Hayek does not elevate ethics to having a status of independent good. He is thinking more instrumentally. Ethics simply lubricates trade. And while a game theory exercise can show that, in the long run, when practicing ethics, we can obtain more material goods, Hayek argues that it is more efficient if ethics are taught as independent goods—having their own independent value apart from their instrumental value for trade—by traditional moral institutions such as religion and education. This creates a paradox: ethics helps economics the most when ethics is valued apart from its economic value, a paradox that will suffuse discussions arising out of this book.

Another dimension of shareholder theory argues that the free market may cause painful dislocations: plant closings and other relocations where people are adjusting to what's the most efficient country to produce a product, or the most efficient company, or what product for a company to market. At the same time, the free market efficiently allocates assets and opportunities, according to free market theory, so in the long run ends up producing more wealth for more people.

There's one final aspect of shareholder theory that is revealed in corporate legal history. Sometimes, as already suggested, we think that the duty of maximizing shareholder profits came down the mountain with Moses or it's stitched into our biological nature that Darwin discovered. However, corporations are creations of society; those laws and rules concerning them change. Reuven Avi-Yonah, a law professor at the University of Michigan, has written a wonderful article that traces how the law has changed with respect to corporations, dating all the way back into Roman antiquity and how it evolves with each society from a shareholder model to a stakeholder model.[27]

The important point is that the law changes. It's not static. In fact, if you go back to the time that the U.S. was founded, the only way that individuals were able to obtain incorporation—and of course, incorporation is valuable because it provides limited liability for investments, transferability of shares so that one can sell a part of your company while retaining ownership, continuity of life so that even if the sole proprietor dies that the company could continue. It doesn't die with the sole proprietor.

The only way to obtain incorporation was if a state legislature met and determined that the business was serving the public good. This is why the only corporations that existed in the late 1700s, early 1800s were for companies that built or operated bridges or ferry boats or municipalities themselves.

Two things changed this approach to incorporation. In the late 1820s, populist pressures culminated in the election of Andrew Jackson as President. Jackson and his allies noted that it was quite ironic that those individuals who were able to achieve this very valuable status of incorporation for their businesses either were the legislators

---

27 *Corporations, Society and the State: A Defense of the Corporate Tax*

themselves or very close friends of the legislators. Jackson called this state of affairs "cronyism." He and his colleagues called for a change in corporate law so that it should be open to everybody as long as a person's business pursued a legal objective. As a result, incorporation changed from being a legislative act to a more administrative process: fill out the right government forms, pay the necessary fee, and make annual reports. Anybody could incorporate and run their business.

The time of these developments is also forty to fifty years after Adam Smith wrote his famous *Wealth of Nations*. His argument was that everyone pursuing their own self-interest would end up making society stronger economically. This view was becoming popular, increasing confidence that if incorporation was made available to everybody, the country would end up stronger as a result.

Having said that, there has always been an expectation that businesses should be very much interested in the public good. If you look in small towns like where I grew up in Illinois or you look far back into the early 1900s or the 1800s, separate from the big organizations, businesspeople were also the community activists. They funded and ran the youth sports teams. They ran for mayor. They advocated for civic improvements.

Indeed, one can make a pretty good argument that the shareholder-only formula is a bit of an aberration historically. Even today, in twenty-eight states in the United States, corporate constituency statutes allow or require managers to take into account non-shareholder constituents in making corporate decisions.[28] This is simply another indication of this expectation that we don't want our business leaders to simply be focusing on economic profitability. Society tends to expect more of them.

Questions:

1. Now that you have read more about the history of shareholder theory, do the *Dodge v. Ford* and *Wrigley v. Shlensky* cases make more or less sense? In each of those cases, you were to predict how you think the case was going to come out. Having seen these cases and read a bit about shareholder theory, how do you think cases like this will come out in the future? What is the direction of the duties of managers to shareholders? For a much more detailed set of materials related to this question, please see Part IV where questions about "The Vision of the Firm" are presented as to how this area will develop.

2. How would you compare, contrast, or connect Hardin's *Lifeboat Ethics* vignette with the discussion of F.A. Hayek's economic theory?

3. As indicated in the materials, there is a significant amount of evidence showing that, in the long-term, ethics has a real benefit to businesses and their economic

---

28 *Whom the Corporation Serve? An Argument for the Constitutionality of Non-Stockholder Constituency Statutes*

value, but ethics is harder to quantify in the short-term. What are the pressures that force business leaders into managing for the short-term rather than the long-term? Apart from ethics, what could be done to try to orient businesses toward the long-term and away from the short-term?

CHAPTER 6

White Collar Crime

I N THE WAKE of the turn-of-the-century corporate scandals, many called for increased emphasis on ethics instruction in business schools. University of Texas professor Robert Prentice, however, wrote an insightful *New York Times* op-ed in which he argued that ethics wasn't really the problem. The problem was the outright flouting of the law. It is a good point. Many corporate ethics issues are legal issues. Moreover, what is called "ethics" in the press, government, and business are often laws concerning things like conflicts of interest. If one looks at "ethics" issues in government especially, they tend to revolve around misuse of public or campaign funds or using one's office—or former office—to gain personal, financial advantages.

This conflation of ethics and law can go a bit too far, however, as happened with me once with a government agency in Washington who had hired me to undertake a year-long ethics education program. In our first, day-long session, my team focused on issues of building community, emotional intelligence and some psychological biases we tend to have (such as those we looked at in Part I). However, the executive members of the organization had no use for discussion on emotional intelligence or building trust in organizations; they simply wanted to know whether or not they could accept an outside gift without violating "ethics laws." We all agreed that if that was what they wanted, they had hired the wrong people for the job.

I do not wish to claim that the law is the only thing one has to concern oneself with in making ethical judgments. But neither do I go to the opposite extreme to suggest that the law is not what ethics is about. They interact in significant ways. This chapter focuses heavily on legal issues and how the law will step in to enforce principles that the public might also think has strong ethical content. The law can do this through the application of criminal as well as civil mechanisms.

A. General Notions of Corporate Liability

Criminal prosecutions arise from some government entity against a person (a natural person or an artificial one, such as a corporation) for violating a law enacted to protect the public. In a tort case, the "prosecutor" is an individual plaintiff who seeks monetary damages or other forms of equitable relief, such as an injunction in nuisance cases, for injuries caused by the defendant. In a criminal case, the prosecutor really is one: an Attorney General, a States Attorney, a District Attorney, etc. Because the prosecutor acts on behalf of the state, it is the state and the system of justice that is, in a sense, the plaintiff and victim in a criminal case. It is possible that a criminal defendant will also be subject to suit by the victim through a related civil suit. One famous example of this is the O.J. Simpson civil and criminal trial, where he was acquitted for criminal charges but still found liable for civil damages.

In any criminal case, there must be an act (the *actus reus*) and some measure of intent (the *mens rea*) depending on the type of the crime. The action component rarely causes difficulty. Some act had to cause the criminal violation or else there would not be a crime to begin with, though the action need not always result in victimization (e.g. attempted murder). The standard of required intent, however, may be subjective, objective, or nonexistent (strict liability crimes).

A subjective intent occurs where the alleged criminal either knows what she is doing or is reckless in her actions. If the intent is purposeful (willful), knowing or reckless, then a higher level of punishment is warranted because what the defendant is doing is no accident. Someone trying to blackmail (extortion) another person doesn't do so accidentally; they purposefully devise a scheme to try to extort money from another person. Embezzlement is another example of a purposeful crime because it would be nearly impossible to achieve without the actual purpose to embezzle.

An objective intent occurs when the subjective intent of the defendant cannot be known or, at least, cannot be proven, but the actions of the defendant indicate a disregard for others. This is a negligence standard and would apply to issues such as careless or drunken driving. Sometimes negligence may err into gross negligence and even recklessness. The defendant may not have set out to drive carelessly, but objectively speaking, they can be determined to have driven negligently by expressing a lack of regard for others through their choices. If so, they still may be guilty of a crime, but it may result in a lesser offense and involve a more lenient punishment because of the lack of provable, subjective intent.

Then, there are some crimes that require no intent at all; these cases are known as strict liability crimes since merely committing the *actus reus* regardless of intent results in a violation. In these cases, the defendant may not have intended any criminal violation at all, but still ended up violating a statute. One example of strict liability that arises with relative frequency is in the context of statutory rape crimes because the crime does not require that the defendant have any knowledge of the victim's age. Age restrictions on pornography and child pornography crimes are also strict liability. Each state has laws against pornography and the Supreme Court has given great deference to how local communities set their own standards for what constitutes pornography. Yet, the Internet crosses state lines by its very nature. So, what happens when someone under the age of eighteen accesses pornography? The following case illustrates that issue and the issue of criminal violations with no intent. It deals with a unique kind of business—pornography—which often raises new legal and ethical issues as new technologies become available for its distribution. In the following case, what may be most interesting is the Court's determination of "community" and how new technology can create unforeseen liability because of the community one unexpectedly finds oneself in.

U.S. v. Thomas

74 F.3d 701 (6th Cir. 1996)

EDMUNDS, District Judge.

* * *

Robert Thomas and his wife Carleen Thomas began operating the Amateur Action Computer Bulletin Board System ("AABBS") from their home in Milpitas, California in February 1991. The AABBS was a computer bulletin board system that operated by using telephones, modems, and personal computers. Its features included e-mail, chat lines, public messages, and files that members could access, transfer, and download to their own computers and printers.

Information loaded onto the bulletin board was first converted into binary code, i.e., 0's and 1's, through the use of a scanning device. After purchasing sexually-explicit magazines from public adult book stores in California, Defendant Robert Thomas used an electronic device called a scanner to convert pictures from the magazines into computer files called Graphic Interchange Format files or "GIF" files. The AABBS contained approximately 14,000 GIF files. Mr. Thomas also purchased, sold, and delivered sexually-explicit videotapes to AABBS members. Customers ordered the tapes by sending Robert Thomas an e-mail message, and Thomas typically delivered them by use of the United Parcel Service ("U.P.S.").

Persons calling the AABBS without a password could view the introductory screens of the system which contained brief, sexually-explicit descriptions of the GIF files and adult videotapes that were offered for sale. Access to the GIF files, however, was limited to members who were given a password after they paid a membership fee and submitted a signed application form that Defendant Robert Thomas reviewed. The application form requested the applicant's age, address, and telephone number and required a signature.

Members accessed the GIF files by using a telephone, modem and personal computer. A modem located in the Defendants' home answered the calls. After they established membership by typing in a password, members could then select, retrieve, and instantly transport GIF files to their own computer. A caller could then view the GIF file on his computer screen and print the image out using his printer. The GIF files contained the AABBS name and access telephone number; many also had "Distribute Freely" printed on the image itself.

In July 1993, a United States Postal Inspector, Agent David Dirmeyer ("Dirmeyer"), received a complaint regarding the AABBS from an individual who resided in the Western District of Tennessee. Dirmeyer dialed the AABBS' telephone number. As a non-member, he viewed a screen that read "Welcome to AABBS, the Nastiest Place On Earth," and was able to select various "menus" and read graphic descriptions of the GIF files and videotapes that were offered for sale.

Subsequently, Dirmeyer used an assumed name and sent in $55 along with an executed application form to the AABBS. Defendant Robert Thomas called Dirmeyer at his undercover telephone number in Memphis, Tennessee, acknowledged receipt of his application, and authorized him to log-on with his personal password. Thereafter, Dirmeyer dialed the AABBS's telephone number, logged-on and, using his computer/modem in Memphis, downloaded the GIF files listed in counts 2–7 of the Defendants' indictments. These GIF files depicted images of bestiality, oral sex, incest, sado-masochistic abuse, and sex scenes involving urination. Dirmeyer also ordered six sexually-explicit videotapes from the AABBS and received them via U.P.S. at a Memphis, Tennessee address. Dirmeyer also had several e-mail and chat-mode conversations with Defendant Robert Thomas.

On January 10, 1994, a search warrant was issued by a U.S. Magistrate Judge for the Northern District of California. The AABBS' location was subsequently searched, and the Defendants' computer system was seized.

On January 25, 1994, a federal grand jury for the Western District of Tennessee returned a twelve-count indictment charging Defendants Robert and Carleen Thomas with the following criminal violations: one count under 18 U.S.C. § 371 for conspiracy to violate federal obscenity laws—18 U.S.C. §§ 1462, 1465, six counts under 18 U.S.C. § 1465 for knowingly using and causing to be used a facility and means of interstate commerce—a combined computer/telephone system—for the purpose of transporting obscene, computer-generated materials (the GIF files) in interstate commerce, three counts under 18 U.S.C. § 1462 for shipping obscene videotapes via U.P.S., one count of causing the transportation of materials depicting minors engaged in sexually explicit conduct in violation of 18 U.S.C. § 2252(a)(1) as to Mr. Thomas only, and one count of forfeiture under 18 U.S.C. § 1467.

...

B.

Defendants ... challenge venue in the Western District of Tennessee for counts 2–7 of their indictments. They argue that even if venue was proper under count 1 (conspiracy) and counts 8–10 (videotapes sent via U.P.S.), counts 2–7 (GIF files) should have been severed and transferred to California because Defendants did not cause the GIF files to be transmitted to the Western District of Tennessee. Rather, Defendants assert, it was Dirmeyer, a government agent, who, without their knowledge, accessed and downloaded the GIF files and caused them to enter Tennessee. We disagree. To establish a Section 1465 violation, the Government must prove that a defendant knowingly used a facility or means of interstate commerce for the purpose of distributing obscene materials. Contrary to Defendants' position, Section 1465 does not require the Government to prove that Defendants had specific knowledge of the destination of each transmittal at the time it occurred.

"Venue lies in any district in which the offense was committed," and the Government is required to establish venue by a preponderance of the evidence. This court examines the propriety of venue by taking " 'into account a number of factors—the site of the defendant's acts, the elements and nature of the crime, the locus of the effect of the criminal conduct, and the suitability of each district for accurate fact finding ...' "

Section 1465 is an obscenity statute, and federal obscenity laws, by virtue of their inherent nexus to interstate and foreign commerce, generally involve acts in more than one jurisdiction or state. Furthermore, it is well-established that "there is no constitutional impediment to the government's power to prosecute pornography dealers in any district into which the material is sent."

...

C.

Defendants further argue that their convictions under counts 1–7 of their indictments violate their First Amendment rights to freedom of speech. As the Supreme Court noted in Bose, when constitutional facts are at issue, this court has a duty to conduct an independent review of the record "both to be sure that the speech in question actually falls within the unprotected category and to confine the perimeters of any unprotected category within acceptably narrow limits in an effort to ensure that protected expression will not be inhibited."

1. Defendants' Right to Possess the GIF Files in their Home

Defendants rely on *Stanley v. Georgia,* 394 U.S. 557 (1969), and argue they have a constitutionally protected right to possess obscene materials in the privacy of their home. They insist that the GIF files containing sexually-explicit material never left their home. Defendants' reliance on *Stanley* is misplaced.

The Supreme Court has clarified that *Stanley* "depended not on any First Amendment Right to purchase or possess obscene materials, but on the right to privacy in the home." It has also recognized that the right to possess obscene materials in the privacy of one's home does not create "a correlative right to receive it, transport it, or distribute it" in interstate commerce even if it is for private use only. Nor does it create "some zone of constitutionally protected privacy [that] follows such material when it is moved outside the home area."

Defendants went beyond merely possessing obscene GIF files in their home. They ran a business that advertised and promised its members the availability and transportation of the sexually-explicit GIF files they selected. In light of the overwhelming evidence produced at trial, it is spurious for Defendants to claim now that they did not intend to sell, disseminate, or share the obscene GIF files they advertised on the AABBS with members outside their home and in other states.

2. The Community Standards to be Applied When Determining Whether the GIF Files Are Obscene

In *Miller v. California*, 413 U.S. 15 (1973), the Supreme Court set out a three-prong test for obscenity. It inquired whether (1) " 'the average person applying contemporary community standards' would find that the work, taken as a whole appeals to the prurient interest"; (2) it "depicts or describes, in a patently offensive way, sexual conduct specifically defined by applicable state law"; and (3) "the work, taken as a whole, lacks serious literary, artistic, political, or scientific value."

Under the first prong of the *Miller* obscenity test, the jury is to apply "contemporary community standards." Defendants acknowledge the general principle that, in cases involving interstate transportation of obscene material, juries are properly instructed to apply the community standards of the geographic area where the materials are sent. Nonetheless, Defendants assert that this principle does not apply here for the same reasons they claim venue was improper. As demonstrated above, this argument cannot withstand scrutiny. The computer-generated images described in counts 2–7 were electronically transferred from Defendants' home in California to the Western District of Tennessee. Accordingly, the community standards of that judicial district were properly applied in this case.

Issues regarding which community's standards are to be applied are tied to those involving venue. It is well-established that:

[v]enue for federal obscenity prosecutions lies "in any district from, through, or into which" the allegedly obscene material moves, according to 18 U.S.C. § 3237. This may result in prosecutions of persons in a community to which they have sent materials which is obscene under that community's standards though the community from which it is sent would tolerate the same material.

Prosecutions may be brought either in the district of dispatch or the district of receipt, and obscenity is determined by the standards of the community where the trial takes place. Moreover, the federal courts have consistently recognized that it is not unconstitutional to subject interstate distributors of obscenity to varying community standards.

3. The Implications of Computer Technology on the Definition of "Community"

Defendants and Amicus Curiae appearing on their behalf argue that the computer technology used here requires a new definition of community, i.e., one that is based on the broad-ranging connections among people in cyberspace rather than the geographic locale of the federal judicial district of the criminal trial. Without a more flexible definition, they argue, there will be an impermissible chill on protected speech because BBS operators cannot select who gets the materials they make available on their bulletin boards. Therefore, they contend, BBS operators like Defendants will be forced to censor their materials so as not to run afoul of the standards of the community with the most restrictive standards.

Defendants' First Amendment issue, however, is not implicated by the facts of this case. This is not a situation where the bulletin board operator had no knowledge or control over the jurisdictions where materials were distributed for downloading or printing. Access to the Defendants' AABBS was limited. Membership was necessary and applications were submitted and screened before passwords were issued and materials were distributed. Thus, Defendants had in place methods to limit user access in jurisdictions where the risk of a finding of obscenity was greater than that in California. They knew they had a member in Memphis; the member's address and local phone number were provided on his application form. If Defendants did not wish to subject themselves to liability in jurisdictions with less tolerant standards for determining obscenity, they could have refused to give passwords to members in those districts, thus precluding the risk of liability.

...

III.

For the foregoing reasons, this court AFFIRMS Robert and Carleen Thomas' convictions and sentences.

The Thomas case tends to surprise people. What happened to privacy in one's own home? What happened to free speech? How can a Tennessee investigator spark a prosecution of someone in California who never (as far as we know) stepped foot into Tennessee? The Court deals with all of these issues in the opinion and shows the degree of oversight society—here through the government and its laws—has over business conduct. To be sure, this case does involve a unique industry of pornography, but the point is that businesses can be held legally liable for their actions when they reach across borders into other jurisdictions. In the Thomas case, that happened to be pornography, but in other cases, businesses can run afoul of advertising,[29] employment, or other types of laws that make what are legal activities in one jurisdiction illegal in another. One could simply dismiss these issues as things for the lawyers to deal with, but (a) by the time lawyers get involved, it may be too late for a company to get itself out of trouble and (b) laws imperfectly represent the cultural norms of a society.

What do you think the relationship of law to ethics is? Can you think of examples where the law provides an indication of what a society's norms are? Can you think of times and places where the laws do not represent a culture's norms? What accounts for

---

29   For instance, at one point, a "money back guarantee" was illegal to offer in some parts of Germany. Thus, American companies like Lands' End would offer a money back guarantee that was illegal when the product was offered to German customers.

the difference? Are there times and places when a business should ignore the law? What reasons would you then give for doing so?

B. Representative Examples

The number of laws businesses are subject to is, of course, vast, and better addressed in a business law course. Yet, the point is that paying attention to legal issues, and the complexity that arises in doing so, pertains to ethics as well. The remainder of this chapter looks at three important issues that impact business internationally: bribery laws (as articulated through the U.S. Foreign Corrupt Practices Act), some miscellaneous U.S.-based White Collar regulations, and Privacy Issues (following from the EU Privacy Directive).

1. Foreign Corrupt Practices

One of the most controversial laws applicable to international business is the Foreign Corrupt Practices Act ("FCPA"). Passed into law in 1977, after the discovery that hundreds of U.S. companies were paying bribes, the FCPA makes it illegal for any U.S. company to pay—or even offer to pay—a bribe to a foreign official in order to obtain or retain business. It also prohibits making a payment to a foreign political party or to a candidate for political office. The law also applies to foreign corporations that have securities listed on a U.S. securities exchange. The following excerpt provides an example of the enforcement of the FCPA.

U.S. v. Kozeny

638 F.Supp.2d 348 (S.D.N.Y. 2009):

SHIRA A. SCHEINDLIN, District Judge.

* * *

The Government's allegations in this case are complex, and it is unnecessary to recite them here. The relevant facts are as follows: SOCAR is the state-owned oil company of the Republic of Azerbaijan ("Azerbaijan"). In the mid-1990s, Azerbaijan began a program of privatization. The program gave the President of Azerbaijan, Heydar Aliyev, discretionary authority as to whether and when to privatize SOCAR. Bourke and others allegedly conspired to violate the FCPA by agreeing to make payments to Azeri officials to encourage the privatization of SOCAR and to permit them to participate in that privatization.

* * *

Bourke contends that the Government has failed to prove that Bourke's intent in agreeing to transfer money overseas was to violate the FCPA rather than to purchase vouchers and options, which he notes is lawful.

As an initial matter, there is no dispute that Bourke invested in Oily Rock in March and July 1998. In order to sustain the money laundering conspiracy charge against Bourke, the Government must present evidence that Bourke had the "knowledge or awareness of the illegal nature of the charged activity and [that he intended] to advance the illegal objective." After a review of the evidence admitted at trial, I conclude that a reasonable jury could draw the inference that Bourke agreed with others that the intended use of his investment would be, in part, for the purpose of bribing Azeri officials.

Hans Bodmer, attorney to co-defendant Viktor Kozeny during the period of the privatization scheme, testified that he had a conversation with Bourke in early February 1998 regarding the bribery of Azeri officials. Bodmer testified that during one trip to Azerbaijan, Bourke asked him, "what is the arrangement, what are the Azeri interests." After obtaining Kozeny's approval to speak to Bourke about the specifics of the "arrangement," Bodmer then met with Bourke the following day. He testified that he then told Bourke that two-thirds of the vouchers had been issued to the Azeri officials under credit facility agreements at no risk to them. He also identified the Azeri officials who received these vouchers as Barat Nuriyev and his family and Nadir Nasibov and his family. It would certainly be reasonable for the jury to conclude that Bourke was aware of the bribery arrangements as early as February 1998.

In addition to Hans Bodmer, the Government also called Thomas Farrell, one of Kozeny's employees, as a witness. Farrell testified that some time after Bourke had invested in Oily Rock, Bourke requested that Farrell leave his office with him so that they might have a conversation. During that conversation, Bourke asked about the status of the privatization venture and whether President Aliyev or Barat Nuriyev had given any indications to Farrell about possible approval. Farrell testified that at one point in the conversation, Bourke had asked: "Has Viktor given them enough money?"

Farrell testified that Bourke raised the subject with him a second time during a trip to celebrate the opening of the Minaret offices in Baku, Azerbaijan in April 1998. Farrell testified that Bourke asked him about privatization and whether Farrell had heard anything from the officials in charge, such as Nuriyev. After Farrell gave Bourke a short status report, Bourke asked: "Well are-is Viktor giving enough to them?"

The testimony of Bodmer and Farrell, when considered in the light most favorable to the Government, is sufficient to prove beyond a reasonable doubt that Bourke agreed and intended that his investment not only be used for the purpose of purchasing vouchers and options, but also to ensure that the privatization of SOCAR occurred, by bribing the officials involved in the decision-making process. At oral argument, Bourke argued that proof that he knew that the investment money was being used partly to bribe officials is not enough; intent is required to sustain a conviction for conspiracy. However, even if *Bodmer's testimony* shows only *knowledge* of the bribery arrangements, a reasonable jury could infer from *Farrell's testimony* of Bourke's statements that Bourke *intended* that part of his July 1998 investment money be used to bribe officials.

* * *

The FCPA does allow for what are known as "grease payments." These are payments made to a foreign official to expedite the performance of duties the person is already bound to perform. In the following case, the judge undertakes a long legislative history of the FCPA on possible variants of what constitutes grease payments.

U.S. v. Kay

359 F.3d 738 (5th Cir. 2004)

WIENER, Circuit Judge:

* * *

Given the foregoing analysis of the statute's legislative history, we cannot hold as a matter of law that Congress meant to limit the FCPA's applicability to cover only bribes that lead directly to the award or renewal of contracts. Instead, we hold that Congress intended for the FCPA to apply broadly to payments intended to assist the payor, either directly or indirectly, in obtaining or retaining business for some person, and that bribes paid to foreign tax officials to secure illegally reduced customs and tax liability constitute a type of payment that can fall within this broad coverage. In 1977, Congress was motivated to prohibit rampant foreign bribery by domestic business entities, but nevertheless understood the pragmatic need to exclude innocuous grease payments from the scope of its proposals. The FCPA's legislative history instructs that Congress was concerned about both the kind of bribery that leads to discrete contractual arrangements and the kind that more generally helps a domestic payor obtain or retain business for some person in a foreign country; and that Congress was aware that this type includes illicit payments made to officials to obtain favorable but unlawful tax treatment.

Furthermore, by narrowly defining exceptions and affirmative defenses against a backdrop of broad applicability, Congress reaffirmed its intention for the statute to apply to payments that even indirectly assist in obtaining business or maintaining existing business operations in a foreign country. Finally, Congress's intention to implement the Convention, a treaty that indisputably prohibits any bribes that give an advantage to which a business entity is not fully entitled, further supports our determination of the extent of the FCPA's scope.

Thus, in diametric opposition to the district court, we conclude that bribes paid to foreign officials in consideration for unlawful evasion of customs duties and sales taxes *could* fall within the purview of the FCPA's proscription. We hasten to add, however, that this conduct does not automatically constitute a violation of the FCPA: It still must be shown that the bribery was intended to produce an effect—here, through tax savings—that would "assist in obtaining or retaining business."

* * *

We conclude that, as important to the statute as the business nexus element is, it does not go to the FCPA's core of criminality. When the FCPA is read as a whole, its core of criminality is seen to be bribery of a foreign official to induce him to perform an official duty in a corrupt manner. The business nexus element serves to delimit the scope of the FCPA by eschewing applicability to those bribes of foreign officials that are not intended to assist in getting or keeping business, just as the "grease" provisions eschew applicability of the FCPA to payments to foreign officials to cut through bureaucratic red tape and thereby facilitate matters.

* * *

Without trying to make a bad pun, relying on the grease payment exception to justify a bribe is, well, slippery. Exactly what falls within or lays outside of the FCPA will be a matter for businesses and their lawyers to wrestle with, but from an ethical point of view, three important points arise. First, one will quickly find consensus that bribery is bad. It tends to be hidden from public view exactly because it is something that is not well thought of. So a question for you to consider is what is wrong with bribery? Why does it elicit negative judgments? And if it is perceived negatively, what does that mean for the company?

Second, many business people argue that laws such as the FCPA—and especially the FCPA—hinder them in a competitive market where companies from other countries. And so, the application of it to companies with U.S. interests seems unfair. Other companies disagree saying that it frees them from the mess entailed in bribery so they can focus on competing on the basis of price and quality. What do you think? Is a legal restriction on bribery a good thing—economically—or bad thing and given your answer, what does that say about ethical considerations in business.

Third, what is it? The excerpt from the court case above had to leave things fairly murky in your head as to what actually counts as bribery. Expand that with cultural differences. Does gift-giving to establish a relationship before "getting down to business" equate to bribery or is it simply culturally acceptable relationship-building? Where does one draw the line? At one point in my career, I spoke to the business-side of a major university. There were accountants, security personnel, investment analysts and dozens of other "industries" present. What quickly became clear was that the industry from which these employees came from had different ideas of what constitutes an unacceptable gift. An employee managing the university's billion-dollar investments would not think twice about a golf outing with a potential investment analyst or a day in the skybox for an NFL game. The value of such an entertainment day might be $10,000, but it is part of the way business is done. Provide something of the same economic value to a security guard and one would have a front page story in the local newspaper. What constitutes these differences in perception? Are they fair?

Given all of the above, if you think they are unfair, what do you do? Break the law? Change the law? Are your standards for changing a law prohibiting bribery the same as your objections to a law perhaps permitting discrimination or even a sex trade? On what grounds and when would you take a stand against a law you believe to be unjust?

2. RICO and Other Examples of White Collar Crime

Originally, the Racketeer Influenced and Corrupt Organizations Act[30] ("RICO") was designed as a tool to fight organized crime. Enacted in 1970, RICO imposes stiff civil and criminal penalties for an organization found guilty under it.

There are nine categories of state crimes and more than criminal offenses under RICO. Consistent with the aim of fighting organized crime, these offenses include drug dealing, extortion, bribery, mail fraud, kidnapping, murder, and arson. If within a ten-year window, an organization has violated two of these criminal statutes—known as "predicate acts"—then RICO can be triggered and criminal penalties of up to $25,000 per violation and prison terms of up to twenty years can be applied. Though designed for organized crime, regular businesses sometimes fall into committing two predicate acts, and so RICO has been applied to them as well. The RICO statute has been used in many business cases, especially with respect to investment fraud situations.

There are numerous examples of White Collar crimes. Following is an illustrative—and certainly not exhaustive—list.

- **Bank Fraud:** Engaging in an activity with the purpose of defrauding a bank
- **Computer Fraud:** Hacking into databases holding information such as credit card numbers, social security numbers, or proprietary company information
- **Credit Card Fraud:** Unauthorized use of a credit card, usually via theft
- **Environmental Fraud:** Overbilling government contracts for environmental work
- **Health Care/Medicaid/Insurance Fraud:** Overbilling for health care treatment in excess of the treatments provided
- **Insider Trading:** Use of securities information inaccessible to the public

---

30 18 U.S.C. § 1961-1968.

(inside information, advance notice of an announcement that will affect stock price)

- **Money Laundering:** Hiding illegal commercial activities by making them appear to be part of a legitimate business enterprise

- **Ponzi Scheme:** An investment scheme where the originator encourages investment with the promise of very high rates of return. The originator does not invest the money, but uses newly invested money to pay the large returns to the earlier investors. Eventually, the scheme falls apart when an insufficient number of investors can be recruited to continue to pay the large returns. Pyramid Scheme: Similar to a Ponzi scheme except while Ponzi schemes are associated with investments, pyramid schemes generally are associated with businesses such as a franchise.

A European Example

While the United States receives a large amount of attention for its laws and for the reach of those laws overseas, it is not the only political body that significantly impacts business affairs, nor the only one that enacts laws that have an extraterritorial reach. The European Union has passed laws with a much stronger emphasis on the protection of customer privacy. This law impacts companies doing business in the EU, which given the size of that market, requires company to take into account a legal and ethical concern for personal privacy in the design and use of information-gathering tactics, usage, and policies. The following is an excerpt from an EU case that examined the practices of Tyco Healthcare in France.

National Commission on Informatics and Liberties

Deliberation No. 2006-281 of 14 December 2006 sanctioning Tyco Healthcare France[31]

The National Commission on Informatics and Liberties, held in restricted, under the chairmanship of Mr. Alex Türk...

Finds the following facts:

1. The Tyco Healthcare France has declared to the CNIL September 22, 2004 one processing of data for the purpose of "managing international career." By letter dated 21 February 2005, the CNIL asked him to send some information that is vital to this

---

31   This is a French-to-English translation of the original opinion performed via Google Translate. This may result in some syntax errors, but the meaning of the opinion is quite clear.

investigation. The Tyco Healthcare France has provided no satisfactory response to the Commission's requests repeated in its letters of 19 September 2005 and 21 March 2006.

Indeed, the reply of Tyco Healthcare France SAS 4 April 2006 has failed to provide answers to all the questions raised by the services CNIL under the instruction of the declaration file (the precise description of the purpose accuracy sought, the precise circumstances in which personal data are sent to Great Britain and the United States, the exact locations of implantation servers and systems, the precise capabilities of the application, the exact recipient Data security measures to ensure the confidentiality of data and the length of data retention).

2. In view of the foregoing, the Commission, by resolution adopted on May 10, 2006 warned the company Tyco, within ten days to respond to questions posed by the CNIL in his letters (letters of 21 February, 19 September 2005, 21 March 2006) or to indicate that the above treatment has been abandoned.

3. In response to the notice, Tyco Healthcare France indicated by letter dated June 1, 2006: "The group at Tyco International was split four sectors which are currently independent entities. This split must be made by the end of the calendar year. Therefore procedures and inquiries that had been implemented in the current circumstances are suspended. "

4. CNIL did not consider themselves sufficiently informed by the response of the exact fate finally being reserved for the treatment purpose of the notice was to make a mission control on site July 12, 2006 in the premises of Tyco Healthcare. On this occasion, the services of the CNIL noted that the purpose of the treatment setting remains, contrary to what had been said, was well used by Tyco Healthcare France.

In light of the documents submitted ("Project Update International Database, Data Auditing and Next Steps, June 2006 "and" Administrator's Guide, and Administration data processing for the international database "), the above treatment appears as an essential management tool at the global level, the wage policy Tyco group whose goals go far beyond the purpose of "reporting" referred to in the declaration of 22 September 2004. During the mission control on site, it was also found that strict and timely procedures were implemented for the Tyco Healthcare France regularly feeds the database with information for French employees.

5. He emerges from the foregoing that the facts found on site July 12, 2006 were contradiction with the reply of Tyco Healthcare France June 1, 2006 since it has no "suspended" the implementation object of the treatment setting notice or respond to all questions concerning the exact terms of operation of the above treatment. Indeed, in the case of the first precise description of the purposes sought and functionality of the application, in its letter of 4 April 2006 Tyco Healthcare France states that "the purpose of this database is purely that of a" reporting "towards our European hierarchy human resources. " An internal document dated June 2006 release services at the CNIL mission control July 12, 2006 shows, however ("International Database Project Update, Data Auditing and Next Steps, June 2006 "), for the treatment above that it is used to manage stock options, vocational training, the level of salaries, professional communication, etc.. At the meeting of 14 December 2006, counsel for Tyco Healthcare France has also indicated verbally the purpose of treatment implementation was also intended to manage the "mobility house. "

Therefore, the Commission considers that it does not always informed about the precise description of purposes sought by treating said September 22, 2004 by Tyco Healthcare France as it was asked yet in the notice of 10 May 2006.

Turning to the specific case in which personal data are sent to the local Tyco group in Britain and the United States, e4 April 2006 merely states that "these data can be transmitted in the United Kingdom to the United States if our hierarchy considers it appropriate to do so. " If control of 12 July 2006 has established a briefing concerning the treatment of the subject notice from Tyco Healthcare France and local Tyco group in England and the United States, it has not been possible to obtain accurate information on the grounds of sending this information.

Therefore, the Commission considers that it does not always properly informed of the specific cases where of personal data are sent to the local group Tyco Great Britain and the United States as though it was requested in the notice of 10 May 2006. Regarding still exact locations of servers and implementation of systems, only one diagram technique has been communicated to the Commission ("Scheme computer operation Tyco Healthcare France "), but the exact addresses of centers computer has not been reported so far.

Regarding questions about the recipients of accurate data and the duration data retention, the Commission has so far no answer.

Finally, as regards security measures to ensure the confidentiality of data, if mission control July 12, 2006 has established that access to computers in the Tyco Healthcare France is secured by a password, the Commission has today no accurate technical information on security conditions related to data retention in England and the United States.

Therefore, the Commission considers that it does not always properly informed on the premises exact location of servers and systems, recipients of accurate data, duration of data retention and security measures to ensure the confidentiality of data as though it was requested in the notice of 10 May 2006.

6. In its response of 24 November 2006 and at the meeting of 14 December 2006, Tyco Healthcare France argues that the proposed sanction proposed by the rapporteur would be ill-founded in law insofar as it does be based on any prior notice but only on the realization of mission control July 12, 2006. On this point, the Commission notes that penalty proceedings may be initiated when the data controller fails to comply with the notice that it is addressed (Article 45 of the law of January 6, 1978 August 6, 2004). This sanction procedure is thus based on the notice issued by the CNIL May 10 2006 and the reply by Tyco June 1, 2006. It should also be noted that in the context of the analysis of the response sent by the Tyco June 1, 2006, the CNIL was entitled to conduct a mission on-site verification in order to verify the reality of the information which had been communicated. The Commission considers in this respect that the information provided by the Tyco Healthcare France in its letter of June 1, 2006 did not allow know the exact fate was reserved for the purpose of processing the notice of 10 May 2006.

In addition, Tyco Healthcare France in its observations of 24 November 2006 that the decision of Mission Control No. 2006-074C was not formally formal notice of 10 May 2006. On this point, the Commission considers that the existence of a formal procedure has, in this respect, no impact on the formalism respect for the realization of such a mission control.

The Commission therefore considers that the sanction procedure is fully regularly.

7. Tyco The company has also argued in its observations of 24 November 2006 at the meeting of 14 December 2006 that the information provided in the Mission Control does not concern the same treatment as described in the application notice of 10 May 2006.

The Commission observes that the checks carried out on site July 12, 2006 by services CNIL found that the treatment declared by Tyco Healthcare France September 22, 2004 ("managing international career")included, as noted above, other features related to the management of human resources such as management stock options, training professional level of remuneration, professional communication and the internal mobility. These features, which can be attached to an end of career management international, were not described in the statement sent by Tyco Healthcare France September 22, 2004.

The Commission also notes that the screenshots made by services CNIL when checking the July 12, 2006 are consistent with regard to the categories of data collected and used with the "fields" computer in the declaration addressed by Tyco Healthcare France September 22, 2004 (data demographics of employees, data on the administrative employees, Data on the geographical location of employees, compensation data of employees, etc..).

Therefore, the Commission considers that the checks carried out by the CNIL on July 12 2006 were well under treatment in the formal notice of 10 May 2006.

8. He is clear from all the foregoing that Tyco Healthcare France did not complied with the notice of the CNIL on 10 May 2006 as it did not provided the information requested by the CNIL on the treatment declared 22 September 2004 (the precise description of the exact purposes sought, in case which personal data are sent in Britain and the United States, the exact locations of servers and implementation of systems, specific features application, recipients accurate data, the security measures to ensure

the privacy and data retention time) and it has not stopped implementation thereof. The Commission notes in this regard that Tyco Healthcare France has clearly not taken the measure of the seriousness of the breaches alleged against him for its lack of cooperation and transparency.

Accordingly, the Commission decided to apply the provisions of Articles 45 and following the law of January 6, 1978 August 6, 2004 and rule against Tyco Healthcare France located 2 rue Denis Diderot, The key of St. Peter Elancourt (78), given the seriousness of the infringement committed, a penalty of 30,000 euros.

In addition, the Commission directed Tyco Healthcare France to respond in ten days from the date of notification of this decision to all applications made by the CNIL in its notice of 10 May 2006.

This decision will be made public.

President, Alex Türk

Should laws apply only within one jurisdiction? Is an attempt to regulate businesses' work overseas unfair? Should the U.S. only regulate U.S. businesses in the work they do within the U.S.? Or, for that matter, should the U.S. not apply the FCPA to companies from other countries when they do business within the U.S.? Similarly, should the EU restrict its privacy protections only to EU companies? What are the challenges to global business if the U.S. and the E.U. restrict their reach? Are these examples of "ethical imperialism" or do they level the playing field so that businesses compete on the same basis and terms? Is it a competitive disadvantage to be prevented from bribing or could a company be better off if everyone knows that it cannot compete on that basis?

Corporate criminal law is purely "law" as opposed to "ethics." Yet, we often put the two of them together in exactly the kinds of situations described in this chapter. Corruption and bribery issues have strong ethical content to them as do pyramid schemes. Privacy issues are more subject to legally unsettled debate in the United States, but sufficient consensus on the need to protect consumer privacy allows for the European Union to go beyond public, ethical consensus to legal prohibition. Even among ethicists, there can be a tendency to flinch when putting law and ethics together, but form the standpoint of practical business conduct, the two stand more along a continuum than residing in separate spheres. That becomes even more true when it comes to reflexive laws, which is the subject of the next chapter.

CHAPTER 7

Reflexive Models of Corporate Ethics:
A Bridge Between Law and Ethics

INTUITIVELY, one thinks of criminal law in terms of the government prosecuting wrongdoers. But increasingly, both Congress and the Courts have sought to find ways to achieve governmental purposes without creating more cases to be heard in court. They have created incentives for corporations to be actively involved in the administration of public policy, including criminal issues. As one commentator said of the Federal Sentencing Guidelines, the law amounts to the deputization of corporations.[32] The Federal Sentencing Guidelines ("Guidelines") are not the only reflexive law to do this, but they are among the most important and are illustrative.

You might think of this chapter as a bookmark. Because reflexive laws—which (for our purposes) are laws that set up a framework within which a company has some discretion to take internal, policy-related actions to comply with the overarching law—are part of complying with the law, I include them in this Part II of the book. However, these laws become even more important in Part III of the book when we examine the contours of building ethical corporate cultures, a requirement that these reflexive laws also call for.

In 1984, Congress established the Federal Sentencing Commission with a mandate to provide guidance to federal judges in criminal cases. In particular, the aim was to make federal punishments for crimes more rigorous and more consistent. The Commission established the Guidelines. It is important to note that these Guidelines are exactly that: guidelines. Judges need not follow them with every "i dotted" and "t crossed." The same is true for corporations with respect to the organizational aspect—the deputization part—of the Guidelines.

The 1984 Guidelines established expectations for the sentences judges would impose. Indeed, if one listens to a news report as a criminal is about to be sentenced for a crime of which they have been convicted, one will hear commentators mention that under the Guidelines, the convicted defendant would receive, for example, a penalty of ten years with a fine of $500,000, or whatever the Guidelines would mandate for specific cases.

In 1991, Congress amended the Guidelines to create provisions applicable to organizations. These provisions extend to a wide variety of organizations, including nonprofit as well as for-profit corporations. They provide incentives for a corporation to set

---

32   *See,* David Hess et al., *The 2004 Amendments to the Federal Sentencing Guidelines and Their Implicit Call for a Symbiotic Integration of Business Ethics,* 11.4 FORDHAM J. CORP. & FIN. L. 725, 726 (2006).

up compliance programs that make it less likely for employees in the organization to violate the law. These include a statement of the standards and mission of the corporations, which typically results in a Mission Statement or a Code of Conduct. A high-level official in the organization is to oversee the program. There should be a forum—such as a hotline or an ombudsperson—where employees can safely report a violation without fear of reprisal. Corporations are benefitted by self-reporting violations rather than waiting for a violation to be discovered. There should be training programs so that employees understand the specifics of the laws applicable to them and the methods for compliance.

These steps comprise a compliance program. The incentives for a corporation to set these up are that there are major monetary issues involved. If a company violates a criminal law, a judge can see the relevant base fine that applies to it based on the severity of the offense, as demonstrated in the following chart (U.S. Sentencing Guidelines Manual § 8C2.4(d)):

OFFENSE LEVEL	AMOUNT	OFFENSE LEVEL	AMOUNT
6 or less	$5,000	23	$1,600,000
7	$7,500	24	$2,100,000
8	$10,000	25	$2,800,000
9	$15,000	26	$3,700,000
10	$20,000	27	$4,800,000
11	$30,000	28	$6,300,000
12	$40,000	29	$8,100,000
13	$60,000	30	$10,500,000
14	$85,000	31	$13,500,000
15	$125,000	32	$17,500,000
16	$175,000	33	$22,000,000
17	$250,000	34	$28,500,000
18	$350,000	35	$36,000,000
19	$500,000	36	$45,500,000
20	$650,000	37	$57,500,000
21	$910,000	38 or more	$72,500,000.
22	$1,200,000		

The amount of the fine will decrease if the judge sees that the corporation has made a good-faith effort in implementing the compliance program pursuant to the Guidelines. On the other hand, a fine could increase if there is no program or if there is no evidence that there has been a good faith effort to comply with the Guidelines. The Guidelines actually use a series of criteria to determine a culpability score, which is then added to the number of violations to determine the fine.[33]

These differences in monetary punishment can become significant and so, while not formally mandated as a law to follow, every major company has implemented a corporate compliance system. Indeed, in the *Caremark* case, 698 A.2d 959 (Del. Ch. 1996), the court held that it was a breach of fiduciary duty to shareholders to not have a compliance program in place. Under examination by the Court as to whether the directors met their duties to monitor employee actions and comply with their fiduciary duties as well as the Sentencing Guidelines, the Directors came out rather well. But the important aspect of the case was not whether or not the Directors breached their duty, but instead, whether failure to institute a compliance program in accord with the Federal Sentencing Guidelines could be held to be a breach of their fiduciary duty. That legal point provides a precedent for future shareholders to hold directors liable to the corporation itself. In *Caremark,* the Court said:

> "Modernly this question has been given special importance by an increasing tendency, especially under federal law, to employ the criminal law to assure corporate compliance with external legal requirements, including environmental, financial, employee and product safety as well as assorted other health and safety regulations. In 1991, pursuant to the Sentencing Reform Act of 1984, the United States Sentencing Commission adopted Organizational Sentencing Guidelines which impact importantly on the prospective effect these criminal sanctions might have on business corporations. The Guidelines set forth a uniform sentencing structure for organizations to be sentenced for violation of federal criminal statutes and provide for penalties that equal or often massively exceed those previously imposed on corporations. The Guidelines offer powerful incentives for corporations today to have in place compliance programs to detect violations of law, promptly to report violations to appropriate public officials when discovered, and to take prompt, voluntary remedial efforts. * * *
>
> [A] corporate board has no responsibility to assure that appropriate information and reporting systems are established by

---

33   *See*, U.S. Sentencing Guidelines Manual § 8(c)2.5.

management-would not, in any event, be accepted by the Delaware Supreme Court in 1996, in my opinion. In stating the basis for this view, I start with the recognition that in recent years the Delaware Supreme Court has made it clear-especially in its jurisprudence concerning take-overs, from *Smith v. Van Gorkom* through *Paramount Communications v. QVC*, the seriousness with which the corporation law views the role of the corporate board. Secondly, I note the elementary fact that relevant and timely *information* is an essential predicate for satisfaction of the board's supervisory and monitoring role under Section 141 of the Delaware General Corporation Law. Thirdly, I note the potential impact of the federal organizational sentencing guidelines on any business organization. Any rational person attempting in good faith to meet an organizational governance responsibility would be bound to take into account this development and the enhanced penalties and the opportunities for reduced sanctions that it offers.

In light of these developments, it would, in my opinion, be a mistake to conclude that our Supreme Court's statement in *Graham* concerning "espionage" means that corporate boards may satisfy their obligation to be reasonably informed concerning the corporation, without assuring themselves that information and reporting systems exist in the organization that are reasonably designed to provide to senior management and to the board itself timely, accurate information sufficient to allow management and the board, each within its scope, to reach informed judgments concerning both the corporation's compliance with law and its business performance.

Obviously the level of detail that is appropriate for such an information system is a question of business judgment. And obviously too, no rationally designed information and reporting system will remove the possibility that the corporation will violate laws or regulations, or that senior officers or directors may nevertheless sometimes be misled or otherwise fail reasonably to detect acts material to the corporation's compliance with the law. But it is important that the board exercise a good faith judgment that the corporation's information and reporting system is in concept and design adequate to assure the board that appropriate information will come to its attention in a timely manner as a matter of ordinary operations, so that it may satisfy its responsibility.

Thus, I am of the view that a director's obligation includes a duty to attempt in good faith to assure that a corporate information and reporting system, which the board concludes is adequate, exists, and that failure to do so under some circumstances may, in theory at least, render a director liable for losses caused by non-compliance with applicable legal standards. I now turn to an analysis of the claims asserted with this concept of the directors duty of care, as a duty satisfied in part by assurance of adequate information flows to the board, in mind.

Thus , through a reflexive legal measure, governments can provide incentives so significant for corporations to follow that management really has little choice but to implement them. Empirical studies have also now been undertaken to determine what makes for effective compliance programs. In a series of articles written by Linda Trevino, Gary Weaver and Phillip Cochran, they identify two key factors crucial to an effective compliance program.[34]

The first concerned whether a common set of standards applied throughout the organization. If employees perceived that there were a set of standards for high-ranking officials in the organization and another set of standards for the rank-and-file, the compliance program was not as effective. This led to a second, related, finding: that procedural justice issues were the most important factors in creating an effective compliance program. That is, whatever the particulars of a company's program, its effectiveness mainly depending on whether the standards were enforced.

Effective compliance, then, is not simply the drafting of rules and having employees sign a statement that they have received and read the applicable rules, though that may be a step in the compliance process. Effective compliance has been empirically shown to depend on other factors as well. Complicating things further were a set of amendments to the Guidelines in 2004 that mandated that these programs should create "organizational cultures" leading to "ethics" as well as legal compliance. With these, the ante was further upped for companies to go beyond legal minimums and to consider how to create ethical corporate cultures in order to meet the applicable legal requirement of creating effective compliance programs.

Before discussing what ethical corporate culture may mean, it is worth noting that the Guidelines are not an aberration. A similar reflexive model was implemented with respect to sexual harassment cases in a 1998 U.S. Supreme Court case, *Burlington Industries v. Ellerth*, 524 U.S. 742 (1998). That case clarified a point previously mentioned in this chapter: that employers could be vicariously liable for the actions of their employees.

---

34 *See*, Cochran et al., *Corporate Ethics Programs As Control Systems* 42.1 Academy of Management J. 41 (Feb. 1999); Cochran et al., *Integrated and Decoupled Corporate Social Performance* 42.5 Academy of Management J 539 (Oct. 1999); Cochran et al., *Corporate Ethics Practices in the Mid-1990's: An Empirical Study of the Fortune 1000* 18.3 J. Business Ethics 283 (Feb. 1999).

In a sexual harassment case, that means that a company could be liable for the sexually harassing actions of one of its employees. While the case confirmed that rule, it also provided a way for employers to reduce the likelihood of having such cases go through the long, expensive court process. That alternative was to provide a compliance program directed toward sexual harassment issues that included training programs as well as a forum for resolving the cases.

In short, these reflexive methods of having corporations improve their culture in order to head off legal and ethical indiscretions create significant pressures on corporations to address issues of culture and ethics as well as compliance.

Ethics, the Law, and Corporations

On the one hand, the idea of businesses having ethical obligations is very old. Legal historian Reuven Avi-Yonah has shown that social obligations of business, grounded in the law, date back to Roman antiquity.[35] In early American legal history, one could only obtain a corporate charter if a legislature determined that the corporate purpose served some kind of public good.[36] In smaller towns and urban neighborhoods around the country, the currency of a businessperson very much depended on the extent to which that person was a leading citizen in the community.

For a variety of reasons, the connection between ethical, social engagement of businesses and their profit-making function was perceived to be more tenuous. Part of that reason may have been because the rise of large corporations made it difficult for any one person in the organization, except perhaps the CEO, to see their own obligations extended beyond their job performance. One of the prominent philosophers of the Twentieth Century, Alasdair MacIntyre, has decried "managerialism" that does not ask ultimate questions of whether a business action is bad or good, but simply whether one has completed one's job description.[37]

Liquid markets also play a role because today, a stockholder who has a computer can change positions in the market a dozen or more times a day. Many academic studies—and meta-studies of those studies—conclude that there is a slight correlation between good ethics/social performance and good business/financial performance.[38] But those studies look at long-term business performance. In the long term, concepts such as reputation, goodwill, and social capital have genuine economic value. In the short term, it is much harder to calculate the value of goodwill when determining the company's

---

35   *See*, Reuven S. Avi-Yonah, *The Cyclical Transformations of the Corporate Form* 20 Del. J. Corp. L. 767, 773 (2005).

36   *Id.* at 785.

37   *See*, Alasdair MacIntyre *After Virtue* 75 (2007).

38   *See*, Joshua D. Margolis, Hillary Anger Elfenbein, and James P. Walsh, *Do Well by Doing Good? Don't Count on It* 86.1 *Harvard Business Review* 19 (Jan. 2008).

quarterly forecast on which basis shareholders will make decisions to buy and sell as well as to retain or fire a CEO.

A third factor has been the rise, both in law and in business, of an economics movement, primarily drawing on the Chicago School of Economics, that sidelines notions of corporate responsibility. As Milton Friedman argued, a CEO who spends corporate assets on philanthropic purposes commits theft; stealing shareholder money. Unless that philanthropy leads to a measureable economic benefit—which Friedman acknowledges that it might—then executives should maximize profit and let the shareholders choose what to do with their own money. Similar economic models, especially within Finance, have developed precise statistics models that measures mechanism that enhance profitability that leave hard-to-measure issues of ethics and social goods out of the equation.

These factors triggered a reaction. Depending on where one begins the history, that reaction could be located in a famous debate between Adolf Berle and E.M. Dodd in the Harvard Law Review where they debated whether corporate leaders should manage for the benefit of the shareholders or for the benefit of the general public.[39] In the 1960s, one began to see studies by academics of what businesspeople say about ethics.[40] In the 1970s, in the aftermath of political scandals such as Watergate and then with corporate scandals like the bribery scandals of Lockheed,[41] public and institutional pressure built on business schools to address ethical issues.

In the 1980s, that pressure gave rise to the major effort of philosophers entering into business schools who took classic philosophical frameworks and applied them to business. This included scholars such as Ed Freeman, who brought to life the idea of Stakeholder Theory, a play on the focus on Shareholders. Following principles of the German philosopher Immanuel Kant, Freeman argued that all people should be treated as ends, not as means to an end (a corollary of Kant's Categorical Imperative), and so, businesses should not look at employees as "labor inputs," but as flesh-and-blood beings with dignity. The same logic applied to anyone else who was affected by a corporate action (the definition of a stakeholder). Kant was also followed by those who advocated for a human rights standard within business, such as Patricia Werhane. Thomas Donaldson invoked the work of social contractarian John Rawls and argued for a meta-bargain between businesses and society, with businesses owing obligations to society in exchange for its existence. Donaldson later partnered with Thomas Dunfee to expand that social contract to consider not only philosophical social contracts, but practical,

---

39 A.A. Berle, *Corporate Powers as Powers in Trust* 44 Harv. L. Rev 1049 (1931); E. Merrick Dodd, *For Whom are Corporate Managers Trustees* 45 Harv. L. Rev. 1145 (1932).

40 See, Raymond Baumhart *Ethics in Business* (1968).

41 *see* William Hartung, *Prophets of War: Lockheed Martin and the Making of the Military-Industrial Complex* 115 (2011),

political, and legal social contracts that already exist around the world. Robert Solomon and Edwin Hartman drew on Aristotle to argue for a virtue-based philosophy of business ethics and a community-based one, respectively. William Frederick drew upon naturalist notions and applied them to business to create a more pragmatic version of business ethics; drawing on different sources, Richard DeGeorge similarly articulated a pragmatic model.

Though these rich formulations were being developed, notions of ethics and social responsibility were fairly marginalized in business schools until the mid-to-late 1990s. At that point, more scandals erupted, especially just after the turn of the century with Enron, Worldcom, and others. This placed more pressure on business schools. Their accrediting body, the AACSB, responded with a requirement that all business schools have some method of teaching ethics. Perhaps more influentially, cell phones and the Internet appeared. When those technological tools became available, it became quickly apparent that a corporate indiscretion could be captured on a hand-held cell phone and placed for worldwide view on the Internet within a matter of seconds.

Suddenly corporations realized that actions matter, just as they might for a business in a small town or in an urban neighborhood. Corporations began to create public relations departments that focused on issues of corporate responsibility. Perhaps as or more importantly, business school students drove the faculty and deans to address the issue of ethics, corporate social responsibility, and environmental responsibility. Thus, by 2005 or so, business schools had been pushed by students and businesses to address corporate responsibility issues by technology, scandals, and accrediting bodies. The previously mentioned Federal Sentencing Guidelines also added to this mix.. By 2005, studies were showing that paper programs and legal-only based compliance programs were ineffective. Amendments to the Guidelines were, in light of the scandals of Enron and others, requiring attention to "organizational culture" and "ethics."

With this history in mind, one has an answer to the question of why a company would bother to undertake an ethics initiative or social responsibility project. One reason is economic. No less an authority than former Federal Reserve Chairman Alan Greenspan testified before Congress that in today's economy, the only thing a business may bring to the market is its reputation; if that reputation is damaged, so is the company.[42] Protection of reputation has become a vital issue for today's modern businesses, whether in the form of a public relationship campaign, partnering with an NGO to address social ills, or hiring employees or consultants to "scrub" damaging statements about the company placed on the Internet.

The economic calculus is not merely concerned with damage control. It also brings opportunity. Some firms seek to differentiate themselves in the market by appealing to a segment that values identifiable corporate reputation. Ben and Jerry's ice cream

---

42   Alan Greenspan, The Assault on Integrity, 2.8 *The Objectivist* Newsletter 31(1963).

was the forerunner of this, but today that niche—and it can be a big niche—is filled with companies such as Whole Foods, Timberland, and Starbucks. Without canonizing these companies, other companies have had more mixed results in achieving this niche-status, but their effort in trying to do so is indicative of the value reputation has in today's market. Thus, one sees extractives such as Chevron, Shell, and even Exxon touting their corporate social responsibility programs, even though each has been the target of major, public demonization in the not-so-distant past. Diamond companies, such as Tiffany's and DeBeers, embraced a certification program (the Kimberly Protocol) that attempted to assure a customer that diamonds were not mined with the assistance of child soldiers. Wal-Mart gets hammered in the press for its labor practices one day and then is touted for its environmental programs the next. Johnson & Johnson was one of the great champions of ethical conduct in the 1980s, but its reputation suffered under continuous recalls and lawsuits so much that its shareholders filed a derivative lawsuit demanding that the board of directors bring the company back to its moral roots. In short, companies today see an opportunity for preserving or gaining market share by being a company that seeks to do good as well as to maximize profits.

These considerations spill over into two other reasons for why a company might take ethics and social responsibility seriously. Legal reasons also are important. Companies get sued for breaches of conduct. Internet companies, such as Google and Yahoo have been sued in U.S. courts for the actions of their subsidiaries in China following the Chinese legal system's requirement to identify users who might use words like "democracy" and "freedom" in their postings. Some of those users have ended up in Chinese jails as a result. The Internet companies have claimed that they are only following local law, but human rights groups have sued them under the Alien Tort Act (28 U.S.C. § 1350) on behalf of the litigants.[43] While the U.S. Supreme Court limited the reach of the Alien Tort Act in a 2013 decision, the effort to hold corporations accountable for their actions in other courts should be anticipated.

More domestic policy questions may include: why would a company undertake a sexual harassment training policy? Well, one clear reason is fear of litigation. And, of course, litigation's bite is economic damages. So to get out ahead of potential litigation, one might adopt an ethically driven policy. Studies also show that harassing workplaces tend to be less productive. After all, the harasser isn't working; he is harassing. And targets of the harassment aren't working either; they are trying to get away from the harasser. Neither lends itself to economic productivity.[44]

That leads to the third reason for why one might bother: identity reasons.

---

43 *See, Wang Xiaoning, et. al., v. YAHOO! Inc., et al.* 2007 WL 1908759 (N.D. Cal.).

44 *See,* Roy Whitehead, Jr. and Walter Block, *Sexual Harassment in the Workplace: A Property Rights Perspective* 4 J. L. & FAM. STUD. 229, 243 (2002).

Continuing with the sexual harassment example, most companies would prefer not to be known as the sexual harassment company. It also leads to some of the earlier examples of wanting to be known as a clean diamond company or a shoe company (Timberland) that gives its employees forty hours a year off from work to do volunteer work in the community. In an Internet age where reputation is important, so is identity. Indeed, companies recruit on the basis of their identity and so if a company does not consistently manage with that identity in mind, it can have an impact on the morale of the employees recruited to work in "that kind" of company.

A final reason to bother with ethical issues is simply a moral one. At the end of the day, human beings, even at work, have moral sentiments. They have a hardwired desire to want to help those in need and they take pride, even joy, in treating others well. At times, organizational incentives do not reward such actions; they may even punish such considerations. But there is an aspect of human nature that wants to be proud of the ethical content of the work one does.

CHAPTER 8

The Philosophers' Formula/Stakeholder Theory

Nestlé's Use of Slave Labor in the Ivory Coast
Brian Reisman[45]

As Cynthia McMullan maneuvers the crowded aisles of her local superstore, her 7-year-old son whines about the length of his mother's shopping excursion. Much to her own dismay, Cynthia's son has already wreaked havoc during her afternoon grocery run. Upon entering the store, little Johnny McMullan dropped a can of olives from a promotional stand. A few minutes later, he stepped on a box of strawberries and proceeded to leave fruity footprints throughout the produce section.

Cynthia, normally a calm and collected mother, is beginning to lose her patience. After a long day at work, she is too tired to adequately reprimand her son for his inappropriate antics. Johnny is growing equally impatient and begins to sing his favorite cartoon theme song in an infinite loop. By the time little Johnny begins the 9th repetition of the jingle, Cynthia snaps.

"Cut it out, Johnny! Mommy had a very long day at work and needs to finish shopping before Daddy gets home. You're really getting on my nerves and I need you to cool down. I'll make you a deal. Go to the candy aisle and choose something you want. If you behave for the rest of the time we're here, I'll buy it for you when we check out."

Within seconds, Johnny has disappeared from the frozen goods aisle, leaving his mother in a state of newfound calm. Meanwhile, Johnny scans the numerous sweets available to him. After a long period of deliberation, he snatches a Nestlé Crunch Bar and sprints back to his mother's side. He throws the bar into the shopping cart and remains silent for the remainder of the shopping trip. He wants nothing more than to enjoy a Nestlé Bar.

On the other side of the world, an African boy slightly older than Johnny accidentally slices his hand with a machete he was given to retrieve cocoa beans. He looks for something to wipe the blood off his hand, but finds nothing. He considers walking back to his supervisor to get medical care, but fears returning without a sufficient cocoa yield. He thinks about the dire situation he has been forced into and tears run down his face. The young boy knows he is worse off on his own, and therefore cannot run from the

---

45   This case was prepared by Brian Reisman as an adaptation of a paper he wrote in 2013 for my ethics class. A copy of that paper appears in the Appendix.

injustice of slavery. He is stuck. The boy sighs and continues to hack at the cocoa plants in front of him. His blood and tears trickle onto the sweet beans he is harvesting.

When Cynthia finally gets home after a long drive from the superstore, Johnny starts acting up and rubs his strawberry-coated sneakers on an antique rug. Cynthia sits him down and disciplines him as she wipes the soles of his shoes with a washcloth. Johnny demands the Crunch Bar he earned be given to him immediately. Cynthia, defeated from tiredness, caves in. She begrudgingly hands the candy bar to Johnny and heads to the kitchen to prepare dinner. *He could have it so much worse, she thought to herself.*

Introduction

As of March of 2013, Nestlé Company was the World's largest food distributor. Specializing in everything from snack foods to health supplements, Nestle is a huge multinational company that has branded itself as a healthy and reputable player within the food distribution industry.

Within the spectrum of Nestlé's many market offerings exists Nestlé Chocolate, sometimes referred to as Nestlé Confectionery. This division of Nestlé, one that competes with companies such as Cadbury and Mars, is internationally known for products such as the Crunch Bar, the Kit Kat Bar, and the Butterfinger Bar.

In 1998, pressure from social activists led to widespread investigation of the cocoa harvesting industry. As a result of the investigation, allegations arose suggesting that large chocolate companies were using child labor in production, and moreover, that some child labor was a product of enslavement. These allegations led to further investigation and more bad news for large chocolate companies. By 2000, it had been revealed that many of those working in the cocoa industry were trafficked or coerced into unfair labor conditions on West African plantations. While the legitimacy of these reports was questioned, the breadth and scope of investigation surrounding the cocoa industry led to serious problems for large-scale chocolate manufacturers.

During this time, Nestlé was involved with cocoa plantations under investigation. Nestlé, which was responsible for the purchasing of approximately 10 percent of all global cocoa output, obtained more than one third of its cocoa from the Ivory Coast. The investigations surrounding enslavement and child labor within the cocoa industry focused largely on the Ivory Coast, as the country is known for unfair labor practices and lenient trade rules that allow for exploitation of workers. While Nestlé faced little scrutiny during the early 2000s, it was aware of the investigations taking place as well as the potential for reputational damage to the firm.

In 2005, the International Labor Rights Fund filed a lawsuit against Nestle claiming that young children had been trafficked to the Ivory Coast by the company in order to work on cocoa plantations. Although the lawsuit was later dismissed, the public attention surrounding the case propelled Nestlé into the spotlight and branded the company as one that exploited young workers in West Africa.

In the late 2000s, NGOs and social activists targeted Nestlé utilizing the idea that it is most effective to fight an industry's worst offender. Suddenly, Nestlé Chocolate experienced widespread boycotts of its products and large demonstrations in metropolitan areas. At this point, the company knew it had to react. In 2009, Nestlé consulted the Fair Labor Association and asked for guidance on the issue of slave labor in the Ivory Coast. The FLA conducted an investigation on Nestlé's involvement and sent back a report detailing their objectives for the company. In an effort to form a strategic ally, Nestlé publicized its response to the report and outlined a plan for improvement based on the FLA's findings. Among the changes promised by Nestlé were better definition of employee roles, better communication of labor expectations, improved grievance and remediation procedures, and perhaps most importantly, the mapping and monitoring of Nestlé's entire supply chain. In taking on this last measure, Nestlé aimed to form relationships with all suppliers and to track the flow of labor in West Africa. In 2012, Nestlé became a member of the Fair Labor Association, demonstrating a commitment to fair working conditions within in its operations.

As of late 2012, however, both the Fair Labor Association and critics of Nestlé's continued use of child labor claimed that Nestlé was still facilitating the exploitation of workers in the Ivory Coast. As most of the company's monitoring policies and supply chain models were opaque and made private, some firmly believed the company was creating an image that represented a false reality.

Nestlé's Reaction

Although Nestlé aimed to reduce activist pressures and to make meaningful change in West Africa by partnering with the Fair Labor Association, the company saw little change in public opinion during the year following implementation of the FLA's recommendations. Small and large pressure groups alike continued to attack Nestlé, asserting that the company had created a mirage that allowed for continued abuse of workers.

During this time, Nestlé felt threatened by the potentially disastrous allegations made against the company, but did not take further action for a number of reasons. First and foremost, the company did not see itself as the only responsible actor contributing to the problem. As "slave free chocolate" groups cited Hershey and Cadbury as offenders in the same region, Nestlé saw its participation as a contribution to the issue instead of the sole reason for it. Furthermore, the company believed that its actions reflected the best interest of the small African country. While many activist groups claimed that Nestlé was not investing enough time or money to make serious social change in the region, Nestlé's long-standing presence within the region gave the company little reason to be optimistic. Shortly after the first lawsuit was filed against Nestlé Chocolate, the Chief Executive of the entire corporation made this idea clear.

"Nestlé is not the owner of any plantation," said Peter Brabeck-Letmathe." ...There might be a lot of other human rights abuses than just the ones that have been picked up."

While it may be easy to dismiss Brabeck-Lemathe's claim as a desperate business maneuver intended to sway public opinion of Nestlé's actions, there is legitimacy in his words that demand consideration. According to a report by the U.S. State Department published during the 2000s, the Ivory Coast is a country where an estimated 215,000 children live on the streets at a given time. The report also lists numerous forms of observed corruption, most notably the performing of sexual acts within schools in return for passing grades. These problems are made worse by the fact the Ivory Coast lacks a law against human trafficking.

Referring to the country as "basically a civil war situation", Nestlé's chief executive made clear that he doubted his company's ability to make change within the region. Investing large sums of money and time not only threatened the company financially in the short-term, it also posed a long-term investment risk in that any positive societal change would likely require sustained investment for a number of years. As Nestlé felt falsely accused in many cases, the company wondered which route would be more expensive: doing nothing and suffering profit loss from reputational damage or investing for social change in an uncertain political and legal environment

Perhaps most importantly, Nestlé's lack of further response was intended to deny guilt and to shift blame away from the company. In taking on additional action in the Ivory Coast, Nestlé felt it was accepting a burden it was not entirely responsible for. In addition to bearing cost from the corporate side, improvement plans would also draw public attention. While the company knew it could leverage any socially responsible action in a targeted marketing campaign, the decision on whether to take action in the Ivory Coast remained extremely difficult.

An Interesting Dilemma

Because West Africa was a critical component of Nestlé Chocolate's supply chain, and thus ability to produce its product, the company did not see exit from the region as a viable strategy. While the company considered abandoning the region entirely and investing in less controversial harvesting partners, the company also feared what would happen to young children on plantations once the company exited. As many children in the Ivory Coast long for basic resources and shelter, Nestlé urged the public to consider the context surrounding the ethical issue of worker exploitation. Although it is difficult to understand, Nestlé felt that a secure life with minimal or no pay was better than a fight for survival in what can be a very unstable region.

Since its inception, Nestlé has aimed to "...positively influence the social environment in which they operate as responsible corporate citizens, with due regard for those environmental standards and societal aspirations which improve quality of life".

Promising to provide quality food to help people of all ages thrive in life, the company prides itself as a reputable and socially responsible company. With attention surrounding the worker abuse in West Africa rising, the corporation realized that its corporate credo and reputation were on the line.

Regardless of guilt, Nestlé found itself battling the perception that it provided for children in International markets at the expense of children suffering from slavery and illegal working conditions. Moreover, the company needed to defend the exploitation of children in the first place. As young children in West Africa are an especially vulnerable party, Nestlé's involvement in any form of abuse looked even more irresponsible. With public perception of Nestlé's reputation in jeopardy, the company knew it needed to do something. Although the company was working to track all components of its West African supply chains, the public demanded more. With critics growing in number and charges increasing in severity, the company feared that proving it was slave-free was no longer enough.

Management weighed its options. Was there a solution that was beneficial for all parties involved? Was there a way to make lasting social change in the Ivory Coast without breaking the bank? Would socially responsible corporate action provide a return on investment or would it draw negative public attention from previously unaware consumer segments? Most importantly, did the company need to do anything at all if it wasn't responsible for the dilemma in the first place? Management considered the issue at hand and thought about these questions. What was the company going to do?

Stakeholder Theory

Stakeholder theory is where most of the action is in business ethics for the last quarter century. Stakeholder theory obviously starts off as a play on words. What is the responsibility of the company? Is it to its shareholders or is it to its stakeholders?

The key originator of stakeholder theory is **Ed Freeman** of the Darden School of Business at the University of Virginia, who we mentioned before. Freeman argued that all stakeholders should be treated as an end and not as a means to an end. They are not labor inputs. They are not interchangeable parts. They are flesh-and-blood human beings with their own families, their own joys, sorrows, aspirations, own ideas of good and bad. They are independent human beings and we should treat them as an end and not as a means. Why? Freeman draws upon Immanuel Kant, who arguably is the most influential philosopher in the Western world, who developed something called the categorical imperative.

Kant's categorical imperative says that for any law to be a moral law, it needs to be able to be applied with a degree of universality. That means that we should be willing to apply a law or principle to ourselves, since that really is where the rubber meets the road. Are you willing to say that people should be honest to everybody, for instance?

How do we want to be treated? Do we want to have people treat us in an honest way, in a compassionate way?

One of the formulations of the categorical imperative is that human beings are people with dignity and should be treated as an end as opposed to a manipulable means to an end, which is easier said than done. I think that we've all probably manipulated others to our own ends. But Kant suggests you wouldn't like that if that happened to you.

R. Edward Freeman, University Professor; Elis and Signe Olsson Professor of Business Administration; Academic Director, Business Roundtable Institute for Corporate Ethics

For corporations then, how should corporations be operated? They should be operated so that anyone who is affected by their corporate action be treated as an end. What would those people affected by an action be called? A stakeholder, because they have a stake in the company. That is obviously true if they're shareholders. Shareholders are stakeholders, though they frequently are not thought of that way. So too are employees, consumers, suppliers, local governments, national governments, the environment. Because of the logic of stakeholder theory, one might say that if we have forgotten anybody, then add them too. The corporation should make decisions so that any person affected by their action, any stakeholder, is treated as an end and not as a means to an end.

Norman Bowie took these Kantian arguments even further. Arguing for a Kantian principle of "respect for persons," Bowie agreed that individuals should be treated as ends rather than means to an end. He also believe that the corporation could serve as a relevant moral community that would further provide empowerment for those associated with it. Pursuant to the categorical imperative, moral principles should be followed if they are universalizable. Bowie argues, in fact, that the failure to follow such principles doesn't just make for bad decisions, but it makes for incoherency because we are not willing to abide by

Norman Bowie, Professor Emeritus, University of Minnesota; Elmer L. Andersen Chair of Corporate Responsibility

distortions of moral rules when they apply to us. We may want to write a bad check, but we don't want to live in a society in which people do write bad checks. In this and in many other respects, Bowie takes Kant's duty-based ethics quite seriously and argues for the logic of Kantian principles in business.

The first step in applying stakeholder theory is to figure out who the stakeholders are. Who are the people, individuals, and organizations that are affected by the proposed corporate action? Then the real work begins. How do you prioritize among stakeholders? So many people are stakeholders that one has to find some mechanism of knowing who is most important at a particular time and place. To answer that question, I propose a formula, adapted from William Frederick, an Emeritus Professor at the Katz School of Business at the University of Pittsburgh.

Frederick characterized the stakeholder approach to business as ethical business behavior (EBB) being a function of rights (particularly Kantian rights), plus justice (particularly Rawlsian justice), plus utilitarianism. So,

$$EBB = R_K + J_R + U$$

This stands for the proposition that EBB is "Ethical Business Behavior" and it is a result of Kantian Rights, Rawlsian Justice, and Utilitarianism. Frederick offers this whimsically, which is the way that I use it, but it's not a bad way of remembering the various dimensions of stakeholder theory. Frederick also proposed his own theory for business ethics that is rooted in evolutionary principles. Frederick argued that there are naturally recurring value clusters of ecologizing, economizing, and power-aggrandizing values that businesses draw upon. I will build upon Frederick's principles in Part III when looking at issues of corporate culture, but for now, it's worth attending to the dimensions of Frederick's characterization of rights, justice, and utilitarianism.

William C. Frederick, Professor Emeritus of Business Administration

Rights

The first element of stakeholder theory is **rights**. The primary expositor of rights theory is **Patricia Werhane**. Werhane cautioned that people use rights theory kind of indiscriminately. We like to talk about having rights to all kinds of different things. We may casually say, "By golly, I have a right to a good football team this year. I have a right to a good seat when I go to the concert." Werhane was worried about such emotive assertions. Instead, she created a framework anchored by two different kinds of rights. One is a **basic right or a primary right,** and the other one is a **secondary right or a non-basic right.** She wants to say, "Corporations, I know that you are used to doing cost-benefit analysis in order to determine what your course of action should be, and you do that pretty well, and I'm not going to interfere with that being your primary way of making decisions. But I want you to jump through some hoops first to make sure that you're not violating anybody's basic rights, and those rights become a way to prioritize stakeholder interests."

Patricia Werhane, Ph.D.; Professor, Northwestern University

How does one know whether a stakeholder has a basic right or not? Werhane says that a basic right is something without which life would be intolerable. Her list includes life itself, some basic health—she's not talking about whether you have coverage under a PPO versus comprehensive care, but some very basic health-related issues—food, water, shelter, freedom from torture.

Could a corporation possibly impact an employee's life and health? Well, yes. Consider studies reported by LaRue Hosmer, concerning battery restorations in the 1980s. To restore a battery, the accumulated lead acid must be dumped and then refreshed. Those jobs were outsourced from the U.S. to Taiwan; investigators found factory workers in Taiwan working knee-deep in lead battery acid, which has been shown to result in health defects as well as various kinds of cancer. [46]

One could say that that factory worker consented to the risk. Even if that were true, the children later born with health defects didn't consent to the risk of having their parents working knee-deep in lead battery acid. This is one example of how corporations can have an impact on a person's health and even life.

If we have a sense of basic rights, what are non-basic rights? Other things, such as my demand that my alma mater fields a good football team every year, don't really qualify as a right at all. But could there be an intermediate set of rights in between an alleged right to a good football team and a clear, basic right to life? According to Werhane, this category would be comprised of non-basic rights, such as, private property ownership. She says that people in history have been able to live happily and successfully without the right to private property. In many societies, particularly if you look back in hunter-gatherer times, there was a collective ownership of property and people lived quite well, at least in terms of seeming to be happy. So property and the right to income would be an example of a non-basic right. Should we have laws that protect property interest? Yes, so there should be laws against trespassing. There should be laws against theft. Property should be protected. But in a test between a right to property, including corporate income, and a basic right of an employee's death or health, basic rights win.

Sometimes, one has a situation in which there is a contest between rights of equal stature: basic versus basic, secondary versus secondary. An example of two competing secondary rights would be a labor negotiation, where employees want more money and corporate headquarters doesn't want to meet their demands. Both parties have rights to income. Those are non-basic rights. In Werhane's model, one must come up with a compromise to try to honor both. Similarly, if one had basic rights of equal stature, which is more important? Again, both of them are essential, so you try to compromise to honor both.

Werhane provides a caveat. She says that businesspeople are prone to saying that without the service provided by a business, people will starve. So they therefore convert

---

46   LaRue Tone Hosmer, *Moral Leadership in Business* (1995).

the providing of a job to a basic right. She says she is open to that analysis because it is possible that without a job, an unemployed person will indeed suffer due to a lack of clean drinking water, an insufficient food supply or because of health issues. But she says she wants actual evidence. It may well be that the unemployed person goes to another job or perhaps reverts to a subsistence lifestyle; perhaps not optimal, but not starving either. Thus, economic development could provide a basic right, but she wants to see evidence to demonstrate that this is really true.

A question that often arises today concerns the environment. Does the environment have a basic right? Under Werhane's theory, the environment does not have a basic right because rights apply, again following a Kantian analysis, to human beings, sentient beings. However, she would be the first to say that since human beings can be very much affected by environmental degradation, then derivatively, one should protect the environment because ultimately human beings, and their basic rights, are affected by it.

Another approach comes from **Mark Starik**, who does claim that the environment is imbued with basic rights.[47] Or you could rely on ecofeminist theory which argues that the Earth is a living creature, the so-called "Gaia hypothesis."[48] The earth literally inhales and exhales; there are exchanges of gases occurring in the ecosystem. The earth literally gives birth to creatures. Viewed this way, the earth would have basic rights to be protected in and of itself as well as derivatively because of the negative impact it would have on others.

Mark Starik

If one still has not been able to resolve the dilemma, then one attempts to find the formulation that creates the least harm to an affected stakeholder. Go back to the issues of jobs and labor disputes. It may well be that property rights (and derivatively , the rights to income) are secondary rights. A person laid off from a job will not starve, but they will be adversely affected. Is there a way to create a lesser amount of harm to the employee in the process of laying her off? It may well be that the company must reduce costs to stay in business or it may be true that the employee is not doing a good job and really needs to be fired. But a company could create less harm by giving notice to the person that a layoff will occur, to provide funds for retraining, or to lay the person off in a way that is respectful rather than one that is demeaning. All of these would create less harm.

Finally, if the situation still cannot be resolved, then Werhane allows for a cost-benefit analysis.

---

47 *See, e.g. Should Trees Have Managerial Standing? Toward Stakeholder Status for Non-Human Nature*

48 *See, e.g.,* Jon Turney, *Lovelock and Gaia: Signs of Life* (2003).

Justice

The application of Rights is one Stakeholder Theory analysis. Justice and Utilitarianism come next. Frederick does not specify how these are applied; his formula is more of a whimsical characterization of the leading ways of how Stakeholder Theory ends up playing out on the literature. But for our purposes, the idea is for each one of these sub-frameworks (Rights, Justice and Utilitarianism) to be given its due and then the decision-maker makes a judgment as to which is the most relevant and/or persuasive to the situation at hand.

With that in mind, the second element within Stakeholder Theory is Justice. There are a couple of different elements of justice theory. One focuses on equality: equal people with equal talents and equal opportunities ought to be paid and treated equally. For instance, if a man and a woman have the same degrees and grade point averages and experience, they should be paid the same. There is an injustice there if they are not. This is an example of an equality version of justice.

A second kind of justice is distributive justice and is articulated by a famous American philosopher, John Rawls. Rawls says that people want to be treated fairly. What does that mean? We all have different ideas of what fairness means. So how do we know whether something is fair and whether it's not?

So he undertook a thought experiment. Suppose that a person—many persons really—put themselves behind what he called a veil of ignorance and are in "the original position." In other words, a person knows she will be born, but beyond that, she don't know any of the particular defining characteristics that you have. He could be male or female, he doesn't know what skin color he will have, whether he is going to be smart or dumb, whether he going to be tall or short, whether he is going to be a good athlete or a bad athlete, whether he going to be musically talented. She (I intentionally use alternating pronouns here because gender identity becomes one of the unknowns) doesn't know any of those things. She just knows that she is going to be a person.

If you had 100 people in the original position—you can make it a thousand people or a million people or whatever number you want—what kind of deal would they construct for what a fair society would look like? Using psychological studies of risk assessment, Rawls argues that human beings would want to make sure that if they're not well off, they're not made worse off. Applied to corporate actions, this would be a principle to protect the most vulnerable members of a given situation.

The corporate action may well make the rich richer. If you're going to make the rich richer, you need to lift all boats. But if the rich are getting richer at the expense of the poor, then you've got a problem. The corporate action in question needs to account for the most vulnerable stakeholder. That's fair. That's just. Rawls' approach is a social contract approach because it hypothethically assumes a negotiation among parties in the Original Position.

Two prominent expositors of social contract theory in the field of business ethics are **Tom Donaldson** and the late **Tom Dunfee**, who were both at the Wharton School of Business. They used something called an integrative social contracts theory of business ethics. This is a complicated theory of business ethics that blends a philosophical kind of social contract, akin to what Rawls proposes, together with the social contracts, the real ones in place throughout all human societies. Donaldson and Dunfee's approach tries to navigate a way to be respectful of the rights of local communities to be free to make decisions that are appropriate for their time and culture, while also holding all societies to some basic philosophical demands of justice.

Let me start with an example. When I was at the University of Michigan, I was fortunate to have Linda Lim as a colleague. She was an international business professor who

did her dissertation on the plight of women workers, particularly in Southeast Asia. She expected to find that they felt abused and harassed in horrific working conditions. Instead, she found that everyone she talked to was incredibly grateful for the job. Of course, one has to worry about whether the boss was looming in the background, and so they may have spoken more glowingly than they would otherwise, but Linda really didn't think so. She cautioned that when we're making judgments of what a fair working condition is, we should ask the people who are working there.

*Thomas Donaldson, top;
Tom W. Dunfee, bottom.*

Similarly, Donaldson and Dunfee recognized that when you're applying a moral value, you need to give a degree of moral free space so that individual societies and cultures are free to develop their own moral norms. If people in that society consent to that moral norm, then the norm is what Donaldson and Dunfee call "authentic." It has some level of credibility. At the same time, Donaldson and Dunfee are not willing to just let everything be relative. Even if people allegedly consent, there still may be some things that violate what they call cross-cultural "hypernorms" that still make it wrong and require some sort of an action.

For example, I once wrote an article with Dunfee on the blood diamond industry. The extraction of diamonds in certain African areas is all about who has control of the geographical space that has the diamonds in it. Warlords provided AK-47 automatic weapons to six- and seven-year-olds and tell them to shoot the opposition. The warlords, of course, didn't care about whether the six- or seven-year-old got killed. They simply want to have someone shooting bullets at the other side. If the child refused, they warlords would cut off the child's arm or leg. Two students in my undergraduate class said, well, if that's what the culture is then we shouldn't say anything about it because we don't want to be imperialistic. I was shocked. A child just lost his arm because he wouldn't shoot somebody else and you're going to say we shouldn't interfere because of wanting to avoid being a cultural imperialist? Be an imperialist!

I further said that I doubted if it's really a society's judgment or moral tradition to let a child have their hands cut off if they didn't shoot the other side. I don't think that there was Donaldson and Dunfee-like consent. Sometimes, in fact, things do require one to say no, that's wrong, we must do better. How else do you progress?

Donaldson and Dunfee recognize this as well. They argue for a sense of moral free space for societies and communities to develop their own moral norms. If people consent to them, fine, but one should not simply take at face value claims that "this is the way things are here." Cutting off children's limbs is unlikely to be considered good in any society, no matter what the rulers at the time say. At the same time, deferring to local custom is one level of respect that is due to a given society.

These extant social contracts should still be evaluated according to a larger, philosophical social contract that are anchored by hypernorms. What are those hypernorms? The first answer is that they are something of a work in progress. Donaldson and Dunfee believe that we will continue to find norms that cut across cultures through additional empirical research. As a provision holding spot—and this isn't Donaldson and Dunfee's position, this is argument of some of their interpreters—basic rights might well have a lot of overlap with hypernorms.

Thus, in justice theory, there's an equality dimension and then there's a vulnerability dimension because people aren't born equal. They're born with all kinds of different characteristics and advantages, and so we have to account for what happens when people are born differently. In protecting the vulnerable, however, one can neither simply project one's own norms as to what should happen nor automatically defer to a local culture. Instead, the Donaldson and Dunfee model call for a blend of respectful deference to existing social norms while also holding those norms accountable to cross-cultural hypernorms.

Utilitarianism

The third framework is utilitarianism: the greatest good for the greatest number. Or if you're a devotee of *Star Trek*, you can think of Spock: the needs of the many outweigh the needs of the few. Utilitarians like Bentham and Mill said we all have different preferences, which they called *utiles*. One person has one preference and another person has another preference; how do we decide one from the other? We can't. But we can take such actions that tend to make the most people the most happy as much as we can.

Capitalism has utilitarian dimensions where you're trying to create additional profits and generate additional economic growth to benefit more people, and not just for the rich. While the rich may become richer, capitalism also lifts the poor out of poverty, thereby making them happier as well, at least in theory. Democracy is an example of utilitarianism where the greatest good for the greatest number is defined by votes. Whoever gets the most votes—another kind of utile—ends up being elected.

We use utilitarian thinking a great deal, but there's always a concern with utilitarianism: the majority wins and the minority loses, which is why typically in a utilitarian decision-making process, whether it's economic or political, there's some sort of protection for the rights of minorities. Politically, just because the majority thinks a person's religion is nuts doesn't mean it can be banned. This is why we have the Bill of Rights protecting freedom of religion, freedom of speech, and other freedoms. Even if the majority thinks that your speech is stupid, you still have that freedom to speak stupidly.

There are other examples of utilitarian calculations. We know in the United States, for instance, 30,000-50,000 people a year will be killed in an automobile accident. (Fortunately, the numbers have been going down in recent years.) We've made a societal judgment that the greater good is achieved by having highways and cars as opposed to going back to horses, which were a lot slower and which may result in some broken bones, but not as many deaths.

The corporate application of utilitarianism frequently ends up looking a lot like long-term shareholder value. If a company takes care of all its stakeholders, it will likely generate the kind of goodwill, reputation, and social capital that will end up paying off for the corporation in the long run.

Having said that, one may not find such a happy correlation or blending of these theories. Rights theory and Justice theory often will be arguing directly opposite of utilitarian theory. Rights and Justice may go directly against shareholder theory. Together, however, these three frameworks provide a thorough way of defining the obligations of managers to the corporation's stakeholders.

CHAPTER 9

Virtue Theory

THE THIRD ETHICAL framework is Virtue Theory. Chapter One provided an introduction to virtue theory when you were to think of virtues that you would like an organization you are part of to have.

Applying virtue theory requires three things. First, one needs to identify the relevant virtues that are applicable. There are at least three ways one can figure out the pool of virtues from which one can select those that are relevant. One of those ways is to consult the philosophers who study and work with ethics. Classically, that would begin with someone like Aristotle; in contemporary business ethics, Robert Solomon and Ed Hartman would be scholars to consult. Focusing more on corporate life, one can look to a given company's list of virtues. Many will list a set of virtues or values in their mission statement that one could draw upon in assessing a problem. Finally, one can gather a group of people—such as members in a class—and have them elect a set of virtues they think are most important. That last way of determining virtues is what I have generally used in asking members of a class to tell me what they believe are important virtues (Chapter One's exercise), and then we work with the virtues that receive the most votes. As we saw in Chapter One, the virtues elected tend to be fairly constant, suggesting that human beings share a sense of these core values. Further, having students express their sentiments rather than having them didactically prescribed tends to generate more buy-in on the legitimacy of those virtues. As a result, I won't give away the punch line of what students say are the most important; the process of discovery is itself part of the very point of the exercise.

Once one has a pool of virtues, one can then determine which one(s) are relevant. In a given situation, some virtues are relevant and some are not. Two or three may be very relevant. The next step is to define them. Remember the story from the first chapter of the difference between honesty to a car dealer when trading in an old car as opposed to honesty to your nephew when selling the car to him. Honesty can be defined differently according to the nature of the underlying relationship. The effort to define what the virtues mean is important. Companies sometimes fall prey to the idea that once they have listed what virtues are important to them in a mission statement, their work is then done. But actually, that is just a step. Virtues do not self-define and in the process of determining what they mean—especially in discussion with other people—one picks up skills of refinement in what the virtues are, how they apply, and shades of meaning people attach to them.

Once one has determined the relevant virtues and defined them, the final step is to apply them. How does the virtue in question apply to the issue at hand? The application itself is fairly straight-forward once one has gone through the process of determining the relevant virtues and defining them.

Robert Solomon.
Photo: Ted S. Warren

Let me, though, provide a little bit more context on virtue theory. Virtue theory has been primarily brought to bear in the field of business by **Robert Solomon** and **Ed Hartman**. Solomon emphasized an Aristotelian approach to business ethics which doesn't ask what one's duty is, what one can get in trouble for, or what one can avoid. It doesn't ask how does one avoid trouble. It asks instead what would be beautiful? What would be powerful? What would be admirable? What would be excellent? If you fall short of excellence, it doesn't mean that you're a bad person; it means there is more work to be done. With duty-based theories, there's a connotation of failure.

Edwin M. Hartman,
Rutgers University

Aristotle said that the only way to be a good person is to be a part of a good community. Business ethicist Ed Hartman emphasized the dimensions of community that lead to a good life, especially as related to business and the community which it creates for itself. A good person learns to be a good person because they are in a good community that teaches them what it means to be a good person. That may seem circular, but it doesn't mean that there isn't truth within the description. Think in terms of your family. A four-year-old will need to be told what things to do or what things not to do. Sometimes, she needs to be punished. Other times, she needs to be praised. Both can be effective. We build people's character through this reinforcement from their community; the community, in this case, being a family. The four-year old doesn't just figure things out on her own; she has help through other people who teach, punish, and praise her. As she matures, she may increasingly exercise more independence in determining issues of right and wrong on her own, but she her moral character has much to do with the mediating institutions that have formed her.

People tend to react to this emphasis on community as taking away individual decision-making. Let me emphasize that, over time, that individual then decides what dimensions he or she is going to internalize, what things they are going to push and elaborate, and maybe what kinds of communities that they want to be part of. They may desire not to be part of that particular family, but you know what? Human beings don't go away to live as hermits very often. They go to live in another kind of a community that appeals to them. Even as adults, human beings depend on a community.

There is a good deal of scientific, evolutionary evidence that shows that we are social beings; some people have gone so far as to say that we are moral beings. I'm not quite so sure about whether we are innately moral, but we certainly are social. If you're going to live with other people, there will be certain rules of behavior to follow in order to stay in a relationship with others with whom you live.

In fact, a quick and dirty way of defining ethics would be the rules and principles that sustain relationships. That's true between a husband and a wife, between friends, between coworkers, between nations. A relationship requires certain rules and principles to maintain that relationship. The same is true of any community.

We can apply this to business organizations as well. Businesses are communities. People do adapt their behavior in order to be a member of that community. Sometimes that means bad behavior occurs. An article in the Academy of Management Journal several years ago called "Monkey See, Monkey Do," [49] analyzed how people mimic the behavior they see at work so they can fit in. This adaptation to our business environments and the behaviors practiced in them has consequences for the question of whether one can teach ethics to an adult, a criticism that is sometimes made against the presence of ethics in a business school. The charge, actually, is rather silly; we teach and absorb community norms of behavior all our lives, even when we are elderly living in a nursing home. A virtue approach recognizes this dialectic between community and individual, and it recognizes that will be certain behaviors that are championed and others that are disapproved of. If we more mindfully think of what those are, then we can bring to bear and introduce the behaviors that we really value as opposed to the ones that are practiced but we really don't think that are important or that we don't think are particularly good.

This explanation provides a student-friendly way to apply virtue theory: one identifies the relevant virtues, defines them, and then applies them. And by doing so, you're fitting in to a larger sort of a naturalistic dimension of human nature that has this dialectic going back and forth between individual and community. As with the other frameworks in this part of the book, I have tried to do enough justice to the framework so that it strikes a balance of useful student applicability and consistency with the expositor's theory. This explanation of virtue theory, however, is a bit too simplistic and so what follows is a far more masterful and comprehensive understanding of virtue theory as applied to business from Ed Hartman.

Hartman's article is specifically about an Aristotelian approach to ethics, but his article—reprinted in full —also provides a comprehensive conclusion to his Part II of the textbook and also brings together with Part II many of the issues raised in Part I as well .

---

49 *Monkey See, Monkey Do: The Influence of Work Groups on the Antisocial Behavior of Employees*

Can We Teach Character? An Aristotelian Answer

Edwin M. Hartman, Rutgers University

Business ethics courses can help improve our students' ethics by teaching them about character, as opposed to just principles, the application of which creates difficulties. In particular, we can help our students consider their values and realize them in practice. According to Aristotle, ethics is about virtue, which is a matter of one's own well-being primarily, but as we are rational and social creatures, this state of well-being entails having what we would consider good moral values. Does good character really serve the agent's interests? Yes, if the agent has the right interests, and interests can be cultivated to some degree. One's values must be coherent, and one must be able to discern the salient moral features of the situations with which one deals. These are marks of good character, which the culture of one's organization may nurture or undermine. We arrive at principles supportive of good character by reflective equilibrium, a process like what Aristotle calls dialectic. Case studies assist our students in developing good character and learning to bring it to bear in complex situations, as some recent research has suggested is possible. One way to protect one's character, our students may learn, is to choose a workplace that does not undermine it.

What We Can Teach

What Ethics is About[50]

One might wonder whether business ethics courses are of any value. We sometimes hear this: If character is formed in childhood, how can a course improve a student's character? The question whether good character is teachable, and if so by whom, is as old as Socrates (see the *Meno*, Plato/Bluck, 1961). The issue for us here is whether character can be taught in business school. One is tempted to add, "of all places." I shall argue for an affirmative answer.

The assumption that teaching business ethics entails improving character is at odds with the widespread view that ethics is not about character primarily but about principles that an agent can apply to situations in business or elsewhere to find the right thing to do. But so-called virtue ethicists, following Aristotle's *Nicomachean Ethics* (hereafter *NE*), argue that the moral principles on which we can reach a consensus are usually vague, often in conflict, seldom unexceptionable, hence not reliably

---

50 Thanks go to Katherina Glac, a most valuable research assistant. Dennis Moberg, Amanda Anderson, and Dennis Patterson offered helpful advice on different essays of mine on related issues. Mikhail Valdman gave me good ideas on several topics. James Bailey, Mark Seabright, Patricia Werhane, Geoff Moore, and Robert Audi offered feedback useful to the readers of this essay as well as its author. Thanks also to the Prudential Business Ethics Center at Rutgers, which supported the re- search on this work.

action-guiding. MacIntyre (1981) is the best known of these, though Anscombe (1997) and Foot (1997) were pioneers. Williams (1981, 1985), Slote (1983, 1992, 2001), McDowell (1997), and Hursthouse (1999) have been influential as well. Solomon (1992), Koehn (1998), Walton (1997, 2001, 2004) and Moore (2002, 2003) emphasize virtues and character in business ethics.

Even most of these virtue ethicists do not entirely rule out principles, however. A generous person acts according to principles derived from the nature of generosity; so Hursthouse argues concerning what she calls v-principles. For ex- ample: a generous person happily lends money to needy friends even if they may not be able to pay it back. As generosity is a virtue, one ought to act on the principle (among others) that one should happily lend money to needy friends even if they may not be able to pay it back. An ungenerous person can know the applicable principles but be stingy anyway; so what good is mere knowledge of the principles?

Even if an ethical person is one who acts according to certain principles, it does not follow that the best way to teach Smith to be ethical is to give her principles to follow. By analogy, we can show that she is an excellent employee by stating her sales figures, but a training professional will focus on her knowledge and skills as a way of improving her sales figures. The analogue in ethics is improving Smith's character as a way of causing her to act according to appropriate moral principles (see Hartman, 1998: 547f.).

A virtuous person is a person of good character. We may define character as one's standard pattern of thought and action with respect to one's own and others' well-being and other major concerns and commitments; so, approximately, Kupperman (1991: 17). Character includes virtues and vices and entails certain values, dispositions, and emotions as well as actions. Aristotle suggests not only that one's character ought to be consistent over time and coherent at all times, but also that character is essential to personal identity. In a person of good character, virtues and values are reinforced by appropriate dispositions and emotions. And why is character important? What could be more important? Maintaining your character is tantamount to continuing your life (see NE IX 4: 1066a13–29, b7–14).

According to Aristotle, we have certain enduring desires that can serve as premises of so-called practical syllogisms—in effect, as good reasons to act. These desires have to do with our well-being and with our most important concerns and commitments. So a person of generous character acts generously, wants to do so, and thinks it good to do so. If you are generous, you are and want to be motivated by thoughts like this: "Jones needs help, so I want to help him," although one need not be quite so self-conscious. The next-best thing, short of a generous character, is mere acceptance of one's moral obligation: "Jones needs help, so I suppose I ought to help him, so all right, here I go." To be a person of truly generous character is to have and to want to have a settled disposition to help a friend in need, with emotions to match. It entails wanting to be consistently motivated by a friend's need. (A desire to have a desire is what Frankfurt, 1981, calls a second-order desire.) Some of our enduring desires and dispositions, especially those concerning the sort of person we want to be, we call values.

Parents tell children not to lie, as employers tell new employees not to be late for work. Beyond that, however, many parents raise children to be honest—that is, to be inclined not to lie, to feel some repugnance when lying even in circumstances that justify it. A v-principle that proscribes lying will be fairly unresponsive to utilitarian considerations. Employers, similarly, want employees to work well out of genuine loyalty. Virtues involve certain dispositions and attitudes. Consider gratitude: When you give me a generous gift, I ought not only to thank you but also to be actually grateful. Ethicists who rely just on principles have a hard time saying why one ever has an obligation to be grateful, or to care about one's employer's success. But those who believe that one has an obligation to be grateful must defend the view that one is morally responsible for one's feelings, which are not typically voluntary. Aristotle suggests that while you cannot make yourself feel grateful on a particular occasion you can over time become the sort of person who is grateful on appropriate occasions (see NE I 3: 1095a2-13). If he is right, it is not absurd to try to help make a student a certain sort of person.

Teaching Ethics

Even if we cannot mold our students' character, business ethics courses have some value if they help students who already want to be ethical businesspeople get better at it. Business ethics courses can encourage morality by raising critical questions about the standard economist's definitions of morally significant concepts (utility, maximization, and rationality, for example) and presuppositions about behavior (facile egoism, for example). We can also teach well-meaning students some techniques for deciding what the right thing is. We can teach them how to create organizations that encourage rather than punish doing the right thing. All this is worthwhile, but recent corporate scandals suggest the need for business ethics courses that will improve the character even of those future businesspeople that are not clearly predisposed to work and play well with others. My claim is that a business ethics course can improve students' character by helping them think critically about their values and realize them in practice. Those two activities are essential to character development.

Still, no ethics course will much affect a student who, after careful consideration, believes that the one who dies with the most toys wins in the zero- sum game that is business and that s/he wants to be such a person. Nor can we do a great deal for people incapable of developing any skill in dealing with complex situations, or those incapable of doing anything other than what nearly everyone else is doing. Not every student is in such bad moral condition, however, and we can reach the ones that are not.

Aristotle on Well-Being and Ethics

Character and Interests

In Aristotle's view, every substance, including the human being, has an essence and an associated end or purpose. We are essentially social and reasoning creatures; our natural end is therefore to live in communities and to think and act rationally. If you reach your actuality as a person, you are virtuous (or, on an alternative translation, excel- lent). You are in a state of *eudaimonia*, a particularly broad, deep, long-lasting form of well-being characteristic of good character and psychological health—health being a normative notion (see especially Prior, 2001). Aristotle would find asking what reason I have to be virtuous as odd as asking what reason I have to be healthy.

Aristotle holds that your character is a matter of what you enjoy doing (NE II 3: 1104b5ff.): good things if you are a good person, bad things if you are a bad one. Good character is therefore a matter not only of doing the right thing but also of having the right desires and emotions (NE X 8: 1178a9 –24, etc.). You should be grateful for kind- nesses, angry if and only if you are seriously wronged, sympathetic toward the wretched. If you do the right thing while gritting your teeth, you are not really a per- son of good character, and virtuous action is not in your best interests. The person of good char- acter has an enjoyable life, acting rationally and doing good things, unless misfortune intervenes.

Elster (1998), who acknowledges a debt to Frank (1988), argues that certain emo- tions supplement rationality. His view is similar to that of Aristotle, who believes that desires may be rational or irrational, whereas Hume and those that he has influenced believe that rationality is a characteristic only of the way in which we choose means when the desired ends are given. In any case, there is broad support for the view that appropriate emotion is required to support moral behavior. Psycho- paths typically know what is right, but their knowledge has no emotional support; so say Cleckley (1976) and Hare (1993). The brain-damaged Phineas Gage, described by Damasio (1994: 3–33), is an excellent and appalling example.[51]

Aristotle's view raises an obvious question for us, who think of ethics as encom- passing others' interests, not just one's own. What reason is there to believe that being a person of good character in Aristotle's sense is good not only for that person but for others too? To put it another way, why is a virtue like generosity, for example, good for the agent? Aristotle's answer is that, since human beings are social creatures, the good life, hence good character, involves living satisfactorily in a congenial community. So your virtues cause you to benefit your family and friends and people in your community. We can think of an organization as a community—arguably the emerging preeminent

---

51 Haidt (2001, esp. 824) discusses these works in an article on emotion and reason. Walton (1997) notes similar- ities between Aristotle's views and Damasio's.

kind of community. Virtue ethics in the Aristotelian tradition takes status in the community seriously, does not presuppose equality as a good, and deemphasizes rights. So it fits well with how most people view organizations and their employees. As Walton (2001, 2004) notes, in NE III Aristotle describes a good polis—not unmanageably large, united in purpose, with distributed but not necessarily democratic decision-making authority—much as we would a good organization.

Aristotle's form of egoism is useful in dealing with business students, who want to know how studying ethics can add value to a career in business. Kantians would argue that morality needs no support from self-interest, but Aristotle's claim that psychological health and good character coincide speaks to our students' self-regarding concerns. Aristotle argues that if you behave stingily, you will become a stingy person. But what if you want to be a stingy person? Won't you enjoy your stinginess? Why then should our students try to be people of good character? Getting to Aristotle's answer requires considering his moral psychology. In doing so I largely agree with Irwin (1988), but Nussbaum's (1990) and Sherman's (1994) accounts are useful as well.

Values and Strength of Character

We say that people of good character have good values. That formulation does not distinguish be- tween values in the moral sense—the usual meaning of the term values—and what one considers good for oneself. From the point of view of Aristotle's brand of egoism, however, it makes sense to say that the two are identical. This is not absurd. Many people who give values any thought would prefer to be driven by morally good ones (Jones & Ryan, 2001). We have enough self-respect that we like to think of ourselves as wise, mature, rational, and courageous. I perform a vindictive act and tell myself that it is just. I lose my nerve in confronting the boss and tell myself that I am being diplomatic. So we provide students with motivation as well as information when we teach them that, for example, courage requires not acting impulsively in a macho culture.

Wise and mature people have desires largely determined by their values. In fact some philosophers (e.g., Watson, 1982) regard this determination as definitive of autonomy. Ideally we would want to be so strong in character that we can choose to be a person with emotions, values, and desires that are consistent and good for us. That degree of autonomy is rare, like being able to decide to crave salads more than doughnuts. Aristotle claims that the right upbringing in a good community and long practice are necessary, though not sufficient, to make us value and choose the right things. So one way to choose to be a certain sort of person is to choose to be in a certain sort of community.

Most of us have limited strength of character. We cannot choose to enjoy courage and generosity at all times; we find them occasionally burdensome. And while one can habituate oneself to like doing the right sort of thing, there are limits: No normal person can learn to like root canal surgery. Good people will not suffer the discomfort of pretending to be, say, congenial, but virtues sometimes impose costs. Courage would not be courage if the courageous person did not sometimes pay a price for it. Honesty entails opportunity costs. But despite whether doing the honest thing always pays, if you are a virtuous person you think yourself better off on the whole for being the sort of person who is inclined to do the honest thing.

What Is Good About Character: Choosing One's Interests

But why, a business student might ask, is it in my interest to be a person of good character rather than a stingy person? How do I know I'll enjoy it more? On the Aristotelian view, those are wrong- headed questions. Here is a better one: Given that you want to serve your own interests, what do you want your interests to be? Do you want to be the sort of person who enjoys only overwhelming financial success? Or the sort of person who enjoys a life in which work plays an important but not dominant role and in which that work offers challenge, variety, growth, association with interesting people, and compensation that lets you live comfortably? The question is not which one our students prefer. It is a higher-order question about which one they would choose to prefer if they could choose. That question cannot be readily answered by reference to self-interest, since it is hard to see what would count as a straightforwardly self-interested answer to the question, "What do you want your interests to be?" (see Hartman, 1996: 80–83 and 134f. and Elster, 1985: 109–140 on what the latter calls adaptive preference formation).

There is a wise answer to that question if, as is probable, most MBA students who give the second answer are happier in the end than those who give the first. Huge wealth is hard to come by, and many people who achieve it enjoy it less than they expected to. Many who have retired from a successful career say that if they had it to do over again they would spend more time with their families. Why didn't they? Perhaps they were committed to a conception of the good life based on peer pressure rather than reflection.

Students need to understand that things can go wrong because they can have mistaken beliefs about the benefits of what they want. Most people are not very good at "affective forecasting," as it is called. Gilbert, Pinel, Wilson, Blumberg, and Wheatley (1998), Loewenstein and Adler (2000), and others offer evidence that we cannot accurately estimate how happy or unhappy some future event, or our future success, will make us. Hence it is not easy to know what sort of life you can enjoy. We can begin to teach our students the necessary self-knowledge and self-control by encouraging them to reflect on their assumptions about what will make them happy.

What should their reflection tell them about choosing a conception of the good life if it cannot be done just on the basis of self-interest? The Aristotelian view is that a wise person will choose to be rational and social because that is the nature of the human being. Indeed, we would probably reject the life of an animal or a happy idiot as being unworthy of a human being, and would probably not choose a life so barren that the smallest gains make us feel wealthy and the most humdrum activities excite us (see Sen, 1987: 45f). Aristotle sees no necessary connection between desire fulfillment and happiness, and he would invite us to infer that we are better off consulting human nature, rather than our own unreliable expectations and desires, on the question of what will make us happy. In any case, a life empty of what is characteristically human falls short of Aristotle's conception of happiness—and ours too, since few of us envy happy idiots.

Even if we can never agree on an appropriate conception of the good life, our consideration of the issue shows how facile is the usual talk about one's interests and one's pursuit of them, and helps undermine students' unreflective assumptions about them. Perhaps under the influence of economists, we tend to believe that interests are fixed and easily identified. We also tend to believe that ethics is opposed to self-interest—that if Jones is an ethical person, he characteristically puts others' interests ahead of his own. (And if Smith does the same, how will she and Jones deal with each other?) These tendencies make it easy for our students to assume that success is a matter of satisfying one's greed and that it has little to do with ethics.

Coherence and Integrity as Reasons for Good Character

Whatever life you choose, Aristotle believes, it should have a certain wholeness, as he suggests in saying that the continuation of character is the continuation of one's life. Just as a substance is not a mere pile of stuff but has a certain form and purpose, as Aristotle argues in the Metaphysics, so a life is more than just a succession of experiences. Part of his message is that happiness requires desires that are consistent with one another and with one's values, and actions that are consistent with one's desires (so he says at NE IX 4: 1066b7–11). In this he is echoed by psychologists like Festinger (1957), who argues that people desire coherence in their views. Chaiken, Giner-Sorolla, and Chen (1996: 557) argue, similarly, that one wants all of one's attitudes and beliefs to be "congruent with existing self-definitional attitudes and beliefs."

If you are in that state of coherence, we would say, you have integrity. If not, you will sometimes desire, and may get, what you do not value. Valuing courage, you wish that you looked forward to making the crucial presentation or did not dread giving the boss negative feedback, but you are less courageous than you would like to be. You are better off as well as more virtuous if your values and desires are consistent throughout. Most of us, alas, are not like that. Valuing good health and attractiveness, we wish the doughnut were not so tempting. Valuing success, we envy those who look forward to the required challenges. Or worse, as Luban (2003, esp. 281–283) has argued, we may re- arrange our desires and even restate our values to rationalize our actions. That is the kind of coherence that Luban finds in Festinger. What is required, and difficult, is choosing values rationally and with some detachment from what is immediately attractive and then acting on them—or at least, when we have not acted on them, accepting that we have not.

Integrity in this sense is probably not sufficient for good character or for happiness, but it goes some distance in the right direction. It is not possible to be both stupid and wise, or both irrationally risk-averse and courageous. On causal rather than logical grounds, there are difficulties in prizing both idleness and personal achievement, or heavy drinking and fitness, or feeling free to be offensive and having many friends. But can't you do well if you hide your hostility or rapacity? Aristotle says no. If you do it for strategic reasons, as when people are watching, you will be doing something that you don't enjoy (NE IX 4: 1066b7–14). In any case, like it or not, you are a communal being, and your happiness depends in part on your being a productive and congenial member of the community. So you have good reason to be virtuous, and not merely to act sometimes as though you were.

Most of us would recognize a greater variety of possibly satisfying lives than does Aristotle. In fact, most of us think that the room for choice among possible lives is itself a good thing. At the same time we respect the limits on that variety that are implied by the requirements of our nature. As our students plan their lives, we should encourage them to consider their strengths and limitations, their opportunities, and what they can and cannot learn to enjoy. Some of them really will turn out to enjoy a life of intense competition and high risk, but we should not let them thoughtlessly assume ahead of time either that whatever they happen to want is possible or that they will enjoy it if they get it or that it would be a good thing if they did.

Community and Culture

Organizations Affecting Character

We are essentially social creatures, and our character is malleable and vulnerable to some degree, for organizations exert a powerful socializing and sometimes corrupting influence. Sennett (1998) argues that this influence is usually inhospitable to good character, but it need not always be. We can teach our students how corporate culture, as well as structures and systems, can be deployed to encourage and accommodate good character. Aristotle argues in NE I 2 that politics is the culmination of ethics insofar as it creates a state that teaches and supports good characters (see Walton, 2001, 2004, and Moore, 2003, against Koehn, 1998, on this point). A community goes a long way toward determining its citizens' values—what they count as success, for example—for better or worse. By providing role models and in other ways, the culture of a community may make a citizen want to be a certain kind of person, motivated by certain considerations and not others. We can say the same of corporate communities, and perhaps infer that management rather than politics is today the culmination of ethics.

There is voluminous evidence that organizations support or oppose ethical behavior. Fritzsche (1991) argues that organizational forces may drive decisions more than personal values do and (2000) that organizational climate can raise or lower the probability of ethical decisions. Jones and Hiltebeitel (1995) find evidence of the effects of organizational expectations on ethical choices. Sims and Keon (1999) argue that the organizational characteristics that most influence employees are situationally determined, so the organization can foster both ethical and unethical decision making. Trevino, Butterfield, and McCabe (2001) offer a detailed and complex account of the effects of ethical climate. I have argued (1994, 1996) that corporate culture can affect an employee's second-order as well as first-order desires: People in the grip of a powerful culture adopt the local values and definition of success and want to be motivated by what motivates their colleagues.

So great is the influence of the organizational setting on employee behavior that Harman (2003) and Doris (2002) argue that character does not matter. They base their conclusion in part on the arguments of social psychologists such as Nisbet and Ross (1991) and invoke the familiar works of Mil-gram (1974) and Haney, Zimbardo, and Banks (1973). But as Solomon (2003) points out, even in the Milgram experiment there were a number of people who walked away. Trevino (1986) seems judicious in arguing that both organizational and personal attributes affect behavior. Many of the arguments of those who dismiss character as an independent variable would work equally well against the concept of rationality, which Aristotle takes to be a great part of good character (see Rabin, 1998, and especially Haidt, 2001: 827f.). That people act irrationally in ways not emphasized by most economists is a familiar truth with a huge literature attached (Kahneman & Tversky, 2000, are preeminent on this issue) but not one that leads us to discount it in all explanations.

We teach our students about organizational culture because we believe that as employees they will be able to respond to it by recognizing it and taking its possible effects into account. Few people who know of the Milgram experiment would be so obedient if they were subjects in a rerun of it. Former students who have learned about the experiment in a business ethics course testify that they do sometimes think of it when they are in similar situations, and act accordingly. Beaman, Barnes, Klentz, and McQuirk (1978) show that people can be inoculated against crowd-induced culpable indifference by being taught to recognize the crowd's influence and to act appropriately despite it (see Slater, 2004: 109f.).

One might object that the available evidence shows only that one's behavior and immediate desires are affected by the ambient culture; one's character is a different matter, a harder thing to change and hard to measure as well. But what Aristotle means by character encompasses not only values but also the readiness to act on them and the ability to see how to do so in a particular situation, however complex or difficult it may be. Some people sincerely espouse a certain value—say, the importance of courage—but do not act on it because they do not recognize that speaking one's mind in this situation is what courage requires. They are sincere, but they are not courageous. An organization can do that to you. On the basis of a number of studies of the impact of corporate culture, Chen, Sawyers, and Williams (1997) conclude that ethical behavior depends on the ability to recognize ethical issues and that this ability appears to be a function of corporate culture more than of individual employees' attributes.

This is an important finding about culture and character. According to Aristotle, understanding morally complex situations under salient descriptions and having the appropriate emotional reactions to them are central to character.

> *Ethical behavior depends on the employee's ability to recognize ethical issues and this ability appears to be a function of corporate culture more than of individual employees' attributes.*

Character and Its Development

Ethical Knowledge and How It Fails

Aristotle says that having a virtue entails knowing (though not necessarily being able to state) a principle of the form "It is a good thing for a person to act in a certain way." For example, "It is a good thing for a person to eat dry food." This is not to say that Aristotle believes that dry food is appropriate for all human beings in all circumstances, or that in general his first premises are foundational or unexceptionable principles of either nutrition or morality. Specifications of principles of that sort typically function as first premises of practical syllogisms. So you may start your deliberation with this thought: "Eating dry food is good (i.e., nourishing) for a human being." Since Aristotle assimilates the prudent and the ethical, he would also accept as a first premise "Respecting other people's property is good (i.e., just) for a human being." But Aristotle wants to explain a phenomenon that we may regard as a mystery: We can claim with apparent sincerity to value something—to know that it is good—but intentionally act against our value.

Imagine a person well informed about nutrition having breakfast. The choices are granola and a doughnut. The breakfaster knows that granola is better for human beings than are doughnuts, but eats the doughnut because it is delicious. Similarly, the person who knows that it is good to respect others' property may dump some garbage in the neighbor's field even though s/he knows that that is no way to achieve long-term psychic satisfaction, just as eating doughnuts is no way to achieve long-term health. In both cases the agent acts against his or her values.

What has gone wrong? According to Aristotle, one can intentionally do what one does not value because there is something to be said for, as well as against, eating doughnuts and running from the enemy. One common form of weakness of the will is a matter of acting on the wrong one of conflicting principles. Indeed, in ethics, multiple considerations push us in conflicting directions, and there is no algorithm for choosing the right principle every time. That is a problem about ethics based on principles. If you are a loyal employee of a generally good company in which people whom you respect decide to do something that you con-sider sleazy, how do you apply appropriate moral principles as you decide what you should do about it? That one should be loyal to one's generally good employer and that one should be courageous in confronting immoral behavior are two good moral principles, good v-principles in Hursthouse's sense. According to Aristotle, in many such cases the best we can do is to rely on the intuitions of an experienced person with a good moral track record—that is, a person of practical wisdom (phronesis; the word is sometimes translated as prudence). If s/he says, "I'm just not comfortable with that," Aristotle takes the discomfort seriously, for that emotion has cognitive weight.

Perceiving Correctly

One can act on a wrong principle as a result of choosing an action under a description that, al- though accurate as far as it goes, is inappropriate, often because it focuses on the short term and the narrow gauge. If I had practical wisdom in Aristotle's sense, I would not crave the doughnut so much, because I would not focus so much on its positive properties; hence, I would not act on the principle, "If something will taste delicious, one should eat it." In the same way, Arthur Andersen's auditors might have described their misdeeds in the Enron case as "good client service" or "aggressive accounting" or even "billing a lot of hours." Those characterizations were accurate, but less salient than "misrepresenting the financial position of the firm." It is common enough: Darley (1996) describes the phenomenon of ethical rationalization, which Jones and Ryan (2001) attribute to a desire to be, and be considered, moral. Auditors with higher professional standards would act on the ethically salient description of the action. Most auditors could not have offered a coherent argument from their own values that the short-term gain made by giving good client service justified misrepresenting the financial position of the firm. So why did the Arthur Andersen auditors do it? Because they were ignoring the salient descriptions and focusing on the ethically inessential ones, as one might wolf down a delicious, satisfying doughnut without giving adequate attention to one's need to lose weight.

It is Aristotle's view that the person of good character perceives a situation rightly— that is, takes proper account of the salient features of a situation. As you perceive that a particular figure is a triangle, so you perceive that a particular act is a betrayal, though the latter is harder to do with assurance. According to Aristotle, perception involves imagination (the standard translation of the Greek *phantasia)*: The faculty of imagination is operating when you understand what a perceived object is, or when you grasp the moral quality of an act; in either case you grasp the essence of the item. You are morally responsible for understanding the act correctly. If you get it wrong—that is, fail to apprehend the morally salient features of the situation—then you have a character flaw (NE III 5: 1114a32–b3). A person of good character will perceive that a certain act is courageous rather than foolhardy, generous rather than vainglorious, right rather than wrong, and will act accordingly. An irascible or phlegmatic person will take offense, or not, inappropriately. Moral imagination is the faculty that correctly "frames" morally significant states and events. Johnson (1993) has an influential book on the subject. Werhane (1999), Moberg and Seabright (2000), and Hartman (2001) assess its importance for business ethics. Vidaver-Cohen (1997) considers how organizations can encourage moral imagination. Chen, Sawyers, and Williams (1997), noted earlier, show how they can do the opposite.

One advantage that persons of good character have in assessing a complex situation is that they have certain fairly inflexible v-principles to apply. For example, a consultant may be honest and therefore have a personal rule against ever lying to a client. When a situation arises in which failing to lie would damage the consultant's relationship with the client and lead to avoidable bad consequences for the client, the consultant must take "lying to the client" to be a salient description of any action of which it is true. "Preserving the relationship" or "preventing consequences A, B, and C" cannot be salient for such a person. This inflexibility may not give the best result in every case, but it is best in the long run for the agent's character, and it is a barrier to rationalization (see Luban, 2003: 307f.).

Moral imagination involves intelligence and rationality, although it is not a matter of finding an algorithm for deciding among moral considerations. That is all right with Aristotle, who, though he distinguishes intellectual virtues from moral ones, understands how closely they are related. Practical wisdom shows up in both moral and prudential guises. He does not give points merely for meaning well. The Aristotelian position gets sup- port from Haidt (2001), who relies on the findings of Blasi (1980) and Kohlberg (1969) to argue that intelligence is a causal factor in good moral reasoning and behavior.

Ethical Vocabulary and Perception

Vocabulary is one of the prime vehicles of culture, as Schein (1985) and others have argued. In an organization in which people are called decisive and risk accepting with approval, the culture may create peer pressure that encourages shortsighted disregard of possible costs. One who acts on impulse will be called strong. One who prefers moderation or consideration of alternatives will be known as a wimp. A European at Salomon Brothers who goes home at the end of the afternoon rather than stay and be seen working late is a Eurofaggot (Lewis, 1989: 71).

A person of good character in Aristotle's sense knows genuine strength and cowardice when s/he sees it. The ethical manager cannot readily change an employee's character, but s/he can help that person to consider the difference between (say) courage and the readiness to succumb to macho peer pressure. A business ethics course can begin that educational process. One of its most important functions is to help students become more fluent in the language of right and wrong, of virtues and vices, without which their moral imagination will be impoverished, and there is little chance that they will give salient descriptions of morally significant situations.

The vocabulary of character is not a foreign language to businesspeople, despite what they have been taught in economics courses about utility and rationality and other such concepts. Most businesspeople do regard honor, courage, and respect for fellow workers and competitors as virtues. Most would say that it is the legitimate purpose of financial statements to give a clear picture of the financial condition of a firm. But some people in Enron who might have objected on ethical grounds if a secretary had taken some office paper home did not see anything wrong with creating special purpose entities whose special purpose was to hide losses.

A good business ethics course can give students practice in seeing and describing states and events in ethical terms, as a first step toward understanding their morally salient features. Questions like "Would I want my act to be publicly known?" invite students to consider how others might describe the action. But such questions, like the principles that they presuppose, must be accompanied by a mature sense of right and wrong and of what is salient in a particular case. That sense needs to be exercised and developed, given a language, and sharpened by critical analysis. Even then it may be overridden by social pressure or inattention or anything that causes people to perceive and describe their actions inadequately, particularly if the corporate vocabulary and emotional reaction become their own. The Milgram experiment shows how readily people deal with conflicts between their values and some immediate pressure. So if their moral language is impoverished or insufficiently exercised, they may latch on to some other, nonsalient description of the situation: "I am helping Dr. Milgram, who knows what he's doing," rather than "I am torturing innocent people." They may ignore their emotional re- action, and in due course it will go away.

Virtues and Principles: Dialectic and Reflective Equilibrium

This may leave us still wondering how, exactly, a virtuous person is supposed to act. Telling someone to be honest sounds like good advice, but in the absence of quite specific principles there may be a question about what an honest person should do in this or that difficult case, such as whistle-blowing.

To begin with, as I have stated, Aristotle does not reject principles, which in his case are typically essential descriptions of virtues. So, for example, to act courageously entails acting because one understands that a certain act needs to be done in spite of the risks involved, although the principle identifying this act as courageous may not come explicitly to mind at the moment of action. Our account thus far suggests that Aristotle believes that one ought to act on principles consistently, that the principles themselves should remain in force over time, and that a good person's principles form a coherent body. He does not, however, believe that their application is always straightforward. He takes them seriously as a carpenter or a navigator (NE III 3: 1112a5–7) or a physician or a comedian (NE IV 8: 1028a23–34) must take seriously the principles of carpentry or navigation or medicine or comedy, but not as the geometer takes seriously the principles of geometry (NE I 7: 1098a29 –34). The difference is important: We know just how to apply the principles of geometry to a geometry problem, even a problem in actual space and time. But although ethics is not geometry, Aristotle believes that principles have something to do with sound moral judgments. Many present-day virtue ethicists agree. Nussbaum (1990), Hurst-house (1999), Foot (1997), and others argue that we can apply principles but must be wise about it. McDowell (1997) dismisses principles, but his is a minority view.

Aristotle holds that one arrives at acceptable principles—necessary but not sufficient conditions of acting out of good character—by the process of dialectic. This process usually starts with common opinions, with the intention of finding as moral premises principles that are consistent with those opinions and explain them, or improve on them insofar as they can be proved wrong (see NE VII 1: 1145b4–8, for example).

One wants to reach a state in which one's beginnings (*archai*) form a coherent whole. When Aristotle speaks of beginnings, he sometimes has in mind what we would consider moral principles, while at other times he is thinking of particular moral judgments. The ambiguity is confusing, but he explicitly claims that a starting point of an argument that leads to a principle is called a be-ginning while the principle itself is a beginning in a different sense: It is the starting point of the justification of a particular judgment (see NE I 4: 1095b6 and I 7: 1098b2, for example). Here we may think of Rawls's (1971: 48-1) reflective equilibrium: One compares one's principles and one's considered judgments about particular cases and ad-justs both in an effort to make them consistent. Neither the principles nor the judgement are prior; each is subject to adjustment by reference to the other. If our principles are nothing more than the result of rationalizing the intuitions on which we act, as Luban (2003) is led by Festinger (1957) and others to think may often be the case, then our intuitions are prior in an impermissible way, and likely not very good. In the case of wide reflective equilibrium, so called by Daniels (1979), we bring in pertinent science, settled beliefs about human nature, and other facts as background.[52] Wide equilibrium seems to represent Aristotle's views pretty well. At our moral best we have a set of back-ground beliefs, intuitions, and principles that co-here, with emotions to match.

Hursthouse (1999) and Irwin (1988) take an approach similar to reflective equilibrium as a way of thinking about virtues. We might say, in the spirit of Aristotle, that a person is virtuous when s/he has intuitions and perceptions and emotions and

---

52 See Calkins (2004: 34f.) for an application to wide equilibrium to virtue ethics.

principles that cohere, and acts in a way that expresses them. Rawls has in mind logical rather than psychological coherence, whereas Aristotle seems to be thinking of both, although he does not sharply distinguish them. When Aristotle says that understanding should be part of our perception, he implies that the intuitions of a moral person will incorporate the right principles into a particular judgment. Arras (1991) makes a similar point in discussing the advantages of casuistry in medical ethics. Among business ethicists Nielsen (2001) sounds similar to Aristotle here, as does Van Hooft (2001).

We do not make sound moral judgments by be-ginning with a certain notion of, say, fairness and then applying it to business or politics or any other area of life. The notion of fairness has little substantive content if separated from all these areas. Suppose we say that it is unfair to treat talented people differently from the way we treat untalented ones. So those whose talent lets them con-tribute more to the economy do not deserve more votes. But many of us do think that employees should be paid according to what they contribute to the bottom line—a principle that is utilitarian in that it creates an incentive to do what they can to contribute. Whether they deserve better medical care is not immediately obvious. In fact, philosophers have always struggled with the notion of desert. If we ever do reach a consensus, it will be hard-won from experience.

Reflective equilibrium should have some appeal for both principle and virtue ethicists. While the former emphasize principles, the latter have an interest in judgments—in Aristotle's case, those of wise and experienced people—about particular situations. Aristotle holds that virtuous people must trust their intuitions where principles compete or are hard to apply. People of inferior character often do the wrong thing not because they have bad principles, though many do, but because their intuitions do not lead them to apprehend the situation under the right principle. They may act on a principle that social pressure forces on them, or one that rationalizes their previous behavior.

Experience and Its Wisdom: Learning and Living

Aristotle does not claim that dialectic is either necessary or sufficient for good character. The usual process of moral growth is a gradual one, part of a life lived in a good community. Experience of that sort is the best teacher. There were some wise old heads at Arthur Andersen who did grasp the salient descriptions of the sleazy actions of their auditors and others at Enron (see Chicago Tribune, 2002) and no doubt had emotional reactions that supported their view. Unfortunately in the Enron case the winning intuitions were those of people of bad character, who acted on the principles that were not morally salient.

If Aristotle is right, business ethicists should have great respect for the opinions of intelligent people of good character who are experienced in business. The moral philosophers' contribution will be to compare these intuitions to one another and to moral principles with a view to sharpening both. We want our students to have values that are coherent and achievable without catastrophic cost. We want them to have principles and intuitions that form a fairly coherent set, and to learn how to apply the principles appropriately with the help of the right emotional reactions. We also want them to have desires that are consistent with their values insofar as possible. An accountant of good character will value both good client service and transparency for the benefit of the public, but will normally give the second consideration priority when they conflict.

How does one come to apprehend courage? One is told as a child that this or that act is courageous, or not courageous but cowardly. Over a period of time one comes to have a pretty good sense of what courage looks like, and then through dialectic—that is, roughly, philosophical conversation about the concept—one acquires a real understanding of courage and its contraries, cowardice and foolhardiness, and reliably identifies instances of them. In the best case, the moral intuitions are consistent with the principles—for example, definitive statements about courage and cowardice—although one's understanding of courage will never lead one to a principle that gives the precise necessary and sufficient conditions of courage, since that kind of precision cannot be expected in ethics (NE I 3: 1094b23–27). So Aristotle says (NE VI 11: 1143a35–b5) that the correct perception (*aisthesis*) of a particular act as being the sort of act that it is—say, perceiving that a certain act is cowardly, hence not to be done—involves the faculty of understanding (nous). In the ethical case it also involves emotion, which entails cognition: The emotions of a person of good character are an indicator of the moral quality of an actual or possible act. So, for example, an unjust injury to a courageous person provokes his or her indignation, which leads to a response that is appropriate given the risks involved.

From this we might infer, as Aristotle does, that a long life in a good community is a necessary condition of becoming a person of good character. So what does a course in business ethics do to help in developing the kind of character that generates morally salient descriptions of complex situations with emotions and motivations to match? It plays the part that dialectic plays in Aristotle's under-standing of moral education. First, we offer students case studies that sharpen their moral perception much as experience does, and we offer analysis of them based on wide reflective equilibrium, and we thereby enhance moral maturation. Second, we encourage students to engage in critical analysis of their values with an eye to what is coherent and sustainable. As a result of this analysis, our students will be better equipped to choose courses of action, and even a career path, that will support rather than undermine or alter their values.

Ethics and Strategy: The Value of Case Studies

We already have at hand a way of teaching business ethics so that our students begin to learn to see business issues as moral issues and grasp their salient features.

The case study method suits business ethics as it suits strategy, both of which require practical wisdom in Aristotle's sense. In a typical strategy course the students read a text and then consider case studies that challenge them to apply the principles in the text to a real situation. This is the beginning of the process of developing their intuitions about strategy. In real-life corporate strategy, as I learned as a management consultant, there is much to be said for trusting the intuitions of an intelligent and experienced person with a good track record. When a manager makes decisions about the strategies to be undertaken by certain strategic business units, there will be some easy cases. Where the market is teeming with opportunity and the SBU is stronger than any of its competitors in all important respects, the strategy of reinvesting for growth is obvious. But there are non-obvious cases, as when a group of weak SBUs can together achieve economies of scale or use slack resources. Even if there were an algorithm permitting the strategist to infer the correct strategy from the available numbers, it is not clear that the value of finding the algorithm would justify its cost. At a certain point the experienced and wise manager must satisfice and make an intuitive decision.[53] Some managers are consistently better than others at knowing which of the many accurate descriptions of a strategic situation is the salient one, although they often cannot say in any detail how they do it. Their track record is evidence of their practical wisdom.

When one of our former students goes on to join an organization that is an ongoing Milgram experiment, we hope that there will be a spark of recognition.

By using case studies we give students experience that supports the development of their moral imagination. We teach them the warning signs of rationalization and ethical anesthesia. We show them cases in which machismo and courage are opposites. Complex case studies exercise their moral judgment about particulars, as when justice and economic efficiency conflict. In looking at a case and considering what its salient features are, we are helping students develop moral imagination and thus practical wisdom and thus good character.

Authors of textbooks do not usually alter the principles that they espouse to accommodate the complexities of business. A business with high entry barriers is not always more profitable than one in which growth quickly attracts new competitors, but we do not expect Porter (1980) to try to list all of the possible exceptions to his general principles. Most virtue ethicists acknowledge that there are situations in which (say) lying would be a useful move for all concerned, but most of them would say that one should not lie even then, be-cause it is bad to be a liar. An analogue in strategy would be the advice that an organization should usually stick to doing what it does

---

53 Simon (1954) invented the concept of *satisficing*; Winter (1971) argued that we must satisfice in deciding when to satisfice.

best even when the organization does business in a suboptimal way but change would be disorienting.

Our objective is to help our students get better at answering the question, "What shall I do?" The moral imagination required to put one's values into practice is a necessary but not sufficient condition of an adequate answer to the question. The students need a critical understanding of their actual and possible values.

An Aristotelian would take the view that in business, as anywhere else, a life of integrity is a fulfilling life on which one will be able to look back with satisfaction. In spite of the advantages of good character, however, choosing one's character is no easy task under any circumstances. One cannot readily choose which desires to have: Many people are tempted by doughnuts; some are tempted by dishonesty. We can, however, ask students to reflect on what is most important to them and how to protect it. Reading Michael Lewis's Liar's Poker (1989), for example, provides an opportunity for this. Does Dash Riprock lead a good life? Is the Human Piranha's approval a good thing? Is selling equities in Dallas inappropriate for anyone with any self-respect? Why? How does Salomon Brothers of that era differ from the Milgram experiment? Knowing about Salomon or Milgram may enable one later to stop and reflect on one's situation, and to do a little moral reasoning rather than rationalization.

There is some encouraging evidence about the possibility of doing that. Beaman et al. (1978) show that people who are taught certain effects of social pressure will act better thereafter. Nickerson (1994) argues that little of the moral reasoning that is taught in the classroom is transferred, but Lieberman (2000) claims that continued discussion in an appropriate environment—what Aristotle would call dialectic in a good polis—can make a positive difference. At least we can disabuse the students of the notion that ethics is by its nature opposed to their interests, show how certain virtues are compatible with a good life, and argue that integrity is a necessary condition of it. If, as I suggested ear-lier, students tend to have some good values already, that should not be impossible

Fairly Hopeful Conclusion: Choosing a Job and Choosing a Character

Even for those who remember Milgram, corporate culture may be very powerful. By holding out a certain notion of success, a bad culture can thwart people's ability to reflect on their values and to identify salient characteristics, as it can thwart the strategist's attempt to maintain a long-term perspective and see events from that perspective. But if a strong organizational culture can affect one's character in that way, then the choice of an employer is a most important one. Having been in a certain organization for a while, I may like being the sort of person who enjoys acting ruthlessly, or perhaps the sort of person who takes satisfaction in maintaining a professional attitude. If Aristotle is right, by acting ruthlessly or professionally I can become that kind of person. For some of our students, choosing an employer (or a career; that is a different essay) will in effect be choosing which desires to cultivate, hence choosing a character. The least that we can do is help students under-stand the importance of that choice and not make it thoughtlessly. If Harman and Doris are right, advocating that form of adaptive preference formation may also be the most that we can do. Aristotle would not accept that choosing the right polis is a sufficient condition of developing a good character, but he does believe that it is a necessary condition.

We can intervene here. We can help students examine what their values really are at the moment of choice of a job. We can raise questions about why someone would want to pursue a certain sort of career or join a certain sort of firm, and about whether getting a certain job will be as satisfying as one has anticipated. In so doing, we may help expose the reasons given as incoherent or based on self-ignorance or peer pressure.

Think of Smith, who is considering entry-level positions as she completes her MBA. She has two options: a job in finance at a large manufacturing firm known for good ethics, or a job in an investment banking house known for its competitive environment and its contempt for its customers. Call them Johnson and Johnson and Salomon Brothers. Maybe she is already the sort of person who will be happy in one of those environments but not the other. Maybe, on the other hand, Smith is wrong in thinking that she could not be happy if she were not making a lot of money as the biggest swinging dick in the house. Maybe she has bought into the pecking order in her second-year MBA cohort with-out considering what sort of life in business would satisfy her. She might indeed go with the investment house and come to feel contempt for those who settle for equities in Dallas, or she might take a job in a high-ethics company and come to enjoy it and be quite happy that she did not go with the invest-ment house. But if Lewis is right about life at Salomon Brothers and the researchers on affective

forecasting are right in general, she might achieve success at Salomon Brothers but never find it quite satisfying. Like Dash Riprock, she might always be looking for the next fix. But by the time she learns this about herself, she may not be the sort of person who could enjoy life at Johnson and Johnson, either.

We cannot choose her job for her, but we can help her think about whether a prospective career and even a prospective life can be compatible with values that will sustain her happiness. After she has made the choice, we hope that she maintains the values appropriate to good character and the moral imagination to put them into practice.

REFERENCES

Anscombe, G. E. M. 1997. *Modern Moral Philosophy.* In R. Crisp & M. Slote (Eds.), *Virtue Ethics:* 26–44. New York: Oxford University Press.

Aristotle. 1894. *Ethica Nicomachea.* I. Bywater (Ed.). Oxford: Clarendon Press.

Aristotle. 1985. *Nicomachean Ethics.* T. H. Irwin (Trans.) Indianapolis, In: Hackett Publishing Company.

Arras, J. D. 1991. *Getting Down To Cases: The Revival of Casuistry In Bioethics.* The Journal of Medicine and Philosophy, 16: 29–51.

Beaman, A. L., Barnes, P. J., Klentz, B., & Mcquirk, B. 1978. *Increasing Helping Rates Through Information Dissemination: Teaching Pays.* The Personality and Social Psychology Bulletin, 4: 406–411.

Blasi, A. 1980. *Bridging Moral Cognition and Moral Action: A Critical Review of the Literature.* Psychological Bulletin, 88: 1–45.

Calkins, M. 2004. *Casuistry, Virtue, and Business Ethics.* Unpublished.

Chaiken, S., Giner-Sorolla, R., & Chen, S. 1996. *Beyond Accuracy: Defense and Impression Motives In Heuristic and Systematic Information Processing.* In P. M. Gollwitzer, & J. A. Bargh (Eds.), *The Psychology of Action: Linking Cognition and Motivation To Behavior:* 553–578. New York: Guilford.

Chen, A. Y. S., Sawyers, R. B., & Williams, P. F. 1997. *Reinforcing Ethical Decision Making Through Corporate Culture. Journal of Business Ethics* 16: 855–865.

Chicago Tribune. 2002. Tribune Special Report: *A Final Accounting.* September 1–4.

Cleckley, H. M. 1976. *The Mask of Sanity* (5th Ed.). St. Louis: Mo:

C. V. Mosby.

Damasio, A. 1994. *Descartes' Error: Emotion, Reason, and the Human Brain.* New York: Putnam.

Daniels, N. 1979. *Wide Reflective Equilibrium and theory Acceptance In Ethics.* Journal of Philosophy, 76: 256–282.

Darley, J. M. 1996. *How Organizations Socialize Individuals Into Evildoing.* In D. M. Messick, & A. E. Tenbrunsel (Eds.), Codes of Conduct: Behavioral Research Into Business Ethics: 13–43. New York: Russell Sage Foundation.

Doris, J. 2002. *Lack of Character: Personality and Moral Behavior.* New York: Cambridge University Press.

Elster, J. 1985. *Sour Grapes: Studies In the Subversion of Rationality.* New York: Cambridge University Press.

Elster, J. 1998. *Emotions and Economic Theory.* Journal of Economic Literature, 36: 47–74.

Festinger, L. 1957. *A Theory of Cognitive Dissonance.* Stanford, Ca: Stanford University Press.

Foot, P. 1997. *Virtues and Vices.* In R. Crisp & M. Slote (Eds.), *Virtue Ethics:* 163–177. New York: Oxford University Press.

Frank, R. H. 1988. *Passions Within Reason: The Strategic Role of the Emotions.* New York: W. W. Norton & Company.

Frankfurt, H. G. 1981. *Freedom of the Will and the Concept of A Person.* In G. Watson (Ed.), Free Will: 81–95. New York: Ox- Ford University Press.

Fritzsche, D. J. 1991. *A Model of Decision-Making Incorporating Ethical Values.* Journal of Business Ethics, 10: 841–852.

Fritzsche, D. J. 2000. *Ethical Climates and the Ethical Dimension of Decision Making.* Journal of Business Ethics, 24: 125–140.

Gilbert, D. T., Pinel, E. C., Wilson, T. D., Blumberg, S. J., & Wheatley, T. P. 1998. *Immune Neglect: A Source of Durability Bias In Affective Forecasting.* Journal of Personality and Social Psychology, 25: 617–638.

Haidt, J. 2001. *The Emotional Dog and Its Rational Tail: A Social Intuitionist Approach To Moral Judgment.* Psychological Review, 108: 814–834.

Haney, C., Zimbardo, P., & Banks, W. C. 1973. *Interpersonal Dynamics In A Simulated Prison.* International Journal of Criminology and Penology, 1: 69–97.

Hare, R. D. 1993. *Without Conscience: The Disturbing World of the Psychopaths Among Us.* New York: Simon and Schuster.

Harman, G. 2003. *No Character Or Personality.* Business Ethics Quarterly, 13: 87–94.

Hartman, E. M. 1994. *The Commons and the Moral Organization.* Business Ethics Quarterly, 4: 253–269.

Hartman, E. M. 1996. *Organizational Ethics and the Good Life.* New York: Oxford University Press.

Hartman, E. M. 1998. *The Role of Character In Business Ethics.* Business Ethics Quarterly, 8: 547–559.

Hartman, E. M. 2001. *An Aristotelian Approach To Moral Imagination.* Professional Ethics, 8: 58–77.

Hursthouse, R. 1999. *On Virtue Ethics.* New York: Oxford University Press.

Irwin, T. H. 1988. *Aristotle's First Principles.* New York: Oxford University Press.

Johnson, M. 1993. *Moral Imagination: Implications of Cognitive Science For Ethics.* Chicago: University of Chicago Press.

Jones, S. K., & Hiltebeitel, K. M. 1995. *Organizational Influence In A Model of the Moral Decision Process of Accountants.* Journal of Business Ethics, 14: 417–431.

Jones, T. M., & Ryan, L. V. 2001. *The Effect of Organizational Forces On Individual Morality: Judgment, Moral Approbation, and Behavior.* In J. Dienhart, D. Moberg, & R. Duska (Eds.), *The Next Phase of Business Ethics: Integrating Psychology and Ethics:* 285–300. New York: Elsevier Science Ltd.

Kahneman, D., & Tversky, A. (Eds.). 2000. *Choices, Values, and Frames.* New York: Cambridge University Press.

Koehn, D. 1998. *Virtue Ethics, The Firm, and Moral Psychology.* Business Ethics Quarterly, 8: 497–513.

Kohlberg, L. 1969. *Stage and Sequence: The Cognitive-Developmental Approach To Socialization.* In D. A. Goslin (Ed.), Handbook of Socialization Theory and Research: 347–480. Chicago, Il: Rand-Mcnally.

Kupperman, J. 1991. *Character.* New York: Oxford University Press.

Lewis, M. 1989. *Liar's Poker: Rising Through The Wreckage On Wall Street.* New York: W. W. Norton.

Lieberman, M. D. 2000. *Intuition: A Social Cognitive Neuroscience Approach.* Psychological Bulletin, 126: 109–137.

Loewenstein, G., & Adler, D. 2000. *A Bias In The Prediction of Tastes.* In D. Kahneman and A. Tversky (Eds.), *Choices, Values, and Frames:* 726–734. New York: Cambridge University Press.

Luban, D. 2003. *Integrity: Its Causes and Cures.* Fordham Law Review, 72: 279–310.

Macintyre, A. 1981. *After Virtue.* Notre Dame, In: University of Notre Dame Press.

Mcdowell, J. 1997. *Virtue and Reason.* In R. Crisp & M. Slote (Eds.), *Virtue Ethics:* 141–162. New York: Oxford University Press.

Metcalfe, J., & Mischel, W. 1999. *A Hot-Cool System Analysis of Delay of Gratification: Dynamics of Willpower.* Psychological Review, 106: 3–19.

Milgram, S. 1974. *Obedience to Authority: An Experimental View.* New York: Harper and Row.

Moberg, D. J., & Seabright, M. A. 2000. *The Development of Moral Imagination.* Business Ethics Quarterly, 10: 845–884.

Moore, G. 2002. *On the Implications of the Practice-Institution Distinction: Macintyre and the Application of Modern Virtue Ethics To Business.* Business Ethics Quarterly 12: 19–32.

Moore, G. 2003. *Corporate Character: Modern Virtue Ethics and the Virtuous Corporation.* Unpublished.

Nickerson, R. S. 1994. *The Teaching of Thinking and Problem Solving.* In R. J. Sternberg (Ed.), *Thinking and Problem Solving*: 409–449. San Diego, Ca: Academic Press.

Nielsen, R. 2001. *Can Ethical Character Be Stimulated and Enabled: An Action-Learning Approach To Teaching and Learning Organization Ethics.* In J. Dienhart, D. Moberg, & R. Duska (Eds.), *The Next Phase of Business Ethics: Integrating Psychology and Ethics:* 51–77.

Nisbet, R., & Ross, L. 1991. *The Person and the Situation: Perspectives of Social Psychology.* New York: Mcgraw-Hill.

Nussbaum, M. C. 1990. *Finely Aware and Richly Responsible: Literature and the Moral Imagination. In Love's Knowledge: Essays On Philosophy and Literature,* 148–167. New York: Oxford University Press.

Plato. *Meno.* 1961. R. S. Bluck, (Ed.). New York: Cambridge University Press.

Porter, M. 1980. *Competitive Strategy: Techniques For Analyzing Industries and Competitors.* New York: Free Press.

Prior, W. 2001. *Eudaimonism.* Journal of Value Inquiry, 35: 325–342.

Rabin, M. 1998. *Psychology and Economics.* Journal of Economic Literature, 36: 11–46.

Rawls, J. 1971. *A Theory of Justice.* Cambridge, MA: Harvard University Press.

Schein, E. H. 1985. *Organizational Culture and Leadership.* San Francisco: Jossey-Bass.

Sen, A. K. 1987. *On Ethics and Economics.* New York: Basil Blackwell.

Sennett, R. 1998. *The Corrosion of Character: The Transformation of Work In Modern Capitalism.* New York: W. W. Norton & Company.

Sherman, N. 1994. *The Role of Emotions In Aristotelian Virtue.* Proceedings of the Boston Area Colloquium In Ancient Philosophy, 9: 1–33.

Simon, H. A. 1954. *A Behavioral Theory of Rational Choice.* Quarterly Journal of Economics, 69: 99–118.

Sims, R. L., & Keon, T. L. 1999. *Determinants of Ethical Decision Making: The Relationship of the Perceived Organizational Environment.* Journal of Business Ethics, 19: 393–401.

Slater, L. 2004. *Opening Skinner's Box: Great Psychological Experiments of the Twentieth Century.* New York: W. W. Norton.

Slote, M. 1983. *Goods and Virtues.* New York: Oxford University Press.

Slote, M. 1992. *From Morality To Virtue.* New York: Oxford University Press.

Slote, M. 2001. *Morals From Motives.* New York: Oxford University Press.

Solomon, R. C. 1992. *Ethics and Excellence: Cooperation and Integrity In Business.* New York: Oxford University Press.

Solomon, R. C. 2003. *A Defense of Virtue Ethics In Business.*

Business Ethics Quarterly, 13: 43–62.

Trevino, L. K. 1986. *Ethical Decision Making In Organizations: A Person-Situation Interactionist Model.* Academy of Management Review, 11: 607–617.

Trevino, L. K., Butterfield, K. D., & Mccabe, D. L. 2001. *The Ethical Context In Organizations: Influences On Employee Attitudes and Behaviors.* In J. Dienhart, D. Moberg, & R. Duska (Eds.), *The Next Phase of Business Ethics: Integrating Psychology and Ethics:* 301–337. New York: Elsevier Science Ltd.

Van Hooft, S. 2001. *Overcoming Principles: Dialogue In Business Ethics.* Teaching Business Ethics, 5: 89–106.

Vidaver-Cohen, D. 1997. *Moral Imagination In Organizational Problem-Solving: An Institutional Perspective.* Business Ethics Quarterly 7: 1–26.

Walton, C. 1997. *Brain, Feeling, and Society: Damasio and Aristotle On Neurobiology and Moral Psychology.* Unpublished.

Walton, C. 2001. *Character and Integrity In Organizations: The Civilization of the Workplace.* Business and Professional Ethics Journal, 20: 105–128.

Walton, C. 2004. *'Good Job,' Bad Work: Aristotle and the Culture of the Workplace.* Unpublished.

Watson, G. 1982. *Free Agency.* In G. Watson (Ed.), *Free Will:* 96–110. New York: Oxford University Press.

Werhane, P. H. 1999. *Moral Imagination and Management Decision-Making.* New York: Oxford University Press.

Williams, B. 1981. *Moral Luck.* New York: Cambridge University Press.

Williams, B. 1985. *Ethics and the Limits of Philosophy.* Cambridge, Ma: Harvard University Press.

Winter, S. G. 1971. *Satisficing, Selection, and the Innovative Remnant.* Quarterly Journal of Economics, 85: 237–261.

The following case is an unusual one. It is a sexual harassment case set in the 1980s; it is not likely a similar case would be decided the same way today. But other than the oddness of the case, the real value of it is to use it as a way to work through the Shareholder and Stakeholder models of the Hosmer framework. First, read the case, think about it and talk about whether the Malibu Grand Prix (a company that makes go-carts for use at entertainment places that might also have baseball batting cases or miniature golf). Then I will provide a hypothethical extension of the case to serve as a way to practice the application of the Shareholder and Stakeholder frameworks.

Marvelle Dornhecker, Plaintiff-Appellee, v. Malibu Grand Prix Corp.,

828 F.2d 307 (5th Cir. 1987)

Before GEE, GARWOOD, and JONES, Circuit Judges.

EDITH H. JONES, Circuit Judge:

The behavior of a co-worker at the Malibu Grand Prix Corporation proved too racy for Marvelle Dornhecker. She worked there in a corporate staff position for four days in December 1984 before resigning because of sexual harassment to which, she felt, the company was insensitive. This Title VII lawsuit followed, and the district court awarded her $25,000 compensatory damages. Malibu appeals.

We shall assume, without deciding, that Mrs. Dornhecker was the victim of unwelcome sexual harassment that was sufficiently pervasive to alter the conditions of her employment and create an abusive working environment. The perpetrator was one Robert Rockefeller,*a contract consultant to the corporation in marketing, who was slated to attend a series of out-of-town presentations with Mrs. Dornhecker and other Malibu representatives during December 1984. Rockefeller's conduct in the presence of Mrs. Dornhecker was public, clownish and boorish. During two days of her first business trip with the company to Cincinnati and Miami, Rockefeller put his hands on her hips in an airport ticket line and dropped his pants in front of the passengers while waiting to board the airplane. He touched her breasts. Finally, when a number of Malibu employees attended a business dinner at the Downunder Restaurant in Fort Lauderdale, he put his stocking feet on a cocktail table directly in front of her and "playfully" choked her when she complained. The co-workers were appalled.**

---

*   Despite the gilded surname, Rockefeller is unrelated to its wealthy holders and, at the time of trial, was in bankruptcy.

**   On more than one occasion during these two days, Rockefeller had used the expression "Let's get naked and go to my room." As Mrs. Dornhecker admitted, this offensive expression was not, however, necessarily directed at her.

The events most pertinent to this appeal commenced when Mrs. Dornhecker, overcome by Rockefeller's disgusting lack of professionalism, rushed to the ladies' room immediately after this last incident and dissolved, in her words, into hysterical tears. Her immediate supervisor, Krysia Swift, followed and tried to console her. Although Swift had not seen the choking incident, she agreed to talk to the company president about it. The next morning, December 6, Mrs. Dornhecker herself addressed Peabody, the president, and the court found that he "told Plaintiff that she would not have to work with Rockefeller after the Florida trip." The Florida presentations were then scheduled to last one-and-a-half more days. It is undisputed that Rockefeller did not attend the remaining presentations in Fort Lauderdale, and his contract with Malibu went un-renewed at the end of December. Mrs. Dornhecker was not present to savor these events: she believed management was unresponsive, and shortly after talking to Peabody on December 6, she left Fort Lauderdale, explaining her departure only with a brief note in her supervisor's hotel mail slot.

The critical issue in this case for purposes of Title VII liability is whether Malibu, knowing about Mrs. Dornhecker's claims of sexual harassment, failed to take prompt remedial action. The district court found that Malibu did not. This is clearly erroneous. Since the demise of the institution of dueling, society has seldom provided instantaneous redress for dishonorable conduct. In this case, the district court found that Malibu's president personally reassured Mrs. Dornhecker that Rockefeller would not be working with her after the Florida trip. This assurance occurred approximately 12 hours after Mrs. Dornhecker had tearfully confronted Krysia Swift in the ladies' room and first acquainted her with Rockefeller's behavior. Considered in terms of the speed with which the company addressed Mrs. Dornhecker's complaint or the length of time it proposed to resolve that complaint, Malibu's remedial action was unusually prompt.

Mrs. Dornhecker resigned before she ever saw or worked with Rockefeller again after dinner at the Downunder Restaurant. Thus, we do not know whether Rockefeller, ashamed by his performance or by conversation with Malibu employees, or by the prospect of being summarily booted out of the rest of the business trip, might have left Mrs. Dornhecker alone for the remaining one-and-a-half days in Florida. Where the offending conduct spanned only two days to begin with, it is not unreasonable for the company to offer ending it virtually overnight. And, although we do not condone Rockefeller's conduct, it was not as aggressive or coercive as that underlying a number of hostile sexual environment claims that have been unsuccessful in court. Mrs. Dornhecker was not propositioned, she was not forced to respond to Rockefeller, she was not placed in any threatening situation. The company's remedy to Mrs. Dornhecker's complaint may be assessed proportionately to the seriousness of the offense. A company's lines of command, organizational format and immediate business demands cannot be wholly extracted from the analysis of its manner and promptness in resolving a claim of sexual harassment. The remedy was prompt.

Malibu's handling of the problem was also decisive. Ordinarily, an organization requires time to respond to embarrassing, emotional and often litigation-spawning claims of sexual harassment. Careers and corporate image rest on the company's handling of such charges. Here, Krysia Swift witnessed an hysterical outpouring from Mrs. Dornhecker, whom she had known and worked with for only two days, and whose reaction to offensive conduct Swift could hardly have been expected to assess in a moment. Whether Swift brushed off the charges or was just trying to defuse Mrs. Dornhecker's condition in the ladies' room is unclear but irrelevant. The next morning Peabody informed Mrs. Dornhecker that Rockefeller would only work with her one-and-a-half more days. Had Malibu believed it needed more time to consider Mrs. Dornhecker's complaints or what to do about them, it would have been reasonable. Rockefeller, despite his faults, had helped to purchase Malibu for its owners and held an employment contract. In this case, one cannot reasonably demand the employer to ignore its experience with the alleged offender or to examine a charge of sexual harassment based on one side of the story, in a vacuum. Malibu speedily evaluated Mrs. Dornhecker's complaints.

For these reasons, we find that the court clearly erred in its determination that Malibu did not promptly remedy Mrs. Dornhecker's predicament. A similar analysis leads to the conclusion that she was not constructively discharged. The district court asserted that Malibu's "inaction" upon Mrs. Dornhecker's complaints and her subsequent resignation effected a constructive discharge. Because Malibu's prompt response was the antithesis of "inaction", Mrs. Dornhecker was not constructively discharged. Moreover, constructive discharge occurs only "when the employer deliberately makes an employee's working conditions so intolerable that the employee is forced into an involuntary resignation.... [T]he issue is whether a reasonable person in the employee's position and circumstances would have felt compelled to resign As the Eleventh Circuit recently put it, "[P]art of an employee's obligation to be reasonable is an obligation not to assume the worst, and not to jump to conclusions too fast." Under all the circumstances, Mrs. Dornhecker did not give Malibu a fair opportunity to demonstrate that it could curb Rockefeller's self-destructive exhibitionism.

The judgment of the district court is REVERSED.

Several questions arise from this case. Most fundamentally, do you think the company acted responsively (as the Appellate Court found) or not (as the Trial Court determined)? Why didn't any of the co-workers, appalled as they may have been, do anything to challenge Rockefeller? Is it unusual that the President of the company is on the telephone the next morning to someone who has been working for the company less than a week? Are the last two questions, in particular, two sides of the same coin?

In addition to these questions, let's suppose that Malibu was in trouble. Nearing bankruptcy—remember, this is a hypothetical; I have no idea of its financial status—it badly needed to land new contracts at this event. If new contracts are not landed, then the company may fold and all the good people who work for Malibu might lose their jobs. For better or for worse, Rockefeller was deemed to be crucial to the sales efforts. With these variations in mind, how would you analyze this case under Shareholder Theory and under Stakeholder Theory? That is, what should happen —both long-term and short-term, to accord with what the shareholders want? In Stakeholder Theory, how do Rights, Justice, and Utilitarianism play out? How would the Virtues you have identified as being relevant apply to this case? You will find that this is a very good case to practice the frameworks from this Part II of the book!

PART III:

ETHICAL CORPORATE CULTURE

I N MY EXPERIENCE, to the extent consider the importance of ethics, it is in terms of making ethical business decisions, the topic of Part II. But the institutions we live and work in have a great deal to say about the kinds of decisions we make. Part III focuses on this dimension of business ethics: How do we create ethical cultures that are prone to make good decisions. Sometimes cultures lead people to make poor decisions and those organizations, which also need to be recognized. Yet organizations can be positively oriented as well. Making them so requires issues of leadership to be sure, but organizations exist beyond a given leader. They also must attend to building trust with the constituents of the organization, a topic that Part III will focus on.

There is an old adage that the best way to be ethical in business is to have a good boss. While easier said than done, it is a good bit of advice. To provide an example, former CEO of Robert Galvin came to my class in the early 1990s to give a talk about business ethics. (I have heard him give this same presentation elsewhere, so by revealing it, I am not breaking any confidences!) He said that when he was a rising executive at Motorola, the company was negotiating with a government to build a telecommunications network. The contract would add significant revenues. Galvin's assistant brought him the good news that the government liked Motorola's proposal and was ready to sign the contract. But to seal the deal, a gift to the Minister in charge of the contract would need to be made. Even in pre-FCPA days, Motorola had a policy against bribery and the assistant wanted to know what Galvin wanted to do.

Galvin's response was that (1) Motorola would not pay the bribe, (2) the negotiations for the network were off, and (3) there would never again be negotiations as long as the current regime was in power. One could ask if Galvin was nuts, but he had a firm explanation. Motorola was not going to pay a bribe. Getting into business with an organization that expected to be paid bribes was going to have a bad future. It did no good to refuse the bribe and do business with the government because no one is actually going to admit they paid a bribe so any public pronouncement that Motorola refused would not be believed if the government's norm was to get a bribe.

One of my students in the back of the room raised his hand and complimented him on the presentation, but also asked if it wasn't easier to take such a strong stand when your father was the CEO. And he was; Paul Galvin was Robert Galvin's father. To his credit, Galvin said that it certainly was easier, but the organizational point was that if you want to have good ethics, pay attention to the ethics of the organization you are going to work in so that you will find leaders who will back your ethical stances just as Galvin's father did. That organizational insight is the topic of Part III.

CHAPTER 10

When Culture Goes Awry:
Interview with Sherron Watkins

T HOUGH THE MAIN Enron characters have received their prison sentences, there's no closure for corporate fraud. Sherron Watkins, Enron's sentinel, describes the debacle's details and warns that it could happen again.

Dec. 3, 2001. Black Monday. The day that Enron declared bankruptcy. CEO Ken Lay had left a voice mail on the phones of all Enron employees asking they come into the office regardless. Nearly 5,000 were called to a massive meeting and told that the paychecks that they had recently received would be their last. Three weeks before Christmas.

In August of that year, Sherron Watkins, an Enron vice president, had sent an anonymous memo to Lay that read, "I am incredibly nervous that we will implode in a wave of accounting scandals."

Of course, that's exactly what happened. After the company's demise, the investigating U.S. Congress discovered Watkins' memos to Lay and other top executives. (After sending the memos, she had met with Lay with no results.) Watkins was soon lauded as an "internal whistle-blower," brought before Congressional and Senate hearings to testify against her former bosses, and heralded by TIME magazine as a "Person of the Year," with WorldCom's Cynthia Cooper and the FBI's Coleen Rowley.

Five years after Black Monday, Sherron Watkins talks with *Fraud Magazine* about what went wrong, why it could happen again, weakening moral underpinnings, and the lack of ethical business leaders.

Q The Enron debacle was anything but simple, but what were a few of the reason\why it happened? Had management lost its way or was it a ticking time bomb from the beginning?

A Many experts summarize "what happened" at Enron using two words, greed and arrogance. An accurate summary, I agree, but it fails to help others learn from Enron's demise. How did greed and arrogance run amok at Enron? How did a company's culture breed not only corruption from its own employees but also disreputable behavior from the outside auditors, lawyers, consultants, and lenders?

Enron was at one time the seventh largest company in the United States, based on Total Revenues. It collapsed into bankruptcy without ever reporting a losing quarter. More than $60 billion of shareholder investments became worthless; Enron owed $67 billion to its creditors, 20,000 of them who will or have received on average, 14 to 25 cents on the dollar. Nearly 5,000 employees lost their jobs with no severance pay or medical insurance, and far too many of Enron's employees also had all their retirement monies invested in Enron, losing not only their jobs but also their retirement savings.

What happened? It was a complete breakdown in moral values. But the scary part is that the breakdown was not done by outright intention but more by small steps in the wrong direction.

W*ere laws broken? Yes. Were lives devastated by it? Yes.*

Certainly, Enron was not a ticking time bomb from its beginning; in fact, the company started life in 1985 as a merger of two large U.S. regulated gas pipeline companies that had been in existence for decades. One of Enron's early mission statements was "to become the premier natural gas pipeline company in North America," a laudable, non-arrogant goal. However, by the mid-90s, Enron had changed that mission statement, first, "to become the world's first natural gas major" and then in 1995, "to become the world's leading energy company." Pay attention to the words a company uses to define itself and its goals. A great deal of arrogance can be seen in the 1995 mission statement. Enron was a large company, but primarily it was still a natural gas company and nowhere near the size of the Exxons and Shells of the energy world. [In 2001, Enron's mission statement was "to become the world's leading company."]

By 1995, the company had been very successful. It had transformed itself from a stodgy regulated pipeline business to a state-of-the art energy trading shop, which eventually handled more than 25 percent of the country's gas and power transactions. The natural gas market had deregulated and Enron came out on top of the newly created energy trading industry. Folks were fairly cocky at Enron. The company was the top dog in energy trading; competing companies either moved to Houston or at least moved their trading operations to Houston. Enron made the city of Houston the Wall Street of energy trading.

Enron's ability to evolve and shape the energy markets in the United States earned the company accolades from many sources. Harvard University did a case study; Business Week, Forbes and Fortune routinely covered the company in a favorable light. In fact, Fortune named Enron the most innovative company in America for six years in row, beginning in 1996. Unfortunately, the dark side of innovation is fraud.

Enron's leaders set the wrong tone, so did Arthur Andersen's leaders. [Arthur Andersen was Enron's external auditor.] In the end, both companies put revenues and earnings above all else —the means by which those earnings were generated did not matter. Were laws broken? Yes. Were lives devastated by it? Yes.

Q You've said that <u>Ken Lay</u> would force all Enron employees to book corporate travel through his sister's travel agency even though it was more expensive than more competent agencies. Can you tell me your thoughts about the importance of a proper "tone at the top"?

A What I've come to realize is that leadership is tough " very tough." All eyes are on you and the slightest erosion in values at the CEO level is magnified in the trenches.

Ken Lay was well known for his charitable giving and his verbal commitment to Enron's four core values —respect, integrity, communication, and excellence —but he was not quite walking the walk. He always had us use his sister's travel agency. Trouble was that it was neither low cost nor good service. Domestically, you could manage, but when it came to international travel —that agency was very nearly incompetent. I was stuck in Third World countries where I didn't speak the language without a hotel room or with an insufficient airline ticket home despite paperwork that indicated otherwise. The incompetence was hard to understand. I would try using a different agency, but after one or two expense reports, I'd get a finger-wagging voice mail or e-mail reminding me that I needed to use Enron's preferred agency, Travel Agency in the Park; we all called it Travel Agency in the Dark.

Ken Lay was setting the wrong tone. He was in effect letting his managers know that once you get to the executive suite, the company's assets are there for you to move around to yourself or your family. In some perverse way, Andy Fastow [Enron's CFO who was originally indicted on 98 criminal counts], could justify his behavior, saying to himself, "Well, my creative off-balance-sheet deals are helping Enron meet its financial statement goals. Why can't I just take a million here and there for myself as a 'structuring fee,' just like Lay has been taking a little Enron money and transferring it to his sister for all these years?"

The CEO of a company must have pristine ethics if there is to be any hope of ethical behavior from the employees.

Q CFO Andy Fastow operated (and partly owned) LJM partnerships. He used these partnerships to mask hundreds of millions of dollars of losses on Enron investments. How was Fastow able to construct such complicated deceits with the tacit approval of top executives plus accountants and attorneys inside and outside Enron?

A That's an excellent question that many still do not understand, me included. How in the world did a qualified and talented independent board of directors waive Enron's code of conduct twice, to allow Fastow, to form and run an investment partnership [named LJM] which for the most part did nothing but buy, sell, and hedge assets with Enron?

Enron had allowed Andy Fastow to enter into an unprecedented conflict of interest. Because he was CFO, his fiduciary duties included looking out for the best interests of the company while also becoming the general partner of this investment partnership, LJM, where he raised $500 million of limited partner monies and was charged with maximizing returns for limited partners.

Trouble was that LJM's business was to do business with Enron. In every transaction Fastow had to choose: Enron or LJM. No human being should be put in such a conflict. Why did Enron's board allow such a conflict of interest? I must conclude that their judgment was severely clouded by the fees they received as directors. Each director received nearly $350,000 per year for serving on Enron's board. That amount was double the high end of normal large public company director fees. The board routinely bragged about Enron's management team. How much of their "Enron can do no wrong" attitude was impacted by the fees they received?

The reason so many Enron executives, and finance, legal, and accounting professionals went along with the questionable —and, in some cases, fraudulent —off-balance-sheet vehicles is multi-faceted. Sometimes, their reasoning was similar to the board's: their judgment was clouded by high salaries, bonuses, and stock option proceeds. Another cause was diffusion of responsibility; it was Arthur Andersen's job to opine on complicated accounting structures, or the lawyers' job to vouch for the legality of certain arrangements, or the board of directors' role, etc.

When these structures were created, intimidation was used to keep people silent.

Besides money-clouded judgments and the diffusion of responsibility, I often explain how Fastow and his team got away with it by recounting the "Emperor's New Clothes" fable. In that fable there is an emperor focused on his appearance not his kingdom —that fits Ken Lay. And there is the swindle —incredibly beautiful cloth but it is impossible to see it if you are stupid or not fit for your office. The swindlers play into people's insecurities. The emperor sends a minister to check on the progress of the weaving. The minister panics when he doesn't see any cloth. He knows he's not stupid, but maybe he's not fit for his office so he lies and says he sees it. Ditto for the second minister, and so on, until the whole town exclaims about the beautiful new clothes the Emperor is wearing in the parade.

Fastow's team of accountants, bankers, and lawyers devised very complex structures —so complex, in fact, that when I was first looking into them in July of 2001, it took two hours for a business manager to walk through just one of them with me. When these structures were created, intimidation was used to keep people silent. CEO Jeff Skilling was well known for his accusation that those who didn't understand Enron or a particular structure were not smart enough to "get it."

Q You once said that you had no desire to take your fears of fraud outside Enron. In "The Smartest Guys in the Room," you were quoted as saying, "When a company cooks the books, their only chance of survival is to come clean themselves." Do you still believe that about the Enron situation or any corporate fraud situation? Creating a highly competitive environment where employees did not want to appear weak or unintelligent was a root cause of Enron's problems. Smart people stopped asking questions for fear of looking like they didn't "get it."

A Yes, I do. I think when a company has committed fraud, its most meaningful chance of survival is to find it, disclose it, and fix it themselves. By the year 2001, Enron was primarily a financial trading house. A financial trading house lives on its investment grade rating and its reputation. Any hint of trouble and business disappears like water through a sieve. When I met with Ken Lay, I was both optimistic and naive. I not only expected that a thorough investigation would occur but I also expected Enron to establish a crisis management team to address the financial peril Enron would face when the accounting was exposed, which in my opinion was sure to happen. In the long run, companies rarely get away with "cooking the books." But no other top executives came forward to back me up and Ken Lay gravitated toward good news and didn't quite accept what I was saying.

Q Many probably think that you wrote just one memo to Ken Lay but you actually sent seven pages of memos to him and memos to other top executives. In many of those memos you listed intricate details of the situation with several recommendations. And then you met with Lay face to face. How could it be that in a company of that size there was no one else who was willing to, as that old adage says, "speak truth to power"?

A After all of the Enron investigations and trials were completed, I did discover that others had sounded the warning bells and some very early on. There were managers within Enron, actually in the room when Enron's questionable accounting structures and schemes were hatched, and they complained —they tried to stop their birth. But in every case that person was shot down. Others soon realized to protest was fruitless and they just left the company. Or they reacted the only way they knew how —they posted comments on Yahoo's message board. LOL

On April 12, 2001, the following message appeared on Enron's message board: "The Enron executives have been operating an elaborate con scheme that has fooled even the most sophisticated analysts. The first sign of trouble will be an earnings shortfall followed by more warnings. Criminal charges will be brought against ENE executives for their misdeeds. Class action lawsuits will complete the demise of Enron." And that's when Enron was selling for $50 to $60 per share.

Q You had a final meeting with Lay, at which you actually gave him one more memo with proposed action steps: "My conclusions if we don't come clean and restate: All these bad things will happen to us anyway; it's just that Ken Lay will be more implicated in this than is deserved and he won't get the chance to restore the company to its former stature." What made you finally realize that he, too, was implicated in the fraud?

A The last meeting I had with Ken Lay was at the end of October. The company had written off the structures I was concerned with but as a current period write-off, not in the correct fashion, as a prior period restatement. The Wall Street Journal had run very lengthy exposé-style articles, the stock price was tanking and Enron, primarily Ken Lay, was not being honest about things. Ken Lay was making comments like, "We have no accounting irregularities." "Now is a good time to buy the stock." "I have the utmost faith in Andy Fastow." "We could have done the related party transactions with an outside third party." These were all statements that eventually helped the Department of Justice win a criminal conviction against Lay.

Q Mary Jo White, former U.S. attorney for the Southern District of New York, once said that executives at companies in the "90s engaged in group rationalization" an extrapolation of the third leg of the renowned fraud triangle developed by Dr. Donald Cressey. Despite the changes so far in this century, is that still the case?

A I do believe that executives rationalize their pay packages as well as aggressive accounting and other problem areas. My biggest concern for corporate America right now is that we have so few truly ethical leaders. The Enron scandal was the first, followed by a whole slew of others and we discovered with each scandal that the watchdog groups that are in business to protect investors failed: auditors, outside lawyers, Wall Street research analysts, and the nation's largest banks.

After all the corporate scandals, we had the Wall Street scandals —tainted stock research, among other things. Then the mutual fund scandal with money managers trading against their own customers for personal gain, trading after hours, and giving preferential treatment to larger customers. Next we had the insurance industry scandal unearthed by Elliot Spitzer. Now its outsized CEO pay packages and option backdating.

What has happened? It is very ironic that we get on our high horse and claim to have the world's most moral and fair system and try and force other countries to conform, when in actual fact we have such a broken system.

In order to flourish, a successful capitalist system —really any system, be it education, medicine, business or government —must be predicated on fairness, honesty, and integrity. In fact, many scholars describe the capitalist system as a three-legged stool —one based on economic freedom, political freedom, and moral responsibility. A weakness in any one leg and the stool topples.

Michael Novak, a former Catholic priest, wrote "The Spirit of Democratic Capitalism" in 1982. In his well-regarded book, he praises the virtues of a democratic capitalist system for its ability to raise the standard and quality of life for those less fortunate, for the poor. He assumes, however, that an appropriate system of checks and balances actually exists such that a challenge or a weakness to either the economic and political freedoms within a capitalist system or the moral fiber of its leaders would be almost immediately corrected.

We have seen morality problems in the past addressed with new laws, most notably that of child labor abuse, environmental pollution, and worker safety. Business leaders in those days complained about the restrictions and about the government killing our economic system with overly burdensome regulations. Same song, different verse. But we all survived. However, I see a slight difference today; there is less moral outrage about the pure materialism involved in capitalism. Instead of more outrage about CEO pay packages, there seems to be more envy.

Q Jeff Skilling and Ken Lay appeared to show no remorse nor accepted any responsibility for their actions. Even at his sentencing, Skilling said, "I believe, deep down, and this is no act, I believe I'm innocent." But even Skilling's mother, as quoted in Newsweek, said, "When you are the CEO and you are on the board of directors, you are supposed to know what's going on with the rest of the company." And when your own mother has suspicions, you know you're in trouble. Can you conjecture what causes that type of faulty thinking in top executives?

A I think there are difficult moments of truth when leadership is tested. And if these moments are not faced honestly, if the hard decision is not made at that point, it becomes next to impossible to return to the right path. It is that rationalization we spoke of before. Once you start to rationalize, you're stuck.

I am sure you have heard of the analogy of a frog in boiling water. If a frog is thrown in a pot of boiling water it will jump out and save itself. If a frog is in a pot of cool water that is slowly heated, he'll stay in the pot until he boils to death.

Leaders and employees will never choose wrong when faced with a clear-cut choice between right and wrong, but there are those gray areas that involve rationalization to stop your gut from bothering you. For instance, when Enron's accounting moved from creative to aggressive, the pot of water moved from cool to lukewarm. Unfortunately, nobody protested and those involved with the creative transactions soon found themselves moving onto the aggressive transactions and finally in the uncomfortable situation of working on fraudulent deals. The water was boiling and they were stuck.

From bosses to managers to staff, we must realize when we are in a pot of water that has gone from cool to lukewarm. We must recognize that moment of truth; we must address it and then act. Once the water is heated past lukewarm, we won't have the willpower to jump out.

Q What are a few of the major points of your talks to groups now and how do they differ from those talks you gave shortly after you left Enron?

A The major point I stress now is how and why company leaders must have a zero tolerance policy for ethically challenged employees. It is probably the hardest role of a CEO, but when he or she discovers that an employee has violated the company's value system, that person must go.

That's a tough one for most. Often we feel it's compassionate to forgive and forget and give them a second chance. And if the violator is a star, a superstar, who is great with the customers, or great generating revenues then you really want to forgive and forget.

Trouble is that once you do that, you've sent the message throughout the organization that the value system is second to producing the numbers, second to being great with customers. Go ahead, push the edge of the envelope; if you get caught, you'll get a second chance.

A company's system of internal controls is not supposed to be bulletproof. It should expose ethically challenged employees so you can fire them. If a company does not have a zero tolerance policy for unethical employees then its internal control system will eventually be worthless.

An organization just cannot afford to keep ethically challenged individuals. It is too much of a risk. Giving them a reprimand and stern marching orders to never break the rules again just solidifies for these type of folks that they got away with it. Now they just go into more of a stealth mode, making it harder to catch them before they've wreaked havoc with the company.

> *An organization just cannot afford to keep ethically challenged individuals. It is too much of a risk.*

Q Back in 2002, you told the 13th Annual ACFE Fraud Conference that "the financial accounting system has become too rule-based and not principle-based." In addition to the passage of the Sarbanes-Oxley Act, what do you think has changed in the ensuing five years since Enron collapsed?

A   As a result of Enron and other similar companies —WorldCom, Tyco, HealthSouth, Adelphia, and the like —we have a law in the United States, the Sarbanes-Oxley Act of 2002.

The Sarbanes-Oxley Act, in effect, tries to specify, to make totally clear just what existing laws and regulations actually mean. It seeks to make into law what are considered the "best practices" in the area of corporate governance, internal controls, and financial transparency.

The act basically calls for a culture change within companies to a culture that truly attempts to live by the spirit of existing laws and regulations and away from a culture of form-over-substance compliance.

I am afraid that although the purpose of SOX was to legally discourage form-over-substance compliance, what we've got is just more rules to use or justify behavior that still doesn't comply with the spirit of existing laws. I'm not sure we've come very far.

Q   Where were all the fraud examiners at Enron? Were internal controls emphasized anywhere? Were any departments ever audited for fraud? Today, what would a fraud examiner specifically look for to begin uncovering the types of fraud at Enron?

A   Enron had no fraud examiners. In fact, Enron had no internal audit department; it was outsourced to Arthur Andersen in the mid-1990s. When I speak across the globe, that fact alone always brings gasps of surprise and shock from audiences. The typical response is: No wonder the Enron fraud occurred.

As for where a fraud examiner would start at Enron, it would be the spotty cash flow from operations. Why did all the cash flow from operations come in during the fourth quarter of the year? Why the need for so many related-party transactions, the LJM transactions? Why the waiver of the code of conduct? Why such large audit and consulting fees to the outside auditors? Also, I often suggest answering a set of questions that Fortune once listed for boards of directors. If a company has difficulty answering these questions, then a fraud examiner has identified an area worth investigating.

Q   What could a courageous CFE, with his or her skills, have done to help head off such a disaster? In the wake of Enron, what's the single most important bit of advice you could give fraud examiners?

A   I am afraid that a courageous CFE would have been fired at Enron. If folks run into Enron-like behavior, I always suggest finding peers who will join you in your quest to correct things. Never go it alone.

Q How does an organization like the ACFE help train anti-fraud professionals to help prevent the conditions that could spawn another Enron?

A An organization like the ACFE exposes anti-fraud professionals to all the tricks, the prior frauds, the outlandish schemes that have been tried in the past. I think most professionals don't really believe what they're seeing. The founder of the ACFE, Joe Wells, has seen it all. Realizing that life is stranger than fiction is more helpful than most realize. I didn't react correctly to all that I was exposed to at Enron because frankly I didn't realize the gravity of some of the actions I was witnessing. I also didn't grasp the depth of the rationalizations and their ability to prevent people from accepting truth. War stories help educate anti-fraud professionals.

I started my career in the early 1980s at Arthur Andersen & Co. as an auditor. I have to say that it bothered me that we were told it was not a public accountant's job to detect fraud. We were told to maintain a healthy degree of skepticism, but our audits were not specifically designed to find fraud. The trouble is that most shareholders believe the opposite: that an audit does in fact mean auditors looked for signs of fraud.

I am deeply appreciative of the ACFE. It takes passion and loads of blood, sweat, and tears to start and build an organization like the ACFE. Joe Wells firmly believed that it was the job of an accountant to find and prevent fraud. Because of that passion and hard work, the ACFE is a healthy, thriving, fraud-busting machine, with more than 38,000 members in more than 125 countries.

I often repeat to audiences the saying that, "all it takes for evil to prevail is for good people to do nothing." The ACFE stands for good people doing something and I encourage the organization to keep up the good work. Your organization does more good and "prevents more evil" than you probably realize.

Q If you ever were to go back to a corporate executive position, what kinds of things would you ensure would be set in place before you took the job?

A In addition to the zero tolerance policy I've already mentioned for ethically challenged employees, I'd be sure that the company had a mechanism for bad news to get to the top and had effective policies and procedures for dealing with that bad news. I would also verify that the company's control and risk personnel had autonomy and equal power with top revenue executives. I would want to see that top management values the control and risk management function. I would want to make sure they recognize that control and risk personnel will not be the most popular and that the problems the company avoids as a result of the work of these groups will never be quantified.

Q You said that Skilling's sentencing of 24 years and four months in prison "feels like closure." What does closure mean to you? How do you reconcile all that happened and move on?

A The Department of Justice went after the top executives at Enron. They did the right thing. Without Jeff Skilling, I don't believe the Enron fraud would have occurred. If the DOJ had stopped with Enron's CFO, I don't think justice would have been served.

Q The media furor has subsided. What kinds of reactions do you get from people now?

A People respond very favorably to me. I think most folks see themselves taking the same actions I did at Enron, if they found themselves in my shoes. And just in case they ever do need to follow in my footsteps, they sure like hearing the story directly from me and hearing what I might have done differently, etc.

Q Do you correspond with other corporate sentinels?

A I keep in touch with Cynthia Cooper, formerly of WorldCom; and Colleen Rowley, formerly with the FBI.

Q What are your plans for your consulting firm?

A I am starting a leadership development program, collaborating with other leadership experts and executive coaching firms, to hone the next generation of leaders. The program is designed for those knocking on the door to the CEO suite. It is a multi-month program, involving peer interaction along industry lines. The goal is to equip these leaders with a peer network and an experience that prepares them for anything, even the perfect storm that was Enron.

Q What are some of the latest books that you've read? Who are you listening to these days?

A I have read many Christian books, most notably by Derek Prince and Watchmen Nee. As for business books, I recommend Bill George's "Authentic Leadership," Mike Useem's "Leadership Moments", and "The Go Point: When It's Time to Decide:

Knowing What to Do and When to Do It." Also, a must read is "The Thin Book of Naming Elephants: How to Surface Undiscussables for Greater Organizational Success," by Sue Hammond and Andrea Mayfield. "Naming Elephants" dissects the Columbia shuttle disaster and the Enron debacle very effectively. It is a fabulous book to improve the chances that elephants in the room will be recognized and dealt with. You can also read it in 45 minutes. It is a must!

Q You've been asked this one numerous times, I'm sure, but what's the moral of the story?

A Being an ethical person is more than knowing right from wrong. It is having the fortitude to do right even when there is much at stake.

Mammoth dilemmas often have no clear answer. The best a company can do is to follow the least worst alternative. This was demonstrated in other headline-grabbing events as well. In 1989, the Exxon Valdez ran aground in Prince William Sound off the coast of Alaska. Once oil floats in the water, there is no good way to get it out. There may be crisis-management strategies to skim oil off the water. Successfully doing that will depend on well-developed plans with people practicing putting those plans into action. Often the expense of both the planning and the practice are significant, and so they are not both done, leaving an underdeveloped capability in place when a disaster strikes. This was true in the Valdez case when the emergency response plan for cleaning up oil spills—managed by a consortium of oil companies organized through a state agency named Aleyeska—had been downsized prior to the spill.

Without denying that crisis management and response programs are essential, there is also a reality that the best way to make sure water is not polluted with oil is to make sure that the oil doesn't get there in the first place. Or to prevent a massive unwinding of hidden debt doesn't occur in the first place as with Enron. That requires another kind of planning—preventative planning—that reaches into the depths of the company's culture. On a daily basis, how are people in the company rewarded? What incentives do they have? What goals do they pursue?

The answers to these kinds of questions can be disturbing. Here are two scholars looking at such issues. The first comes from the practice of law, but the excerpt itself is readily applicable to nearly any major business organization today. The author, Patrick Schiltz, holds an impeccable pedigree. A graduate of Harvard Law School and a law clerk to a Justice of the U.S. Supreme Court, Schiltz also practiced law in a large law firm before heading to academia and then becoming a judge himself. In the following excerpt from a landmark—and controversial—law review article, Schiltz shows how subtle signals lead new lawyers down a path that makes keeping to moral standards of practice difficult.

Symposium: Attorney Well-Being In Large Firms: Choices Facing Young Lawyers

On Being a Happy, Healthy, and Ethical Member of an Unhappy, Unhealthy, and Unethical Profession[1]

by Patrick J. Schiltz *

* * *

B. Big Firm Culture

I t is hard to practice law ethically. Complying with the formal rules is the easy part. The rules are not very specific, and they don't demand very much. You may, on rare occasions, confront an extremely difficult conflict of interest problem that will require you to parse the rules carefully. You may even confront a situation in which some ethical or moral imperative compels you to violate the rules. But by and large, you will have no trouble complying with the rules; indeed, you are unlikely to give the rules much thought.

Acting as an ethical lawyer in the broader, non-formalistic sense is far more difficult. I have already given you some idea of why it is hard to practice law in a big firm (or any firm that emulates a big firm) and live a balanced life; I will return to that point in a moment. But even practicing law ethically in the sense of being honest and fair and compassionate is difficult. To understand why, you need to understand what it is that you will do every day as a lawyer.

Most of a lawyer's working life is filled with the mundane. It is unlikely that one of your clients will drop a smoking gun on your desk or ask you to deliver a briefcase full of unmarked bills or invite you to have wild, passionate sex (or even un-wild, un-passionate sex). These things happen to lawyers only in John Grisham novels. Your life as a lawyer will be filled with the kind of things that drove John Grisham to write novels: dictating letters and talking on the phone and drafting memoranda and performing "due diligence" and proofreading contracts and negotiating settlements and filling out time sheets. And because your life as a lawyer will be filled with the mundane, whether you

---

1   Patrick J. Schiltz, *On Being a Happy, Healthy, and Ethical Member of an Unhappy, Unhealthy, and Unethical Profession,* 52 VAND. L. REV. 871-951 (May 1999).

practice law ethically will depend not upon how you resolve the one or two dramatic ethical dilemmas that you will confront during your entire career, but upon the hundreds of little things that you will do, almost unthinkingly, each and every day.

Because practicing law ethically will depend primarily upon the hundreds of little things that you will do almost unthinkingly every day, it will not depend much upon your thinking. You are going to be busy. The days will fly by. When you are on the phone negotiating a deal or when you are at your computer drafting a brief or when you are filling out your time sheet at the end of the day, you are not going to have time to reflect on each of your actions. You are going to have to act almost instinctively.

What this means, then, is that you will not practice law ethically—you cannot practice law ethically—unless acting ethically is habitual for you. You have to be in the habit of being honest. You have to be in the habit of being fair. You have to be in the habit of being compassionate. These qualities have to be deeply ingrained in you, so that you can't turn them on and off—so that acting honorably is not something you have to decide to do—so that when you are at work, making the thousands of phone calls you will make and writing the thousands of letters you will write and dealing with the thousands of people with whom you will deal, you will automatically apply the same values in the workplace that you apply outside of work, when you are with family and friends.

Here is the problem, though: After you start practicing law, nothing is likely to influence you more than "the culture or house norms of the agency, department, or firm" in which you work. If you are going into private practice—particularly private practice in a big firm—you are going to be immersed in a culture that is hostile to the values you now have. The system does not want you to apply the same values in the workplace that you do outside of work (unless you're rapaciously greedy outside of work); it wants you to replace those values with the system's values. The system is obsessed with money, and it wants you to be, too. The system wants you—it needs you—to play the game.

Now, no one is going to say this to you. No one is going to take you aside and say, "Jane, we here at Smith & Jones are obsessed with money. From this point forward the most important thing in your life has to be billing hours and generating business. Family and friends and honesty and fairness are okay in moderation, but don't let them interfere with making money." No one will tell you, as one lawyer told another in a Charles Addams cartoon, "I admire your honesty and integrity, Wilson, but I have no room for them in my firm." Instead, the culture will pressure you in more subtle ways to replace your values with the system's.

Here is an example of what I mean: During your first month working at the big firm, some senior partner will invite you and the other new associates to a barbeque at his home. This "barbeque" will bear absolutely no relationship to what your father used to do on a Weber grill in your driveway. You will drive up to the senior partner's home in your rusted Escort and park at the end of a long line of Mercedeses and BMWs and sports utility vehicles. You will walk up to the front door of the house. The house will be enormous. The lawn will look like a putting green; it will be bordered by perfectly manicured trees and flowers. Somebody wearing a white shirt and black bow tie will answer the door and direct you to the backyard. You will walk through one room after another, each of which will be decorated with expensive carpeting and expensive wallpaper and expensive antiques. Scattered throughout the home will be large professional photographs of beautiful children with tousled, sunbleached hair.

As you enter the partner's immaculately landscaped backyard, someone wearing a white shirt and black bow tie carrying a silver platter will approach you and offer you an appetizer. Don't look for cocktail weenies in barbeque sauce; you will more likely be offered pate or miniature quiches or shrimp. A bar will be set up near the house; the bartender (who will be wearing a white shirt and black bow tie, of course) will pour you a drink of the most expensive brand of whatever liquor you like. In the corner of the yard, a caterer will be grilling swordfish. In another corner will stand the senior partner, sipping a glass of white wine, holding court with a worshipful group of junior partners and senior associates.

The senior partner will be wearing designer sunglasses and designer clothes; the logo on his shirt will signal its exorbitant cost; his shorts will be pressed. He will have a tan—albeit a slightly orange, tanning salon enhanced tan—and the nicest haircut you've ever seen. Eventually, the partner will introduce you to his wife. She will be beautiful, very thin, and a lot younger than her husband. She, too, will have a great tan, and not nearly as orange as her husband's. You and the other lawyers will talk about golf. Or about tennis. After a couple hours, you will walk out the front door, slightly tipsy from the free liquor, and say to yourself, "This is the life."

In this and a thousand other ways, you will absorb big firm culture—a culture of long hours of toil inside the office and short hours of conspicuous consumption outside the office. You will work among lawyers who will talk about money constantly and who will be intensely curious about how much money other lawyers are making. If you want to get some sense of this, leave your tax return on the photocopier glass sometime. (At least one hapless lawyer seems to do this every spring at most firms.) Every lawyer in the firm will know how much money you made last year in about fifteen minutes, and every lawyer who joins the firm during the next quarter century will hear the story of your tax return.

The lawyers in your firm are not unique. Thirty or forty years ago, talking about income and clients and fees " 'just wasn't done,' " even among Wall Street lawyers. Today, "the legal profession . . . has become extraordinarily self-conscious about making money," and "the new legal journalism has honed this self-consciousness to a sharp comparative and competitive edge." Just about every issue of the National Law Journal or the American Lawyer seems to include at least one article about how much money some lawyer somewhere is making. A couple times a year, these journals publish extensive surveys of lawyers' incomes—focusing in particular on the incomes of associates and partners in big firms. These surveys are pored over by lawyers with the intensity that small children bring to poring over the statistics of their favorite baseball players. Want to know what a first year associate at Irell & Manella in Los Angeles makes? $88,000. How about a sixth year associate at Dewey Ballantine in New York? $166,500, plus a $26,500 bonus. 263 Profits per partner at McDermott, Will & Emery in Chicago? $700,000. Reading about the incomes of your rivals will bring on either intense envy or smug *schadenfreude.*

Big firm culture also reflects the many ways in which lawyers who are winning the game broadcast their success. A first year male associate will buy his suits off the rack at a department store; a couple years later, he will be at Brooks Brothers; a few years after that, a salesperson will come to his office, with tape measures and fabric swatches in hand. Similar ostentatious progress will be demonstrated with regard to everything from watches to cell phones to running shoes to child care arrangements to private social clubs. When lawyers speak with envy or admiration about other lawyers, they do not mention a lawyer's devotion to family or public service, or a lawyer's innate sense of fairness, or even a lawyer's skill at trying cases or closing deals, nearly as much as they mention a lawyer's billable hours, or stable of clients, or annual income.

It is very difficult for a young lawyer immersed in this culture day after day to maintain the values she had as a law student. Slowly, almost imperceptibly, young lawyers change. They begin to admire things they did not admire before, be ashamed of things they were not ashamed of before, find it impossible to live without things they lived without before. Somewhere, somehow, a lawyer changes from a person who gets intense pleasure from being able to buy her first car stereo to a person enraged over a $400,000 bonus.

* * *

Most likely, when you were a child, your parents or grandparents told you that money does not buy happiness. They were right. Even scientists now say they were right. In part, they were right because much of what determines whether you will be happy is outside your control. You cannot control your genetic makeup—upon which happiness seems in part to depend (according to recent studies)—nor can you control many of the events in life that, for better or worse, will affect your subjective well-being (for example, you cannot control whether you will be permanently injured in a car accident or whether your spouse will perish at a young age). But the main reason your parents or grandparents were right about money not buying happiness is because—well, because money does not buy happiness.

Research has shown that, with the exception of those living in poverty, people are almost always wrong in thinking that more money will make them happier. "Once people are able to afford life's necessities, increasing levels of affluence matter surprisingly little." When people experience a rise in income, they quickly adjust their desires and expectations accordingly—and conclude, once again, that more money will bring them more happiness. (Psychologists Philip Brickman and Donald Campbell aptly refer to this process as the "hedonic treadmill.") Thus, when, as is true in law firms, more money almost always means more work, money not only fails to buy happiness, but it actually buys unhappiness. As one study of lawyers found, "after a certain time commitment (for most people, working more than 225 hours per month), even substantial income cannot negate the reduced quality of life. Because of this . . . the net impact of income on career satisfaction is negative." Note that the reference is to working 225 hours per month, and not to billing 225 hours per month.

* * *

When you are at that barbeque at the senior partner's house, instead of wistfully telling yourself, "This is the life," ask the senior partner some questions. (I'm speaking figuratively here; you probably don't want to actually ask these questions aloud.) Ask him how often he sees the gigantic house in which he lives. If he's honest, you will find out that he hasn't seen his home during daylight for almost four weeks, and that the only reason he came home at a decent hour tonight is to host the barbeque. Or ask him how often he's actually sat on that antique settee in that expensively decorated living room. You will find out that the room is only used for entertaining guests. Or ask him about his beautiful wife. You will find out that she is the third Mrs. Partner and that the lawyers for the first two Mrs. Partners are driving him crazy. Or ask him about those beautiful children whose photographs are everywhere. You will find out that they live with their mothers, not with him; that he never sees one of them because she hates his guts; and that he sees the other two only on holidays—that is, when he is not working on the holidays, which isn't often. And then ask him when is the last time he read a good book. Or watched television. Or took a walk. Or sat on his porch. Or cooked a meal. Or went fishing. Or did volunteer work. Or went to church. Or did anything that was not in some way related to work.

This is the best advice I can give you: Right now, while you are still in law school, make the commitment—not just in your head, but in your heart—that, although you are willing to work hard and you would like to make a comfortable living, you are not going to let money dominate your life to the exclusion of all else. And don't just structure your life around this negative; embrace a positive. Believe in something—care about something—so that when the culture of greed presses in on you from all sides, there will be something inside of you pushing back. Make the decision now that you will be the one who defines success for you—not your classmates, not big law firms, not clients of big law firms, not the *National Law Journal*. You will be a happier, healthier, and more ethical attorney as a result.

* * *

True, Schiltz's concern is about lawyers and, in particular, lawyers in big law firms. Yet, when it comes to issues of competitiveness and thirst for money, would we expect that other business organizations are all that different? What is your experience with firms, and especially, their subtle message of what one needs to do to fit in? How about your college or university? Do they count work outside of big corporations? (Actually, because entrepreneurship is so popular in business schools, students from MBA and BBA programs do have a decent shot of having their aspirations being valued but doing so requires conscious effort in making sure those values suffuse the business.) Does the competition, the culture signaling, the money, the work ring bells? Do companies lie in their recruiting practices as Schiltz alleges of law firms? What signals do companies give to you in their recruiting or during their internship? As Schiltz argues, it is not just the hard signals during the day that matter; it is also the soft signals of what one has to do—your attire, your car, your living space—that also can get wrapped for what counts and how the culture defines what is important.

Many of the things Schiltz uses to characterize big law firms were also used to characterize firms like Enron, so lest you think that business students are immune from the kinds of organizational, culture pressures Schiltz describes, the following interview of Robert Jackall, who wrote a famous book entitled *Moral Mazes*, demonstrates that these these issues persist in corporations as well. Notice in this interview with Jackall how his research finds that accountability is often completely absent. One might think that a business organization would have strong structures specifying accountability, but large corporations are political organizations with diffuse responsibilities for a given project. Credit and blame can be arbitrarily assigned and that makes a difference for whether people in the organization believe their actions make a difference....or not.

Interview with Robert Jackall

Hervé Laroche. EMJ, Editor

ROBERT JACKALL is the Class of 1956 Professor of Sociology & Public Affairs at Williams College and the founding Director of the Williams in New York program (www.williams.edu/go/newyork). He is the author of Workers in a Labyrinth (1978); *Moral Mazes: the World of Corporate Managers* (1988); *Wild Cowboys: Urban Marauders & the Forces of Order* (1997); *Image Makers: Advertising, Public Relations, and the Ethos of Advocacy* (2000, with Janice M. Hirota); *Street Stories: the World of Police Detectives* (2005), and many essays and reviews, including "Moral Mazes: Bureaucracy and Manage-rial Work" (1983), which received a McKinsey Award from the *Harvard Business Review*. He is the editor of *Worker Cooperatives in America* (1984, with Henry M. Levin), *Propaganda* (1995), the book series *Main Trends of the Modern World* (1995— present, with the late Arthur J. Vidich), and of the forthcoming collection of essays by German émigré Hans Speier, *Intellektuelle und Moderne Gesellschaft* (2007). He is currently working on a book entitled *The Demonics of Terror & Bureaucracy*, based on fieldwork with counter-terrorism experts. His undergraduate syllabus on violence won an international competition sponsored by the Harry Frank Guggenheim Foundation in 1998.

Q What is it that corporate managers do?

A Although managers' specific tasks vary depending on the industries in which they work, managers are always administrative experts whose essential functions are to coordinate substantive experts whose knowledge and skills create value and to direct interpretive experts whose expertise with symbols makes that value publicly known, both inside and outside an organization.

Q You study occupational communities. In addition to this book on managers, you've written about men and women in advertising and public relations; police detectives; public prosecutors and judges. Why did you choose to study managers and what's particularly important about their world?

A All of my studies are part of a larger project. This is a long-term examination of the social, institutional, cultural, moral, and epistemological foundations of modern American society, seen through ethnographic studies of occupations and professions. Each study focuses on a different piece of the larger puzzle. The study of managers explores how bureaucracy shapes moral consciousness by examining corporate managers' occupational moral rules-in-use, that is, their occupational ethics. Managers constitute the quintessential bureaucratic work group in modern society because they both create bureaucratic rules and are bound by them. To the extent that bureaucracy is a key organizational form of modernity, to that extent managerial work yields insights into today's experience of human affairs in general.

Q What is the "managerial ethos?" What are the key forces within the corporation that form it?

A By "managerial ethos," I mean the particular habits of mind and accompanying social behaviour that corporate bureaucracies foster by placing premiums on some attitudes and actions, and not on others. Corporations want men and women who are smart, quick-witted, well-dressed, cool under pressure, ambitious, team players willing to subordinate themselves to their bosses' judgments, capable of discerning 'what has to be done' in particular situations, adroit enough to avoid trouble or to extricate themselves from it quickly, and morally flexible, able and willing to live with constant ambiguity. Corporations generally get lots of those kinds of people precisely because of how they are structured, that is, as hierarchical, but interlinked, layers of men and women bound to each other through personal and social ties, common work experiences, and political alliances. In corporations, people look up and they look around for cues on what to think and how to behave. If you don't do that, you don't get very far and, generally, you don't last very long. It's important to note that this is an entirely voluntary process. People submit themselves to such a regimen and internalize the managerial ethos because they want to get ahead and reap the rewards that come with that.

Q You say that the "world of corporate managers" is marked by, among other traits, "self rationalization, emotional aridity, psychic asceticism, and narcissism." Can you comment on the development of such traits?

A This follows on the remarks I just made. Self-rationalization, Karl Mannheim's conceptual extension of Max Weber's larger treatment of rationalization as the key process of modern society, means simply self-streamlining. One looks for, recognizes, and internalizes the premiums stressed in a given organization or situation. Then one moulds one's public face, external behaviour, and projection of attitudes, all to fit the expectations embedded in those premiums in the hopes of garnering the rewards promised. Not everybody wants to or can do this. Some drop out entirely or accept a fixed role in an organization that doesn't require this kind of relentless subjection of self to others' expectations. But there are always some people who do respond to organizational premiums for self-rationalization and they make themselves into the men and women that their organizations desire and require. It's my observation that those who persevere in such self-rationalization are generally highly self-conscious men and women who are used to guarding their emotions and expressions of sentiment. Generally speaking, they shield themselves from others. And they see themselves as lead actors in a drama, even as they simultaneously watch that drama from front-row seats.

Q Would you see the Enron case or similar scandals as a consequence of the moral mazes that managers get lost in?

A I gave a talk at the University of Notre Dame right after the Enron story broke. The talk was entitled "Take the Money En Ron". There are a few key recurring observations in Moral Mazes that speak to what happened at Enron and at many other corporations caught up in public scandals. First, corporations foster in their managers a short-term mentality, best characterized by the old joke among salesmen: "I know what you did for me yesterday, but what have you done for me lately?" Or, as one manager said to me, "Our horizon is today's lunch." There's no mystery to this. People think in the short term because their bosses expect short-term, immediate results.

Second, there is no tracking system for credit or blame in the big corporation, none whatsoever. Credit or blame depends on where one happens to be located when something good or bad happens. So one has the phenomenon of "being in the right place at the right time" or, its sad opposite, of "being in the wrong place at the wrong time."

Third, when there is short-term pressure and no measurable accountability for one's actions, one might as well "take the money and run" when money is there to be taken. So, with few exceptions, one doesn't think of the long-run needs of the organization or, even less, of the world outside of the organization that might be affected by one's actions. One comes to focus on the here and now. Within such a framework, even smart, well meaning people lose track of things. Looking closely at the Enron catastrophe, one can argue that anyone with any inside knowledge of the corporation's operations either knew or should have known that something was terribly wrong. Instead, it took a young journalist, Bethany McLean, a 1992 alumna of Williams College, to say after a quick review: "Wait, the numbers simply don't add up." How could so many smart, talented people preside for so long over what was in the end an elaborate Ponzi scheme? Well, if people are judged only by quick returns, if they are not held accountable for the long-run consequences of their actions, then "take the money and run" becomes an occupational virtue.

Q Today's organizations are highly preoccupied with ethics. What do you think of the efforts they make and widely advertise?

A Ethics Incorporated, as I call it, became big business in the aftermath of the 1980s' Wall Street scandals. The ethics industry provides a lot of work for under-employed moral philosophers and for some lawyers with a philosophical bent. One whole wing of Ethics Incorporated specializes in writing codes of ethics for corporations. Another wing specializes in giving ethics seminars and courses to ombudsmen or compliance officers in corporations. Still another wing works closely with established business advocacy groups such as the Business Roundtable to institute simultaneously "ethical standards" for different sectors of the business community and, of course, to convince lawmakers, regulators, United States attorneys, and other major players in the business world that business is regulating itself and needs no help from outside authorities.

It's important to note that Enron, along with virtually every other major corporation, had an elaborate and well publicized "code of ethics" long before the company fell apart. Such corporate codes of ethics can demonstrate how skilled the corporation's advisers or public relations personnel are. But there's no necessary connection between a corporation's public pronouncements of its virtuousness and the day-to-day moral rules-in-use of its executives and managers.

Q You described the modern corporation as a hybrid bureaucracy— that is, a combination of rationalized structures and personalized ties. It is often taken for granted that business organizations have changed a lot in the last 20 years: decentralized, flattened, downsized, reengineered, streamlined, computerized, outsourced. What do you think about these transformations and to what extent have they actually affected the nature of the corporation?

A My primary field sites—a major chemical company that was a subsidiary of an industrial conglomerate, a major United States textile firm, and a major public relations firm—all exemplified the kind of "patrimonial bureaucracy" that I describe. By this term, I mean a hierarchical structure permeated by close personal ties. The most important of these was shared occupational experiences in the same organization. Cohorts of managers who came up through the same divisions in an organization and who shared similar views of what the organization was and should become constituted the primary networks of affiliation that determined organizational fates. If one member of a particular cohort prevailed in the struggle for ascendancy in a corporation, he— and these organizations had almost entirely male managerial hierarchies—almost always reached back to the cohort from which he came for colleagues in the new order that he established. The saying was: "He feels comfortable with these guys." Members of other cohorts were expendable, especially in a time of upheaval and cutbacks.

I've not done extensive fieldwork in newly decentralized organizations. So it's an empirical question to be investigated as to whether occupationally shaped personal ties are as salient in decentralized organizations as those I observed in hierarchical organizations. But on the basis of many conversations with men and women in such decentralized organizations, I'd say that personal ties might be even more important than they are in big hierarchies.

It's also important to note that "decentralization" may be more apparent than real. I am a close observer of one supposedly decentralized, self-governing organization whose workforce consists almost entirely of highly trained professionals. There the CEO continually launches new initiatives in response to needs articulated by some faction in the organization. He establishes elaborate new committees to carry out those initiatives. Those committees work long and hard to produce reports and recommendations. The CEO receives these with acclaim and appreciation, and then promptly moves on to address new crises with yet new committees. The years pass by and the reports on different subjects pile up into small mountains. The recommendations are passed on to still other committees for consultation. Most recommendations die quietly and in a few years become distant memories. The constant turmoil of committee work makes outsiders, and most newcomers to the organization, think that the organization is actually democratic and decentralized. In fact, the "decentralization" cloaks the CEO's and his coterie's centralized direction of the organization.

Q Do you think that female managers are different or do they behave differently?

A We don't have a lot of data about female managers in large industrial corporations so this too remains an empirical question to be investigated. But some businesses, in particular publishing, public relations, and increasingly advertising, are now thoroughly feminized. On the basis of my own close observation of those worlds, women's behaviour there is no different from the behaviour described in *Moral Mazes*.

Moreover, one need look no further than American colleges and universities, all now as thoroughly bureaucratized as the corporations, to explore in depth the question of how female managers/professionals behave in organizations. Because women were largely excluded from the upper levels of corporations until fairly recently, they entered the academy in great numbers and became a powerful force there, especially in the humanities and social sciences divisions and in various deans' offices. What does one find in the academy? One sees identical patterns to those described in

Moral Mazes. Particularly apt examples are internal political struggles involving, say, gender or sexual orientation study programs or promotion of colleagues who specialize in these matters. In such cases, one can readily observe: cronyism based on personal affinities and shared perspectives; the consequent abandonment of universalistic criteria for judging the work of colleagues, including the approbation of specious scholarship provided that it conforms to requisite "progressive" norms; the mobilizing of bloc voting to enforce one's group's will and destroy perceived enemies; adeptness at inconsistency, particularly the use of moralistic rhetoric to keep opponents off balance and on the defensive; and, of course, the requisite ruthlessness necessary to triumph in organizational struggles. The behaviour of managers/professionals does not turn on gender or, for that matter, sexual orientation, race, or ethnicity. Instead, it turns on the extent to which managers/professionals, driven by personal ambitions, subject themselves to the exigencies of their particular organizations. Such ambitious people are always alert to the precariousness of organizational life and they surround themselves with others who, they think, will support them, especially when things go awry.

Q In *Moral Mazes,* you write that "managerial moralities are always situational, always relative." Isn't this a more general characteristic of modern societies?

A Corporate managers are the true revolutionaries of our age, despite their modest, well-mannered, well-dressed, outwardly conservative demeanors and quietly expressed views. They are the shapers, harbingers, and principal carriers of the situational, relativistic moral ethos that defines the modern epoch.

Exactly because of debacles like Enron, Congress passed laws to put incentives on companies to develop "organizational culture" that attends to "ethics as well as compliance." This is important. As we have already seen, in 1984, Congress passed the Federal Sentencing Guidelines. These Guidelines provide instructions to federal judges as to the severity of sentences that should be handed down to those convicted of a federal crime. If you listen to CNN when a famous or notorious criminal is sentenced, you will likely hear a commentator saying that the expected sentence in such a case would be such and such. His or her prediction is most likely coming from the Federal Sentencing Guidelines. In 2004, Congress amended the Guidelines so that now, corporations seeking the benefits the financial benefits from the Guidelines must aim to create "organizational cultures" that lead to "ethics" as well as compliance. This means that the culture of organizations is legally important now as well. Moreover, as we also saw from the *Caremark* case, having an effective compliance program is necessary for the Board of Directives to uphold its obligations to the company's shareholders.[2]

Exxon, Enron, and BP provide the basis for doubting the possibilities of ethical business culture. Then again, there are times when companies seem to get things right. No case in the history of business ethics is as celebrated as Johnson & Johnson's response to the tainting of Tylenol in 1982.

Johnson & Johnson pulled all the product off the shelves nationwide within days, even though the company had seemed to do nothing wrong. Indeed, pulling the product off the shelves was a curious decision: isn't that the same as admitting guilt? But J&J's President James Burke said the company could not live up to its Corporate Credo, which placed the well-being of customers first among the companies list of obligations and aspirations (followed by employees, suppliers, community, government, and finally shareholders), by doing otherwise.

In the long run (actually, in the medium run), the decision turned out to be a brilliant defense of the Tylenol brand, and the case remains the single brightest light of corporate responsibility in public annals. J&J's reputation was burnished and, in talking to J&J employees, one had to be struck by how seriously they reported the Credo to be to the company and how it saturated the culture.

This is not to deify J&J. Over the years, things have seemed to slide at Johnson & Johnson. There were more recalls and lawsuits and questions about J&J's business practices. This became so much an issue that the Board of Directors was sued by some shareholders in a derivative suit demanding that the Board institute practices to return the company to its ethical culture. While the Board never admitted wrongdoing, they did reach a settlement with the shareholders, below, which interestingly shows not just the ethical importance of corporate culture, but the *legal* importance of ethical corporate culture.[3]

Empirical studies have also now been undertaken to determine what makes for effective compliance programs. In a series of articles written by Linda Trevino, Gary Weaver and Phillip Cochran, they identify two key factors were found that were crucial to an effect compliance program.

The first concerned whether a common set of standards applied throughout the organization. If employees perceived that there were a set of standards for high-ranking officials in the organization and another set of standards for the rank-and-file, the compliance program was not as effective. This led to a second, related, finding that procedural justice issues were the most important factors in creating an effective compliance

---

2   *In Re* Caremark International, Inc., 698 A.2d 959 (Del. Ch. 1996).

3   United States District Court, District Of New Jersey *In Re* Johnson & Johnson Derivative Litigation Civil Action No. 10-2033 (FLW) *In Re* Johnson & Johnson FCPA Shareholder Derivative Litigation.

program. That is, whatever the particulars of a company's program, its effectiveness mainly depending on whether the standards were enforced.

Effective compliance, then, is not simply the drafting of rules and having employees sign a statement that they have received and read the applicable rules, though that may be a step in the compliance process. Effective compliance has been empirically shown to be depending on other factors as well. Complicating things further were a set of amendments to the Guidelines in 2004 that mandated that these programs should create "organizational cultures" leading to "ethics" as well as legal compliance. With these, the ante was further upped for companies to go beyond legal minimums and to consider how to create ethical corporate cultures in order to meet the applicable legal requirement of creating effective compliance programs.

Discussion Questions:

1. How different are your values from an important community to which you belong, such as your family or an important campus organization (a fraternity, sorority, team, or music group)?

2. What are these organizations' blind spots? How do these blind spots differ from or are similar to those of BP, Exxon, or Enron?

3. What should be done when corporate culture goes awry? To be sure, changing a culture is a leadership responsibility, but can leaders who are not in formal positions also make a difference? In other words, even if you are not the CEO, what might an employee do to improve the culture?

4. John Mackey, CEO of Whole Foods, argues that every business person (especially entrepreneurs and including employees) has an objective in working in addition to making money. What's yours?

CHAPTER 11

Ethical Business Culture

A T THE END of Part II, we saw an article by Ed Hartman on the importance of virtue and its relationship to the organization. In a similar article, Hartman compared a corporation to a commons, with much the same importance for virtues. Fellow Aristotelian, Robert w, endorsed Hartman's argument, but in the following article, Solomon seeks to make the idea of business being a community more central, an idea that this Chapter will build upon in identifying possibilities for positive business culture.

———

The Corporation As Community: A Reply to Ed Hartman[4]

Robert C. Solomon

Robert Solomon,
University of Texas at Austin.
Photo: Ted S. Warren.

What is a corporation? Ed Hartman momentarily hesitates, commenting that "the last thing we need is another metaphor for organizations." The truth is that we can all too easily imagine—and will no doubt get—much worse than another metaphor or model for organizational structures, functions and behavior, but the critical question is, of course, how apt a metaphor is "the corporation as commons"? excitement about a subject can be measured by the number of current metaphors—witness the current overuse and abuse of the "information superhighway" image—then the nature of the corporation would still seem to be a vibrant topic. But whether a metaphor depicts business organizations as teams playing games, as free-for-alls, as military hierarchies or as "dog-eat-dog" jungles makes all the difference, not only in our understanding of organizations but in the way that the people in those organizations understand themselves and, consequently, behave and treat one another.

Hartman suggests that corporations and other large organizations are a lot like, in fact are (at least metaphorically) identical to, "a commons." This is, admittedly, not a very pretty or exciting metaphor. It is rather rural for such an urbane subject, and the metaphor of sheep farming may suggest some unintended and unfortunate images in

4   ©1994. *Business Ethics Quarterly*, Volume 4, Issue 3. ISSN 1052-150X. 0271-0285.

the corporate world. But, nevertheless, the metaphor of "the commons" has the virtue of being an old, rather established philosophical and political metaphor. Indeed, it is so well established that it is no longer considered to be a metaphor. Literally, the commons is publicly owned land on which any villager's sheep may graze. It is obviously a finite resource, and its maintenance is in the interests of all.

But the commons is not just a piece of shared public property. It is so fundamentally because it is understood to be such by those who share it, and that raises a number of often neglected issues about the nature of that shared understanding. Is it simply taken for granted, rather thoughtlessly, as just "the way things are," the way a fish takes for granted the water as its natural medium, or more appropriate, as the sheep take the grass? Very likely, when the population is small, the common is large and lush and habits and traditions rather than philosophy and strategic thinking dictate the attitudes. Could the commons rather be conceived of as the product of a tacitly negotiated agreement, perhaps "a social contract," in which each farmer agrees to restrain his use of the commons to protect the general interest? Yes, but this represents a rather advanced and not entirely happy form of thinking in which personal self-interest and the likelihood of mutual conflict have already come into focus and the dangers of depletion are clearly in view. Could the commons be viewed as shared, not with a suspicious eye to possible exploitation but with a real shared concern for its preservation, above all, perhaps because of its social rather than narrowly economic significance, because of its aesthetic and symbolic importance to the community? Again the answer is yes, but here the attitudes involved, whether or not articulated as such, display a more profound appreciation of the nature of the commons, one in which, most likely, the commons will continue to flourish. Such understanding presupposes a certain amount of reflection, and it has a kind of moral significance. Preservation and cultivation of the commons is a virtue, not just a matter of long-term mutual advantages.

I applaud Hartman's metaphorical analysis of corporations as organizations in which morality and the virtues are essential, in which reflection plays an important role and the definitive ties are emotional, not legal or merely prudential. I also share his Aristotelean viewpoint, that is to say, this emphasis on the virtues and their cultivation within a community, but, predictably, I think that he does move not far enough in that direction. The metaphor of the commons still smacks of compromised egoism and does not take into account what Arnita Etzioni, myself and many others have emphasized as the spirit of community as such. Indeed, what was most obvious to Aristotle (as to most of us) can be found in what he did not say, what he saw no need to say. Thus Aristotle talked very little about community as such; was simply the framework of his thinking. And Aristotle talked very little about self-interest, not that he didn't (as we all do) witness greed and avarice firsthand but rather because he didn't see such behavior as what we call self-interest. It was rather a vice, a defect in character, *pleonexia*, greed or "grasping." But this isn't an essay on Aristotle and Greek ethics—Professor Hartman could provide that much better than It is an essay on the nature of corporations. And if I seem to disagree with Hartman on a number of points and paint the Aristotelean picture in a somewhat different way, that should not be construed as either vice or defect nor as a violation of our own shared sense of community.

The Corporation as Commons

The corporation is not just a "legal fiction," an instrument for consolidating and protecting capital and limiting liability. In the flesh, corporations are organizations of people, people with (more or less) shared assets and interests. Legally, a corporation may exist apart from its people, but in any meaningful or practical sense a corporation is its people. This includes, of course, the stockholders, although the notion of "stock" once again takes on an unfortunate ambiguity in light of the metaphor of the commons. But any corporation—apart from those individual enterprises for whom incorporation is no more than a tax strategy—lends itself to the commons metaphor insofar as it consists of shared assets and interests and therefore requires collective understanding, a shared sense of purpose and cooperation.

Corporations, like public land, can be simply taken for granted, rather thoughtlessly, as just "the way things are." Life in many American corporations was very much like this, only a few decades ago, before global competition, hostile takeovers, leveraged buy-outs and epidemic "downsizing" virtually killed that sense of security which defined corporate life for many a "corporation man," in the old sociology's now dated terminology. The corporation was a shared community with shared wealth and shared purposes and responsibilities, and one entered into a corporation much as one entered into a traditional community, by quickly assimilating and internalizing its traditions, customs and expectations. One did not show "constraint" so much as one simply did what was expected of him. It would have been a rare and already pathological case in which a new manager or employee had to quash selfish impulses in order to do his job. What one wanted, in the standard case, was to "fit in," to be accepted, and to be recognized, eventually, for a job well done. In return for taking the existence and interests of the corporation for granted, one could, for the most part, take one's job for granted as well.

Today, of course, that idealized picture has radically changed. More and more employers are talking the language of "employment at will," which is strategically presented as the worker's right to quit but, in this economy, virtually always refers to the employer's right to fire or, according to one of today's many noxious euphemisms, "make redundant." In virtually every industry, and at virtually every level, no job is secure. Thus contingency replaces security, and contingency plans take the place of what once was called loyalty. Nothing is left to trust. Clear and explicit understandings are demanded where mere member ship once sufficed. No wonder that the language of so many editorials and business ethics books favors the philosophical language of "the social contract"—that mythical, primal agreement when mutually suspicious and competitive men and women decided to live together in society, giving up certain rights and powers but gaining a modicum of security and cooperation in return. Never mind that the myth is nonsense, and never mind that the nonsense is subject to radically different understandings and interpretations. The point is rather that such talk represents a response to a social catastrophe, the loss of precisely those tacit understandings and agreements according to which pre-historical (pre-contractual) societies did manage to live together in all sorts of complex organizations.

Among its several other liabilities, social contract theory tends to be radically ahistorical, and not only in the technical sense that Robert Nozick charges against his colleague John Rawls, that is, because it doesn't take adequate ac count of prior claims, rights and inequalities. It is also ahistorical in the much graver sense that it doesn't recognize that it is itself the product of a very special (and quite unhappy) historical circumstance, the disintegration of the commons, or in business, the moral collapse of the traditional notion of the corporation. To employ such a metaphor in defense of the commons and the corporation is, therefore, a mixed blessing at best. The fact that it is almost always so defended by tenured academics, who are the one group not (thus far) prone to the insecurity gripping the rest of the working world, makes it all the more suspicious.

Is it desirable to view the corporation as a commons? Perhaps, but it is a real community as well. It is not just commonly shared land, as is a commons. A community involves, first and foremost, the people who share that land. Community is not to be simply taken for granted (no one can afford that luxury anymore) and in or out of the corporation community is not ordinarily viewed as a primarily economic and contractual device either. Hartman's metaphor betrays this traditional economist's bias, even though he follows it up with more Aristotelean considerations. His is a strong *moral* conception of the corporation. But such significance cannot be squeezed from the thin concept of the commons, only from the ethically rich concept of community. Of course, there are both good and bad, successful and unsuccessful, benign and evil communities. But all communities have what Hegel called *ethical substance,* holding them together. Obligation, responsibility and loyalty are essential to community. A certain amount of freedom is certainly required, including, presumably, the freedom to leave or "exit" the community. But this is not what defines community, and emphasizing the freedom to leave ("love it or leave it") tends both to neglect the strong bonds of membership involved and too readily lends itself, once again, to an implicit social contract metaphor, in which a community is nothing more than mutual agreements which can, under certain conditions, be annulled. is certainly not enough that one can exit. One wants to know the nature of the virtues that entice one to stay.

Nor is it clear how a commons as such encourages reflection. A conniver may come to see the commons in a game-theoretical way, forcing everyone else to either stop him in his tracks or hare his degenerate mentality, but this is hardly the same as moral sensibility. A crisis or impending depletion may stimulate collective concern for the preservation of the commons, but it does not follow that the people who thus share this concern will also reflect on themselves, their relationship and their behavior. It is certainly not evident that mutual self-interest will inspire loyalty, fellow-feeling or any number of other, community-related emotions. If anything, mere mutual self-interest-which is very different from shared concern-would suggest the pure contingency of cooperation and loyalty. A commons as a piece of shared property, in other words, gives us very little to go on, for it says very little or nothing about the relationships between the people who share the commons. In a corporation, relationships between people, whether of affection, friendship, loyalty, power, position or expertise, define the organization. Social contract theory only muddles this picture because it suggests, almost always falsely, that the primary relationships involved are predominantly contractual. This is a sure way to misunderstand the notion that corporations are communities.

This suggestion that corporations are communities is often willfully misunderstood. The idea is not, as I so often hear (with that familiar ring of sarcasm), "should a corporation and its executives then forget about profits, ignore the legitimate expectations of the shareholders and simply make themselves and their employees happy, enjoying the corporate life with all of its perks and advantages?" (One thinks of the scandalous stories of E. Hutton, in the days before its collapse.) The question betrays a failure to understand the notion of community, which, according to Alasdair Macintyre as well as Aristotle, presumes some higher purpose, a *teleology*, which includes the cultivation and improvement (by whatever standards) of its members as well as its own perpetuation. One of the purposes of a corporation—by no means the only one but the one that is most often ripped out of context and overly-celebrated—is profit. Indeed, one might even argue that corporations need profits the way people need air, but that doesn't mean that one should go around thinking about nothing but breathing all the time. Profits may be "the bottom line," but that should be read as a ground for doing what the corporation is doing rather than the ultimate purpose to which all corporate and individual activities should be driven. Nor man Bowie popularized an ancient philosophical paradox some years ago as "the profit-making paradox." Just as the ancient philosophers noted that one should not try to become happy by intently trying to be happy but rather by living a good life and doing what one is supposed to do and does well—from which happiness will emerge "like the bloom of youth,"—corporations that fixate on the bottom line and ignore the interests and concerns of their employees, their customers and the surrounding community are often doomed to fail. Talk about community is not antagonistic to making a profit. It is, in any successful corporation, rather one of its prerequisites.

The new wisdom, in the wake of the recent calamities, is that if a company takes care of its employees, satisfies its customers and acts as a good citizen of the community, it will flourish. Thus a new and radical concept has entered into and virtually taken over corporate life, *values*. To talk about values is to say that there are certain activities and ways of behaving that are *worth* doing, not just for the sake of some other end (e.g., profits), but for themselves. The paradox, of course, is that such action for its own sake, in the context of a properly-structured organization, will achieve these other ends as well. Looking at the corporation as a community, looking after the well-being of employees and the emotional health of one's managers, going the extra bit to satisfy customers and insisting on being a good citizen are not just supererogatory luxuries which successful corporations can afford. They are the prerequisites of a successful corporation. Thinking in terms of values is thinking of the corporation in a different way, not as a culture with a tradition whose origin and nature need not be explained or justified, not as a network of legal agreements about who will do what and for how much and how long. It is to share a tradition whose purpose is reflection and self-understanding. "This is what we stand for." It is to question that tradition and current practices that do not measure up to the values that one recognizes according to that same tradition and the traditions of business and community in general. It is to look beyond one's legal obligations to one's personal responsibilities, to the unwritten and perhaps unspoken customs and policies of the company, the shared values and understandings that define the organization. This is the key to success in the nineties, and this is the importance of Hartman's metaphor of "the commons." But let us call it by its proper ethical, not agrarian name. It is the sense of community, and citizenship in the larger community as well.

What is a Community?

One of the running arguments that dominates social and political philosophy runs on the rails of a false polarity whose names are "liberalism" and "communitarianism." There are many other alternative views, of course, but now that the socialists have (if only temporarily) discredited themselves and libertarians, sometimes with a six figure income and a five-watt imagination, tend to ignore or dismiss any form of community outside of Ivy walls anyway, academic discussions tend to stick to the rails, inviting an occasional Marxist and/or libertarian for some welcome relief from the tedium. Liberals, of course, are by no means in agreement about what they stand for, and even the name went into eclipse as a *Schlimmwort* during most of the last decade. John Rawls' much-admired treatise was picked to pieces and, though still admired, largely abandoned as a practical model of communities. Not surprisingly, the focus has shifted to the communitarians. I mention this not just as an excuse to toss off a couple of political insults but in order to distinguish what I am arguing here from this more popular alternative.

For many communitarians, the celebrated concept of "community" is too often kept immune from analysis, covered in a mystical haze, as often as not described or even defined in religious terminology. So disguised, who could be against "commu-nity"? But what kind of community are we talking about—a primeval prehistorical tribe? a small puritanical New England town? a university community? an association such as the Rotarians, the Optimists or the local chapter of the NRA or the Ku Klux Klan? An awful lot of oppression, small-mindedness, blind uncritical loyalty and down-right evil can slip into the discussion under the guise of "community." Such abstract talk of "community" all-too-often resembles the recent discussion of the politically-explosive phrase, "traditional family values." (The two often go together.) Who could be against traditional family values? is neither tradition nor family nor values that are in question, but rather the very narrow and sometimes malignant agenda that gets hidden behind that innocent phrase, condemnation and persecution of homosexuals, de facto economic sanctions against single parent families, the assumption that every-one is or ought to be a member of a narrowly designated church-going Protestant com-munity. "Community" has become a buzz-word, an excuse for the persecution and/or exclusion of minorities, a plea for protection, a demand for immunity and isolation, a warm and cozy metaphor for some mythical extended family left over from the com-mune days of the late sixties. (No wonder Hartman hedges his bets with "commons.")

Michael Sandel attacks John Rawls for two hundred pages in the name of "com-munity" without ever suggesting what a community might be. Alasdair Macintyre has written three rather brilliant books attacking liberalism in the name of traditions and communities[2]. His most recent and protracted discussion focusses on the nature of alternative forms of "practical reason," which threatens to turn the notion of com-munity into an intellectual concern, properly stressing the importance of reflection (even in non-philosophical communities) but nevertheless neglecting the prereflective substance—his discussion of the virtues—to which his best book, *After Virtue*, was devoted. To make matters all the more confusing, Macintyre denies being a "com-munitarian," on the good grounds that "there are good and bad communities." But he thus gives us little help in under standing his project. Charles Taylor has written a great deal on communities and the formation of the self in communities, but, again, he remains very much on the high intellectual plain and one is left with the impression that communities are ultimately to be defined only in terms of such intangibles as the Hegelian Geist, an appealing suggestion for some of us, perhaps, but hardly a help in the more mundane analysis of the corporation and its nature.

A community is, first of all, an open-ended and immensely complex set of rela-tionships between its members, who may, within that context, be called "individuals." (An "individual" outside of any and all communities, a staple hero of American folk-lore, tends to be a pathological and often pathetic creature, hardly the ontological unit out of which societies are supposedly composed by way of "contract.") A corporation is about as well-defined and tangible as a community can be. The particular individuals may come and go. Indeed, in that sense the corporation is rarely the same from one day to the next. But the relationships, always forming, being reinforced and reforming, even in the midst of traumatic "restructuring," retain a certain resiliency. And they are by no means, as communitarians often imply, relationships between equals or between people who are essentially the same. Indeed, let's make this point loud and clear: communities and the spirit of community are fundamentally concerned with complementarity and differences, out of which emerge relationships of reciprocity and cooperation. The corporate budget, and for that matter even the organizational chart, are entirely secondary to the flesh and blood exchanges that take place in the halls, offices and lunchrooms of the corporation. These relationships consist, first of all, in a shared sense of belonging, a shared sense of mission or, at least, a shared sense of mutual interest. To say that a corporation is a community is, then, to say nothing mysterious. It is to say that the corporation consists primarily of its people, its share-holders and its customers as well as its executives, managers and employees. Like Hegel's Geist, it also includes its products and means of production, its buildings and its other assets, but more as a matter of identity and expression than as independent and merely dead "matter." The corporation might be viewed as a commons in the sense that virtually all of its people have, in some more or minimal sense, private lives, lives outside of the company, but they share the bulk of their waking time and energy and a major dependency on each other and the company and how well it flourishes. It is these multifaceted and complex relationships between people that raises the real questions about community and the nature of the "good" organizations, and this is what I find missing from Hartman's analysis. He is so focused on the relationship between the individuals and the organization that he overly neglects the psychodynamics that constitute communities.

People who join a corporation do not simply find themselves, once hired, members of a social collective. There is a conscientious effort, to become a member, to internalize the appropriate shared attitudes. One also comes to accept—or forces oneself to accept—the idea of being there indefinitely, or, at least, giving up the thought of leaving, of being somewhere else, of doing something else. This is where the importance of "exit" can too easily be misunderstood. It is an evil organization that allows no one to leave, but it does not follow that a good organization is not one which no one wants to leave. (John Grisham's *The Firm* comes to mind here.) People in corporations are rarely just "doing their job," and when we meet someone who does so, we know that their membership in the community is already compromised and their relationships antagonistic rather than cooperative. Nor is this membership merely a matter of mutual agreement, a fleshless theory that allows no recognition of the "spiritual" ties that are essential community. There is value, albeit somewhat opaque and pretentious, in the Hegelian notion of "Geist" or "spirit," which he uses to describe the shared self that holds together a family, a community, and ultimately all of humanity. But "spirit" here does not refer to "religion." rather refers to that sense of secular transcendence, of an entity larger than ourselves of which we are a part, and the sense of membership I get from most members of most corporations, even the not-so-good ones, is just this. But these need not stay on the level of a philosophical abstraction. Hartman rightly brings it down to earth (Aristotelean that he is) in terms of ordinary human emotions. To put a complex matter very simply, emotions are the ties of mutual identity that form any relationship, including community, which presupposes first of all a feeling of mutual identity (however hostile, envious or jealous as well).

Such feelings presuppose and include concepts, ways of thinking and judging, and these should not be thought of merely as "feelings" in the more vulgar sense, mere matters of felt warmth or tingles or any of those physiological disturbances that many philosophers (following Descartes) have called "agitations" and some psychologists (following William James) have called "bodily commotions." In the specific terms of the corporation, community is formed, as Hartman suggests, by virtue of a variety of mutual emotions, only one of which need be loyalty as such, but all of them have to do with a sense of personal identification. I am tempted to say that this includes the tendency to like and trust someone, just because they are part of the same organization, except this is prone to so many counter-examples. The tough point is, however, that insofar as distrust and dis like are pervasive in an organization, that organization will almost certainly prove to be dysfunctional. More on the level of sociology, however, even those corporations that are dysfunctional (by any reasonable measurement of efficiency and success) are defined by a surprisingly strong sense of camaraderie and sense of belonging. The alienation shows predictable fault lines, middle managers against one or two specific executives or upper management, manufacturing *versus* finance or sales *versus* accounting. What keeps the corporation going—and holds out the promise of a dramatic turnaround and success—is precisely that set of emotions, the "glue" that holds the organization together even when it may be falling apart.

The Problem of Self-Interest

The problem is that any of these views and attitudes towards the commons and toward one's corporation can be corrupted by the intrusion of self-interest. Self-interest is not the natural attitude which we bring to every situation and transaction. Self-interest, like compassion and cooperation, is cultivated and encouraged by the environment, by the culture, by the corporate culture in particular. One of the places in which I disagree with Hartman, despite our shared Aristotelean leanings, is the nature of that self-interest. I don't deny self-interest, of course. I see it all around me. (I see it in me.) But I think that self-interest is far more complex—along with the self that is interested—than Hartman suggests. But before we get into those weighty matters, let us just look at the damage that self-interest, Adam Smith's "invisible hand" aside, can do.

Any given individual can use the commons more or less, and thought might well have been raised to think in terms of fair or fixed allotments there can always appear that spark of evil energy that is the temptation to crowd all of one's sheep onto the commons, saving one's own land. Of course, if everyone did the same, the commons would soon be destroyed. The usual rationalization is that most of them will not do that. (This is the meaning but not the origin of the term, "free riding"—again, an unfortunate mix of metaphors, more appropriate to bus and subway riders than to sheep farmers.) The evil and eventually destructive solution to this problem is, "let's get there first." The result is the depletion of the commons, or the bankruptcy of the corporation. But too many writers write as if this degeneration is all but inevitable, unless of course, some Hobbesian lawyer steps into the chaos and suggests a contractual arrangement agreeable to all. I would suggest that this Hobbesian situation is rather the result of a communal breakdown, not the prior "state of nature" Hobbes (and many others) make it out to be. The notion of self-interest enters in as an intrusion, a destructive fragmentation of what was formerly and unchallenged system of "oughts" and expectations.

But according to the Hobbesian metaphor, we face a range of familiar problems, most of them having to do with the false or only occasional antagonism between self-interest and the public good. raises all of those old philosophical questions about selfishness, altruism, "free riders" and collective prudence. The usual game-theoretical plot unfolds: if everyone is a rational self-maximizer, they will rush to get their sheep out on the commons first. Disaster, not to mention sheep grid-lock, will ensue. On the other hand, if other people are cooperative and restrained, one might easily take advantage of them. But there are much deeper questions that are too rarely asked in the search for new and ingenious solutions to the free rider problem: in what kind of a society is free riding to be worried about, is it rational or even imaginable to free ride? Too many economists, and at times Hartman, I fear, take rational self-interest to be a given, indeed, the very meaning—if only part of the meaning—of rationality.

In an article on Buddhist ethics, Joel Kopperman wisely points out that there are some ethical questions that simply should not be raised. Perhaps, at least often, the common question, "what's in for me?" is one of them. (Think of the destructive impact of that simple question in a marriage, for example.) And yet, we often debate as if that is the first (and only) question that people ask. The truth is, people more often ask, what am I supposed to do? More often than not, they don't ask any question at all. They just do what has to be done. On the commons, before the self-interested question appears, the farmers take out their sheep as routinely as the sheep do their grazing. They do not think, "how much can I get away with?" They do not think, "what would be the best for all?" And they certainly do not need an economist or a game theorist to straighten them out about their interests.

Of course, the economic model of self-maximization, like most uncritical economic models, fails to take into account the social dynamics of the small village. Common interest is not the same as simply "shared" or mutually-effected interest. The metaphor of the commons in fact points to a much grander philosophical metaphor, of community and shared identity, not only land and lamb food. Profit and self-interest undoubtedly play a role, even in sheep farming, but calculating self-interest does not even begin to compare with the social sanctions engendered by a bad reputation in the village. Your sheep may eat well at public expense, but you yourself will most likely not be invited to dinner for a long, long time.

This small slight against economic models is intended, in fact, as a deep rejection of a common way of thinking, a way of thinking in which the dilemma of the commons, and those games that game theories call "the prisoner's dilemma" (non-zero, non-cooperative games with considerable uncertainty) play an unfortunately central role. There is, of course, the by now rather established criticism that prisoner's dilemma models misleadingly emphasize the single game context. In business ethics, this would be tantamount to talking about corporate culture in terms of the snake-oil salesman passing through town. The fact is that virtually any business and every institution thrives (or not) on the basis of repeated exchanges with any number of "players," and the "one-shot deal" is almost never a fair example, even in such dubious and marginal contexts as mail-order shopping from the daily newspaper. ("Just send ten dollars …,") It is now also accepted, by most authors in the field, that in such repetitive competitive games the best strategy, both in terms of individual maximization and general optimality, is what Robert Axelrod calls the "tit-for-tat" strategy. That is, presume cooperation, but hit 'em hard if they cheat. The best strategy, in other words, is an efficient and judicious combination of cooperation and punishment.

That is the best strategy, that is, if you think in a way that only game theorists (at least when they are on the job) and a few psychopaths (on or off the job) actually think. What such talk of self-interest and the public good, maximization and optimality tend to leave out is the dimension of the social, where this does not just mean life as a game played with and against other people but, in a deeper "Aristotelean" sense, life embedded in and defined by a community. For stalwart individualists, this distinction, between life with a collection of other people and life as a member of a community, will seem like no distinction at all. But it is just this that the metaphor of "the commons" is meant to capture, and so I think it is unfortunate that it has become so bound up with sheep (who form a herd but hardly a community) and individual farmers who are part of a tight-knit community but are seriously misunderstood by the alienated urban philosophers who interpret them as individualistic self-maximizers. What means to be a part of a community is something more than cooperation, something more than having something ("a commons") in common. It is, among other things, to identify yourself and your interests in and with the community. It is. simply. to become a different person.

This does not mean, as rugged individualists and/or followers of Nietzsche would insist, that one gives up one's sense of autonomy and independence, that one becomes an anonymous drudge, foregoing personal ambition and wallowing in the pseudo-virtue of self-sacrifice. (Ayn Rand here.) And within the corporation. I shall argue, this does not mean that one gives up one's sense of moral autonomy and becomes a corporate drudge, caught up in what Robert Jackall calls "moral mazes" and incapable of making a decent decision. Perhaps the author that has seen this most clearly, or in any case most precociously, is the renowned "father of capitalism" Adam Smith, who perhaps also deserves credit as one of the parents of business ethics.

Adam Smith, Aristotelean

Adam Smith is best known, of course, for his *Wealth of Nations*, published in 1776. But he is also the author of *A Theory of the Moral Sentiments* (1759), and I have argued[1] that Smith himself was much closer to the Aristotelean viewpoint (as we might expect from his friendship with Hurne) than the Friedmanesque parodies and according to what Patricia Werhane calls "the prevailing view."Smith's notion of "self-interest" is not at all the self-maximizing sentiment that it is usually made out to be. is certainly not Hobbesian, nor even Rousseauian (that is, benign indifference rather than open hostility). is intrinsically social and a genuine source of pleasure for its own sake. Smith did not hold that radical individualist view to which so many of his colleagues in Great Britain and France subscribed. Adam Smith's theory of human nature was not at all the view of Thomas Hobbes. at whose feet so much of the current literature on the many virtues of selfishness and the rational need for a social contract have been laid. For Smith as for Hume, people are naturally social and benevolent.[3] They seek one another's approval and by nature "desire of being what ought to be approved of, or of being what he himself approves of in other men." They sympathize with each other's interests and misfortunes and care about the prosperity of all. Smith also displays a keen sense of justice, both in a personal and an institutional sense, and both, it must be said, militate against the individualist viewpoint. His personal virtue of justice is mainly negative, a natural aversion to harming others. But it is also a sense of fair play and, institutionally, justice is "the main pillar that upholds the whole edifice of society." Conservatives who invoke Smith's name may rail against "social justice," but Smith does not. In fact, what is "social justice," if not the "commons," that is, the shared wealth that is, ultimately, the province of all of us? It is justice that upholds the legitimacy of contracts, and the interpersonal virtues and society, not the isolated individual out to make a buck and believing as his excuse that some invisible hand will make it come out alright.

Smith does speak, of course, about self-interest, and one would be a fool not to recognize the prevalence of a certain competitive attitude, but more often in competitive times. But human nature must be understood, first of all. in terms of social solidarity and cooperation. It may be true. as Smith himself argues that self interest is our strongest motivating principle, but what this means is not that we are "selfish" or in any way antagonistic to one another. Our self-interest is constituted within society and tied to that system of virtues which make us good citizens and contribute to the well-being and happiness of others as well as to our own. Since for Smith, the primary ingredient in self-interest is not personal advantage as such but rather the desire for approval and the respect of our fellows. "Nature, when she formed man for society, endowed him with an original desire to please, and an original aversion to offend his brethren." It is the importance of the personal virtues that lead Smith to make the very Aristotelean claim, that acts of benevolence give us pleasure not because they serve our own interests but for their own sake.

The Examined Corporate Life: The Importance of Self-Reflection

"The unexamined life is not worth living," said Socrates. This is no doubt unfair, even outrageous. Trillions of animals have perfectly meaningful lives without a moment of self-examination, and the amount of reflection engaged in by most people is minuscule compared to the amount of effort they expend in self-deception. But it raises an important set of questions, first of all the nature of reflection, second the role of reflection in the moral—not the intellectual or the literary—life. As Aristotle pointed out, the prerequisite of a moral education is a good upbringing, being raised to act virtuously and celebrate the virtues before one could conceivably have any understanding of them. Indeed, a person who has to debate and wrestle within before acting properly has thereby already raised serious doubts about his or her virtue. Acting virtuously should be second nature. A salesman who has to think about whether or not to lie to a customer or a manager who has to think about whether or not to lie to an employee is less than virtuous even if he ends up telling the truth. (Of course, a salesman who can lie to a customer or a manager who can lie to an employee "by second nature" raises a different kind of question, but that does not concern us here.) But then what is the role of reflection and self-understanding in ethics? Sometimes (as in Aristotle), it seems like an intellectual afterthought. In cases of ethical conflict, however, reflection may well be necessary as a second order attempt to straighten out a first order confusion. But to limit reflection to such cases is surely to rob ethics and the moral aspects of the corporation of one of their most important dimensions.

It is into this Socratic-Aristotelean line of questioning that one might best understand Harry Frankfurt's now famous (in philosophy) notion of "second order desires." Such desires become manifest when one is wrestling with oneself about what one wants. But, then, doesn't this imply that when one is not wrestling, when one is simply doing what is expected of him or her, such reflection is unnecessary and, in fact undesirable? Doesn't reflection thus pose a threat to efficiency in an organization, a possible threat to its very existence where one's own values are clearly out of kilter with corporate expectations, a benign but nevertheless unnecessary bit of self-reinforcement when personal values and corporate expectations are in harmony? I think such questions throw into doubt the simple "two layer" conception of human reflection. It does, of course, make an important point, essential to virtually every philosopher (even Nietzsche, who ruthlessly challenged it.) The point is that we are creatures capable of reflection on our own emotions and motives, indeed, creatures who are virtually incapable of not reflecting on our own emotions and motives. But what this means is by no means simple, and I think Hartman's welcome emphasis on the importance of emotions makes this quite clear, particularly in the emotionally complex set of relationships that constitute the corporate community.

This notion of community and this complex relationship between personal ("self-interested") and social (but not "altruistic") desires suggest what is wrong with thinking in terms of first and second order desires. While desires can be shared, I would argue, the sense of desire that is so clearly indicated here (and exemplified in virtually every illustration of the thesis) is individual desire, personal desire. The thesis, which comes recently from Harry Frankfurt but is clearly evident in the writings of Aristotle and Confucius, is that what is important is not just what one wants but what one wants to want. (This is, in addition, part and parcel of Frankfurt's definition of "freedom," but that is not of great importance here.) But what one wants is too often taken as a fairly basic, even vulgar desire—the desire to have a cigarette is the most often used example—and the second order desire is too often taken as a merely prudential consideration, in terms of one's long term interests (one's health, for example). (The second most common example, used almost exclusively by men, is the [first order] desire to have an affair, which conflicts with the [second order] desire to "be faithful," to maintain one's marriage and one's moral reputation.)

It is to Hartman's credit that he expands this overly narrow focus to include the sorts of desires that one might properly call "social" desires, which means not only that they are cultivated in a certain culture or society but they involve and are concerned with that culture or society, what was once typically meant by the very word "socialization." To enter a corporation is to be socialized in just this way, which in Frankfurt's now-established jargon might be stated as being inculcated with the appropriate secondary desires (to fit in, to want what is good for the company) which in turn tend to encourage the right kind of first order desires (wanting to be accepted). The problem, first of all, is that the above examples make it fairly evident that the neat division between first and second order desires (like Locke's seemingly neat division between primary and secondary qualities) will not bear much weight or scrutiny. Except for those easy examples, where one desire is a physical craving and the other a somewhat sophisticated medical judgment or a powerful social prohibition, our desires do not fall neatly into hierarchical levels, and socialization—including the cultivation of the virtues—involves a dynamic psychosocial network of emotions, attachments, psychological needs, long-term prudential outlooks, very short-term threats of punishment, an evolving ability to empathize with others and under stand their perspectives and problems. Hartman's own examples make this quite evident, and I would suggest that while it is certainly valuable to emphasize the importance of how people talk and think about their desires and their behavior, the emphasis on levels only reinforces the already prevalent practice of overly separating thought and action, talk and behavior.

I think that such an emphasis also leads Hartman to overemphasize the distinction between rationality, which he tends in non-Aristotelean fashion to elevate to an impersonal ideal, and appeal to the emotions, which he unfortunately conflates at one point in his essay with brainwashing. I would suggest that an overly impersonal conception of rationality is precisely what leads "practical minded" people to what they inevitably call "realism" instead and results in the vulgarized notion of rationality as maximizing individual self-interest which is then taken for granted by economists and game theorists. On the other hand, there are both rational and irrational emotions, what Nietzsche called "life-enhancing" and "life stultifying passions," and one need not look very far to see how these function the corporate setting. Loyalty, fellow-feeling, pride in the company as well as in one's own work are obviously life-enhancing as well as enormously beneficial to the bottom line. Mutual distrust and envy, fear and resentment—not to mention moral outrage—are collectively life-stultifying and pave the road to bankruptcy. Impartiality and autonomy have their place, as Hartman rightly argues, but so do personal attachments, commitments and what Kant unflatteringly called "heteronomy" as well. The virtue of a virtue ethics such as Hartman's is precisely that it need not force an inhuman division be tween reason and the passions, prudence and collective interest. The practical importance of the concept of the commons—or better, community—is that it discourages those walls and barriers within companies that stimulate the wrong kind of competition (holding the other back rather than everyone doing his or her best), encourage envy and resentment and cause the stagnation that comes of mutual distrust and hostility.

And yet Hartman puts such distinctions to good use too, for example, when he emphasizes such Aristotelean questions as, "do I want to be motivated by this kind of consideration?" and "do I want to become the kind of person that this organization will surely make me?" But does he need different levels or "orders" of desire to encourage such reflection? Such distinctions also give him a way of distinguishing good organizations from bad ones, by appealing to an ideal rationality that transcends all organizations. But what is the difference between a good corporation and an awful one? Is it really a matter of internal reflection and loyalty or over-reaching rationality? I was thinking again, as I studied Hartman's essay, of John Grisham's popular novel, *The Firm*, in which a perfectly congenial and certainly successful law firm turns out to be a snake pit of corruption. Of course, due to the ingenious disloyalty of the book's hero, the scoundrels get their comeuppance. But, if we take away the obvious illegality that condemns the firm in the book, such examples make it much less clear where the goodness in organizations lies. There are organizations that are wonderful to work for but corrupting, even evil, nevertheless. There are organizations that offer very little by way of fun and fellowship, but they are certainly virtuous nonetheless. The connection between community and morality is not always so obvious.

One of the most important moral questions has not to do with the relationships and activities between people within the organization but relations with and impact upon those who are no part of the corporate community. Aristotle, after all, accepted and defended the institution of slavery. His conception of the virtues did not extend as far as that majority of the population who made his aristocratic life so leisurely and comfortable. That should always be a warning to Aristoteleans who put all of their emphasis on integrity within the company. One danger in thinking about the corporation as commons is that it leaves wide open any question about obligations and responsibilities to those who do not now share the commons. Thomas Aquinas was rather eloquent on this point, namely, that one has a duty to share what one has with those who have not. But the current emphasis on the privacy of property has overwhelmed this simple humanist attitude, and the history of many of the actual small towns on which Hartman's metaphor is based shows all too clearly the limits of local cooperation. So, too, many corporations. All too often, management sees itself as "the company," as opposed the employees, who merely "have jobs" there. And, of course, there is still that horrible, slow-to-die Gordon Gekko and T. Boone Pickens argument about the company consisting wholly of the stockholders. We have seen where that devil argument leads, although the alternative, I hope I have made amply clear, is not neglect of the stockholders, who are (and should think of themselves more as) moral members of the corporate community as well. If the corporation is to be a good community, it must be an all-embracing community.

One of the proper objections to communitarianism as often conceived is its implicitly exclusive nature. Internal fellow-feeling is a wonderful thing, but when it become "us against them" it is no longer so wonderful. In the corporate world, it is once again the promise of community that gives us some insight into our way past the psychologically devastating activities of the past few years, but if that promise of community only reinforces a new division between the haves and the have-nots, the interests of the corporation versus the interests of every one else, then we have just bought our way back into the prisoner's dilemma and the game theorists will again eclipse the Aristotelean wisdom of which Ed Hartman has once more reminded us.

NOTES

1 The beginning of the turn can be seen in Vance Packard's three-decade old best-seller, *The Pyramid Climbers*, published in 1962. The fast curve of the turn became evident in Michael Maccoby's classic, *The Gamesman*, in 1975. The end of turn from cozy corporate life to what some have come to see as an amoral snakepit is brutally portrayed in Robert Jackall's recent *Moral Mazes*, 1990.

2 See my *Ethics and Excellence* (Oxford, 1992) and Patricia Werhane's *The Legacy of Adam Smith* as well as my review of Werhane (this journal, Vol. 3, No. 4).

3 I think Macintyre misrepresents them on this when he claims that they were essentially egoists hiding behind a facade of philosophically manufactured "sympathy."

Solomon, a professor at the University of Texas in Austin, died in 2007—a loss still felt in the business ethics community. Though coming from a much different focus, both philosophically and in terms of him being an entrepreneurial CEO rather than an Aristotelian philosopher, Whole Foods founder John Mackey captures a strong sense of Solomon's conception of business being a community with his notion of Conscious Capitalism.

John Mackey's 'Conscious Capitalism': 'Simply a Better Way to Do Business[5]'

by Michael Connor

Whole Foods Market practically created the large-scale market for organic foods in the U.S. With some 342 stores, last year it boasted more than $11 billion in annual sales. The company is often included in lists of most ethical/sustainable businesses. It supports and distributes Fair Trade goods. And it has a reputation as a responsible employer, one of only 13 companies included in *Fortune* magazine's list of "100 Best Places to Work For" every year since the list was created in 1998.

Yet Mackey clearly doesn't fit the typically progressive political stereotype of an executive focused on corporate

John Mackey
CEO, Whole Foods Market

---

5   Michael Conor, John Mackey's 'Conscious Capitalism': 'Simply a Better Way to Do Business,' business-ethics.com (Jan. 27, 2013), http://business-ethics.com/2013/01/27/1154-john-mackeys-conscious-capitalism-simply-a-better-way-to-do-business/.

social responsibility. A self-described libertarian, he acknowledges having been heavily influenced by free-enterprise thinkers including Friedrich Hayek, Ludwig von Mises, Milton Friedman and Ayn Rand. Fiercely anti-union, he has successfully resisted labor organizers at Whole Foods Markets. And just this month he amended a previous criticism of Barack Obama's health care law, volunteering to an NPR interviewer that it was not "socialism" but, instead, more like "fascism." (Mackey later said his characterization was a "poor use of an emotionally charged word.")

In a new book, *Conscious Capitalism: Liberating the Heroic Spirit of Business*, Mackey takes shots at multiple targets on the left and right. While he worships free-market capitalism as "unquestionably the greatest system for innovation and social cooperation that has ever existed," he also challenges the "myth of profit maximization" as espoused by Milton Friedman and embraced by many to justify short-term financial goals for American business. While he opposes unnecessary regulation—a favored mantra of American business—he also attacks "the cancer of crony capitalism" in which "crony capitalists and governments have become locked in an unholy embrace, elevating the narrow, self-serving interests of the few over the well-being of the many."

Whole Foods Market is Mackey's day job, but for him conscious capitalism is a serious avocation. He has been involved in several organizations dealing with related subjects and is a director of Conscious Capitalism Inc., a non-profit organization headed by his co-author, Raj Sisodia, who is also a professor at Bentley University.

According to the authors:

Conscious Capitalism is not about being virtuous or doing well by doing good. It is a way of thinking about business that is more conscious of its higher purpose, its impact on the world, and the relationships it has with its various constituencies and stakeholders. It reflects a deeper consciousness about why businesses exist and how they can create more value...

Our dream for the Conscious Capitalism movement is simple: *one day, virtually every business will operate with a sense of higher purpose, integrate the interests of all stakeholders, elevate conscious leaders, and build a culture of trust, accountability and caring.*

And the aspirations are enormously high:

Picture a business built on love and care rather than stress and fear...Think of a business that cares profoundly about the well-being of its customers...Envision a business that embraces outsiders as insiders, inviting its suppliers into the family circle...Imagine a business that exercises great care in whom it hires, where hardly anyone ever leaves once he or she joins...Imagine a business that exists in a virtuous cycle of multifaceted value creation, generating social, intellectual, emotional, spiritual, cultural, physical and ecological wealth and well-being for everyone it touches..."

In addition to Whole Foods Market, companies currently practicing conscious capitalism, according to the authors, are The Container Store, Patagonia, Eaton, the Tata Group, Google, Costco, Amazon.com, Panera Bread, Southwest Airlines, Bright Horizons, Starbucks, UPS, Wegmans, Nordstrom, Trader Joe's, REI, Zappos, Twitter, POSCO (a South Korean steelmaker) and "many others."

Notably absent from that list are most Fortune 500 companies and a number of firms that regularly appear on lists of those excelling in sustainability and corporate responsibility. In fact, Mackey and Sisodia include an Appendix to their narrative which attempts to explain how conscious capitalism is different—and, in their view, superior-to "corporate social responsibility," the "triple bottom line," "shared value," and other popular terms used to describe most long-term corporate citizenship and corporate responsibility practices.

While the book's narrative alternates between "I" and "we," the voice heard most clearly is Mackey's and the examples used are by far those of Whole Foods Market. The tenets of conscious capitalism seem to suit new ventures and entrepreneurs far more than mature businesses with decades of corporate cultural baggage. And it's often difficult to sort out what's critical to the practice of conscious capitalism and what's particular to John Mackey.

For example, according to the book, in addition to contemplative practices such as meditation and Tai Chi, it is "imperative" for an executive interested in becoming a "conscious leader" to eat a wholesome diet which includes being "plant-strong," eating "primarily foods such as raw and cooked vegetables, fruits, whole grains, legumes, and nuts and seeds, with no more than about 10 percent of calories coming from animal foods." (That would presumably eliminate many martini-drinking meat-loving candidates for CEO positions, even if they are skilled in strategies to save the planet.)

If you can filter out that kind of practical and philosophical arrogance, Conscious Capitalism contains a bold statement of optimism about the role of business in society in an age when cynicism often merits out-sized rewards. In fact, Mackey and Sisodia are certain their dream will come true. "One day," they write, Conscious Capitalism will no doubt become the dominant business paradigm for one simple reason: it is simply a better way to do business. It just works better, and over the long term it will outcompete other business philosophies."

Discussion Questions

1. What do you make of Solomon's argument? Of Mackey's argument?

2. What would it take to make companies into a community or one that practices Conscious Capitalism?

3. After reading Solomon, how would you define a "community?"

4. Do you see your self-interest any different, after reading Solomon Do you see your self-interest defined solely in economic terms? If not solely economic, in what other terms?

5. Do you know anyone who works at Whole Foods? To what extent do they see it as a "Community?"

6. What are the most prominent features of that community, and how would they compare to others they have known?

Now that you have seen examples of problematic corporate culture, academic articles outlining what a good community/culture might look like and a concrete example of culture building from a successful CEO, how would you analyze and assess corporate culture?

The following case was written by a student of mine, Benjamin Besse, who wanted to examine an example of a positive organizational culture. The original paper he submitted can be found in the Appendix. Here he presents the issues confronted by a company trying to make its culture one that would supports its constituents—especially its employees—in making ethical choices.

As you read this case, keep in mind the materials presented so far in this Part III of the book in order to answer Besse's questions posed at the end of the case.

Costco: A Commitment To Conscious Capitalism[6]

Prepared by Benjamin Besse

Background

C ostco Wholesalers was founded in 1983 by Jim Sinegal and Jeff Brotman, the first store opening in Seattle, Washington. Both partners brought significant experience to the table—Jim Sinegal a successful career in wholesale distribution and Jeff Brotman a background in law and retail. By the company's 10th anniversary in 1993, Costco was publicly traded, over 100 warehouses had opened across the United States, and Costco shareholders approved a merger with rival membership retailer Price Company. The merger effectively doubled the size of the company and senior executives set their sites on international expansion.[7] Since 1983, Costco has grown to be the largest warehouse retailer in the United States, with over 450 locations and just under $100 billion in revenues.[8]

Costco's Ethical Standards

When Jim Sinegal and Jeff Brotman opened the first Costco warehouse in 1983, they envisioned a company built upon an unshakable commitment to customers, employees, and shareholders.[9] From the day of their founding until the present, Costco has remained true to its core ethical principles, offering employees some of the most coveted salary and benefits packages in the industry and restricting product markups to no more than 14% on goods sold in the warehouse stores.[10] In their 2005 letter to shareholders, Brotman and Sinegal remarked:

> We remain committed to running our company and living conscientiously by our Code of Ethics every day: to obey the law; take care of our members; take care of our employees; respect our suppliers; and reward you, our shareholders.[11]

Costco's mission statement is "To continually provide our members with quality goods and services at the lowest possible prices." Hand-in-hand with Costco's mission statement is the company's Code of Ethics, which directs management to: (1) Obey the law, (2) Take care of our

---

6 Benjamin Besse, Costco: A Commitment to Conscious Capitalism.

7   Costco Wholesale Corporation, History

8   Yahoo! Finance, Costco Wholesale Corporation Stock

9   Costco Wholesale Corporation, History

10 Casico, "Decency Means More than "Always Low Prices": A Comparison of Costco to Wal-Mart's Sam's Club," 31

11 Quoted in Casico, "High Cost of Low Wages," 28

members, (3) Take care of our employees, (4) Respect our suppliers, and if those four things are done throughout the organization, (5) Reward our shareholders.[12] (It is important to note that engrained in the company's Code of Ethics is an explicit commitment to the law, members, employees and suppliers *before* the interests of Costco shareholders.)

In upholding these standards, Costco has instituted a number of practices that have been heralded by many as the "conscious" capitalist enterprise. For employees, Costco is committed to a fair wage structure, with the average employee taking home $17 per hour, a staggering amount compared to industry standards, which hover just above minimum wage. Employees also enjoy a wide array of generous benefits options and a supportive work environment. Although labor-related costs account for approximately 70% of Costco's operating costs, the company enjoys a very low turnover rate, limited employee theft, high employee satisfaction, low union participation, and, ultimately, an improved customer experience.

Costco also holds itself to impressive ethical standards in regards to their relationship with customers, or as the company refers to them, members. With a value-oriented approach to product procurement designed to appeal to a high-income clientele, Costco delivers high quality products for some of the lowest prices in the market. The warehouse club abides by a strict policy of maintaining profit margins on all goods at or below 14%, or 15% on Kirkland-brand items.[14]

Sinegal and other Costco leaders believe that the company's strategy of maintaining high ethical standards and fair business practices is rewarding to shareholders as well. According to Sinegal, shareholders can expect long-term strength and performance by Costco as a result of the goodwill and customer and employee loyalty stemming from the company's practices.[15]

Conscious Capitalism

Costco is one of many businesses that has committed to the ideals of Conscious Capitalism, a nonprofit organization founded by Whole Foods co-founder and CEO John Mackey. Conscious Capitalism aims to advance the following notion:

> While making money is essential for the vitality and sustainability of a business, it is not the only or even the most important reason a business exists. Conscious businesses focus on their purpose beyond profit.[16]

---

12   Costco Wholesale Corporation, Costco Mission Statement and Code of Ethics

13   Casico, "High Cost of Low Wages"

14   Casico, "High Cost of Low Wages," 31

15   Costco Wholesale Corporation, Costco Mission Statement and Code of Ethics

16   "OVERVIEW OF PURPOSE." *Conscious Capitalism.*

In an article for *Harvard Business Review,* Mackey provides an explanation of Conscious Capitalism and a characterization of the businesses that have joined his cause:

> "Conscious Capitalism" is a way of thinking about capitalism and business that better reflects where we are in the human journey, the state of our world today, and the innate potential of business to make a positive impact on the world. Conscious businesses are galvanized by higher purposes that serve, align and integrate the interests of all their major stakeholders. Their higher state of consciousness makes visible to them the interdependencies that exist across all stakeholders, allowing them to discover and harvest synergies from situations that otherwise seem replete with trade-offs. They have conscious leaders who are driven by service to the company's purpose, to all the people the business touches and to the planet we all share. Conscious businesses have trusting, authentic, innovative and caring cultures that make working there a source of both personal growth and professional fulfillment. They endeavor to create financial, intellectual, social, cultural, emotional, spiritual, physical and ecological wealth for all their stakeholders. Evidence is mounting that such businesses significantly outperform traditional businesses in financial terms, while also creating many other forms of well-being.[17]

In addition to Costco and Whole Foods, a number of other prominent corporations have joined Mackey in his campaign to bring lasting and ethical values into the realms of market capitalism. Business leaders from Container Store, Starbucks, Nordstrom, Southwest Airlines, UPS, Trader Joe's, and Patagonia are among those who joined the ranks of Conscious Capitalism executives.

Costco's Critics

Despite Costco's commitment to Conscious Capitalism and Jim Sinegal's ethical framework, not all of the company's shareholders are convinced. In 2004 and 2005, in the face of rising costs, Costco faced increased frustration from shareholders and financial analysts, who argued that the public company needed to adjust its policies to realign corporate directives with the interests of shareholders. Bill Dreher of Deutsche Bank argued that at Costco "it's better to an employee or a customer than a shareholder.[18]" Analysts at C. Bernstein & Company echoed these concerns, adding, "Whatever goes

---

17 Mackey, John, and Raj Sisodia. "Conscious Capitalism" Is Not an Oxymoron."

18 Casico, "High Cost of Low Wages," 29

to employees comes out of the pockets of shareholders.[19]" Analysts and shareholders also pointed out that Costco's pricing strategy failed to take advantage of maximum potential for profits.

Costco's response to these criticisms was limited. Company executives made the decision to raise employees' share of health insurance costs from 4% to 8%, compared to the much higher industry standard of 25%. This marked the first increase in employee health premiums in over eight years. Beyond addressing the raising cost of health insurance, Costco made few other changes in response to Wall Street's criticisms.[20]

Sinegal's reaction to the censures of his management style was equally resolute. The CEO rebuffed the criticisms, stating:

> On Wall Street, they're in the business of making money between now and next Thursday. I don't say that with any bitterness, but we can't take that view. We want to build a company that will still be here 50 and 60 years from now.[21]

In defense of his employees and their compensation, Sinegal added, "that's not altruism, that's good business." Costco has not made any notable changes in policy since.[22]

Alternatives

In responding to the shareholder and analyst criticisms of 2004 and 2005, then-CEO Jim Sinegal was faced with three primary courses of action:

Alternative One: Acquiesce to Shareholder Requests

The first alternative course of action available to Sinegal and Costco management in response to the shareholder and analyst criticisms of the mid-2000's is to carry out the directives of those dissatisfied shareholders, lowering costs on employee compensation, raising product prices, and instituting other changes to realign Costco on a profit-centric course. This alternative would likely involve cutting employee compensation to near-industry-standard levels, in the case of Costco, a near 40% drop and dramatically increasing the employee share of other benefits, such as health insurance. Such an initiative would also likely entail eliminating Costco's commitment to low markups in their warehouse clubs, from the current 14% to over 30%, the industry standard.[23]

---

19   Neubert, "Wal-Mart Versus Costco: Is Wall Street Ready for Multistream Strategies?" 17

20   Greenhouse, "How Costco Became the Anti-Wal-Mart"

21   Greenhouse, "How Costco Became the Anti-Wal-Mart"

22   Greenhouse, "How Costco Became the Anti-Wal-Mart"

23   Casico, "High Cost of Low Wages"

Alternative Two: Maintain Current Approach

The second alternative facing Sinegal is to maintain Costco's current approach to management and resource allocation. This is essentially the path Sinegal selected in 2005, when Costco did little more than adjust health insurance premiums for rising costs to address shareholder concerns that labor costs were hurting company performance.

Alternative Three: Compromise

The final alternative available to Costco in this case is to reconcile the interests of concerned shareholders and those of other involved stakeholders, primarily employees and customers. This approach might involve making modest cuts in employee compensation, while maintaining industry-leading status and improving product margins gradually, perhaps in line with rising costs.

Corporate Social Responsibility: A Critique

While Jim Sinegal alleges that practicing Conscious Capitalism has been a cornerstone of Costco's success over the past three decades, a number of distinguished members of the business community—practitioners and academics alike—have denounced the benefits of Conscious Capitalism and other forms of corporate social responsibility.

Milton Friedman, often regarded as one of the greatest economists of the 20th Century and a disciple of free market economics and classical liberalism, was highly critical of most forms of corporate social responsibility. Friedman, in his book *Capitalism and Freedom*, argued:

> There is one and only one social responsibility of business—to use its recourses and engage in activities designed to increase its profits so long as it stays within the rules of the game, which is to say, engages in open and free competition without deception or fraud.[24]

In a later *New York Times Magazine* article, "The Social Responsibility of Business is to Increase its Profits," Friedman again takes a hard stance against corporate social responsibility. Friedman's primary argument against corporate social responsibility involves a violation of the principal-agent relationship by managers—executives act as the agents of shareholders and effectively breach their responsibility to shareholders when diverting resources from profit-maximizing activities. The social responsibilities heralded by reformers, he argues, are strictly individual responsibilities, not business responsibilities. In fact, Friedman goes on to argue that corporate social responsibility, by employing political mechanisms, as opposed to market mechanisms, to allocate scarce resources, is "pure and unadulterated socialism.[25]"

---

24 *Quoted in* Friedman, Milton. "The Social Responsibility of Business Is to Increase Its Profits."

25 Friedman, Milton. "The Social Responsibility of Business Is to Increase Its Profits."

Costco's Financial Performance

While critics of Conscious Capitalism may argue that greater returns could have been achieved, Costco shareholders have not suffered over the course of Sinegal's reign. In terms of rewarding shareholders, Costco has excelled over the long term. Since Costco's initial public offering in 1985, the company's stock has appreciated by nearly 900%. In comparison to Costco's competitors who are more profit-oriented, this is an astounding return. The following chart demonstrates the performance of Costco (COST) stock in comparison to Walmart (WMT), owner of Sam's Club and one of Costco's largest competitors, over the past ten years. This includes the period of 2004 to 2005, when some Costco shareholders and financial analysts issued criticisms of the company's management.

COST vs. WMT, March 2003-March 2010.[26]

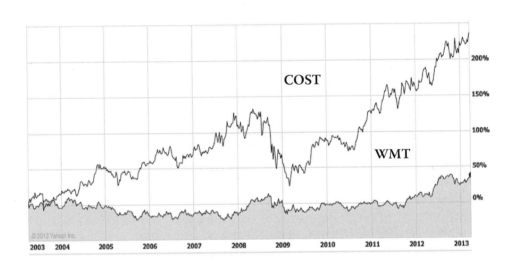

The performance of Costco stock over this period clearly demonstrates that Costco has rewarded its shareholders with astounding stock appreciation and dividends over the long term. Furthermore, the comparison to Walmart demonstrates that the profit-driven approach to business advocated by financial analysts and some shareholders, and adamantly opposed by Sinegal, did not serve Walmart well. During the 2004 to 2005 period, Costco stock appreciated nearly 50%, while Walmart stock dropped in value over the same period.

Costco's impressive financial performance over the past decade would appear to serve as proof that Sinegal's Conscious Capitalism is working. Costco's critics,

---

26   Quoted in Friedman, Milton. "The Social Responsibility of Business Is to Increase Its Profits."

however, offer a different explanation. Bill Dreher, of Deutsche Bank, attributes the performance of Costco's stock to the love of its shareholders for the company—"It's a cult stock," he claims.[27]

Discussion Questions

1. Assume you are Jim Sinegal in the midst of the 2004-2005 criticism of Costco management. What do you believe is the more ethical decision: continue practicing Conscious Capitalism or focus on maximizing profits? Which ethical frameworks did you use to arrive at this conclusion?

2. Based on your answer, which of the three alternatives (listed on page 4) would you choose? How do you believe your selection supports your opinions from question one? Has your answer to question one changed based on your selected alternative?

3. Costco's Mission Statement and Code of Ethics are written and approved by shareholder committees. Both documents incorporate elements of Conscious Capitalism. If these are considered the lawful directives of Costco shareholders, do the arguments of Friedman liberalism against corporate social responsibility apply? Why or why not?

WORKS CITED

Cascio, Wayne F. "Decency Means More than "Always Low Prices": A Comparison of Costco to Wal-Mart's Sam's Club." *Academy of Management Perspectives* 20.3 (2006): 26-37. *JSTOR*. Web. 24 Mar. 2013.

Cascio, Wayne. "The High Cost of Low Wages." *Harvard Business Review*: Web. 24 Mar. 2013.

Costco Wholesale Corporation. *Audit Committee Charter*. Rep. Issaquah: Costco Wholesale Corporation, 2011.

Costco Wholesale Corporation. *Corporate Governance Guidelines of Costco Wholesale*

Corporation. Rep. Issaquah: Costco Wholesale Corporation, 2011.

Costco Wholesale Corporation. *Costco Mission Statement and Code of Ethics*. Rep. Issaquah: Costco Wholesale Corporation, 2010.

---

27   Quoted in Greenhouse, "How Costco Became the Anti-Wal-Mart"

Costco Wholesale Corporation. "History." *Costco*. Web. 24 Mar. 2013.

Costco Wholesale Corporation. *Nominating and Governance Committee Charter*. Rep. Issaquah: Costco Wholesale Corporation, 2011.

Friedman, Milton. "The Social Responsibility of Business Is to Increase Its Profits." *The New York Times Magazine* 13 Sept. 1970: n. pag. *The New York Times Company*. Web. 4 June 2013.

Greenhouse, Steven. "How Costco Became the Anti-Wal-Mart." *New York Times* [New York] 17 July 2005.

Mackey, John, and Raj Sisodia. "Conscious Capitalism" Is Not an Oxymoron." *HBR Blog Network*. Harvard Business Review, 14 Jan. 2013. Web. 04 June 2013. <http://blogs.hbr.org/cs/2013/01/cultivating_a_higher_conscious.html>.

Neubert, Mitchell. "Wal-Mart Versus Costco: Is Wall Street Ready for Multistream Strategies?" *Management in Practice*. By Bruno Dyck. Boston: Houghton Mifflin Harcourt, 2010. 17.

"Overview of Purpose." *Conscious Capitalism*. Conscious Capitalism, n.d. Web. 04 June 2013. <http://www.consciouscapitalism.org/purpose>.

Whitford, David. "Can compassionate capitalists really win?" *Fortune*. [New York] 30 March 2011.

Yahoo! Finance. "Costco Wholesale Corporation Stock." *Yahoo!*. Web. 24 Mar. 2013.

At the beginning of this Part of the book, I suggested that trust might be particularly important for building an ethical culture. The following is a transcript from a speech I often give and is itself adapted from my book, *Business, Integrity, and Peace*. I offer it as a model for how to build ethical corporate cultures based upon the notion of Trust. Business people generally understand that trust is essential to their businesses, especially for long-term, repeated sales to customers and loyal, productive employees. This model, which I call Total Integrity Management, has three types of trust: Hard Trust, Real Trust, and Good Trust. The Real Trust/Good Trust combination is one that resonates significantly with Mackey's Conscious Capitalism. The Hard Trust dimension adds in the realities that the law and public opinion demand corporate accountability today whether companies like it or not.

As you will see in this transcript, the Total Integrity Management model flips the formula we used in Part II on its head. Rather than trying to use that formula to solve dilemmas, the Total Integrity Management model applies it in a pro-active way. That is, in a way that tries to prevent problems from happening in the first place. A way to do that is by creating a sense of corporate community—an ethical business culture –that attends to ethical issues prior to them being presented as ethical messes.

Total Integrity Management

(Adapted from "Business, Integrity, and Peace;"
Cambridge University Press, 2007)

Often, people think of ethics as something associated with a dilemma. In fact, many times, managers think that they go about their work with no ethical implications one way or another until suddenly...they stumble onto a dilemma. Then they have an ethics question.

As an ethicist, I must confess that I find this annoying. Dilemmas are dilemmas because there are no clear answers to them. If there was a clear answer, we would call them something else. But there isn't a clear answer and so we call them a dilemma. If we think ethics are only about a dilemma, then ethics questions are, by definition, questions with no clear answer. And so, managers who view ethics this way come to me (or another ethicist) with a question where there is no clear answer. We tell them that, and they walk away wondering why they ever asked us in the first place!

To be sure, sometimes there are questions where one goes to ask someone who specializes in the field for their advice. That could happen in marketing or accounting or law just as well as it could happen in ethics. Managers legitimately view such people as those who might have some expertise to help them with a problem. Ethicists should be able to make dilemmas more clear. Yet, if we simply leave ethics as co-terminus with dilemmas, we won't get anywhere. Aristotle believed that many, maybe most, of our ethical actions are those we are unaware of. They are so much a part of our nature and character and we practice them so habitually, we are not even aware of them as being ethics. Yet, they are and because they are, they are resources for us to draw on when we do come across that dreaded dilemma. Indeed, when companies make ethics part of their culture, they tend to more securely embed ethics as habits of their employees and richer ethical competencies are developed as a result. In those kinds of cultures, businesses become trustworthy not because they concocted a dazzling solution to an intractable dilemma but because they are reliably and habitually organizations that make ethics central to their business affairs.

Thus, the better way to look at ethics is in a preventative fashion. That is, how do we prevent problems from developing into dilemmas? The apt analogy is to quality. After a couple of decades of quality theory –ranging from Quality Circles to Total Quality Management to Open Book Management to Six Sigma—it is now well understood that a company does not ensure the quality of a product by waiting until the end of the manufacturing process to perform a quality check. If a company waits until then and there is a flaw, it is too late. The company is then in a dilemma: Does it ship out a defective product or does it swallow the costs of remanufacturing? Neither is a good answer and that is exactly what happens in a dilemma: One merely tries to figure out the least worst answer.

The same is true of ethics. If the first time a company asks about ethics is when there is a bunch of oil in Prince William Sound, it is too late. There is no good way to get millions of barrels of oil out of the water. Exxon had to look for the least worst way of solving the problem. If Exxon was really concerned about oil spillages it would have done more to *prevent* the problem. Like quality, ethics becomes a preventative solution to potential problems by integrating ethics checks throughout the manufacturing process, not just when there is an intractable dilemma.

Why Don't We Get This?

This seems rather straight-forward, so why don't companies get it? The answer, I think, is that there are real, perceived detriments to raising ethical issues. In their wonderful work, *The Moral Muteness of Managers*, Fred Bird and James Waters surveyed managers about ethical practices. Bird and Waters concluded that managers have a great deal of moral knowledge, but they fear that by raising an ethical issue at work, they will be viewed as "soft." We all know that one doesn't succeed in business by being soft. One succeeds by being "tough." And so, managers mute themselves.

I don't quarrel with Bird's and Water's research. They are probably right. I do think that it is strange to think of ethics as soft. Three of my moral heroes were Martin Luther King, Jr., Gandhi, and Jesus and they all got killed. That doesn't strike me as particularly soft. That strikes me that ethics is the tough stuff and the hard work.

Nevertheless, if one wants to improve ethics in business, one has to take into account the accuracy of Bird's and Water's findings. That means thinking about how one can encourage discussing ethics at work and not intimidating those who think it is important. If ethics is built into the daily work of business, we should expect people to get more skilled at thinking about ethics. Ethics is not, after all, simply an innate trait nor something that stops developing at age six (although detractors of talking about business ethics like to spin these folk tales). Ethics is a skill. If one practices making ethical decisions, one gets better at it. One refines ethical decision-making just as one becomes a better violinist or a better quarterback through rigorous practice. Companies that do this are companies that can be trusted. Companies that do this develop integrity.

An Ethics Equation

How do companies do this? I would like to suggest that they can do this by applying the following formula:

$$\textbf{EBB} = (L_{C/J} + (R_K + J_R + U)\,(M^3)$$

In offering this formula, I must confess great pride. My colleagues in Finance, Marketing, and Accounting have nothing on me. I too have a formula for my classes! Of course, this formula is offered very much tongue-in-cheek. Years ago, I did have colleagues who asked me if I could reduce ethics to a number. Numbers are, after all, hard. Ethics (confirming Waters and Bird) are soft. I thought about this suggestion and thought that there would be something missing if one was able to say that one was, say 22.5 on the ethics scale. Numbers may be "hard" but there are sometimes foundations underlying the numbers that are more important than the numbers themselves. Numbers without foundations are simply arbitrary. The challenge to come up with a formula, though, was too tempting to pass up and it doesn't do a bad job in capturing the academic approaches to corporate responsibility. I borrow the $R_K + J_R + U$ from Bill Frederick, but otherwise, the formula is my own.

The formula stands for the idea that Ethical Business Behavior is the result of complying with the law, provided that the law is just ($L_{C/J}$), attending to stakeholder interests ($R_K + J_R + U$) including attention to notions of rights, justice and utilitarianism, and having motivation to care about either the law or the stakeholders (M^3). If one is faced with making an ethical decision, including a decision about a dilemma, academics use one or a combination of these three approaches. Let me spend a few paragraphs spelling these out a bit more because then I can apply them not reactively, which is what happens when faced with a dilemma-based decision, but pro-actively when one is trying to create a culture of trust that prevents problems.

It is first worth noting that legally, the duty of managers is to carry out the lawful directives of shareholders. Many think that means profitability and profitability only, but the courts have long upheld the legitimacy of non-financial directives of shareholders. For instance, as law-and-economics scholars Daniel Fischel and Frank Easterbrook have noted, if someone was able to prove that the *New York Times* could make more money by having racy, front-page headlines rather than adhering to its sense of journalistic excellence, the company could turn its back on the extra profits. There is nothing illegal about aspiring to journalistic excellence if that is what the shareholders desire. If the Chicago Cubs want to forfeit profits to create a sense of family entertainment by playing more day baseball games than is the norm (as was the case in *Wrigley v Shlensky*), they can do so. If Timberland wants to give its employees time off to work on volunteer causes they can. If Johnson & Johnson wants to jeopardize its brand name in yanking Tylenol off the shelves because it can't live up to its corporate credo, it can. Profitability is essential to the viability of a business, but the law provides a good deal of room to incorporate long-term strategies that may seem initially unprofitable and it also provides room to pursue non-financial directives for their own sake.

Second, most of the action in the field of business ethics is in terms of respect the rights (R_K) of vulnerable stakeholders or pursuing a sense of justice (J_R) or a utilitarian greatest good for the greatest number of corporate constituents. (The subscripts "K" and "R" stand for (Immanuel) Kant and (John) Rawls respectively). This formula is about how business should do its business, but in the process, it shouldn't pollute the environment or sell a product that harms kids for instance, even if in refusing to cause such harms, profitability suffers.

Third, there are typically three reasons why any business will pursue ethical practices: Legal, economic, and moral. Companies pursue ethics because they are motivated by the fear of lawsuits, they see a payoff in good ethics in terms of building social capital, reputation, and goodwill, or they simply want to do something they believe is a good thing to do. That is true if companies are concerned with the misuse of a product and it is true about instances where companies are considering enacting a sexual harassment policy. And so M^3 is about motivation: Why companies institute ethics programs.

This formula can be used to make moral decisions in the midst of a dilemma. But from a preventative standpoint, the formula can be used proactively to create the corporate cultures that enhance trust, integrity, and confidence. Practicing "ethical business behavior" has a reactive feel to it. One is responding to external norms (legal, social, philosophical) for engaging in practices. But if one applies this formula pro-actively, one can create a management approach that integrates ethics in a pro-active, leadership model. Then the formula becomes:

$$\text{Total Integrity Management}^{28} = (L_{C/J} + (R_K + J_R + U) (M^3)$$

The Problems with Integrity and Trust...And Their Benefits

"Trust" and "integrity" are bandied about in business these days with great frequency. Log on to a company's website and it is highly likely that both words will jump off the web page. There is a perception that trust in business is eroding and so in response, business trumpets how this is a time for integrity. What these terms mean is a different story.

Integrity vaguely gets associated with honesty, but it is a much more complex virtue. Integrity, as its root, suggests is about wholeness. An integer is a whole number. To integrate is to bring together. Integrity is not about honesty only; it is about a bringing together many relevant virtues and knowing how and when to apply the most relevant ones to a case at hand.

Each approach to business ethics—the legal, the managerial, and the aesthetic spiritual—have something important to say about ethics. In an isolated case, each independently might provide a satisfactory result. For instance, if a company is faced with an issue of product safety, following the law may be sufficient. On the other hand, it may not be sufficient. To address the complexity of issues that arise in business and to build a "culture" of trust requires more than one single approach. It requires an integrated approach. That integration is one that takes all three approaches and weaves them

---

28   Although I like the acronym Total Integrity Management provides, using it, as my wife says, is disturbingly narcissistic.

together. In some sense, this is bad news, because all that weaving takes time and a good deal of thinking of how it should take place for a particular company. Well, welcome to ethics. It isn't necessarily easy, but by breaking these components into "Hard Trust," "Real Trust," and "Good Trust" one can make a lot of progress.

Hard Trust ($L_{C/J}$)

Hard Trust is about coercively requiring corporations to adhere to standards. It is about law and public opinion. An outside third party provides assurances to the public that business will obey certain standards under the threat of punishment if they do not. Hard Trust is about rules. It is about making clear what is permissible and what is not.

In some cases, custom is enough to create Hard Trust. I grew up in a very rural area of the Midwest. You don't need a lot of written rules there because there is great continuity. Families have lived there for generations and everyone understands the authority of unwritten rules. When I go back to my hometown, for instance, I always remember to wave at any car passing me in the opposite direction on the two-lane highways. The reason is that waving is expected and I don't want to be grabbed by my shirt at the Post Office and asked if I am a stuck-up professor now who thinks he is too important to wave at his old friends. I've been gone long enough now that I don't recognize everyone (although I used to be able to) when I go back, but I wave at everyone anyway. That prompts my five year old to ask:

"Daddy, who are you waving to?"

I respond, "I have no idea."

"Then why are you waving at them?"

"Because I don't want to die."

Well, I doubt anyone would kill me, but the point is that when there is great continuity, you don't need a lot of written rules. But when you work in a mobile work force with people moving to a new job every few years and when in a global economy, people you work with come from all kinds of different cultures, then a company needs rules to fairly alert everyone working for them of the rules they are expected to know and abide by.

This is old stuff for companies by now. In large part because of the 1991 Federal Sentencing Guidelines, companies have adopted all kinds of Codes of Conduct, Mission Statements, and Values Statements by which they operate their company. These compliance programs attempt to get everyone at a company to abide by the rules. The Guidelines have been around now long enough so that studies have been done to determine what makes for "effective" (which is the standard the programs are to meet) compliance programs. Paper programs, of course, don't work very well. But the main problem undermining programs, according to Linda Weaver, Gary Weaver, and their co-authors, is if there is no top-to-bottom accountability. Everyone knows, of course, that lower level workers are accountable to people at the top. But are top level people accountable, if not to the bottom, at least to a code of behavior that everyone from top to bottom must follow? If not, if exceptions are the norm for top management, companies create great cynicism and undermine trust. Let me provide two concrete examples.

Enron had a very well thought-out conflict of interest policy so that high-level executives could not hold ownership interest in related companies. Yet, according to *The Powers Report,* the report of the independent members of Enron's Board of Directors, the Board formally suspended its Code of Conduct three times in order to allow Andrew Fastow to obtain lucrative ownership interests in special purpose entities designed to remove Enron debt from its books and provide a financial windfall for him at the same time. Three times the Board did this! What kind of message does that send?

Or let me give an even more concrete example. In the 1990s, I began to teach Executive Education courses. One evening, I taught a two hour session on ethics with the main theme being how to make ethics a part of the regular, every day life of the workforce. I had one fellow, who got very charged up about the whole idea, and with voice rising, fist pounding, and neck veins bulging, he said

> "I wanna know how my people can know that I mean business!
> And if they screw up, I'm gonna bust their ass and get 'em out of here!"

It was, to put it mildly, a strange scene. I responded that the best thing he could do would be to make sure everyone knew that the rules applied to him too. He got up and walked out of the room! That's exactly what the Trevino and Weaver studies are showing. Corporate rule and corporate policies are fine, but they have to be fairly and evenly applied or else they boomerang.

From a dilemma-based perspective, when one is in trouble, one asks what is legally required. From a preventative-based perspective, one alerts everyone what the applicable laws are in advance and also carefully designs and publishes policy statements so that people know the rules of the road. Putting on my lawyer's hat, these programs are essential. Not only are they essential to comply with laws such as Sarbanes-Oxley or the Federal Sentencing Guidelines, they are essential to give people fair notice of what is expected of them. They need to be accompanied by training programs and measuring mechanisms.

There are two other aspects of Hard Trust. One is public opinion and the other is technological. Law is a coercive weapon to make sure companies behave. So is public opinion. Think of how easy it is today to capture incriminating behavior. How many people have a camera on their cell phone these days? Cameras and communications (Internet, Blogs, television) can turn public opinion against companies very easily, which is why companies today have increasingly developed public relations programs to deal with corporate responsibility.

Cameras are the tip of the technological iceberg. Technology can also make unethical behavior impossible. Think of how companies can simply prevent employees from accessing pornographic websites at work. Technology and public opinion (like the law) are double-edged swords, but the point is that their toughness can be used to force people to abide by certain standards. Used constructively, these tools can be beneficial.

Real Trust ($R_K + J_R + U$)

Real Trust is what most people think of when they think of trust in business. Real Trust is about the business case for building social capital, reputation, and good will through ethical behavior. Real Trust is about aligning rewards and incentives, about garnering the confidence of stakeholders because you keep your word, tell the truth, and produce high-quality goods and services. It is about putting your money where your mouth is, so that when a crunch time comes, you deliver on ethics rather than weaseling out of commitments. It is about making sure than in conducting business, one doesn't trample on the interests of stakeholders who, at the moment of the action, can't protect themselves that well and who trust a company not to do so.

The most lauded case for this is Johnson & Johnson's handling of the 1982 Tylenol crisis. Let me relate that story a bit differently and personally. In 1982, I was a third year law student at Northwestern University living in the Old Town area of Chicago. On the corner of North Avenue and Wells, was (and is) a Walgreen's drugstore. When I was feeling under the weather, my preferred medication was Extra Strength Tylenol Capsules. One Fall day, I wasn't feeling so well, but discovered that I was out of Extra Strength Tylenol Capsules, so I started to put on my coat to go over to the Walgreen's. Fortunately, my roommate said that he thought he had some in his medicine cabinet, so he went up to his room to check and found some to give to me. While I didn't go to the Walgreen's, that same afternoon, an unfortunate flight attendant from United Airlines did go there and purchased Extra Strength Tylenol capsules, went home to her apartment in nearby Sandburg Village, took them, and died from the poison lacing the pills. Thus, began Chicago's Tylenol killings where seven people died.

No one showed that J&J had done anything wrong—nor have they ever since the case remains unsolved—but within a week, J&J had yanked every bottle of Extra Strength Tylenol off the shelves nationwide. Apparently, the company managers first thought about trying to deny that the company did anything wrong, but then J&Js CEO, James Burke, said that in doing so, the company could not live up to its corporate credo, the first provision of which stressed the obligation of the company to provide safe products to its customers. The company couldn't be sure that it could meet that obligation at that moment and so pulled the product. Granted, J&J had some good public relations people, but still, making a decision on the basis of some "credo" seems like a very soft way to run a business. And yet, that is exactly what J&J did to its credit. It put its money where its mouth was, not based on a business case—although their actions ultimately proved to be a brilliant business move—but because of a commitment to a certain way of doing business.

Internally, Real Trust is about aligning incentives and rhetoric. It is one thing for a company to claim it values integrity. It is another thing to structure its affairs to actually reward that integrity. For instance, I frequently teach a case I call "the bug-infested cookie case." Written by LaRue Hosmer, the case tells the story of a recent MBA graduate working in a department store in California. One of her jobs was in the gourmet food section, where the story was selling cookies wrapped in sealed foil. Some of the customers said that when they opened the foil, there were bugs crawling around on the cookies. The manager of the gourmet food section told the recent graduate that they would have to get rid of the cookies. The recent graduate thought that meant they were to throw away the cookies. The manager, though, said no, they weren't going to throw away the cookies. She knew of a store in the inner city where they could take the potentially infested cookies, sell them for cents on the dollar, and get back some of their investment.

Now there are a number of things wrong with this scenario, but from a certain twisted standpoint, it made sense. The standpoint was that the manager's annual bonus was based on a formula of profitability per square foot and her annual allocation of floor space was based on the same formula. All the company's incentives were for her to do exactly what she did: Squeeze every cent of profit she could from the product. I'm sure the store did not want to be known as the bug-infested-cookie-store, but that's exactly what its incentives were leading to. In this case, as in most cases, ethics isn't about personal integrity (although it would have been good for either the recent graduate or the manager to take a firmer stand against the sale of the cookies) and it wasn't about applying a refined philosophical principle. It was about designing a "bad food" category on its accounting books so that the manager wasn't punished for doing the right thing. It is exactly this example that shows that ethics in business is a management issue, not a personal integrity issue.

In the end, J&J's decision was a brilliant protection of its brand, but at the moment of its decision, it was the ethical value more than the "business case" that was important, a message consistently communicated from the top of the organization. That value, in fact, was a better business case decision than a business case analysis. It was a value that arose from an enculturation of the corporate credo. J&J practiced its credo in job interviews, games, and evaluations so that it meant something in the daily live of the company. That enculturation probably headed off a lot of issues that could have ultimately become an intractable dilemma. When J&J was faced with an issue that was not of its making, its culture also generated the way to respond to the problem.

This is not to deify J&J. There are no perfect individuals and there are no perfect companies. At the same time, there is wisdom in its actions. People may trust a company that understands that it can be punished if customers may boycott the product or the government may intercede. But they really trust the company when they know the company is committed to doing the right thing. That leads directly to the final aspect, Good Trust.

Good Trust (M^3)

Good Trust is about caring about ethics. All the legal rules, empirical connections, and philosophical principles in the world only go so far. If people don't care about ethical behavior in the first place, nothing is likely to happen. This is a badly neglected area of business ethics, but it may be the most important one. We tend to be absorbed in the external legal rules to guarantee trust and we want to find a business case for why trust pays. Those are well and good. But the heart of ethical behavior in business gets to how to nourish a sense of caring about the behavior in the first place. That is why in the formula, Total Integrity Management = $(L_{C/J} + (R_K + J_R + U) (M^3)$, if M^3 is zero, everything else ends up as zero.

M^3 is about Music, Mediating Institutions, and More Mediating. In other words, it is about Motivation and how that has an aesthetic, sometimes even spiritual aspect, how our moral sentiments are nourished in mediating institutions, and how the aim of how businesses can contribute to sustainable peace (More Mediation) is an inspiring enough "good" to transform how people approach their work.

To illustrate this, I would like to give a really cheesy example. For eleven years, I was a professor at the University of Michigan, an appointment made more interesting because I am an alumnus of one of Michigan's biggest rivals, Notre Dame. I realize that the biggest football game of the year for Michigan has always been Ohio State and that the biggest game of the year for Notre Dame has always been Southern California. But for me, even before I had dual allegiances, I thought that the best college football game each year was the Notre Dame-Michigan game. They are the two winningest major college programs in football history. Michigan has the most wins, Notre Dame is second. They have been in a virtual dead heat for years in terms of best all-time winning percentage. And in terms of national championships, members of the college football hall of game, and first team All-Americans, Notre Dame is first and Michigan is second. The schools have had legendary coaches, famous stadiums, and even unique helmets. The games are usually very close.

But even if none of this was true, the game is worth going to each year just to hear the two best school songs played all day long. While I know that readers of this article may disagree (and if so, you can simply substitute your favorite rivalry and school songs here), but an awful lot of people will agree that Notre Dame's and Michigan's are the best. John Phillip Souza, the famous "March King" said that Michigan's "Hail to the Victors" was the greatest college march ever written. There is a story that during the Vietnam War, American POWs were unable to talk to each other, but they all knew the tune to the Notre Dame Victory March and so they hummed it. In short, these are just great songs. So here's the test.

Each band (and I have interviewed members of both bands to verify this para-graph's point) have a tradition of first playing the other's song before playing its own. When they play the other's (great) song, you will hear Hard Trust and Real Trust. You will hear all the laws and rules of music followed. You will hear the right notes, right time signature, right key signature, and right rhythm played. The band will do everything "right." That's Hard Trust. You will also see rewards and behaviors aligned. The fans whose band just played aren't going to boo their own band and the fans whose song was just played aren't going to boo their own song. There will be polite applause throughout the stadium as everyone things the band did a "nice" thing. That's Real Trust.

Then listen to the band play its own song. When it plays its own song, it plays it with heart, with pride, with passion, and with identity. It is that rendition that sends chills up one's spine. That's Good Trust.

The same is true of business. There are some companies for whom being ethical means following the law. There's something to be said for that. There are others who align their incentives to live up to their rhetoric. There is even more to be said for that. But there are some companies for whom ethics is so much part of the identity of the company and the reason people come to work that ethics becomes a passion for excel-lence. In those companies, ethics will be talked about on a regular basis and people get good at making decisions. They build a culture so that most ethical problems are headed off before they become problems and even if they still do, the people in the company, like J&J in the Tylenol case, know what to do.

So how then do we get to this place? Do we all going around whistling our favor-ite fight song? Well, let me give three ways to pursue this quest for aesthetic, even spiritual excellence.

One way is to tell stories. Philosophical and legal principles have their merit, but the most natural way for people to connect with ethical behavior is through telling sto-ries. I play on this inclination with my students. In their first assignment, they have to tell me a story about something they saw in business that they thought was good. Then they have to define what good is. The assignment is just a two-pager, but it is a difficult one. Many students struggle with a memory of the good, preferring to write about some-thing they thought was bad. That's too easy. What's more interesting, and harder, is to define what you think is good. The story part connects them to what's in their heart. The explanation part challenges them to articulate their good in a way so that others can evaluate it, think about it, internalize it themselves, or something else.

Indeed, I have used this in consulting assignments with excellent success. I used the assignment with a family business, a leader in its industry. The family shareholders, however, had come to really dislike each other on, in their words, the ethical issues surrounding the family and the business. After hearing me give a speech, they hired me to come in to help them. It was clear, quickly, that each side thought that I would side with "their side" and against "the other side." I didn't side with anyone. I made them do this exercise and then forced them to listen to each other at a weekend retreat. It was painful. It also transformed them because even when the old-style, small-town Calvinists disagreed one of their New Age cousins, they suddenly heard a person with values talking. (The same thing happened when the New Agers listened to the Calvinists.) That "other" suddenly became a person with dreams, values, and goals that were important.

Sometime later, I checked up on them, and they said they weren't sure why they needed to hire me; they all got along so well! I don't have a sophisticated empirical study to prove this assertion, but I believe that if companies put individuals in work groups of fewer than thirty (more on that in a second) and one every three years let those people tell their stories, it would dramatically change the culture of many companies. It would make ethics and values and dreams and goals of everyone relevant to work.

As I argued in my 2001 Oxford University Press book, *Ethics and Governance: Business as Mediating Institution*, a second way is to build Good Trust is to take into account our hardwired, biological propensities for interacting with groups and to thereby maximize the expression of our innate moral sentiments. Within the natural law tradition, there is a long-standing belief that human beings form their moral character in "mediating institutions." These are small organizations where is significant face-to-face interactions and people experience, in one form or another, the consequences of their actions. They are family, neighborhood, religious and voluntary organizations, and potentially business too. No matter how much a sibling may make you mad, you have to figure out a way to get along, to be a good citizen of the family. In these structures, our actions become habits and we develop our moral character.

Anthropologists have also shown that there a certain sizes of groups that we are most naturally "at-home" in. The first three of those numbers are 4-6, 30, and 150. For example, the next time you are at a cocktail party, watch how frequently people will talk to each other in a group size greater than 4-6. It will almost never happen (unless there is someone in that group that everyone else believes is super-important and the rest are trying to suck up to that person). If the number in the group gets larger than this, or even gets close to the top numbers, the group will fission like an amoeba. It is simply too difficult to carrying on a conversation with numbers larger than this. Some management theorists have applied the same numbers to the maximum number of people a manager should supervise.

The next number is thirty. If one accepts evolution, anthropologists tell us that humans lived in hunter-gatherer societies for about 98-99% of human history. The argument is that our brains have evolved to live in the sizes of groups that comprised that history rather than in large urban areas. Even today, as explained by Gregory Johnson, there are "scalar stresses" that limit the number of individuals who can work together on a regular basis: Some studies show that in groups of thirty, for every person added to the group, the number of disputes increase not arithmetically for every person added, but exponentially. Before I learned of this threshold, I frequently noted that the optimum size for an ethics class was thirty. One can still have an entertaining class with numbers beyond that, but there is a community dynamic that is lost once you get above that number. Students are more reluctant to share experiences and to volunteer in larger numbers.

Perhaps my favorite number though is 150. Robin Dunbar, an anthropologist in England, tried to figure out why human beings speak better than other creatures. One possible answer is that we have bigger brains. But whales and elephants have bigger brains than we do and we seem to talk better. However, when one looks at head size in comparison to body mass, we have big heads! Look around you! We don't out-run a lion, we don't out-duke a tiger, we out-think them. That is our evolutionary advantage. Moreover, humans and our primate cousins have a large neocortex in comparison to our body mass. The neocortex is the thin membrane that covers the brain that, somewhat controversially, is believed to be responsible for cognitive processing. The neocortex ratio of primates far exceeds that of other creatures (except dolphins).

Dunbar also possessed data on the sizes of groups primates live in. A given species will only live in a certain size of group. Above that number, the group fissions until it again reaches that ceiling. Dunbar thought there might be a relationship between group size and neocortex ratio, so he plotted the two against each other and then tried to predict the maximum size of a human grouping. The number he came up with was 150.

This is all fun, esoteric stuff, but Dunbar then showed some of its practical dimensions. 150 is the average number of names in an address book. 150 is the average size of the company unit in the military. When Brigham Young moved the Mormons from Nauvoo, Illinois to Utah, he said that he couldn't coordinate 5,000 people, but the people could be organized into groups of 150 and he could coordinate their leaders. Dunbar gives several more examples indicating that 150 represents a maximum of number of individuals who can be in a group where the individuals have an actual, personal awareness of each other. Or as Dunbar colloquially puts it, there are probably 150 in the world who, if you saw them sitting at a bar, you'd feel comfortable pulling up a chair and having a beer with them. (My colloquial example is a wedding. There were 4-6 people who had to be there—bride, groom, witnesses, and officiant). There were thirty that each person thought would just be essential to be on the invitation list. There were about 150 that each thought would be fun to be there and if you get beyond that, the betrothed look at each other and say, "who the hell are they?"

The significance of this is that there are sizes of groups that match our biological comfort levels. Above those levels, we start to lose a sense that our actions make a difference to others, for good or for bad. Listen to someone who got caught embezzling. They will almost always say that they didn't think anyone would pay attention to them—it was such a big place. In smaller groups, one has to care. One has little choice but to know that actions have consequences. This doesn't mean that one loves everyone in the group, but simply that they have to be taken account of. It also doesn't mean that small groups are more ethical than big groups. It means that moral sentiments of empathy and compassion as well as integrity virtues such as truth-telling and promise-keeping are nourished because they are essential to the maintenance of the relationships in the group. *If businesses want to develop cultures of trust where people are habitually being honest and habitually keeping promises, they need to put employees into small "mediating structures" within the company that matches with their neurobiology.*

The more one is in a relationship, the more integrity-kinds of virtues like truth-telling and honesty make a difference. For example, suppose that you had a car with 100,000 miles on it. After driving it for a couple of hours, the car seemed to jerk, as if there might be something wrong with the transmission. Would you feel really, really bad if, when you went to trade the car in for a new one, you didn't mention this possible problem? Some people would. Others would say,

> "Car dealers are big boys and girls. They have mechanics. They can look out for themselves. I won't lie that there isn't a problem, but I am not going to pro-actively offer that there is one."

Now suppose that you were me, back in the 1990s and the car I was ready to trade in had 100,000 miles on it. The person I would going to sell it to wasn't a used car dealer, but my wife's 18 year old nephew. The demands for pro-active honesty go through the roof, if for no other reason than I happened to like Thanksgiving dinner! I didn't want to be carved up by my in-laws after they carved up the turkey because they thought I had taken advantage of the young man. The more one is in an experience of a mediating institution, at work or in a family, the more one has to be concerned with issues of pro-active virtues.

At the same time, more than sentimental caring is needed. Caring sometimes gets limited to other members of the group and precluded from outsiders. That's why just as Hard Trust and Real Trust need Good Trust, so too Good Trust needs the accountabilities to the outside world that Hard Trust (brings through law and public opinion) and Real Trust (though markets) give.

The final aspect of Good Trust is itself a corrective to the negative small groups can generate. That is "more mediation" or, the concept of how to achieve peace through commerce. For several years, I (sometimes with my co-author Cindy Schipani) have developed evidence that suggests that commonly accepted ethical business practices can reduce the likelihood of violence.

Looking at traits of relatively nonviolent societies identified by anthropologists, political scientists, and economists, it became clear that economic development, adherence to the rule of law (particularly with respect to avoiding corruption) and building good community relations between the company and its host society and also within its own corporate walls were the kind of traits that were championed by ethicists as well.

It is not simply that commerce creates peace—businesses sometimes are in the midst of colonialism, imperialism, and project the worst kinds of insensitivities—but rather than a certain kind of business, an ethical business that promotes peace without the negatives (colonialism, exploitation) commerce can sometimes bring. . Those practices, living up to responsibilities to shareholders, promoting contract and property rights, avoiding bribery, and encouraging voice, gender equity, and human rights are consensus-based ethical business practices. And so, it is not that businesses needed to approach business from an entirely different perspective. It is simply that there may be an unexpected payoff to ethical business behavior: It may reduce violence.

Conclusion

Businesses may enhance trust by obeying the law. They may enhance trust by aligning incentives with rhetoric and fostering economic development. But one trusts individuals and one trusts organizations not simply because they *react* to social and market pressures. People truly trust organizations and individuals when they *lead* with moral clarity. Until then, trust is simply responsive and, frankly, risks continually being behind the curve of what society really craves. It is when individuals and companies lead that trust is deeply engendered.

And so, it is good to be ethical and to build trust because one thinks it is a good thing to do. There are also times and places when good ethics can be good business and trust can be reinforced in those happy instances. But companies setting new standards for leadership truly create trust and if companies and their executives need one more reason for being ethical in business, the research now shows that in doing so, they just might prevent a kid from getting his head blown off. I can't think of many more powerful reasons to be ethical today than that.

Discussion Questions:

1. From the materials in this chapter, how would you construct a model that fosters the kinds of ethical corporate cultures that helps people in the organizations make good decisions rather than, as described in the previous chapter, tends to push them into troubling decisions?

2. What strengths and weaknesses do you see of these models (Solomon's, Mackey's and Fort's)?

3. If you are the CEO, how would you go about creating an ethical corporate culture?

4. Even if you are simply a rank-and-file employee, is there anything you can do to generate trust and to foster an ethical corporate culture?

A Return to Economics

At the end of Part I, we looked at the interview with economist David Rose, who argued that there is a strong, essential link between ethics and the optimal functioning of the market. Relying on Adam Smith and others, Rose focused his arguments on duty. The market depends, he argues, on individuals having a sense of moral duty that restrains them from opportunistic behavior, the kind of behavior that can undermine the functioning of the market. To conclude this Part III of the book, I turn to an excerpt from another economist, Javier Aranzadi, who roots his argument on Aristotle and thereby creates an argument that also features ethics in terms of a quest for excellence and virtue.

The questions for you to consider as you read the excerpts from this article are how, exactly do you think that ethical corporate culture helps? Helps an individual employee? Helps a company as a whole? Helps a community? Helps other stakeholders? Helps an economic system? Or does corporate culture, in the final analysis, make that much of a difference.

Aranzadi poses some serious philosophical questions concerning the social role of the firm and its place in fostering individual fulfillment. Hearkening back to early materials in this course, do you believe this is a valid function of the corporation? If so, why? If not, what are your arguments for why Aranzadi (as well as Solomon, Mackey and myself) are wrong? We just might be, though I wouldn't write what I did if I thought so nor would have Aranzadi, Solomon, or Mackey), but if you think so, what are your arguments?

The Natural Link Between Virtue Ethics and Political Virtue: The Morality of the Market[29]

Javier Aranzadi

* * *

The Social Role of the Firm

Let us use the interactive view of creativity to approach the firm. The first thing we note is that entrepreneurial innovation has not only a personal dimension, i.e., the creator, but also a socio-cultural dimension. We now have an interactive view of creativity and entrepreneurship linking the person, the firm, and entrepreneurial culture. We should be clear that these are not three distinct realities but three moments in the same process. These three moments are closely interlinked, so any changes in any one of them affect the creative process. Rather than speaking of what creativity is, we should ask where creativity comes from. In this view, the social importance of the firm is huge: the firm's social responsibility is to enhance the possibilities of [30] persons. The assertion that any person has the ability to create to a greater or lesser extent is not an exaggeration but quite the reverse. It highlights a current problem of great importance when firms need to innovate at high speed. It highlights the fact that in firms there is much wasted talent. Jack Welch, until recently president of General Electric, said:

> The talents of our people are greatly underestimated and their skills underutilized. Our biggest task is to fundamentally redefine our relationship with our employees. The objective is to build a place where people have the freedom to be creative, where they feel a real sense of accomplishment—a place that brings out the best in everyone. (Ghoshal and Bartlett 1997, p. 21).

In this respect, Ghoshal and Bartlett, echoing Welch, define the new social dimension of the firm:

> Rather than accept the assumption of economists who regard the firm as just an economic entity and believe that its goal is to appropriate all possible value from its constituent parts, we take a wider view. Our thinking is based on the conviction that the firm, as one of the most significant institutions in modern society, should serve as a driving force of progress by creating new value for all of its constituent parts. (1997, p. 27)

---

29   Javier Aranzadi, *The Natural Link Between Virtue Ethics and Political Virtue: The Morality of the Market*, J. Bus. Ethics (Dec. 2012).

30   As has been noticed Grassl and Habitsh (2011) the Encyclical-Letter *Caritas in Veritate* emphasizes the same two basic ideas. First, business activity must be understood as personal action, and second management should foster the creativity of employees.

This is a view that implies an extension of economics.[31] Firms occupy a central position as basic institutions in society. It is a dynamic view that shows the firm's importance as a behavior pattern in social relations in which the lead role is played by the person and the driving force is entrepreneurship. To go deeper into the criterion of entrepreneurial efficiency, I define economic efficiency as the enhancement of persons' possibilities for action.[32]

The first aspect of this criterion is that it is dynamic. Its coordination lies in the process of social interaction that progressively eliminates inefficient situations. Thus, an economic, social, and cultural system will be more efficient if it increases personal possibilities for action. That is, a situation will be more efficient where a person's prospects of action increase. And conversely, a social and cultural situation will be more inefficient if the possibilities for action that it affords to persons are more limited.

However, we should supplement this criterion, for if we assert only the first part and stop at an increase in personal possibilities, it could be inferred that the more freedom of individual action we have, the better coordinated society is. Thus, we could reach the paradoxical situation of asserting that the more murderers, drunks, thieves, etc. there are, the better the coordinated society is. Something that no-one accepts. That is, this first formulation of the criterion provides an element that is necessary but insufficient in itself. This first aspect concerns personal freedom of choice. But in the course of this paper, we have argued that all individual action has a social dimension and that, as a result, the institutional order is maintained by personal actions. Therefore, it is necessary to supplement the criterion of coordination from the social perspective and assert that the more entrepreneurial and social coordination it generates, the more efficient personal action will be. Thus, we can assert that all behavior that we normally regard as antisocial or pernicious, such as theft, murder, fraud, or drug addiction, are inefficient because with them it is impossible for society to function, and much less so an economy based on theft.[33]

As we have developed the relationship between personal action, institutions and culture, the criterion may be formulated in three ways. Each one refers to each element's

---

31 And the development of the humanistic management approach (Argandon̄a 2007, 2010; Mele´ 2003, 2009; Spitzeck et al. 2009; Hartman 2011) among others.

32 Koslowski (1996, p. 53) states emphatically that the market allows not only freedom of consumption but also of action and production.

33 This efficiency criterion requires the two formulations in order to correspond to the two views of human freedom. Our first formulation refers to the conception of freedom as "freedom from." In this view, the person is free from institutions to do what he or she likes. It represents the freedom of indifference. One may do this or that. In this view a person who chooses to be a thief is as free as one who chooses to undertake a great enterprise. This first view presents the freedom of indifference. To distinguish between such behaviors, I have introduced the second view corresponding to the concept of freedom as "freedom for." This view presents the person as a generator of positive actions. It presents human's freedom in the search for excellence in action. See Pinckaers (1985).

contribution to the system presented in this paper. That is, as Csikszentmihalyi (1996) says, when speaking of creativity, we must take a systematic view. Instead of asking about individual creativity in isolation, we should consider how to stimulate creativity in personal action in entrepreneurial culture and in existing firms. We may formulate the coordination criterion with reference to each element. (1) Regarding firms: the criterion is the more personal possibilities for action they afford, the more efficient firms will be; (2) regarding entrepreneurial culture: the more possibilities for action they foster, the more efficient cultural transmission mechanisms will be; (3) regarding individual action: the greater its contribution to the firm and to entrepreneurial culture, the more efficient action will be. If we bear in mind that this separation is analytical and that the sole existing reality is the person in action, we may sum up the three criteria in just one: coordination improves if the process of creating culturally transmitted personal possibilities for action in firms is extended.

This systematic criterion allows us to counter a common criticism. It is often objected that the outcomes of an institution and culture are acceptable only from within the relevant institutional and cultural prerequisites. Thus, for example, the working of the market is accepted provided that we accept the validity of private property as an institutional prerequisite. If for moral reasons we reject private property, the outcome of the market is unacceptable and we must regard its supposed efficiency as fallacious, and above all unfair and greedy (Moore 2002, 2005a, b, 2008). Is this objection valid? With the dynamic and systematic criterion propounded above, it may be rejected, as institutional prerequisites are an essential part of personal action. Institutions and culture are not givens external to action, and therefore they are liable to appraisal. With the efficiency criterion, institutions and cultures may be appraised according to the personal possibilities for action that they afford. The only fact that is irreducible, i.e., axiomatic, is action as the primary human reality (von Mises 1996). This primary reality is human action, which consists of the deliberate seeking of certain valuable ends with scarce means.

The Morality of the Market

Market economy is the means to economic development and prosperity. But now our crisis is putting at the stake the market economy, the firm as institution, and the morality of profits. [34]Through this article, we have maintained that the market economy is not captured in the neoclassical model efficient price-clearing process based on the homo economicus. Market economy is based on the acting person within its socio-cultural framework. Value creation, the driving force of the modern organization, cannot be reduced to a factor of production or to objective knowledge. Creativity becomes real in structuring the means and the ends in projects. But it is fundamentally important

---

34   Hartman (2011) makes a pertinent defense of profits from an Aristotelian point of view.

to make it clear that the creative capacity of the person is dynamic. Creativity is not dynamic because it is developed in time, but because it goes beyond what is immediately given. This dynamism which creativity develops is the transformation of the action. This is the basic concept in understanding the capitalistic process; that the end is an imagined reality and that the means must be constituted.

In the previous section, we have presented an interactive view of the value creation process linking the person, the firm, and entrepreneurial culture. We should make it clear that these are not three distinct realities but three moments in the same process. These three moments are closely interlinked, so any changes in any one of them affect the creative process. Rather than speaking of what creativity is, we should ask where creativity comes from. In this view, the social practice of the firm is huge: the firm's social practice is to enhance the possibilities of persons.

As Ghoshal et al. say: "corporations, not abstract economic forces or governments, create and distribute most of an economy's wealth, innovate, trade and raise living standards" (1999, p. 9). The social institutions, in this case, firms, have their own dynamism, which depends on the opportunities that enable their members to exercise their creativity and capabilities. So following Moran and Ghoshal (1999), I can define the economic process as a value-creating process based on the following steps: (1) universe of all possible resource combinations; (2) perceived possibilities; (3) productive possibilities; (4) productive opportunities. And they affirm: "as many firms of different forms and sizes engage in this process, each broadens the scope of exchange in ways that allow it to focus on some fragmented bits of the knowledge that Hayek (1945) talked about" (Moran and Ghoshal 1999, p. 405). Creativity action is the result of our ability to project ourselves and to envisage what may exist in the future (Shane 2000; Venkataraman 1997). The background of action should not be sought in the past but in the attempt to get a more profitable present out of a future that does not exist.[35]

Any person, however, unadventurous, undertakes project outside her immediate area of development. The person has the ability to procure information that motivates her to act. If we reduce the entrepreneurial function to mere knowledge, there is no room for creative capacity, capacity that consists of seeing more possibilities where there is apparently nothing. It is not, as is often said, that person with great creative capacity needs little information in order to create great firms, but rather the other way round: such persons are able to create more practical information than others, which means we cannot confine the entrepreneurial function to great geniuses. Any person, by the fact of being a person, has this ability which is not reducible to objective knowledge (Dew et al. 2004).

---

35   The same idea was masterfully expressed by Professor Marías in the following words: "My life is not a thing, but rather a doing, reality projected into the future, that is argumentative and dramatic, and that is not exactly being but happening" (1996, p. 126). More bluntly, Drucker says: "the best way to predict the future is to create it" (1998, p. 197).

As we have said, the social function of the firm consists of fostering its employees' creative capacity. Not as a form of social benefit or the like. In fact, the firm's essential function is to enhance the real possibilities of its employees. The greater these possibilities, the greater the possibilities of monetary profit. There is a wider range of possibilities to try out. Therefore, we must not reduce the firm's function to that of making money and paying taxes. This is necessary, but not enough. Milton Friedman, Nobel laureate for Economics, says:

> The social responsibility of business is to increase its profits. Few trends could so thoroughly undermine the very foundations of our free society as the acceptance by corporate officials of a social responsibility other than to make as much money for their stockholders as possible. (Friedman 1970)

We may share Friedman's idea, but the following questions arise. How do we increase profits? What is the essence of the productive process? What needs to be encouraged and increased? The answer can be no other than the entrepreneurship of persons. This is the way to increase profits: creating, creating and creating! But this involves taking account of the efficiency criterion that we described in our previous section: entrepreneurial coordination and wealth increase if the process of creating culturally transmitted personal possibilities for action in firms is extended. All the fundamental work of Friedman on micro theory of consumption, monetary policy, and his defense of free market economy can be integrated in a more general and systematic framework. As Freeman says: "Better stakeholder theory focuses us on the multiplicity of ways that companies and entrepreneurs are out there creating value, making our lives better, and changing the world" (Agle et al. 2008, p. 166). Each work is not reduced to a technical command. We do not only make shoes or build houses. In every productive act, we seek something else. We seek to carry out those actions with ease, with the perfection of the specific power, and confidence of aim. Virtue is in this way a connaturality with the acts that belongs to the productive domain. It is a second acquired nature which empowers us with ability, brilliance, mastery, competence, and excellence to make shoes or houses. In other words, virtue is the fulfillment of being human in the dynamism of human action, either "knowing," "making," or "doing." As Rhonhemier points out: "virtue in all its types is a habit for carrying out well the actions of a faculty: an *habitus operatibus bonus*" (2011, p. 193).

In any action, there are external effects, *poiesis, facere*, and internal ones of *praxis, agere.* That is, external goods are achieved at institutional level in the schema: institution (goods)—culture (norms)—individual action (virtues). In this dynamic schema, ethics is the system of goods, norms, and virtues that makes personal action coherent at its societal, cultural, and individual levels. The technical virtue (*habitus operatibus bonus*) is the fulfillment or excellent of the intelligence respect to *poiesis, facere*, i.e., respect the act of "making" external goods. As MacIntyre recognizes: "this making and sustaining of forms of human community—and therefore of institutions—itself has all the characteristics of a practice, and moreover of a practice which stands in a peculiarly close relationship to the exercise of the virtue" (1985, pp. 194–195) In second place, as we have expounded previously, economics does not limit itself to the productive act, it encompasses also the election of ends and means of production inherent to economic action dynamism. This is the realm of prudence (phronesis) which is the fulfillment or excellence respect to praxis, *agere*, i.e., the act of "doing" or the choice of good actions. We are not just "making" shoes or houses; we are "doing" good shoes or houses. As the classic Greeks said that to live the good life one must live in a great city, we agree with Solomon (1992) when he says "to live a decent life choose the right company."

PART IV:

THE VISION OF THE FIRM AND ITS GOVERNANCE

Chapter 12

Corporate Responsibility

T HE TERM "corporate responsibility" means different things to different people. For some, it means environmental stewardship. For others, it means determining what social responsibilities corporations have to a wide range of "stakeholder" interests. For still others, it has to do with whether managers (especially executives) are attending to shareholder needs rather than their own. Yet another group may define corporate responsibility as complying with The Sarbanes-Oxley Act or the U.S. Federal Sentencing Guidelines. And still others may insist that corporate responsibility is about squaring corporate behavior with ethical frameworks that provide guidance for either what corporations should do or at least what they might aspire to achieve. All of the above—and the above is not an exhaustive list of what constitutes corporate responsibility—have legitimate conceptual foundations and literatures to back them up. Because they address different aspects of corporate responsibility, however, one can easily wander into an irresolvable argument as to what a corporation's responsibility really is. As one of my doctoral student once cracked, you never hear someone advocating for "corporate irresponsibility," but the question is the responsibility you are investigating.

This volume will not overcome these differences, but my hope is that it is a start. It is a start because no matter what responsibility one seeks to explore, it has to become a part of a corporation's governance processes if it is to actually apply to real issues. And those processes result from the vision one has of the firm. What is the corporation? What do we want it to do? What does it "look" like to us now? What do we "see" it do? What is our vision of the firm and what is its vision for itself? Knowing that vision informs what responsibilities the firm will undertake and the institutions and practices it will adopt.

Note that the rhetoric of this book addresses "the vision" of the firm, rather than "the theory" of the firm. Both terms refer to the obligations of the firm—especially whether it points to shareholders and the agency problem or whether it is about stakeholders and the prioritization problem—but we hope to take a step beyond that debate (without abandoning it). "Vision" connotes something more than theory; it suggests aesthetic, aspirational possibilities. A vision is more than theory, it is about goal-setting and quests. It is about "seeing" what companies might do. We may see, as Jack London does, that the corporation's purpose is to make a profit and keep shareholders happy or it may, as Per Saxegaard argues, point to a contribution toward global peace that businesses could contribute to through a set of behaviors he calls "businessworthy." Is this debate, then, simply a rehashing of the theory of the firm debates that revolve around shareholder-stakeholder obligations? I don't think so for three reasons.

First, one's vision is based in a reality of what a business deals with. London and Saxegaard, for example, are both successful business executives. They have no patience for idle Ivory Tower ruminations. The divergences between them seem based on a different conception of what the real world is like—or will be like—for businesses. It is a difference of what they see. If the firm is embedded in society and affected by society, more so now because of the Internet, the logical implication is that firms must attend to social demands. Thus Saxegaard frames his "businessworthiness" as essential to the success of the firm in the 21st Century. On the other hand, if the firm is primarily an organizational form where executives have pressures to reward shareholders for their investments, then the glasses through which one makes decisions will aim toward the prioritization of those shareholders. Theory follows vision. Indeed, much of the endless and fruitless debates of "shareholder vs stakeholder" rest upon what we see the firm to be.

Second, just as the definition of corporate responsibility differs, so too do businesses themselves. A small, privately held company is much different that a publicly held multinational corporation. It would not be surprising that they see their place in business and in society differently. Their definition of community, and the long term interests of the shareholders may be quite different. Applying a general "theory of the firm" to these kinds of different entities doesn't work well. If a privately held business wants to comprise its workforce of fifty percent people with disabilities, it is not illegal, but that business surely sees itself differently than a company with a million shareholders working in seventy countries with the pressures of being publicly traded forcing it to maximize short-term profitability. Rather than elaborating a theory of the firm, it seems important to first understand what a company sees itself doing. After that, theories and governance structures can fall into place.

Thus, third, unlike a theory of the firm, the question of considering what businesses "see" clarifies the starting points for the obligations and goals each has for a business. The shareholder-stakeholder argument frequently turns on what the responsibilities "ought" to be, but a vision makes clear that there is an observation point from which one "sees" responsibilities. The contributions to this volume exemplify this difference quite well.

The three chapters that begin the book set a theoretical stage for later discussions. Lisa Fairfax, the Leroy Sorenson Merrifield Research Professor of Law and the George Washington University Law School, draws attention to the idea that whenever there is a perceived breakdown in corporate governance, there are calls for reform. Yet, those calls may not modify primacy of shareholders in a governance model. Many corporate scandals, after all, do not result from corporations taking advantage of stakeholders in favor of shareholders, but result from managers taking advantage of shareholders. Shareholders too have vulnerabilities in large corporations where there is a separation of ownership and management. Many incentives exist for managers to ignore shareholder concerns and simply make as much money as the managers can. This, for example, is one part of the argument over appropriate levels of CEO compensation. Thus, governance reforms may not necessarily augment attention to non-shareholder constituents; instead, they may well reinforce the primacy of shareholders in an environment where that choice of governance model is itself contested.

The Darden School's Edward Freeman and Dean Krehmeyer provide another perspective. Freeman, of course, is rightly credited as one of the seminal thinkers and founders of contemporary corporate responsibility scholarship. He and Krehmeyer founded an Institute for Corporate Ethics at the Business Roundtable. Based on a study conducted by this organization, Freeman and Krehmyer call attention to the problem of short-termism. That is, given liquid markets, where capital can flee from a company in an instance, the pressures for managers to make decisions on the basis of short-term impact is both significant and also tends to leave out considerations for non-shareholder constituents. This, in turn, marginalizes the (empirically documented likelihood) strategic, long-term benefits of practices that foster goodwill and reputation. Hence, their vision of the firm is one aimed at aligning shareholder and stakeholder constituents in the long-term. To do so requires addressing short-termism. With this foundation, they demonstrate how this perspective makes a difference in assessing the issue of CEO compensation. It also provides them with a way to propose a new narrative and vision for business that creates value for stakeholders.

After these theoretical foundations, the subsequent three chapters provide assessments from three business people. Per Saxegaard, the founder and president of Norden Realkapital Group and also the founder and president of the Business for Peace Foundation (both in Oslo, Norway) claims that, as a practical reality, the world is changing. With technology and communications placing individuals in ever-closer possible contact, individuals will be increasingly accountable for the impact of business actions and those actions make a concrete difference around a globalized business environment. Saxegaard calls for a concept of "businessworthiness," which leads to personal fulfillment, and also can contribute to a more peaceful world.

Saxegaard's "golden rule of business" is to only offer a deal that you would like to accept for yourself. This, he argues, is a vision of business that promotes "handshakes" of ethics and responsibility, creating win-win situations for both sides of a business contract. Such win-wins avoid structural violence of exploitation and instead focuses on winning by finding a way for a contracting partner to also win. This, he calls, "businessworthy" and this way of doing business will contribute to an interdependence between business and peace as well as being a way of doing business that builds your own reputation and personal happiness.

Adrian Keevil, a doctoral student at the Darden School of Business responds positively to Saxegaard's vision of the firm. Keevil more explicitly ties Saxegaard's real world experience to philosophical versions of stakeholder theory.

Jack London, Chair of the Board of CACI offers, at least at first blush, a very different depiction of reality. London insists that a company provides goods and services that meet economic needs and create value for the company's owners. Government, not business, is a public institution, but they have—and should have—different goals and purposes. Because of this, London is cautious of calls for companies to adopt corporate social responsibility goals and purposes. Of course, companies should be ethical, law-abiding, and decent citizens; by being profitable, companies provide real value to employees and communities as well as shareholders. He also holds out the possibility that a given company (for instance, an energy firm) might have an interest in environmental sustainability, but insists that the greatest public benefit companies provide is to employ individuals, pay their taxes and spur innovation and productivity; it is only financially successful companies that can afford to engage in other activities.

Thus, London's vision for the firm is to be what he says it has always been: "a value-driven enterprise where goods and services are offered to make profits." This, rather than trying to have corporations take on social endeavors should drive corporate purposes and corporate behavior. Having said this, London is a bit like Milton Friedman, whose work is often misunderstood. Friedman's famous *New York Times Magazine* article, "the Social Responsibility of Business is to Increase Its Profits" frequently gets analyzed in terms of its provocative title. The article itself is more nuanced as Friedman recognizes that actions that benefit a firm's reputation may be quite valuable. Companies also should operate within the bounds of the law and fair play. Of course, strategic CSR, fair play, and obeying the law captures much of the field of corporate responsibility. Similarly, while London demands that companies focus on being profitable, it is with a nuanced view of the many things that go into that equation.

Patricia Kanashiro, a professor at Loyola University Maryland takes a position that more explicitly embracing the need for companies to take stakeholders into account. More so that London's rhetoric, she places importance on corporate constituents and then shows how attention to them can be financially rewarding. At first blush, one would look at the London and Kanashiro opposites much like the contrast between London and Saxegaard, whose position is not unlike Kanashiro's. Reading more closely, one finds a good deal of common ground on the practice of firm activities with rhetorical departures of what each believes firms should do. To be sure, one could describe this dichotomy in different ways, but I would propose that London, on the one hand, and Kanashiro and Saxegaard, on the other hand, articulate different theories of the firm, but their vision of the firm is not all that different because all of them see the firm embedded within a set of relationships that are best served by a multi-tasking of profit-making with attention to their constituents, especially defined long-term. How they articulate that embeddedness, however, because theoretically separate.

Another contribution in this section focuses on financial firms and pharmaceutical companies. Countess Alexandra of Denmark and Timothy Fort look at examples of companies in these industries who have done exemplary work. There are some, but not as many as one would hope and so the Countess—who serves on the Board of Directors of Ferring Pharmaceutical in Switzerland and who also is chair of that company's ethics committee—and Fort sketch a model of how companies in these sectors might improve their work. The heart of their model focuses on sincerity: The instrumental impact of corporate responsibility is most significant when corporate responsibility is undertaken for sincere, non-instrumental reasons. This argument has real importance for the further improvement in pharmaceutical CSR.

David Berdish and Meghan Chappel-Brown round out this middle section. Berdish, the Director of Ford Motor Company's Human Rights Program and Chapple-Brown, Director of Sustainability at George Washington University focus on the importance of "trust" has a critical resource for a company. How one builds trust is based on many behaviors that have both economic and non-economic aspects. Berdish and Chapple-Brown present Ford's efforts to transform from a car company to a transportation company. Such a transformation requires innovation and are successful when they provide genuine value for customers and investors. But what allows companies to move from a current state to a future state is when they have a preexisting reputation for being transparent and trustworthy with those with whom they deal.

Berdish and Chapple-Brown argue that Ford is in the midst of this transformation and their attention to fair labor standards (beginning with Henry Ford's strategy of paying workers enough to afford the company's products to a more recent revitalization of that legacy) and human rights standards has allowed them to build a reservoir of trust with groups that can be helpful, even crucial to the company's efforts to design transporation systems that cut across existing cultural, social, and political landscapes.

Finally, Marc Lavine, a professor at the University of Massachusetts-Boston brings to bear another kind of analysis. His assessment focuses on how scholarly dialogue has historically morphed into a social movement. In particular, Lavine assesses the emerging perspective of "Peace Through Commerce" that argues that businesses can engage in behavior that is linked to reduction of violence. Using theories of social movement, Lavine comments on the ways in which movements that do have an explicit vision of the firm might more concretely develop into social movements given the kinds of dialogues that currently are occurring and where they might develop in the future.

The Financial Crisis and an Other-Regarding Vision of the Firm: Oxymoron or Opportunity?

Lisa M. Fairfax[1]

THIS CHAPTER examines the impact of the global financial crisis and corresponding recovery efforts on the advancement of an "other-regarding" vision of the corporate firm.[2] That is, a vision of the firm that extends beyond the more traditional "shareholder primacy" norm, which focuses on shareholders and short-term profit maximization.[3] The global financial crisis and corresponding recovery effort have resulted in significant changes to our economy and the securities market, including significant corporate governance changes. It is likely too soon to assess the impact of those changes. However, as this chapter will demonstrate, it is entirely possible that some of the corporate governance changes may pose considerable challenges for the advancement of an other-regarding vision of the firm.

Interestingly, the crisis and recovery effort pose somewhat of a conundrum for advancing an other-regarding vision of the firm. On the one hand, the current economic environment may be viewed as an ideal setting for advancing alternative norms regarding the corporation and its primary objective. The global financial crisis and recession exposed flaws in our current economic and financial systems. That exposure, in turn, has prompted questions about the legitimacy of the shareholder primacy norm because many view that norm as a key component of those systems.[4] In other words,

---

1   Leroy Sorenson Merrifield Research Professor of Law, George Washington University Law School. J.D. Harvard Law School, A.B. Harvard College. I would like to thank Timothy Fort for organizing this volume and the Corporate Governance and Vision of the Firm Conference. I also would like to thank the participants of that conference for their comments and suggestions on earlier version of this chapter. All errors, of course, are mine.

2   In corporate literature, theories of the firm that focusing on a corporate obligation to non-shareholder constituents or stakeholders such as employees and the broader community are sometimes referred to as the stakeholder theory or "social entity" conception of the firm.   *See e.g.*, William M. Evan & R. Edward Freeman, *A Stakeholder Theory of the Modern Corporation: Kantian Capitalism, in Ethical Theory and Business* 97, 101-105 (Tom L. Beauchamp & Norma E. Bowie eds., 3d ed. 1988); William W. Bratton, *The Economic Structure of the Post-Contractual Corporation*, 87 Nw. U. L. Rev. 180, 208-15 (1992); Lisa M. Fairfax, *The Rhetoric of Corporate Law: The Impact of Stakeholder Rhetoric on Corporate Norms*, 31 J. Corp. L. 675, 679-80 (2006); Timothy L. Fort, *The Corporation as Mediating Institutions: An Efficacious Synthesis of Stakeholder Theory and Corporate Constituency Statues*, 73 Notre Dame L. Rev. 173, 184-86 (1997); Lawrence E. Mitchell, *A Theoretical and Practical Framework for Enforcing Constituency Statutes*, 70 Tex. L. Rev. 579 (1992); Eric W. Orts, *Beyond Shareholders: Interpreting Corporate Constituency Statues*, 61 Geo. Wash. L. Rev. 14, 16 (1992). This chapter uses the term "other-regarding" in the same vein as such theories. *See also*, E. Merrick Dodd, Jr., *For Whom Are Corporate Managers Trustees?*, 45 Harv. L. Rev. 1145, 1148 (1932) (touching off debate with Professor Adolph Berle regarding the proper focus of the firm).

3   *See* infra note ___.

4   *See* Stephen Bainbridge, *Director Primacy: The Means and Ends of Corporate Governance*, 97 Nw U. L. Rev. 547, 563 (2003); Ronald Chen & Jon Hanson, *The Illusion of Law: The Legitimating Schemas of Modern Policy and Corporate Law*, 103 Mich. L. Rev. 1, 37 (2004); Henry Hansmann & Reinier Kraakman, *The End of History for Corporate Law*, 89 Geo. L.J. 439, 468 (2001).

the financial meltdown has prompted questions regarding whether the shareholder primacy model, with its focus on short-term profit-making, may have incentivized or at least contributed to corporate excess, inappropriate risk-taking, or other forms of corporate misbehavior.[5] Hence, one reaction to that meltdown may be to reject the shareholder-primacy model in favor of one that focuses on ethics, responsibility, and a consideration of how corporate behavior impacts non-shareholder constituents such as employees, creditors, and the broader society. In this regard, the current climate seems an ideal one for re-examining the corporation's role in society, and molding a vision of the corporation that goes beyond short-term profit concerns and towards consideration of other interests and objectives.

On the other hand, the economic crisis itself, as well as reforms generated by the crisis, pose challenges for any such re-examination. Indeed, one of the primary corporate governance reforms aimed at responding to the crisis has been to increase shareholder power.[6] Proponents of increasing shareholder power insist that such an increase makes it less likely that corporate officers and directors will feel free to engage in excessive risk-taking or other inappropriate action, without repercussions.[7] In their view, increased shareholder power enables shareholders to play a role in checking corporate excess and misbehavior. The idea of increasing shareholder power as a means of checking corporate abuses appears to have garnered considerable traction in the legislative arena, as evidenced by various reforms focused on enhancing shareholders' power. The titles of proposed Congressional legislation highlight further this focus. For example, Senator Charles Schumer sponsored the "Shareholder Bill of Rights,"[8] while Representative Gary Peters sponsored the "Shareholder Empowerment Act."[9] Both bills are aimed at increasing accountability of corporate officers and directors by increasing power to shareholders. However, it is entirely possible that increasing power to shareholders could have negative repercussions for the corporation's ability to focus on other non-shareholder stakeholders in the corporation, or otherwise focusing on issues that do not involve short-term profit maximization.[10] In this regard, it is entirely possible that the reforms

---

5   *See* Michael Skapinker, *Responsible Companies' First Duty is Survival*, Financial Times, July 12, 2010 (noting "the blind pursuit of shareholder value was blamed for brining the banking system down"), available at http://www.ft.com/cms/s/0/eba6a20a-8de3-11df-9153-00144feab49a.html.

6   *See* infra notes__ and accompanying text.

7   *See* Lucian Bebchuk, *The Case for Increasing Shareholder Power*, 118 Harv. L. Rev. 833, 836 (2005).

8   *See* Shareholder Bill of Rights Act of 2009, S. 1074, 111th Cong. (2009), available at http://law.du.edu/documents/corporate-governance/legislation/bill-text-shareholders-bill-of-rights-act-of-2009.pdf (bill to "provide shareholders with enhanced authority over the nomination, election, and compensation of public company executives").

9   *See* Shareholder Empowerment Act of 2009, H.R. 2861, 111th Cong. (2009), available at http://www.govtrack.us/congress/bill.xpd?bill=h111-2861.

10   *See* Lisa M. Fairfax, *Making the Corporation Safe for Shareholder Democracy*, 69 Ohio State L. J. 53, 56 (2008) [hereinafter Fairfax, *Shareholder Democracy*] ("one objection of increasing shareholder power is that such an increase

we have chosen bring us closer to a more traditional shareholder primacy model, and thus farther away from alternative, other-regarding, models of the firm.

This chapter will examine that possibility. This chapter begins with a discussion of some of the key corporate governance reforms aimed at increasing shareholder power. In connection with that discussion, it is important to note that there is considerable debate about whether increased shareholder power will increase managerial accountability or otherwise prevent excessive risk-taking or corporate malfeasance.[11] This chapter does not engage that debate. Instead, this chapter highlights reforms that appear to augment shareholder power without addressing the broader question regarding whether that apparent augmentation will achieve its desired result. The second section of this chapter analyzes the manner in which shareholder-centered reforms may pose challenges for a normative or descriptive vision of the firm that favors consideration of non-shareholder constituents. Third, this chapter briefly discusses potential ways in which the other-regarding vision of the firm may remain viable despite such challenges.

A. Shareholder Power as Corporate Governance Reform

The federal government has played a significant role in this current crisis, passing a host of sweeping reforms, and along the way spending hundreds of billions of dollars.[12] Those reforms encompass a variety of different mechanisms designed to address a variety of different issues.[13] However, many of the federal reforms aimed at responding to perceived corporate governance defects focus on enhancing shareholder power.[14] Some of the state corporate governance reforms have a similar focus.[15] In addition, shareholders have been actively engaged in efforts to increase their voice over corporate affairs, and that activism has yielded success.[16] The combination of these federal, state, and

---

would force directors and officers to focus solely on profits to the detriment of stakeholders"). *See also* Bebchuk, supra note __ at 912.

11   Compare Bebchuk, supra note __ at 836 with Stephen M. Bainbridge, *Director Primacy and Shareholder Disempowerment*, 119 Harv. L. Rev. 1735, 1746 (2005); William Bratton and Michael Wachter, *The Case Against Shareholder Empowerment*, 158 U. Pa. L. Rev. 653 (2010).

12   *See* Lisa M. Fairfax, *The Legal Origins Theory in Crisis*, 2009 B.Y.U. L. Rev. 1571, 1590-1603 (discussing legislative response to financial crisis); Steven M. Davidoff and David Zaring, Regulation by Deal: the Government's Response to the Financial Crisis, 61 Admin. L. Rev. 463 (2009).

13   *See id*

14   *See* e.g., Dodd-Frank Wall Street Reform and Consumer Protection Act, Pub. L. 111-203, H.R. 4173, §§ 951 and 971 (2010), available at http://docs.house.gov/rules/finserv/111_hr4173_finsrvcr.pdf [hereinafter Dodd-Frank Act]; Comm. on Capital Mkts. Regulation, Interim Report 93 (2006), available at http://www.capmktsreg.org/pdfs/11. 30Committee_Interim_ ReportREV2.pdf (focusing on the importance of enhanced shareholder rights).

15   *See* Del. Code Ann. Tit. 8, § 112 (supp. 2009) (adopting proxy access procedures) and § 113 (adopting proxy expense reimbursement provisions).

16   *See* Fairfax, *Shareholder Democracy* supra note __ at 61-71.

shareholder-sponsored reforms appears to have generated an altered corporate governance landscape in which shareholders have greater authority within the corporation.[17] This section will discuss four elements of that altered landscape: (1) "proxy access"—shareholders' ability to nominate candidates of their choice on the corporation's proxy statement, (2) "say on pay"—a shareholder advisory vote on executive compensation matters, (3) "majority voting"—a default regime pursuant to which directors are elected only if they receive a majority of the shareholder vote, and (4) changes in the rules associated with discretionary broker voting.

1. Proxy Access

The majority of public company shareholders vote by proxy.[18] Thus, instead of attending a shareholders' meeting and voting in-person, public company shareholders vote by sending a proxy card to the corporation, which card identifies the candidates for whom they have decided to vote.[19] Thus, when public corporations hold a director election, they must distribute a proxy statement, sometimes referred to as a ballot, which identifies and provides information on the candidates for whom shareholders may cast a vote, and contains a proxy card on which shareholders essentially can vote.[20] Because the vast majority of public shareholders vote by proxy, the corporate proxy statement often becomes the primary, if not exclusive, election platform.[21]

Historically, that platform has been the sole province of management-supported candidates.[22] Since their inception, the federal proxy rules have provided that only the names of management-nominated candidates could appear on the corporation's proxy statement; candidates nominated solely by shareholders could not appear on the corporate ballot.[23]

Shareholders who desired to nominate candidates could pursue one of three alternatives. First, they could recommend candidates to management, and convince

---

17 For an interesting discussion of this shift and its impact on boards and executives, *See* Marcel Kahan and Edward Rock, *Embattled CEOs*, 88 Tex. L. Rev. 987 (2010); Martin Lipton, *Some Thoughts for Boards of Directors in 2008*, Dec. 6, 2007, available at http://papers.ssrn.com/sol3/papers.cfm?abstract_id=1090970.

18 *See* Robert C. Clark, *Corporate Law* 360 (1986); *See* Facilitating Shareholder Director Nominations, Exchange Act Release No. 34-62764, Investment Company Release No. 29, 384, 9 and 9 n.28 (Aug. 25, 2010) [hereinafter Final Proxy Access Rule], available at http://www.sec.gov/rules/final/2010/33-9136.pdf .

19 *See* Securities Exchange Act of 1934 Rule 14a-4, 17 C.F.R. §240.14a-4(a)(2) (2010). More precisely, the proxy card grants the corporation the authority to vote on the shareholders behalf in the manner instructed by the shareholder.

20 *See* Securities Exchange Act of 1934 Rule 14a, 17 C.F.R. §§ 240.14a-3 and 240.14a-4 (2010).

21 *See* Final Proxy Access Rule, supra note __ at 9.

22 In this context, this chapter uses the term "management" to include both officers and directors of the corporation.

23 *See* Securities Exchange Act of 1934 Rule 14a-8, 17 C.F.R. 240.14a-8(i)(8) (2007).

management to place those candidates on the corporate proxy statement. Unfortunately, evidence suggests that management frequently declined to endorse shareholder-supported candidates, making this alternative largely illusory.[24] Second, shareholders could nominate candidates at the annual meeting. However, because most shareholders vote by proxy and otherwise do not attend shareholder meetings in person, nominations from the floor of the shareholders' meeting would be tantamount to an empty gesture.[25] Third, shareholders could prepare and distribute their own proxy statement. While this process is likely to have the most realistic impact on director elections, the expense associated with preparing and distributing a proxy statement made such a process prohibitive for most shareholders.[26] Requiring shareholders to prepare and distribute their own proxy statement also involves collective action and other logistical problems.[27] Hence, each of shareholders' available alternatives for nominating director candidates poses challenges that significantly hinder shareholders from truly exercising their nomination authority.

Granting shareholders proxy access—access to the corporate proxy statement for purposes of nominating candidates of their choice—appears to represent an ideal solution for shareholders seeking to play a role in the director nomination process. Proxy access eliminates or reduces the financial and other costs associated with the available alternatives for shareholder nominations.[28] To be sure, critics of proxy access abound. Some insist that such access will impose unnecessary costs on companies, and indirectly shareholders, particularly because such access appears to increase the likelihood of proxy contests.[29] The predicted costs of proxy access not only include the costs of fighting more proxy contests, but also the costs associated with the distraction and

---

24 *See* Security Holder Director Nominations, Exchange Act Release No. 48,626, Investment Company Act Release No. 26,206, 68 Fed. Reg. 60,784, 60,786 (proposed Oct. 23, 2003) [hereinafter 2003 Proposed Proxy Access Rule] (noting that shareholder recommendations to the board's nominating committees rarely translate into actual nominations onto the corporate ballot).

25 *See* Final Proxy Access Rule, supra note __ at 9-10 (noting that most shareholders cast their vote before the meeting, thus nominations at a meeting have no realistic prospects of being effective).

26 *See* Final Proxy Access Rule, supra note __ at 313-320; Lucian Bebchuk, *The Myth of the Shareholder Franchise*, 93 Va. L. Rev. 675, 603 (2007). It was believed that the adoption in 2008 of electronic proxy access rules would provide a cost-effective substitute for proxy access. *See* Internet Availability of Proxy Materials, Exchange Act Release No. 52, 926, Investment Company Act Release No. 27, 182, 70 Fed. Reg. 74, 598, 74, 599 (proposed Dec. 8, 2005); Lisa M. Fairfax, *The Future of Shareholder Democracy*, 84 Ind. L. Rev. 1259, 1279-86 (2009) [hereinafter Fairfax, *Future*]; Jeffrey Gordon, *Proxy Contests In An Era Of Increasing Shareholder Power: Forget Issuer Proxy Access And Focus* on E-Proxy, 61 Vand. L. Rev. 475, 487-90 (2008) However, that regime has confronted obstacles that hinder its utility. *See* Fairfax, supra note __ at 1279-86 (predicting obstacles).

27 *See* Final Proxy Access Rule, supra note __ at 320-322; Fairfax, Future, supra note __ at 1286 (noting potential disadvantage created by having to send separate proxy materials).

28 *See* Final Proxy Access Rule, supra note __ at 312-323 (discussing benefits of proxy access).

29 *See* Lipton, supra note __ at 6.

time-consuming nature of a proxy contests and focusing on shareholder rights.[30] Other opponents fear that proxy access, with its potential for enhanced proxy contests, will dissuade qualified board candidates from participating in corporate elections.[31] Still others express concern that proxy access will enable certain shareholders with special or narrow personal interests to advance those interests to the detriment of the company and the broader shareholder class.[32]

Despite these concerns, many shareholders and their advocates believe that the lack of proxy access strips the shareholder vote of any real power. Because shareholders vote by proxy, excluding shareholder nominated candidates from the corporate proxy statement essentially means that shareholders vote on candidates nominated solely by corporate managers and directors unless there is a proxy contest. However, the expenses and other logistical constraints associated with a proxy contests have made them relatively rare.[33] As a result, the vast majority of director candidates not only are nominated solely by corporate management and the board, but also run without challenge.[34] Shareholder activists contend that such a regime renders shareholders' vote meaningless, and transforms director elections into a rubber stamp of managerial choice.[35]

Shareholder activists further insist that such a regime makes their voting power ineffective as a means of ensuring corporate accountability, or otherwise checking corporate misbehavior. Shareholders' voting rights are believed to be one of the most important mechanisms for shareholders to impact corporate behavior.[36] By decreasing the likelihood that directors need be concerned about shareholders' influence over their board seats, however, shareholders believe that the lack of proxy access also decreases officers and directors need to be concerned with repercussions from shareholders related to their failure to act in a manner that benefits shareholders.[37] Shareholder activists argue that the lack of access therefore significantly undermines the potential power of their vote.

Given the tremendous impact it could have on election outcomes, shareholders have long viewed proxy access as the cornerstone of shareholder rights, and have sought

---

30   *See* Final Proxy Access Rules, supra note __ at 344 (describing and analyzing arguments related to the costs of proxy access)

31   *See id* at 347-348 (detailing concern).

32   *See* Bainbridge, supra note __ at 1754; Romano, supra note __ at 811-12.

33   *See* Bebchuk, supra note __ at 856.

34   *See* Fairfax, Future, supra note __ at 1266-67.

35   *See id* at 1266-67 (discussing shareholder arguments).

36   *See* Bebchuk, supra note __ at 851; Blasisu Inds., Inc. v. Atlas Corp., 564 A.2d 651, 659 (Del. Ch. 1988).

37   *See* Fairfax, *Future,* supra note __ at 1267; *See* also Final Proxy Access Rule, supra note __ at 331-33 (noting potential of proxy access to lead to "greater accountability on the part of incumbent directors to the extent they see a close link between their performance and the prospect of removal").

to secure such access for decades. At least four times in its history, the Securities and Exchange Commission (the "SEC") has proposed such access, but failed to implement it.[38] In July of 2009, the SEC yet again proposed a proxy access regime for shareholders.[39] A little over a year later, in August of 2010, the SEC for the first time in history, voted to implement a proxy access regime.[40] The new rules mandate proxy access for all public corporations. The rules grant proxy access to shareholders who (a) own at least three percent of the voting power of a company's securities, (b) have held the securities continuously for at least three years, and (c) do not seek a change of control of the company.[41] With respect to this final requirement, the rules provide that the maximum number of shareholder-supported candidates that can be nominated pursuant to the rules is one, or the number of candidates representing up to twenty-five percent of the entire board, whichever is greater.[42]

The new rules also allow shareholders to propose their own proxy access structure, which proposal can appear on the corporation's proxy statement and be voted on by shareholders.[43] If shareholders approve the proposal, the new structure would not supplant the SEC's mandated proxy access rules, but rather would provide an additional avenue for shareholders to nominate candidates of their choice on the corporate ballot.[44]

In adopting the proxy access rules, the SEC noted that the financial crisis had "heightened the serious concerns of many shareholders about the accountability and responsiveness of some companies and boards of directors to shareholder interests."[45] Because the proxy process represented a principal way for shareholders to "hold boards

---

38 *See* Fairfax, *Future*, supra note __ at 1273-1277 (detailing previous SEC proxy access proposals).

39 *See* Facilitating Shareholder Director Nominations, Release No. 33-9046, 34-90089 (June 10, 2009) [74 FR 29024], hereinafter 2009 Proxy Access Proposal, available at http://www.sec.gov/rules/proposed/2009/33-9046.pdf .

40 *See* Final Proxy Access Rule, supra note __. Prior to that implementation, and in direct response to arguments that the SEC lacked authority to mandate proxy access, Congress passed a law specifically authorizing the SEC to propose a proxy access regime. *See* Dodd-Frank Act, supra note __ at §971 (a) and (b). *See also* Final Proxy Access Rules, supra note __ at 22.

41 *See* Final Proxy Access Rules, supra note __ at 24-25.

42 *See id* at 26.

43 *See id* at 33.

44 *See id* at 230-32. Importantly, the new proposal rule reverses one implemented a little over two years prior in 2007. That rule made clear that the federal proxy rules not only prohibited shareholder-nominated candidates from appearing on the corporation's proxy statement, but also prohibited shareholder proposals aimed at creating a procedure for allowing shareholder access from appearing on the corporate proxy statement. *See* Shareholder Proposals Relating to the Election of Directors, Exchange Act Release No. 56,914, Investment Company Act Release No. 28,075, 72 Fed. Reg. 70,450, 70,452-3 (Dec.11, 2007) [hereinafter 2007 Final Shareholder Proposal Rule].

45 *See* Final Proxy Access Rule, supra note __ at 7.

accountable and influence matters of corporate policy,"[46] the SEC took the historic step of passing a proxy access rule for the first time in the near seventy-year history of the federal proxy regime. The new proxy access rules not only represent the quintessential example of reforms aimed at enhancing corporate accountability through enhancing shareholder power, but also represent a water-shed moment in securities laws and the effort to augment shareholder rights.

2. Say on Pay

In recent years, groups ranging from shareholders to legislators and the general public have expressed considerable outrage over large executive compensation packages, and what appear to be outsized bonuses and severance arrangements, particularly at companies in financial trouble.[47] These groups insist that there needs to be a tighter connection between executive pay and corporate performance.[48] They also insist that executive compensation structures may have incentivized corporate managers to engage in inappropriate risk, and thereby contributed to the financial crisis.[49]

While there have been a number of reforms aimed at addressing the problems associated with executive compensation, there also has been significant support for "say on pay." The term "say on pay" refers to granting shareholders the ability to cast an advisory vote on executives' compensation packages. To be sure, the vote is only advisory, and hence corporations are free to ignore it. Moreover, opponents not only contend that such a vote is not likely to positively impact executive compensation, but also argue that the complexity of compensation decisions are better left to the board.[50] Nevertheless, in other countries where such votes are required, say on pay appears to have impacted compensation structures, particularly by generating a tighter connection between pay and performance.[51]

---

46   *See id* at 8.

47   *See* e.g., Harris Interactive, *Polls Find Strong Populist Mood in Europe and to a Lesser Extent in the USA*, Harris Poll, tbl. 4, July 25, 2007, available at http://www.harrisinteractive.com/harris_poll/index.asp?PID=791 (revealing that 77% of Americans believe that executives are over-paid); Michael B. Dorff, *Confident Uncertainty, Excessive Compensation and the Obama Plan*, 85 Ind. L. J. 491, 492 (2010); Lucian Bebchuk & Jesse Fried, *Pay Without Performance: The Unfulfilled Promise of Executive Compensation*, 27-31 (2004). For the debate over the extent to which executive compensation can be classified as excessive *see* Dorff, supra, at 493 n.7.

48   *See* Bebchuk & Fried, supra note __ at 27-31.

49   *See* Lucian A. Bebchuk & Holger Spamann, *Regulating Bankers' Pay*, 98 GEO. L. J. 247 (2010); Frederick Tung, *Pay for Banker Performance: Structuring Executive Compensation for Risk Regulation*, available at http://papers.ssrn.com/sol3/papers.cfm?abstract_id=1546229.

50   *See* Jeffrey N. Gordon, *"Say on Pay": Cautionary Notes on the U.K. Experience and the Case for Shareholder Opt-In*, 46 Harv. J. on Legis. 323, 352-353 (2009); Andrew Lund, *Say on Pay's Bundling Problems*, 12-13 (2010), available at http://ssrn.com/abstract=1598384.

51   *See* Fabrizio Ferri & David Maber, *Say on Pay Votes and CEO Compensation: Evidence from the UK*, 20, available at http://papers.ssrn.com/sol3/papers.cfm?abstract_id=1420394. But *see* Gordon, supra note __ 352-53 (questioning

Evidence of this kind of impact has spurred support for say on pay in the US. Federal reforms reflect this support.[52] The federal stimulus bill required companies receiving funds from the troubled asset relief program ("TARP") to grant their shareholders a say on pay vote.[53] The Dodd-Frank Wall Street Reform and Consumer Protection Act (the "Dodd-Frank Act") extended this requirement to all public companies.[54] Under the Dodd-Frank Act, shareholders are entitled to an advisory vote on executive compensation as well as golden parachutes paid in connection with a merger, acquisition, or similar transaction.[55]

By giving shareholders a vote related to compensation packages, say on pay is yet another reform that seeks to encourage accountability by increasing shareholder power over corporate decision-making.

3. Majority Voting

Historically most directors in public corporations were elected under a plurality voting system.[56] A plurality system refers to one whereby directors are elected so long as they receive a plurality of the votes cast, without counting votes that are withheld or cast against them. Under such a system, it is theoretically possible that a director can be elected into office even if ninety-nine percent of the shareholders withhold their vote against the director. Plurality voting is the default voting method under most state corporation statutes, and historically most corporations opted to operate their director elections pursuant to that default rule.[57]

In 2005 shareholder activists began a campaign aimed at encouraging corporations to embrace a majority voting rule.[58] Majority voting refers to a system pursuant to which a director must receive a majority of the vote in order to be elected. Shareholder advocates believe majority voting is important because it ensures that their votes can truly

---

whether the US will experience results similar to the UK).

52   Shareholders also have actively sought to encourage corporations to adopt say on pay at particular companies. *See* Gordon, supra note __ at 338-340. In 2009, say on pay was the most prevalent proposal submitted. *See* RiskMetrics Group, 2009 Proxy Season Scorecard (as of Dec. 12, 2009), available at http://www.riskmetrics.com/knowledge/proxy_season_watchlist_2009.

53   *See* American Recovery and Reinvestment Act of 2009, Pub. L.åNo. 111-5, § 7001, 123 Stat. 516-20 (2009).

54   *See* Dodd-Frank Act, supra note __ at §951(a)(1).

55   *See id*

56   *See* Claudia H. Allen, *Study Of Majority Voting In Director Elections II* (2007), available at http://www.ngelaw.com/files/upload/majority_callen_020707.pdf.

57 See, e.g., Del. Code Ann. tit. 8, § 216(3) (Supp. 2008); Model Bus. Corp. Act § 7.28(a) (2007).

58   *See* Fairfax, *Future*, supra note __ at 1290.

impact election outcomes.[59] Indeed, shareholders have increasingly engaged in "withhold the vote" campaigns whereby shareholders organize campaigns to withhold their vote against a particular director or directors.[60] Under the plurality system, a withhold the vote campaign is essentially symbolic because directors can be elected even when shareholders withhold a substantial portion of their vote from such directors.[61] By contrast, a majority voting system ensures that directors cannot get elected without majority shareholder support, or that directors must tender their resignation when they fail to receive a majority vote.[62] This means that withhold the vote campaigns can have direct repercussions under a majority vote regime. Shareholders also contend that majority voting can impact corporate conduct. In shareholders' view, the plurality system was defective because it failed to embody an actual threat of removal for directors who engaged in misconduct, therefore decreasing the likelihood that directors would feel accountable to shareholders.[63] Majority voting corrects this defect, and thus serves to indirectly encourage greater director to accountability to shareholder concerns.[64]

While there is debate about the effectiveness of majority voting,[65] the majority voting campaign has yielded impressive results. To be sure, Congress proposed, but did not implement, a mandatory majority voting rule under the Dodd-Frank Act.[66] Nevertheless, shareholders have made considerable progress in this area. Indeed, prior to 2005, the plurality system was the dominant voting regime at most public companies.[67] Since that time, shareholders have managed to convince a significant number of corporations to adopt some form of a majority voting regime. Such a regime either requires that a director receive a majority of the shareholder vote in order to be elected, or that a

59 *See* William K. Sjostrom and Young Sang Kim, *Majority Voting For the Election of Directors*, 40 Conn. L. Rev. 495, 463, 468-69 (2007).

60 *See* Riskmetrics Group, 2009 *Postseason Report: A New Voice in Governance: Global Policymakers Shape the Road to Reform*, 10-11 (2009), available at http://www.riskmetrics.com//system/files/private/2009_PSR_Public_final.pdf; Riskmetrics Group, 2008 Postseason Report, 1711 PLI/Corp 89, 102-04 (2009).

61 *See* Joseph Grundfest, *Just Vote No: A Minimalist Strategy for Dealing with Barbarians Inside the Gate*, 45 Stan. L. Rev. 857, 905-908 (1993) (noting that, though symbolic, vote no campaigns could have an impact on corporate behavior).

62 *See* Sjostrom and Kim, supra note __ at 480-81. Despite contentions regarding the influence of majority voting, the authors conclude that "majority voting as implemented in practice [is] little more than smoke and mirrors." *See id* at 463.

63 *See* Fairfax, *Future*, supra note __ at 1294-95.

64 *See id*

65 *See* Sjostrom and Kim, supra note __ at 463.

66 *See* Ted Allen, *Reform Bill Won't Include Majority Voting Mandate*, June 24, 2010, available at http://blog.riskmetrics.com/gov/2010/06/house-agrees-to-drop-majority-voting-mandate.html.

67 *See* Allen, note __ at ii; Kahan and Rock, note __ at 1010.

director tender her resignation if she fails to receive majority shareholder support.[68] By the end of 2009, over seventy percent of S&P 500 companies and more than sixty percent of Fortune 500 companies had adopted some form of majority voting regime.[69] Moreover, in an effort to facilitate majority voting, Delaware (the incorporation home of most public companies) as well as several other states, amended their corporate statute,[70] while the American Bar Association ("ABA") revised the Model Business Corporation Act.[71]

4. Discretionary Broker Voting

In many circumstances, brokers can vote shares held in their control even when shareholders do not provide voting instructions. Shareholders who purchase shares through a broker rely on their broker to vote on their behalf. New York Stock Exchange ("NYSE") and SEC rules require brokers to deliver proxy materials to such shareholders and request voting instructions from them.[72] However, under NYSE Rule 452, brokers are permitted to vote shares in their control for "routine matters" if brokers do not receive voting instructions from the beneficial holders by the tenth day preceding a shareholder meeting.[73] Historically, Rule 452 classified uncontested elections as well as proposal related to say on pay as routine.[74] As a result, brokers cast votes on such matters even when they did not receive shareholder instructions about their voting preferences.

Shareholder activists believe that this kind of broker discretionary voting undermines their voting power and corresponding ability to influence corporate affairs. In 2006, a NYSE working group found that when brokers vote without shareholder instruction, they overwhelmingly follow the voting recommendations of incumbent

---

68 Although some corporations have adopted a pure majority voting rule whereby directors are not elected if they do not receive a majority of the vote, many others have adopted what is known as "plurality plus," pursuant to which the plurality default rule remains the same, but a director must tender her resignation if she fails to receive a majority vote. The board then has the discretion to determine if it will accept the resignation. *See* Fairfax, *Shareholder Democracy*, supra note __ at 65; Sjostrom and Kim, supra note __ at 480-481.

69 *See Calpers Seeks Majority Vote Standard at Top Publicly Traded Companies*, March 15, 2010, available at http://www.calpers.ca.gov/index.jsp?bc=/about/press/pr-2010/mar/majority-vote-standard.xml; Melissa Aguilar, *Shareholder Voices Getting Louder, Stronger,* Compliance Week, Oct. 21, 2008, available at http://www.complianceweek.com/article/5113/shareholder-voices-getting-louder-stronger.

70 *See* Fairfax, *Future*, supra note __ at 1291-92; Allen, supra note __ at v-vi (describing state law changes related to majority voting); *See also* DEL. CODE ANN., tit. 8, §§ 141(b), 216 (Supp. 2008).

71 *See* Comm. On Corporate Laws, Am. Bar Ass'n, *Preliminary Report of the Committee on Corporate Laws on Voting By Shareholders for the Election of Directors* 7 (2006), Available at http://www.abanet.org/Buslaw/Newsletter/0044/Materials/F3.Pdf.

72 *See* NYSE, Inc. Rule 451 (2009), available at http://rules.nyse.com/nysetools/PlatformViewer.asp?SelectedNode=chp_1_2&manual=/nyse/rules/nyse-rules/

73 *See* NYSE, Inc., Rule 452 (2009), available at http://rules.nyse.com/nysetools/Exchangeviewer.asp?SelectedNode=chp_1_2&manual=/nyse/nyse_rules/nyse-rules/.

74 *See id*

boards.[75] Thus, such broker votes likely distort the outcome in favor of management.[76] Indeed, research reveals that broker discretionary votes can influence, and even alter, election outcomes, particularly in elections where there is an organized withhold the vote campaign.[77]

In light of this influence, reforms have narrowed the range of matters upon which brokers can cast discretionary votes. Thus, in July 2009, the SEC voted to eliminate uncontested elections from those matters classified as "routine" under Rule 452.[78] As a result, brokers are no longer permitted to cast votes in uncontested elections when they do not receive shareholder instructions. The Dodd-Frank Act extended this requirement to all national securities exchanges.[79] Dodd-Frank also eliminated broker discretionary voting on compensation matters, while instructing the SEC to eliminate such vote for any matters deemed "significant."[80]

When viewed in the context of other voting reforms, these broker voting changes could have a significant impact on shareholders' power, and their potential to influence corporate conduct. The elimination of broker discretionary voting at those companies that have adopted a majority voting regime may make it more difficult for directors to receive a majority vote, especially when those directors are targeted by shareholders. This difficulty enhances shareholders power over director elections, as well as the extent to which directors feel beholden to shareholders. Along these same lines, the absence of broker discretionary votes may impact the outcome of say on pay votes, increasing the likelihood that compensation packages are rejected, or otherwise enhancing the likelihood that directors feel compelled to engage with shareholders on executive compensation matters in order to avoid such rejection. In these ways, broker voting changes reflect yet another reform that serves to shape corporate behavior by increasing shareholder power over that behavior.

5. Shareholder Power Revisited

Reforms have combined to grant shareholders greater influence over corporate affairs. Proponents of these changes insist that they will inure to the corporation's benefit by ensuring that corporate officers and directors are more accountable for their actions, and hence less likely to engage in misconduct. Opponents disagree that augmenting

---

75 *See* Report and Recommendation s of the Proxy Working Group to the New York Stock Exchange, June 5, 2006, 14, available at http://www.nyse.com/pdfs/PWG_REPORT.pdf.

76 *See* Bernard S. Black, Shareholder Passivity Reexamined, 89 MICH. L. REV. 520, 561 (1990).

77 *See* Report of Proxy Working Group, supra note __ at 9.

78 *See* SEC Release No. 34-60215, available at http://sec.gov/rules/sro/nyse/2009/34-60215.pdf.

79 *See* Dodd-Frank Act, supra note __ at §957.

80 *See id*

shareholder power will enhance corporate affairs, and argue that such augmented power will have a detrimental impact on the corporation.[81] Regardless of one's stance on this disagreement, it is clear that the corporate governance landscape has shifted in ways that could have many different repercussions on the corporation and the relationship between corporate officers and directors, on the one hand, and shareholders and other constituents, on the other. The next section of this chapter explores some of those repercussions.

B. Shareholder Power as Confirmation of Shareholder Primacy

Certainly for those who believe that increasing accountability to shareholders is critical to ensuring greater director and officer accountability, all of the changes identified in section A seem like a positive development. However, they may have some unintended consequences for those seeking to transform the corporation's role in society and adopt a broader vision of its objectives.

1. It's the Economy, Stupid!

Before discussing how reforms could hinder a corporate focus on other-regarding interests, it is important to examine how the economic crisis responsible for such reforms could hinder that focus. Indeed, the economic environment itself poses challenges for efforts to focus corporate attention on alternative visions of the firm. Many corporations must focus on reversing their financial misfortunes and hence enhancing their financial returns. In so doing, corporations may find it difficult to focus on issues beyond profit-making and shareholder wealth maximization. The economic downturn, therefore, may pressure corporations to engage in behavior incompatible with other-regarding impulses.

In fact, research supports the notion that, during economically challenging times, other-regarding behavior may not be feasible for corporations. Indeed, a study of the behavior of Fortune 500 companies revealed a "significant drop" in the number and extent of corporate projects focused on other constituents in the time period after the financial crisis deepened in 2008.[82] This study confirms other data suggesting that corporations with the greatest amount of resources also tend to be those most likely to engage in other-regarding behavior.[83] This suggestion means that when corporations have more limited resources, such as is the case during an economic downturn, they may

---

81 *See* Lipton, supra note __ at 5.

82 *See* Yasemin Karaibrahimoglu, *Corporate Social Responsibility in Times of Financial Crisis*, 4 African Journal of Business Management 382, 383 (2010), available at http://www.academicjournals.org/ajbm/PDF/pdf2010/Apr/Karaibrahimoglu.pdf.

83 *See* Joshua D. Margolis & Hillary Anger Elfenbein, *Do Well by Doing Good? Don't Count on It*, Harv. Bus. Rev., Jan. 2008, at 19 (noting correlation between strong financial performance and contributions to society).

not believe that focusing on other constituents is either necessary or appropriate.[84] As a result, dispensing with other-regarding behavior may simply be a casualty of the financial downturn. Hence, that downturn represents the first stumbling block for advancing an other-regarding vision of the firm.

2. The Shareholder Primacy Norm

Apart from the influence of economic factors, the collection of reforms enhancing shareholder power may strengthen the normative weight of shareholder primacy. There is a long-standing normative debate in corporate law about whether corporations should embrace the shareholder primacy norm and hence focus their attention, primarily, if not exclusively, on advancing the interests of shareholders, or if corporations should focus on advancing the concerns of all corporate stakeholders impacted by the firm.[85] Reforms that shift power to shareholders may be viewed as settling that debate in favor of the shareholder primacy norm, and therefore rejecting or at least marginalizing the normative appeal of an other-regarding theory of the firm.[86]

By appearing to embrace the shareholder primacy norm, such reforms, in turn, strengthen or support directors' belief that their normative obligation is to focus on shareholders and their profit-making concerns. Such reforms also support the normative belief that directors and officers should not focus on concerns of other non-shareholder stakeholders, especially if there is any conflict between advancing the interests of shareholders and the interests of other stakeholders.

3. The Shareholder Primacy Practice

Added to these normative signals, as a practical matter, increasing shareholder power is likely to compel directors to pay heed to shareholder concerns over any other concerns. To be sure, corporate fiduciary law grants directors tremendous discretion to consider the interests of non-shareholder corporate constituents, and in many circumstances, to favor the interests of such constituents over shareholders.[87] As a result, it is not descriptively accurate to contend that corporate fiduciary law compels directors to focus primarily on shareholders, or otherwise to contend that corporate fiduciary law embraces a shareholder primacy conception of the corporation.[88] Instead, that law is

---

84 *See* John Arthurs, *There are Clear Arguments for a Clear Conscience*, Fin. Times, July 28, 2007, at 16 (referring to other-regarding behavior as a "bourgeois luxury" that cannot be sustained during an economic downturn).

85 *See* Henry N. Butler & Fred McChesney, *Whey They Give at the Office: Shareholder Welfare and Corporate Philanthropy in the Contractual Theory of the Corporation*, 84 Cornell L. Rev. 1195, 1195 (1999); Adolf Berle, Jr., For Whom Corporate Managers are Trustees: A Note, 45 Harv. L. Rev. 1365, 1367 (1932); Dodd, supra note __ at 1147-48.

86 *See* Fairfax, *Shareholder Democracy*, supra note __ at 98.

87 *See* Margaret Blair and Lynn Stout, *Director Accountability and the Mediating Role of the Corporate Board*, 79 Wash. U. L. Q. 403, 406 (2001).

88 *See id*

more fluid, allowing directors the discretion to attend to the interests of all of the corporation's stakeholders.[89]

However, increased shareholder power may encourage directors to exercise that discretion solely in favor of maximizing shareholder wealth and interests. Such increased power ensures that shareholders have an increased ability to influence director elections and corporate affairs, making it more likely that directors will feel beholden to shareholders and their concerns, and less likely that directors will deem it advisable to focus their attention on conflicting concerns. When you coupled shareholders' increased voting power with the fact that shareholders are the only stakeholder group that can sue directors for breach of fiduciary duty, it seems inevitable that directors will focus on shareholders and place their interests above others. As a result, the increase in shareholder power may decrease directors flexibility to consider or favor other interests.

The economic environment coupled with the movement to enhance shareholder power may be antithetical to any other-regarding vision of the firm. In fact, corporate scholars, including both opponents and proponents of increased shareholder power, acknowledge that increasing shareholder power could have negative repercussions for stakeholders.[90] In this respect, increased shareholder power may generate a vision of the firm that pushes us away from a genuine consideration of other constituents.

III. Aligning Shareholder and Stakeholder Interests

The previous section suggest that shareholders rise in power necessarily comes at the expense of other stakeholders. This section discusses ways in which that suggestion may prove less salient.

As an initial matter, although the crisis and resulting economic environment may encourage corporations to focus on survival, that focus is not necessarily antithetical to an other-regarding vision of the corporation. Indeed, the crisis has caused some companies to embrace the notion that corporations must focus on sustainability in order to survive.[91] Such a focus demands that corporations pay heed to the interests of other corporate stakeholders as well as issues beyond short-term profit concerns. In this regard, any new or renewed corporate appreciation for the importance of sustainability may pave the way for a new vision of the firm.

In addition, as I have argued elsewhere,[92] the argument that increased shareholder power will necessarily translate into decreased focus on stakeholders is based on a very

---

89 *See id*

90 *See* Bebchuk, supra note __ at 912.

91 *See* Skapiner, supra note __.

92 *See* Fairfax, *Shareholder Democracy*, supra note __ at 79-97.

narrow conception of the shareholder. Instead, shareholders are diverse, and have concerns that may align with stakeholders. There are certainly shareholders who have a short-term perspective and thus may only focus on short-term goals to the detriment of other stakeholders.[93] However, many other shareholders are long-term investors, and literature suggests that long-term investors recognize that corporate officers and directors must consider the interests of stakeholders in order to promote the corporation's long-term viability.[94] Indeed, some scholars insist that even so-called short term investors have an interest in advancing the concerns of non-shareholder stakeholders because such an advancement may enable them to avoid costs associated with harming such constituents.[95]

Diversified shareholders similarly may have a concern that sweeps more broadly than narrow short-term profit maximization. Of course, undiversified shareholders who only hold stock in one company may focus only on policies that impact that company.[96] However, diversified investors comprise a large portion of the shareholder class, and such shareholders should be concerned with the broader ramifications of corporate polices and behavior because they may impact the value of the other shares within their portfolio.[97] Then too, there are some investors who have a non-financial mission, such as faith-based organizations and socially responsible investment funds. These funds embrace investment strategies designed to focus corporate attention on other concerns and issues beyond strict wealth maximization. The fact that there are many shareholders whose interests align with stakeholders means that shareholders' enhanced power may not be detrimental to the corporation's ability to focus on the concerns of other stakeholders.

Perhaps most promising, proxy data reveals that efforts to advance other concerns have increased, along with shareholder activism aimed at advancing governance and other financial concerns. Each year shareholders utilize the shareholder proposal process to call attention to issues concerning other constituents.[98] Not only has the number of such proposals increased, but shareholder support for such proposals has increased in

---

93 Iman Anabtawi, *Some Skepticism About Increasing Shareholder Power*, 53 UCLA L. REV. 561, 580 (2006) (pinpointing short term interest of mutual funds and hedge funds).

94 *See* John H. Matheson & Brent A. Olson, *Corporate Cooperation, Relationship Management, and the Trialogical Imperative for Corporate Law*, 78 Minn. L. Rev. 1443, 1487 (1994); Larry E. Ribstein, *Accountability and Responsibility in Corporate Governance*, 81 Notre Dame L. Rev. 1431, 1459 (2006).

95 *See* Ribstein, supra note __. at 1445.

96 *See* Anabtawi, supra note __ at 579; Lynn A. Stout, *Takeovers in the Ivory Tower: How Academics Are Learning Martin Lipton May be Right*, 60 BUS. LAW. 1435, 1447–48 (2005).

97 *See* Anabtawi, supra note __ at 584-85; Stout, supra note __ 1447-48.

98 *See* Alan Palmiter, *The Shareholder Proposal Rule: A Failed Experiment in Merit Regulation*, 45 Ala. L. Rev. 879, 879-885 (1994).

tandem with shareholder activism more generally.[99] In fact, in 2009, for the first time ever, a shareholder proposal related to environmental issues received majority support from shareholders.[100] This kind of increased support appears to have translated into increased corporate engagement and responsiveness to such concerns. Thus, investors withdrew a record number of social and environmental proposals.[101] Such withdrawal is viewed as a positive signal, indicating successful negotiations between shareholders and the corporation regarding the most appropriate manner in which to attend to particular issues.[102] The proxy data therefore suggest that shareholders not only have interests compatible with other stakeholders, but they act on those interests in ways that influence corporate affairs.

V. Conclusion

This chapter suggests that reforms focusing on increasing accountability by increasing shareholder power may have the unintended consequence of ensuring that corporations cannot embrace a vision of the firm that is not based on shareholders and close attention to their profit making goals, potentially without regard to other issues. However, this consequence is not inevitable. In order to avoid this consequence, those who support a firm vision that is more other-regarding must assess how and to what extent shareholders can be an ally in furtherance of such a vision. In this way, the movement for so-called greater shareholder democracy may be transformed into a movement that increases the full participation rights of all corporate constituents.

---

99 *See* Riskmetrics Group, Inc., *A New Voice in Governance: Global Policymakers Shape the Road to Reform*, Oct. 2009, 15.

100 *See id* at 4, 15 (discussing 51.2% shareholder support for proposal on greenhouse gas emissions).

101 *See id* at 16.

102 *See id*

Three Problems in Corporate Governance[103]

Dean Krehmeyer and R. Edward Freeman
Business Roundtable Institute for Corporate Ethics and The Darden School

I. Introduction

BUSINESS HAS come under enormous critical scrutiny in the last decade. The scandals from Enron to Madoff, coupled with the burst bubbles of the internet and housing, have led to a hue and cry about corporate governance reform. We shall argue that at the center of the calls for reform are three interconnected problems. First of all there is the problem of short-termism, which has long been vilified as the main cause for the unrelenting pressure to meet the expectations of Wall Street analysts on a quarterly basis. Second, there is the problem of executive compensation, which has become a trigger issue for many that symbolizes what is wrong with the corporate world. Finally, there is a problem that we call "the narrative problem" that highlights our view that we need nothing less than a thoroughgoing reform of the way we think about business. Solving one of these problems in isolation will not fix either what is wrong with business, or what is wrong with our thinking about corporate governance.

We proceed as follows. In section II we discuss the problem of short-termism and show how it raises several larger issues. In section III we explicitly address one of these issues: executive compensation and suggest that it is easy to solve once we realize that the underlying narrative of business is badly broken. Fixing the narrative problem leads to the proposal of some principles for corporate governance in section IV.

II. The Problem of Short-Termism

The role of the board of directors, and corporate governance, continues to be analyzed and challenged. The current financial crisis, both on Wall Street and globally, has resurfaced questions from the previous 2000-2002 crisis period marked by Enron, Worldcom, and other corporate governance failures. And while the post-Enron period resulted in increased regulatory requirements from the New York Stock Exchange (NYSE), the Nasdaq Stock Exchange (Nasdaq), and the Securities and Exchange Commission (SEC), along with passage of the historical and far-reaching Sarbanes-Oxley Act of 2002, many continue to question whether such regulatory requirements truly make an impactful, positive difference in the governance of companies. Specifically for the role of boards, the central challenge in reform efforts is in how to leverage corporate governance as a value generator rather than just a regulatory burden (Ide, 834).

---

103 Contact Information: (434-924-6060); KrehmeyerD@darden.virginia.edu © 2010, Dean Krehmeyer and R. Edward Freeman. All Rights Reserved.

A board's responsibilities have generally been evaluated via the perspective of the legal and regulatory obligations relating to management and shareholders. According to both this legal perspective and the literature, boards of directors have two primary functional roles, those of: (1) monitoring and controlling management, and (2) counseling and advising management (Pfeffer and Salancik, 1978; Monks and Minow, 1995).

According to agency theory, a board's primary role is to monitor the executives and managers (agents) who make decisions and manage the day-to-day activities of the organization on behalf of the shareholders (principals) (Jensen and Meckling, 1976; Fama and Jensen, 1983). Managers are assumed to have self-interests that do not align with the interests of the shareholders, therefore boards are necessary to monitor and align such interests.

Supporting the importance of advising management, stewardship theory encourages:

> "insider dominated boards [which] are favored for their depth of knowledge, access to current operating information, technical expertise and commitment to the firm. Stewardship theory predicts that shareholders can expect to maximize their returns when the organization structure facilitates effective control by management." (Muth and Donaldson, 1998: 6).

Although the purpose of both board functions is commonly understood as managing the organization in the best interests of the shareholders, many boards struggle in identifying and practicing the balance between these roles that is necessary to promote, and not impair, the organization's ability to create long-term value.

Embedded in a narrow and oversimplified purpose of maximizing shareholder value rests the peril of myopic governance and managerial decision-making that has contributed to elements of the current financial crisis. This legal duty, requirements, and overall concept of narrow shareholder primacy is being stressed by the increasing complexity of the shareholders that boards represent. In other words, the "best interests of shareholders" is facing at least two issues.

The first issue is the dramatic increase in the influence of short-termism on management decision-making and governance oversight. Short-termism, or "the obsession with short-term results by investors, asset management firms and corporate managers" (Krehmeyer, Orsagh, and Schacht, 2006:1) is being more widely shown as contributing to long-term value destruction. The literature directs most of its attention, and therefore responsibility, at investors and company management.

Analyzing the investor group, Fuller and Jensen (2002) identify fund managers' compensation incentives based on quarterly returns as contributing to the neglect of potential long-term investments. Oyvind, Priestley, and Odegaard (2009) find that the most short-term investors influence a firm's managers into myopic behavior which reduces the firm's value, and further that large holdings by institutional investors induce managers to destroy value, in this case likely due also to the incentive system of fund managers.

Conversely for company management, Graham, Harvey, and Rajgopal (2005), in a survey of corporate financial executives, found that 80 percent of respondents would decrease discretionary spending on such areas as research and development, advertising, maintenance, and hiring in order to meet short-term earnings targets and more than 50 percent said they would delay new projects, even if the delay meant sacrifices in value creation.

Because boards provide the connecting role between company management and investors, and because of the findings in the literature that short-termism may contribute to long-term value destruction, short-termism becomes a critical corporate governance issue due to a shift in prominence of those shareholders with shorter, more immediate time frames for evaluating their return on their investment versus those with longer time horizons. Shareholders are increasingly diverging in their investment timeframes with many institutional or large investors favoring shorter holding periods; thus, the spectrum shift of short-term to long-term timeframes might suggest that board members are influenced to make different governance decisions.

The growth and influence of institutional investors over the last fifty years has provided one of the most significant forces of change in corporate governance (Hamilton, 2000). In 1950, institutional investors—pension funds, investment companies, insurance companies, banks, and foundations—represented $8.7 billion, or 6.1%, of the total $142.7 billion U.S. equity market. By 2000, while the U.S. equity market had grown to $19.4 trillion, institutional investor ownership had grown even faster to represent $12.9 trillion, or 66.3% of the total market. (Brancato and Rabimov, "The 2008 Institutional Investment Report").

Table 1: Institutional Investor U.S. Equity Holdings, 1950—2006

	1950	1960	1970	1980	1990	2000	2006
U.S. Mkt. Value of Instit. Equity Holdings ($Billions)	8.7	52.9	166.4	571.2	1463.1	9059.6	12,879.6
U.S. Mkt. Value of Total Equity ($Billions)	142.7	421.2	859.4	1,534.7	3,530.2	9,059.6	19,431.7
% Instit. Equity of Total Equity	6.1%	12.6%	19.4%	37.2%	41.4%	51.4%	66.3%

Source: Brancato and Rabimov, "The 2008 Institutional Investment Report"

The rise of institutional investor equity ownership has also coincided with the rise in annual turnover ("churn") of equity. Using the NYSE as an example, while the churn rate was largely range-bound between 10-30 percent over the period of 1940-1980, it had increased to over 100 percent by 2005. (See Table 2.) The implication is that, on average, by 2005 each share of company stock on the NYSE had a holding period of less than one year, versus an average holding period of approximately 3-10 years over the period 1940-1980. Such a churn rate imposes costs on a company, its investors, and all of its stakeholders, including higher transaction fees and possible internal company trade-offs against long-term strategic investments. (Krehmeyer, Orsagh, and Schacht, 2006: 11).

Table 2: NYSE Turnover Rate and Institutional Investor U.S. Equity Holdings

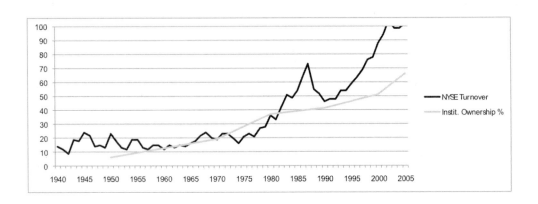

Source: Brancato and Rabimov, Conference Board, "The 2008 Institutional Investment Report"; *New York Stock Exchange Fact Book* (2006).

The impact on management and boards of companies facing increasing short-term pressures from this greatly increased influence of institutional investors, with far shorter holding periods, is often a "laser-beam focus on quarter-to-quarter earnings" (Strine, 2006: 1764) that meet the Street's expectations and thus contributes to an ever-rising stock price. However, managing the company does not equate to managing the stock or the stock price.

Fuller and Jensen (2001) propose that an overvalued stock price can be as damaging to a company's long-term financial health as an undervalued stock, suggesting that "an overvalued stock sets in motion a variety of organizational behaviors that often end up damaging the firm" (Fuller and Jensen, 2001:1). Citing the historic collapse of Enron, "when companies encourage excessive expectations or scramble too hard to meet unrealistic forecasts by analysts, they often take highly risky value-destroying bets. In addition, smoothing financial results to satisfy analysts' demands for quarter-to-quarter predictability frequently requires sacrificing the long-term future of the company." (Fuller and Jensen, 2001: 43).

Lipton, Lorsch, and Mirvis, in a 2009 *Wall Street Journal* editorial, also suggest that excessive stockholder power, particularly among institutional investors, bears responsibility for the short-term fixation in markets and has contributed to the global economic crisis:

> "It is these [institutional] shareholders who pushed companies to generate returns at levels that were not sustainable. They also made sure high returns were tied to management compensation. The pressure to produce unrealistic profit fueled increased risk-taking. And as the government relaxed checks on excessive risk-taking, stockholder demands for ever higher returns grew still further. It was a vicious cycle." (Lipton, Lorsch, and Mirvis, 2009: A15).

The second emerging issue challenging the notion of boards focusing on narrow shareholder primacy is a more contemporary and complex definition of what truly are shareholder interests. This definition extends beyond the time consideration of short-term versus long-term financial performance and indeed, whether just shareholder interests are a sufficient measure of a board's governance responsibilities. Once again, the changing nature of a company's shareholders, and the growth of institutional investor influence, has created a significant change in the board, management, and shareholder relationship (Hamilton, 2000).

Shareholders are becoming more disparate in establishing exactly what are their favored interests, particularly in the use of corporate assets, both tangible and intangible. Even accepting the baseline assumption that shareholders continue to favor above-average share price appreciation and return on their investment, as noted earlier, there are a growing number of shareholder proxy proposals regarding non-stockholder social issues, including employment issues, human rights issues, environmental concerns, and political positions (ISS, 2006). The conclusion appears to be that shareholder interests may no longer be so uniform or easy to identify

What is needed is to rethink the narrow shareholder primacy notion for boards of directors, which is being increasingly imperiled by short-termism. Not just shareholders, but other corporate stakeholder groups are increasingly looking to boards to contribute in more ways to overall performance. Against the backdrop of the economic crisis, Lipton et al observe the following:

> "The stockholder-centric view...cannot be the cure for the disease that it spawned. Though the short-term focus benefited shareholders for a time, when the meltdown happened shareholders weren't the only

people hit. Employees who devoted their lives to building stockholder value felt the pain acutely. Communities, suppliers, and creditors—indeed, the whole range of constituencies who support the creation and maintenance of stock value—were impacted. They have a legitimate stake in this debate" (Lipton, Lorsch, and Mirvis, 2009: A15)

Pushing this notion further, and challenging conventional legal arguments, Lipton and Savitt (2007) suggest that a "director's obligation is to manage the affairs of the corporation to ensure its sustainable long-term growth (2007: 745-6). Since the emergence of the first corporate entities, the construct of incorporation is based on the idea of allowing "thousands or even hundreds of thousands of diverse corporate participants—shareholders, employees, executives, suppliers, customers, and sometimes even the local community" to make commitments and receive stakes in the company's success. (Stout, 2007: 44-45). Directors' duties of loyalty and care are to oversee this corporate construct.

III. Executive Compensation

The problem of short-termism is brought into almost comic relief when it is juxtaposed with the hue and cry over executive compensation. Indeed, there is no more symbolic an issue around the public's trust of business than executive compensation. There has been an outpouring of sentiment that something is dreadfully wrong when executives walk away with lucrative compensation packages from companies that have seen their value decreased over time. The recent global financial crisis has highlighted this issue with the revelations about bonuses paid to executives, particularly in the financial services industry, while the rest of the economy suffers hard times. It is akin, in the public eye, to Nero fiddling while Rome burned.

Chatterjee and Hambrick (2007) have linked executive compensation to visions of grandiosity and narcissism. O'Reilly and Main (2010) suggest that the levels of compensation for executives bear at best a weak relationship to performance. Another earlier survey found that changes in firm performance account for only four percent of any variance in CEO compensation. (Tosi, Werner, Katz, and Gomez-Mejia. 2000). Yet there is strong rhetoric around the necessity of "market forces" and "pay for performance" (Kaplan, 2008). Kahan and Rock (2010) suggest that there is a long-term trend around the loss of power by CEOs fueled in part by the compensation issue. Dillon (2009) and a host of others have claimed that the damage done by the compensation packages of financial executives has only begun to be felt in boardrooms around the world. Indeed in many countries specific restrictive policies or taxes have been enacted which are aimed at restricting compensation or even punishing executives in certain industries.

Embedded in the public calls for reform lies the search for compensation practices that truly link pay with performance, typically identified as "shareholder value" or as overall value creation. For example, Harris (2006) analyzed executive compensation, and the substantive objections to excess pay, from the perspective of three theories of distributive justice. Harris' analysis finds that, despite the different theoretical approaches, they converge on a common theme that compensation processes must fairly appraise an executive based on a "value proposition." From the perspective of both justice as fairness and human development theories—Harris suggests that "executives should be paid commensurate with the true value proposition they bring to the organization;" and from the libertarian idea, he "allows for extraordinary performers to receive exceptional incomes." (Harris, 2006:83). A common element of all three theories is in identifying and further developing what should be the value proposition that such theories of executive compensation are based upon. The problem of short-termism demonstrates that the price of a company's shares may not, in fact, be reflective of a complete value proposition for either the company or the performance of its executives.

The assumption that needs to be questioned is whether or not focusing on the "share price" or even "profitability" leads to sustainable performance. We know that excessive focus on short-termism is self-destructive, i.e. it can destroy shareholder value. Perhaps by correcting "short-termism" we can still rely on these traditional measures of performance, and hence executive compensation. However, we wish to ask a somewhat broader question.

What makes any business successful? The answer is not solely that the business is profitable, else we would not expect to see profitable businesses suddenly failing. We believe that a number of scholars working in the area of business strategy and business and society have evolved a different answer, that is broadly compatible with the idea that businesses must be profitable, but they question whether that is the whole story. While the full explanation of this line of research is explained elsewhere, we want to give an idea of how it is related to these issues in corporate governance in general and executive compensation in particular.

Consider Company A.[104] It is a leader in its industry and it is enjoying record profitability. Its stock is at an all time high. It looks like things couldn't be better. However, upon closer examination, executives in Company A discover that there is a distinct and meaningful downward trend in customers' trust in the main brand of the company. These executives understand, rightly to our view, that sustained profitability is not possible if that trend continues. And, if they wait until profitability begins to decline either because customers have made other choices, new competitors have emerged, or there has been a change in the other fundamentals of the business, it will be too late. They understood that while current profitability was important it didn't tell the whole story about their business. While they were doing many things that were "good management" and led to such record profitability, there was much to be done to insure it.

---

104   The examples we give here are thoroughly disguised and somewhat simplified for our purposes here. They are based on our experience working with companies over the last 30 years, as well as our understanding of the popular conversations about business.

Consider Company B. Over the past several years the executives at Company B have taken a number of steps to boost its profitability. The employees at Company B believe that this increase has come at the expense of a concern for key values that they believe in, and believe have led to the success of Company B, including cutting training and development where Company B had been an acknowledged industry leader. Morale suffers at the company and executives wonder why they have lost employee commitment, and begin what turns out to be multiple attempts to "restate our values". As these attempts sputter, they wonder whether the recent increases in profitability are sustainable, and how they would fare if there were to be a sudden crisis that would require extraordinary employee commitment.

Consider Company C. For the past several years, executives at Company C have enjoyed years of profitability. However, they have ignored the effects of their products and processes on communities in which they operate. Opposition to the company has grown in terms of specific NGOs, dedicated to being critics of Company C. Several local communities have passed ordinances trying to keep Company C out of their community. In addition, there have been several public investigations and resulting lawsuits around employee issues. Several competitors have enjoyed faster growth and better public images. There have recently been documentaries criticizing Company C that have been released to wide public and critical acclaim. Executives begin to wonder whether their business model is sustainable.

Each of these companies is profitable, and is likely to remain so for some time, even if they do nothing. Yet eventually each will lose, and shareholders will lose big. Each example relies on what we call "trade-off thinking" that is encouraged in our current narrative about business and our current narrative about executive compensation.

Ironically, if our short term measures rely only on profitability, these effects will not be understood until it is too late. So, even if we fix "short-termism" we do need some short term measures that will actually give useful advice to executives who want to engage in good management practice. The development of such appropriate short term measures is especially important to address the issue of executive compensation.

Any business is sustainably successful in part because it has great products and services that customers want, can trust and depend on, and that make customers' lives better. The world is littered with the dead bodies of companies that have not heeded this basic truth about business. Measuring customer satisfaction is a tricky business, but let us suppose that it can be measured and let's call that measurement, "Cu".[105]

Reciprocally, any business is sustainably successful in part because it is provided great products and services by its suppliers. Actually having suppliers who are trying to

---

105   Each of the measures that we propose here is complex and may well be multivariate. We save a more methodological discussion of these issues for another occasion.

make your business better creates a great deal of value for both. Let's measure performance with suppliers by "Su". There are similar arguments for employees, "Em", communities, "Co", and financiers, Fi".

Furthermore, when executives can keep all of these interests going in the same direction, even more value is created. Supply chain management offers a great example of how getting employees engaged in creating better, faster, cheaper, greener, ways to connect customer and supplier interests can lead to tremendous value creation.

We want to suggest the following: However we solve the problem of "short-termism" we need some short term measures that give us a finer grained picture of how a company is creating value with its key stakeholders. Fortunately, these measures provide us with an easy answer to the problem of executive compensation.

We propose that compensation schemes be developed that include all five of the measures defined above thus:

$$\textbf{Total Compensation} = \textbf{f(Cu, Su, Em, Co, Fi)}$$

While there is much work to be done to make this more concrete we could imagine something like a market for such "stake options" to emerge. Executives would find some specific measures then try to improve them. Implicitly making tradeoffs would not create as much value as increasing the values of all simultaneously. Indeed we would hypothesize that any one of these measures could be written as an outcome measure of the other four. Profitability is certainly an outcome of how well executives manage customers, employees, suppliers, and communities. But likewise, the value that gets created for employees is an outcome of how the company manages the relationships with customers, suppliers, communities and financiers. What we are suggesting is that compensation be tied to the real underlying business model: the interaction of effects of stakeholder interests.

Our proposal raises some fundamental issues for the underlying narrative of business. And we now turn to addressing these underlying issues.

IV. *The Narrative Problem*

Simply put, we need a new story about business. Unless we are willing to endlessly debate the short-term and long-term consequences of one-dimensional measures such as profitability, we need a story about business that yields a more robust idea of how to govern the modern corporation. There is no conflict, on our view with seeing well managed companies as profitable, and the idea that profitability itself is an inadequate measure for management. Indeed there are a number of research studies that suggest that very well-managed companies are indeed very profitable.

(1) The Managing for Stakeholders Story

One way to understand this new narrative is through the lens of "managing for stakeholders."[106] While this is not the only possible narrative we will use it to illustrate how a different way to think about corporate governance can emerge. The basic idea of "managing for stakeholders" is quite simple. Business can be understood as a set of relationships among groups which have a stake in the activities that make up the business. Business is about how customers, suppliers, employees, financiers (stockholders, bondholders, banks, etc.), communities and managers interact and create value. To understand a business is to know how these relationships work. And, the executive's or entrepreneur's job is to manage and shape these relationships; hence the title, "managing for stakeholders."

Owners or financiers (a better term) clearly have a financial stake in the business in the form of stocks, bonds, and so on, and they expect some kind of financial return from them. Of course, the stakes of financiers will differ by type of owner, preferences for money, moral preferences, and so on, as well as by type of firm. To the extent that it makes sense to talk about the financiers "owning the firm," they have a concomitant responsibility for the uses of their property.

Employees have their jobs and usually their livelihood at stake; they often have specialized skills for which there is usually no perfectly elastic market. In return for their labor, they expect security, wages, benefits and meaningful work. Often, employees are expected to participate in the decision making of the organization, and if the employees are management or senior executives we see them as shouldering a great deal of responsibility for the conduct of the organization as a whole.

Customers and suppliers exchange resources for the products and services of the firm and in return receive the benefits of the products and services. As with financiers and employees, the customer and supplier relationships are enmeshed in ethics. Companies make promises to customers via their advertising, and when products or services don't deliver on these promises then management has a responsibility to rectify the situation. It is also important to have suppliers who are committed to making a company better. If suppliers find a better, faster, and cheaper way of making critical parts or services, then both supplier and company can win.

Finally, the local community grants the firm the right to build facilities, and in turn, it benefits from the tax base and economic and social contributions of the firm. Companies have a real impact on communities, and being located in a welcoming community helps a company create value for its other stakeholders. In return for the provision of

---

106   The material in this section is recast from R. Edward Freeman, "Managing for Stakeholders" in Beauchamp, Bowie, and Arnold, Ethical Theory and Business, 8th edition, 2007; and Freeman, Harrison, and Wicks, Managing for Stakeholders, Yale University Press, 2007. We are grateful to co-authors, editors and publishers for permission to recast these ideas here.

local services, companies are expected to be good citizens, as is any individual person. It should not expose the community to unreasonable hazards in the form of pollution, toxic waste, etc. It should keep whatever commitments it makes to the community, and operate in a transparent manner as far as possible

While any business must consist of financiers, customers, suppliers, employees, and communities, it is possible to think about other stakeholders as well. We can define "stakeholder" in a number of ways. First of all we could define the term fairly narrowly to capture the idea that any business, large or small, is about creating value for "those groups without whose support, the business would cease to be viable. There is also a somewhat broader definition that captures the idea that if a group or individual can affect a business, then the executives must take that group into consideration in thinking about how to create value.

Executives play a special role in the activity of the business enterprise. On the one hand, they have a stake like every other employee in terms of an actual or implied employment contract. And, that stake is linked to the stakes of financiers, customers, suppliers, communities, and other employees. In addition, executives are expected to look after the health of the overall enterprise, to keep the varied stakes moving in roughly the same direction, and to keep them in balance.

(2) Implications for Directors and Boards

This new narrative of "managing for stakeholders" leads to a number of important shifts for members of Boards of Directors and the way they think about governing the corporation. First of all it is important to realize, as we suggested earlier that something like:

$$\text{Total Performance} = g(\text{Cu, Su, Em, Co, Fi})$$

where the variables are defined as in the previous section, is a better measure of performance. And, it follows that director compensation, as well as executive compensation should be based on something like this more comprehensive measure.

Second, no stakeholder stands alone in the process of value creation. The stakes of each stakeholder group are multi-faceted, and inherently connected to each other. How could a bondholder recognize any returns without management paying attention to the stakes of customers or employees? How could customers get the products and services they need without employees and suppliers? How could employees have a decent place to live without communities? Directors and executives need to see stakeholder interests as joint, as inherently tied together.

Seeing stakeholder interests as "joint" rather than opposed is difficult. It is not always easy to find a way to accommodate all stakeholder interests. It is easier to trade off one versus another. Why not delay spending on new products for customers in order to keep earnings a bit higher? Why not cut employee medical benefits in order to invest in a new inventory control system? Directors need to insist that their executives try to reframe the questions. How can we invest in new products and create higher earnings? How can we be sure our employees are healthy and happy and are able to work creatively so that we can capture the benefits of new information technology such as inventory control systems?

In a recent book reflecting on his experience as CEO of Medtronic, Bill George summarized the managing for stakeholders mindset:

> Serving all your stakeholders is the best way to produce long term results and create a growing, prosperous company...Let me be very clear about this: there is no conflict between serving all your stakeholders and providing excellent returns for shareholders. In the long term it is impossible to have one without the other. However, serving all these stakeholder groups requires discipline, vision, and committed leadership. (George: 102)

Third, the primary responsibility of directors and executives is to create as much value as possible for stakeholders. Where stakeholder interests conflict, the executive must find a way to rethink the problems so that these interests can go together, so that even more value can be created for each. If tradeoffs have to be made, as often happens in the real world, then the executive must figure out how to make the tradeoffs, and immediately begin improving the tradeoffs for all sides. Managing for stakeholders is about creating as much value as possible for stakeholders, without resorting to tradeoffs.

(3) Implications for the Debate on Corporate Governance

We wish to propose the following two principles that capture the idea that directors need to pay attention to the effects of their companies on stakeholders, rather than just shareholders:

Directors' Duty of Care

Directors have a duty of care to manage the affairs of the corporation, in a responsible manner.

Directors' Responsibility

Directors are "responsible" if and only if they use reasonable judgment to ensure that, over time and on balance, the corporation creates value for all direct stakeholders.

We would define "the affairs of the corporation" as how the achievement of corporate purpose affects the interests of and creates value (or harm) for shareholders,

customers, suppliers, employees, and communities, i.e., a corporation's direct stakeholders. "Responsible" is a more difficult concept but we would suggest that directors would
not have fulfilled their duty of care in a responsible manner, if the corporation makes
continuous tradeoffs of the interests of one group for the sake of the others. Responsible
directors would seek to use reasonable judgment to create as much value for stakeholders
as possible.

We envision that a body of both "best practice" and case law would emerge to
more clearly define the content of these principles. We do not mean these principles as
"principles of law" though clearly they could be developed along these lines. We offer
them instead as advice to directors and executives who want to create companies that
have a chance to be sustainably great and make a difference in the world.

The current debate in corporate governance is fixated on structural reform to
Boards, better regulation of financial systems and reporting, and other ways to "patch
up" the current dominant business model as primarily concerned with shareholder
value. We believe that a more robust idea of the actual existing business models in
use would yield a story that is more amenable to "managing for stakeholders"[107]. Fixing
short-termism and fixing executive compensation, we believe, involves thinking more
deeply about "managing for stakeholders".

The danger of the current debate is that the "patchwork" solution to the current
dominant business model will not yield any meaningful results in escaping the cycle of
"scandal-outrage-regulation-scandal", and it will continue to penalize companies who
actually create value for their stakeholders. The GFC has raised the stakes here. The
business model is in fact the main issue. We can no longer afford the shopworn story
that business is only about money, profits, and shareholders. Business has always been
our way of creating value and trading with each other, hence, it is a powerful means of
social cooperation. We need to re-embed business in society, via a change in the business model rather than an add-on like CSR, more regulation, and structural reforms of
corporate boards. Anything less is too little, too late.

---

107   Indeed we believe that if we separated out the rhetoric of "shareholder value" from the actuality of what
most successful businesses actually do, we would find that "managing for stakeholders" is far more normal than it is
assumed by most of the participants in the corporate governance debate.

BIBLIOGRAPHY

Bøhren, O., Priestley, R. and Ødegaard, B.A. 2009. "Investor Short-Termism and Firm Value." Presentation. Available at http://finance.bi.no/~bernt/wps/ownership_duration/duration_aug_2009.pdf

Brancato, C.K., Rabimov, 2008. "The 2008 Institutional Investment Report" New York: The Conference Board.

Chatterjee, A. and Hambrick, D.C. 2007. "It's All about Me: Narcissistic Chief Executive Officers and Their Effects on Company Strategy and Performance." Administrative Science Quarterly 52: 351-386.

Dillon, K. 2009. "The Coming Battle over Executive Pay." Harvard Business Review 87(9): 96-103.

Fama, E.F. and Jensen, M.C. 1983. "Separation of Ownership and Control." Journal of Law & Economics 26(2): 301-326.

Freeman, R. E. 2009. "Managing for Stakeholders" in Beauchamp, Bowie, and Arnold, Ethical Theory and Business, 8th edition. Upper Saddle River, NJ: Prentice Hall. 56-67.

Freeman, R.E., Harrison, J.S. and Wicks, A C. 2007. *Managing for Stakeholders.* New Haven, CT: Yale University Press.

Fuller, J. and Jensen, M.C. 2001. "Just Say No to Wall Street: Putting a Stop to the Earnings Game." Harvard Business School Working Paper. Published (2002) in Journal of Applied Corporate Finance 14(4): 41-46.

George, B. 2003. *Authentic Leadership.* San Francisco, CA: Jossey Bass.

Graham, J.R., Harvey, C.R., and Rajgopal, S. 2005. "The Economic Implications of Corporate Financial Reporting." Journal of Accounting & Economics. 40(1-3): 3-73.

Hamilton, R.W. 2000 "Corporate Governance in America 1950-2000: Major Changes but Uncertain Benefits." Journal of Corporation Law 25 (2): 349-373.

Harris, J. 2006. "How Much is Too Much? A Theoretical Analysis of Executive Compensation from the Standpoint of Distributive Justice," in R. Kolb (Ed.), *The Ethics of Executive Compensation*, 67-86. Blackwell: Malden, Massachusetts.

Ide, Bill. 2010. "Self Regulation Can Reform Executive Pay." Corporate Board 31(180): 1-4.

Institutional Shareholder Services (ISS). 2006. http://www.issgovernance.com/

Jensen, M.C. and Meckling, W.H., 1976. "Theory of the Firm: Managerial Behavior, Agency costs and Ownership Structure." Journal of Financial Economics 3(4): 305-360.

Kahan, M. and Rock, E. 2010. "Embattled CEOs." Texas Law Review. 88: 987-1051,

Kaplan, S.N. 2008. "Are U.S. CEOs Overpaid?" Academy of Management Perspectives 22(2): 5-20.

Krehmeyer, D., Orsagh, M., and Schacht, K.N. 2006 "Breaking the Short-Term Cycle." Charlottesville, VA: The CFA Institute and Business Roundtable Institute for Corporate Ethics.

Lipton, M., Lorsch, J.W. and Mirvis, T.N. 2009. "Schumer's Shareholder Bill Misses the Mark." Wall Street Journal. May 12, 2009. 253(110): A15.

Lipton, M. and Savitt, W. 2007. "The Many Myths of Lucian Bebchuk." Virginia Law Review. 93(3): 733-758.

Monks, R. and Minow, N. 1995. Corporate Governance. Cambridge, Massachusetts: Blackwell.

Muth, M.M. and Donaldson, L. 1998. "Stewardship Theory and Board Structure: A Contingency Approach." Corporate Governance: An International Review. 6(1): 5-29.

New York Stock Exchange Fact Book. 2006.

O'Reilly, III, C. and Main, B.G.M. 2010. "Economic and Psychological Perspectives on CEO Compensation: A Review and Synthesis." Industrial and Corporate Change 19(3): 675-712.

Pfeffer, J. and Salancik, G.R. 1978. The External Control of Organizations: A Resource Dependence Perspective. New York: Harper and Row.

Strine, L. 2006."Toward a True Corporate Republic: A Traditionalist Response to Bebchuk's Solution For Improving Corporate America." Harvard Law Review 119(6): 1759-1783.

Stout, L.A. 2007. "The Mythical Benefits of Shareholder Control. Regulation 30(1): 42-47.

Tosi, H. L., Werner, S., Katz, J., and Gomez-Mejia, L. R. 2000. "How Much Does Performance Matter? A Meta-Analysis of CEO Pay Studies." Journal of Management 26(2): 301-339.

Being and Acting Businessworthy

Per Saxegaard, Founding Partner,;
Norden Realkapital Group and
the Norden Investment Banking

A re you businessworthy? I'm going on 25 years as a classical capitalist. My background comes from being an investment banker and a businessman. Today, I want to discuss the concept of being businessworthy, and why marrying quantifiable performance with higher purpose can build values that are essential to sustain business success, in a new global economy where empathy is extending and the human consciousness is expanding leading to a sea change in value orientation.

A few years ago, I founded the Business for Peace Foundation. We wish to spread awareness of the importance of being businessworthy, through showing why successful businesses increasingly will be grounded in ethical and responsible business practices, through a more conscious capitalism if you like. A greater awareness of the dynamic in ethical business practices has personal, professional and societal implications that I will touch upon in this lecture. In fact, as an end benefit, this awareness can contribute to peace, something that is clearly demonstrated by the "Merchants of Peace" and "Peace and stability through Trade" mottos of supporting partners in our venture, the International Chambers of Commerce, ICC and WTC.

Our Ethical Business Challenge

I believe we're facing a challenge, requiring us to unite personal ethics with business ethics in a way that's valued not just by our accountants and shareholders, but by society as a whole. One way of getting more business leaders to accept this challenge, even though it's truly easy to find bad examples from business these days, is to show the many excellent but often silent examples demonstrating that ethical and responsible business practice can lead to both business success and the acceptance of society, and that these need not be in opposition.

The Business for Peace Foundation conducts a worldwide search for excellent examples of ethically responsible business. Through an international nomination process with partners such as the International Chamber of Commerce, seven Business for Peace Honorees are chosen from a worldwide group of nominees, and receive The Just Man statuette. This statuette exemplifies our ethical business challenge: it celebrates ethical and socially responsible business practices, and the commitment of business leaders as individuals towards creating sustainable success.

The members of the award-giving committee, all Nobel Laureates in peace and economics, work independently of our foundation when selecting the seven Honorees. Their participation offers a perspective on business outside of the market, and ensures that the award can be conferred with unquestionable ethical and professional authority. Building on the worldwide nomination process, and the wonderful examples of the award-winners, our vision is to build the highest recognition a business person can achieve outside of making money—with the goal of building a wider acceptance of the wisdom of being ethical and responsible in business.

Ethical Business Is A Partnership With Society

Each year, our committee selects seven Honorees who deserve to receive admiration from all of us. One common theme when they are describing their particular moment of enlightenment in their professional work, is their desire to seek business success in a way that can stand up to the critical eye of society.

The CEO of IKEA, Anders Dahlvig, summed up his philosophy in this manner when accepting The Just Man statuette. "Companies such as IKEA whose purpose and vision have a social ambition that goes beyond the traditional objective of maximizing shareholders' value have an advantage. I believe that most people want purpose and meaning with what they want to do for a living. If this purpose contributes to doing good work for others, it's a tremendous motivator." That is an outstanding example of marrying performance with purpose.

Let me repeat, I am unshakeable in my belief in capitalism. I don't know of any resource or method of organization more powerful in creating value than capitalism. Business is in the business of making the impossible possible and achieves this with a regularity that has made us take this miracle for granted.

Yet, this begs the question: Why are businessmen too often the crooks in the story to the point that even the capitalist system is finding itself in disrepute these days?

A Disconnect Between Theory And Practice

During his entire professional life, in which he held great sway over the conduct of business, Alan Greenspan spoke forcefully in favor of self-regulation and did what he could to reduce government regulation. He stated that government regulation was inefficient compared to what business could do when allowed to self-correct. Yet, at the height of the financial crisis, Greenspan declared "I am in shocked disbelief. I put too much faith in the self-correcting power of free markets." Alan Greenspan had come to lose faith in his own business philosophy.

As businesspersons, we are number crunchers. We measure performance in quanta. We are known to give lower priority to softer values in order to achieve quantity and measurability, in order to deliver hard bottom line results and financial values. In fact, we do not hesitate to denigrate talk of softer values as fluff or irrelevancies. Yet as businesspersons, we are regularly bound to experience situations that are unclear and filled with ethical risk that can challenge our personal values.

As individual human beings we gradually grow to seek and see that quality of life is more than numbers and dollars, and that making the right decision may require more than a calculator and a spreadsheet—we may find that awareness of softer values in fact can lead towards better results.

These are decisions where we risk ignoring that solving the problem demands an awareness and understanding of possible underlying ethical challenges. Instead, we often rationalize, postponing the supposedly inefficient and burdensome ethical questions while focusing on today's quantifiable performance. We compartmentalize the components of the problems between that which is urgent and that which can be left for later. Too often, softer ethical values are left for later.

Thus we risk losing sight of the greater whole. Omitting softer values can have tremendous consequences—if by doing so you betray your integrity through ignoring the bond of trust between your company and society. We may be able to please the stockholders in the short term, but conducting business only according to what is legal while ignoring what is right, is fraught with danger in the long run.

Each of you can probably bring a myriad of examples of business risk gone wrong to the table. Examples that illustrate that short term gains were given priority over long term consequences. Our news media are full of them these days. Is it enough then that we ask what could they be thinking? There are great personal and professional tragedies behind each of these examples and the cost to business and to society is great.

Ethically Responsible Business Builds Trust

We have to accept that what we do as business people will have consequences outside the immediate ones that we are quantifying. What we do and how we do it often has a resounding impact outside our closed circle and the world outside has become painfully aware of it. We need to foster a greater awareness of the far-reaching consequence of our decisions. Let's not pretend otherwise. There's been a strong, lasting and cumulative change in the most important precondition for the conduct of any business: people have gradually stopped trusting business. The only factors that can influence the perception of trust are those of ethical and responsible behavior, and whether your business takes these seriously or for granted.

On February 8 of 2010, Elizabeth Warren, the Harvard law Professor, with a specialty in contract law, bankruptcy law and commercial law, had an op-ed in the *Wall Street Journal* which dealt with the significance of trust in financial relationships. She opened with a blast: "Banking is based on trust. Yet for years, Wall Street CEOs have thrown away customer trust like so much worthless trash. The only factors that can influence perception of trust are those of ethical and responsible behavior. And if a bank is seen to be unethical in its behavior, no amount of advertising can change that."

Yes, we have squandered this priceless asset as if it was an infinite resource. We need to understand that the world is no longer accepting our assurances that we can self-correct. The world—that is consumers, voters, peers, the media, politicians and interest groups—are paying attention to what we are doing and are considering how to make us pay for what we want to do in ways that ensure we do not cause any more damage. This could ultimately mean stricter self-regulation, fines, supplemental taxation, and confiscation of profits, and in view of this looming threat of an avalanche of new regulations, maybe soft values and ethics shouldn't be considered soft at all.

We will have to demonstrate that we are responding to this crisis of confidence in business by regaining public trust—and we do that through demonstrating that we are aware of ethical shortcomings, where they exist.

Marrying Quantifiable Performance With Higher Purpose

I am a businessman. I'm driven by the urge to create value, and I'm not here to point my finger and admonish. I want to increase awareness of the significant potential that lies in ethically responsible business practices, a potential for increased growth and influence. Some will claim that harsh business realities make such beliefs naïve, that promoting quality of life when tasked to deliver quantifiable performance is a luxury we can't afford, or that it is not the business of business to afford such concerns. Well, I am convinced that the truly naïve in this respect are those who continue to refuse to see that behaving in this manner is not an expense. It's an investment in the future success of your business. One of the 2009 Business for Peace Honorees, Mr. Mohammed Jameel from Saudi Arabia, stated that he couldn't possibly have achieved the business success and respect he enjoyed if it wasn't for the strong ethical values instilled in him by his parents, values that told him to place the success of society before personal success.

The Grameen-Jameel Foundation provides microfinance education and mentoring in many Middle East nations. While running one of the most successful businesses in the Middle East, Mr. Jameel still finds time to found and oversee groundbreaking initiatives that are improving the lives of millions in the Middle East.

There is much to be gained in marrying quantifiable performance with higher purpose. We can change increased business risk to greater opportunities for business success. At the Business for Peace Foundation we are promoting the term "being businessworthy" to quickly communicate the increased need to be aware of this higher potential union between performance and purpose. Being creditworthy is a well-established concept that is globally understood, but it's no longer sufficient to establish and build trust. We need to embrace ethical awareness and responsible conduct. By being creditworthy and businessworthy, we will bring more to the table. We show that we are aware of how our activities will affect not only our business, but also the society in which we are acting.

Being businessworthy means you are aware that the value of a business also depends on the ethical values guiding the business, and that this greater set of values is of critical importance if we wish to create financial value that can meet tomorrow's demands. Ethical values come from important and lasting principles that express what is right and desirable in life and that are shared with others in the society in which we are acting. They tell us what we should do and what we shouldn't, and they are constantly evolving to suit new demands. They have relevance as guidelines when we evaluate the quality and sincerity of our relationships, and they become decisive when our ideals are challenged by temptations.

To use the power and potential that comes from being ethical and responsible in business, we need to tear down the artificial distinction between our personal values and our professional values, between our preferred private ethics and required business ethics. In private, we have little trouble understanding that we are responsible for our actions or that we need to be mindful of their consequences. The distinction between the business person and the private individual is being erased—accountability is overlapping the two spheres, to the point where we can't distinguish the business persona from the private person. This was made very clear a few weeks after my lecture, when the CEO of BP in frustration over the Deepwater Horizon oil spill declared on camera: "I want my life back." He made it seem as if he considered having to deal with the spill a great bother, as he would say it. This comment came back to haunt him and BP again and again, as it was replayed in the media, and eventually was cited as a significant factor in why he is no longer the CEO of BP. This disconnect between his personal priorities and his business responsibilities was simply too great for BP to be able to go on with business as usual.

Business Needs Rules

There is a saying: I went to a fight and suddenly a hockey game broke out.

If you try to conduct business without a set of rules and values, it's not business, it becomes "eat or be eaten". A lot of the personal frustrations I have witnessed during my business career are due to the fact that people have tried to be good as private individuals while being ruthless in business. It is worth remembering that great sports performances are ruthless within a given set of rules. When you pretend you can bend the rules as you wish you risk going wrong. The game of golf has a rulebook that would make business leaders cringe if they were to adhere to such strict regulations in business—but adhering to those rules, through a gentleman's ethics, is what makes golf a fantastic sport. Maybe business also needs to accept that there are certain rules you simply can't break when conducting business, and that these are the rules that will make you businessworthy?

We trick ourselves if we believe that we can have one set of rules at work and one at home. Even if your business should be outwardly very successful, you could end up—and I've encountered this many times—you could end up feeling miserable, struggling with frustrations that deeply affect your quality of life.

Many businesspersons solve this problem by living in a bubble, isolated from the turmoil their businesses cause. Living life surrounded by Yes-Men may be convenient, but doesn't it really mean that you aren't up to the challenges posed by doing business in today's world? At any rate, being surrounded by Yes-Men only works if you can't see what people outside think of you, and if people outside can't see what you are up to. That kind of isolation from worldly affairs is no longer possible.

The Value Drivers Of Tomorrow Make Ethically Responsible Business Critical

Surveys show a sea change in values orientation over the past decenniums. As people in industrializing and urbanizing countries become more productive, wealthy and independent, their values orientation shift from materialist values towards self-expression and quality-of-life aspirations of the knowledge- and service based society. Individual security increases empathy. The difference is fundamental.

The digital revolution is accelerating this transformation in a substantive way. The increased transparency of the globally distributed information and communications technologies makes hiding impossible, while creating new opportunities. The distributed network characteristics of the new global economy are leading to a surge of empathy among people and are expanding the human consciousness and values orientation. This drives the need for business leaders to increase their ethical awareness and adjust their business to this growing new reality if success is to be sustained.

The 24-hour news cycle, ever present media intrusions, the expansion of the Internet, and the reach of globalization have removed the artificial distinction between the public and private business personas, and stress the need for increased ethical awareness. The coming tablet revolution and mobile Internet will ensure that we can always connect and always be connected. The opportunities are many and we can clearly see the transformation happening to existing business structures and models.

The social Web, the sites where people participate through sharing and publishing content and opinions in pursuit of greater quality of life, is exploding in size and extension. It is truly transforming relationships, while also redistributing power both on the personal plane, in business relationships, between consumers and advertisers, even between state actors and non-governmental organizations. The Web's ability to rally consumer power has been felt by many businesses that chose to remain comfortably numb and do business as usual. They did not realize that their actions were not universally popular until they had a million consumers telling them they were off track and needed to act in specific ways if they wished to reconnect with their consumers.

These changes in relationships have a potential to transform business, creating deep structural changes. The fact that we call them social media, and stress the relationships they foster, should point us in the right direction. Relationships have always been at the heart of business and are actually more important to business than transactions. During my career as an investment banker, this is an observation I've been able to make daily: Business is, at its core, the synergy that arises from mutually beneficial relationships. I'm convinced that many business leaders are unaware of how extensively the understanding of what constitutes a business relationship is being transformed through the new media and distributed information and communications technologies, moving control from their hands into those of society and consumers. Many are missing out on this opportunity while building risk through remaining ignorant of this change.

The digital revolution has created a tool for communicating what is good. For instance, best practices that force us to improve if we wish to remain competitive. The revolution is also able to widely and quickly communicate scandal and criminal behavior. If the world is not becoming flatter, then it is at least becoming speedier and more closely interwoven. There is no way to hide these days and basically, it's best if you work to avoid having anything to hide.

The Internet and globalization have given people everywhere the tool they need to see deep into the world and into how the business world is working. They are comparing best and worst practices and demanding changes that match the best they see elsewhere. And if they can't have material change, at least they want the assurance that comes from businesses adhering to recognized ethical standards.

Business Leaders Can Choose To Help Create Beneficial Change

Mr. Mo Ibrahim, the 2009 Business for Peace honoree from Sudan, has used the influence and resources he gained through building a multinational cell phone company. He has created an index that measures different African nations against each other on a scale of good governance. Such an index would be inconceivable just a few years ago. Today, citizens in all African nations can consult the index and hold their government accountable where it should fall short of what other nations on the continent have achieved. Or they can feel pride that their nation is doing well in the index.

I think the digital revolution and accompanying surge of human empathy and changes of values orientations observed globally, forcefully discussed and documented in Jeremy Rifkins book "The Empathic Civilization", probably make it possible to speak of an ethical network effect where a wider consciousness is built by better and faster technological reach. Clearly, there is a general increase in awareness of ethics and morals in both business and politics, and we're seeing a cumulative growth in this awareness as well as in the demands being made of those who conduct business.

The Future Holds A Reality Check For
Anyone Who Ignores the Ethical Dimension In Business

If we had cause to complain about strict demands in the past, it will be nothing compared to the demands to come, as society wants a greater say in the conduct of business when such conduct can have harmful consequences. It's not just that the demands have become stricter but also that business scandal now will out much more easily. Previously, delinquent business leaders could rely on their ability to hide their actions from the public eye. Today, sometimes the public knows about the consequences of a transgression before management. At any rate, business practices that we might have expected to get away with 15 or 20 years ago can land you on the front page or in jail today, and there's little reason to expect that things will become easier over the next 20 years—rather the contrary.

Consumers have become a lot more conscious of values beyond the price of purchase and are influenced by more than the amount they pay. They want to know what they are consuming, how it's being produced, and what values the company believes in. They thirst for information, use digital media to gather and exchange information, and are no longer dependent upon advertising in order to choose. They wish to identify with the company they have a relationship with, without having to apologize to others for that relationship.

Adam Smith 2.0—The Invisible Ethical Handshake

Adam Smith's invisible hand is much used to defend the belief that myopic self-interest is to the common good, but that was not what Adam Smith said. Greed isn't good. Gordon Gekko was wrong. Adam Smith was right, but people chose to misinterpret what Smith said and misused his philosophy to defend business wrongs. The recent financial crisis is just one indication that ethical and responsible business awareness has been lacking.

When we glibly refer to "the invisible hand," we are actually misconstruing Adam Smith. The following statement is at the core of his belief in what would make business work best: "Markets could not flourish without a strong underlying moral culture, animated by empathy and fellow-feeling, by our ability to understand our common bond as human beings and to recognize the needs of others."

That statement is far removed from the accepted interpretation of his "invisible hand." Capitalism needs trust to function. Without trust it stops working. Trust is a core consequence of ethical conduct, something Adam Smith was very well aware of. The basic insight of Adam Smith has been sacrificed in an attempt to defend that greed is good, an interpretation that would be repulsive to Smith." Our ability to understand our common bond" is one of Smith's essential insights; it's hard to see how the modern invisible hand interpretation would result from such a statement.

I think more than just capitalism needs to be reintegrated with the values of society if we are to realize the common good that Adam Smith wrote about in *The Wealth of Nations*. We need Adam Smith 2.0, a capitalism that is businessworthy of today's challenges, and those coming. The invisible hand needs a reboot into the invisible handshake of ethics and responsibility. The sincere handshake is the seal of trust in any business. In my opinion, there's an enormous unrealized potential for building value to the common good if we embrace Adam Smith's underlying moral values and dedicate ourselves to being businessworthy.

Win-Lose or Win-Win?

We must recognize that doing great while also doing good, that marrying performance with purpose, can create new business benefits and create new results to an extent not even imagined by regulators made over eager by business malfeasance. But in order to achieve this, we must embrace being businessworthy in our dealings, and it can't just be for show. It has to be sincere and authentic.

During the 2009 Peace Through Trade gathering in Oslo, Dr. Long Yongtu was one of our distinguished speakers. For 10 years he was the leader of the Chinese delegation negotiating China's participation in international trade agreements such as WTO. During his talk, Mr. Long Yongtu said that Chinese businessmen only recently had begun embracing win-win. Chinese business has traditionally been adversarial with win-lose being the recognized and respected dynamic. To him, it was a revelation to adapt to the concept that successful long-term business depends on win-win. His chief message to our gathering was that the new major force driving the economic development in China in the future will have to be, using his term, "the forces of ethics."

Win-lose is a destructive dynamic. When business is seen to be unfairly one-sided the result is division and a destruction of trust. If there ever should be a golden rule of business, it could be: Never offer a deal you couldn't accept yourself. In a societal perspective, business is not a zero-sum game where it's required that one side must lose in order for the other to win. That works well in a tennis match, but it doesn't work in business that seeks to be viable in the long term.

To create value and growth over time, relationships must result in mutual benefits, something that mature businesspersons are well aware of and know how to make use of.

At the micro level, this kind of values building is a de facto peace process. For you to win, the other has to win as well. This is the background for "Peace through Trade"— for claims that peace and stability can result from trade. If the relationship remains adversarial, the result is adversity. Crudely stated, you don't shoot the ones you invoice.

This potential of business to create peace seems not to have been sufficiently understood and utilized by either businesspersons or politicians. Today, we are all becoming interwoven in such complex and mutually dependent ways that we need to expand our awareness of the consequences of the win-win logic. It's not just you and the partner you are doing business with but all those you are having an impact upon that you need to take into account, which is why we need to be aware that for you to win the other, the others must also win. When business promotes conflict such as breaking human rights, silently accepting child labor or corruption, or by contributing to environmental damages or other business transgressions, then we are guilty of business violence, then our business activity does not promote peace, then we are preventing the other parties from also being winners. Such harmful and destructive actions are not businessworthy. They represent an indirect violence that limits creativity and value creation, and which destabilizes and works against peace.

A more conscious capitalism, the benefit that results when business is ethical and aware, can promote stability and peace instead of reducing or limiting them. A conscious capitalism builds upon the framework established in today's CSR movement, and will go beyond the tension between society and business that the present CSR implicitly addresses, towards creating a mutually reinforcing relationship where business and society are partners before they are adversaries.

It's a lot easier to achieve business success when the society in which you are active is also successful. Marrying performance and purpose makes good business sense. It's not just a lofty sentiment; it's down-to-earth, practical and useful.

Three Dimensions to Ethical Business Practices

By being ethical and responsible, as businesspersons we achieve a three-fold return. Ethical and responsible business practice can significantly impact you and your business on the professional, as well as on the societal and the personal levels.

By contributing to society through exploring the mutually reinforcing dependency between business and society, we contribute to higher objectives of stability and peace, and strengthen the business above the bottom line.

At the same time, by fostering win-win relationships, we achieve a future-proofing of our business. By adhering to ethical business practices, we ensure that our business will withstand scrutiny from a world that is becoming ethically more aware and which desires business to be sound and appreciated, instead of worthy of distrust.

Ultimately, a renewed focus on ethical business will help us become aware of our own values and will help us align this with our business practices in a way that reinforces quality of life, our personal fulfillment and happiness rather than placing them at risk.

Through businessworthy achievements, we create value that gains the respect of society, and that is in accord with our conscience.

It helps us gain pride in making a difference as businesspersons.

A Response to: *Are You Businessworthy?*
Working to Create Shared Value between Business and Society;
Marrying Performance and Purpose

Adrian A.C. Keevil
Darden School of Business, University of Virginia

P ER SAXEGAARD has contributed a wonderful chapter to this volume that presents many useful ideas to help restore the relationship between business and society in the wake of the global financial crisis. In his view business people should seek to be what he calls, "businessworthy," by seriously considering ethics as an inexorably intertwined element of business. Saxegaard does not present a vision of the firm as much as a vision for capitalism itself. The core of his argument is that business writ large has misunderstood, or misapplied, Adam Smith's (1776) ideas about capitalism. Specifically, he argues that the "invisible hand" has evolved into a justification for selfishness, when a more useful reading of Smith would show that self-interest was one of many virtues that Smith believed would be essential to a productive economy. Thus, Saxegaard's vision for capitalism does not depend on increased regulation or oversight. It depends on the individual responsibility of people to behave according to a moral standard and for business as a whole to reinforce and promote trust—both performance-based trust and benevolence-based trust. Just as companies and people are judged as creditworthy, he argues, so should they be judged as businessworthy. In this response I will summarize some of the core arguments in Saxegaard's chapter, and discuss them in the context of relevant research in the extant management and organizational and management literature. I then present a vision for the firm that coexists with the vision for business Saxegaard describes—as an inexorable part of society.

Addressing Solvable Problems And Adam Smith 2.0

Being businessworthy is based on a simple idea—the power of collective action and local coordination. Saxegaard's vision is that, through the individual and collective responsibility of businesspeople, we can envision a world in which business and ethics are inseparable, the role of business in society is benevolent, and capitalism fulfills its promise as a system of social progress. This idea of local solutions to local problems is one which has support from scholars. For example, economist Amyarta Sen (2005, 2010) argues that philosophers' and economists' time spent thinking about a theory of "perfect justice" is a significant reason why we tend not to progress towards a more fair society. Sen argues that the path to justice is not through the creation of grand theories, but through the systematic removal of what he calls redressible injustices. These are things that individuals perceive as problems that they can address. Similarly, John Dewey (1927) argued for a pluralist solution to problems in society, arguing for the power of social thought transmitted by word of mouth in the local community.

Local movements require a moral compass to be effective (Dewey, 1927). For this, Saxegaard turns to Adam Smith (1776). One of Saxegaard's core ideas is to move business into what he refers to as, "Adam Smith 2.0." Basically, his argument is that we need new interpretation of *Wealth of Nations*. This argument also has scholarly support. The idea of capitalism was originally conceived by Smith as a part of a broader moral theory, much of which was articulated in his *Theory of Moral Sentiments* (1759) but a lot of which is also contained within Wealth of Nations. But today, the version of capitalism that we observe in practice may have been influenced unproductively by a misreading of Smith (e.g., Werhane, 1991). Self-interest, as Saxegaard argues, tends to be interpreted narcissistically. However, self-interest in Smith's (1776) vision was intended to be interpreted as a virtue, namely the virtue of self-love. As Patricia Werhane argues in her book *Adam Smith and his Legacy for Modern Capitalism*, "According to Smith, human beings are not motivated merely by selfish passions or self-interest; both prudence (the virtue of self-interest) and benevolence are virtues; and the basic virtue is not benevolence but justice" (Werhane, 1991:23-24). Virtues by definition require balance against vices, but also against other virtues. And self-interest was only one of, and arguably the less emphasized of a group of virtues that Smith thought were important to a functional socioeconomic system. Smith's model of the economic actor is a person who embodies the virtues of goodwill, prudence and self-control. Smith emphasizes self-restraint, cooperation, and fairness as principles that work in concert with self-interest. He also describes an institutional environment based on a morality, law, and justice (Werhane, 1991:180). Finally, the invisible hand is in no way portrayed as a perpetrator of morally good economic outcomes (Werhane, 1991: 23). Saxegaard's claim that we "glibly" interpret Smith's work is an accurate one. And in some ways, this misinterpretation foreshadows what he argues is a broader problem of misinterpretation of academic work.

The Shortfall of Academia in Business

Saxegaard is generally critical of academia, and somewhat candidly argues that it has failed to provide vision for capitalism that includes ethics, specifically citing some of Michael Porter's recent writing and Alan Greenspan's recent comments, and that it is somehow partially responsible for some of the divisions we can observe between business and society today. Saxegaard argues that there is a disconnection between theory and practice in business. This is a similar charge as one made by Nobel Laureate Economist Paul Krugman (2009) in the aftermath of the financial crisis. But for practical purposes, the distinction between theory and practice as he characterizes it is perhaps too sharp. Theory is, fundamentally, based on and attempts to describe practice, so at the most basic level theory and practice are always equivalent (Rorty, 1999). But Saxegaard is onto something here. Management and economic theories can be somewhat self-fulfilling in that what is theory today often becomes practice tomorrow (Ferraro, Pfeffer and Sutton, 2005). Therefore, I think Saxegaard's critique of academia might be more powerfully framed not as a disconnection between theory and practice, but as a disconnection between researchers and the real world. And in many ways he is issuing a call for academic researchers to be conscious of the consequences of their research. We seldom hear academic arguments that make this point explicitly (Rorty, 1999). But there is no logical reason that academic research cannot be influential on thought and useful to society (Putnam, 2002). Political philosopher Donald Stokes (1997) described this type of research as inhabiting "Pasteur's Quadrant." Pasteur possessed both the desire to advance basic knowledge and the motivation for research to be useful to society. This is an idea that Rorty (1999) renders in his discourse on the "humanistic intellectual." Rorty (1999) draws a distinction between scholars that conform to "well-understood criteria for making contributions to knowledge" from "people trying to expand their own moral imaginations" (Rorty, 1999: 29). All areas of human activity should strive to improve society, including academic research (Rorty, 1999: xxv).

If we take Saxegaard's depiction of the world as it is, then there is a second failing of business ethics. It hasn't been very good at convincing practitioners that its ideas are useful. This is not unique to business ethics, and applies to academic researchers more generally (Olson, 2009). When Saxegaard argues that we should "redefine business ethics in a way that's valued not just by our accountants and shareholders but by society as a whole," there are two meanings. On one hand this is a call for business practitioners to work ethics into business in a way that isn't just an add-on but is integrated into every decision. But there is a more subtle meaning as well. Notice that his comment is specifically aimed at business ethics. Taking Saxegaard's argument at face value, the field of business ethics, broadly defined, has failed to provide meaningful ways for business practitioners to incorporate ethics into practice. He has an important point here. While it is expedient to lay blame on business for the current environment, in many ways the apparent separation of business and society is as much a failure of ethics. Most of the archetypical frameworks that ethicists use—virtue ethics, deontology, utilitarianism, etc.—were written without taking business into account. And business is largely absent from mainstream ethics journals (Norman, 2011). If business and ethics are separated in the field of ethics, it is not surprising that they are, in Saxegaard's view at least, separated in practice.

This conforms to what R. Edward Freeman (1994) calls the "Separation Thesis"— that the discourse of business and the discourse of ethics can be meaningfully or are usefully separated. But it also speaks to a broader question about the role of ethics in business practice. From one perspective ethics provides frameworks with which to judge right and wrong in business activities, and to establish the duties and obligations that businesses have to society. This is ethics as judgment. If we think about ethics as judgment, we can use ethics to inform decision-making by applying a set of rules. Or that we can render moral judgment on a decision based on a set of rights and wrongs. But to do this requires a redacted version of the world in which right and wrong are clear. Of course the world is much messier than this, and what is "right" and "wrong" is seldom very clear. From another view, which Saxegaard implicitly endorses, we can think about ethics as providing a diverse set of perspectives about business. This is ethics as conversation (e.g., Freeman, Keevil and Purnell, 2011). If we think about ethics as conversation we are saying that within business there is room for moral discourse. We are recognizing that that business is ambiguous and complex and the right and wrong answers are not always clear. Treating ethics as conversation implies that having more points of view (as opposed to fewer). Of course this view of ethics in business tends to make things more complex, but this complexity also helps managers avoid the type of managerial myopia that Saxegaard criticizes (Werhane, 2008). Thus, thinking about business ethics as conversation, instead as judgment, offers not only a means to improve ethical decision outcomes but also a way to incorporate ethics into the everyday discourse of business.

Towards a New Vision of the Firm

The word vision has two meanings. On one hand, it is forward-looking. A "vision of the firm" can be a destination, an idea about where we think the firm should be and how we think it can get there. But vision can also describe what we see now. One of Saxegaard's achievements is that in the midst of what seems like a rift between business and society, he retells stories about how business is making the world a better place. This is a welcomed vision, and it stands in stark contract with the more popular vision of business that we read about in the news. In that version, as Saxagaard writes, "businessmen often become the crooks in the story." In Saxegaard's version, businesspeople contribute to world peace. But in reading Saxegaard's argument, the stiffest impediment to reconciling these two narratives is the need to quantify in business. There is a general prejudicial preference for "hard" versus soft "things" in both business and academia (Putnam, 2002). Saxegaard responds to this when he writes about how we tend to "give lower priority to softer and less determinate values in order to achieve quantity and measurability" (p. 5). Hilary Putnam (2002) also criticized this phenomenon, arguing that it assumes that we can effectively separate all our alleged judgments from inquiry. The consequence of this, Putnam argues, is a market for things which are valuable because they can be measured and the de-emphasis of things that are (by contrast) rendered worthless—aesthetic judgments, metaphysical judgments, and the like—because they cannot be measured in the same way.

But even though we have progressed beyond this version of value, in many ways, I think the idea behind measurement still haunts us as an intellectual ghost (Dewey, 1927). When we think about measuring performance in financial terms, we are implicitly defining the firm in financial terms as well. Literally, if I close my eyes and think about a company, like "Coke" or "Proctor and Gamble" or "Google," I tend to have an image in my mind of an entity that is influenced by the view of the firm from marketing (a brand), from financial economics (a balance sheet), and from the law (incorporation). This vision might have unintended consequences. When a manager has to think about managing, a vision of "the firm" that is neatly parsimonious based on a brand, or a balance sheet, probably leads to an equally parsimonious set of decision possibilities (e.g., Wicks, Keevil and Parmar, under review). And it is this vision that might be what holds us back from living up to Saxegaard's vision for business. The problem, therefore, might lie with our relentless tendency to want define "the firm" as an entity unto itself.

Embedded in the idea of corporation are the ideas of incorporation and excorporation (Trachtenberg, 2007). The idea of corporation implies that an entity can exist in isolation from society, and business people separate from society by association. John Dewey (1927) spends a lot of time in The Public and its Problems trying to reconcile the difference between public and private. He writes:

> A man may be one thing as a church member and another thing as a member of the business community. The difference may be carried as if in water-tight compartments, or it may become such a division as to entail internal conflict. In these facts we have the ground of the common antithesis set up between society and the individual. (Dewey, 1942: 191)

Saxegaard argues a similar point, writing, "...We need to tear down the artificial distinction between our personal values and our professional values, between our preferred private ethics and our required business ethics" (p.11). Corporations have implicit borders, and borders also foster a convenient way to deny responsibility to a broader society (Dewey, 1927).

Scholars writing within a particular class of theories collectively referred to as, "stakeholder theory" (Freeman, et al., 2010) have spent a lot of time thinking about the idea that there are forms of value creation that are important to consider in addition to economic value creation. Stakeholder theory reconciles the idea that we can create value in economic terms in a way that takes external stakeholders into account and values them as ends, and not means. It forces us to ask two questions. First, what is the nature of the firm? And, second, to whom is it responsible? Certainly the nature of "the firm" from a stakeholder perspective has the potential to create usefully inclusive vision of the firm. It potentially allows us to consider people outside the "company", such as suppliers, to whom the success of the company is dependent. Still, the archetypical stakeholder maps depict firms and stakeholders as distinct entities. And I wonder if we can't create a new vision for the firm that incorporates ideas from stakeholder theory and avoids the issue of implicit borders.

Another way that stakeholder theorists have talked the firm is as a nexus of contracts (e.g., Phillips, 2003). Contracts are a central feature of foundational works in organizational economics, such as Klein, et al (1978), Jensen and Meckling (1976), and Fama and Jensen (1983). However, most contract, or nexus of contracts, theories of the firm tend to support a stockholder-centric conception of the firm, and specifically view the firm as a nexus of contracts between shareholders and managers (Boatright, 2002). But this shareholder/manager contract view is a narrow representation of extant theory related to contracts and organizations. For example, Alchian and Demsetz (1972) took a wider position, arguing that the firm was a contractual organization of inputs in which there is: (a) joint input production; (b) several input owners; (c) one party who is common to all the contracts of the joint inputs; (d) who has the rights to renegotiate any input's contract independently of contracts with other input owners; (e) who holds the residual claim; and (f) who has the right to sell his contractual residual status. Similarly, Freeman and Evan (1990) explain stakeholder theory through the lens of Williamson's (1979) contract view of the firm. Accounting scholar Shyam Sunder (2002) uses contracts to explain a theory of management accounting which is inclusive of many external parties. He describes contracts as, "an understanding (implicit or explicit) for mutual benefit among two or more agents about one another's actions" (Sunder 2002). Of course, contracts have implicitly been at the center of management theory since the origins of organizational research (e.g., Barnard, 1936; Cooper, 1951; Cyert & March, 1963; Simon, 1947). All of these are similar in that they use an expanded view of what "contracts" are. From these perspectives they are simply the expectations surrounding the exchange of value between multiple parties. For example, shareholders contribute equity capital, and expect to receive a dividend. Managers contribute tacit skills, and receive some form of monetary compensation. Customers give cash, and receive goods and services. Lenders give capital, and expect interest and eventually principal repayment. Agencies provide important services, and expect fees. While this view represents a minority of management and organizational scholarship, it is useful in this context because it provides a logical framework within which firm and stakeholders to be considered part of the same group.

Chester Barnard (1936) argued that when a collection of people realize they can do things more effectively as a group than individually, they will voluntarily work together to achieve mutual ends. Based on this idea, he defines organizations as: a system of consciously coordinated activities or forces of two or more persons (p. 10). There is no reason we have do think about "the firm" as a corporation. We don't need to base our vision on whom owns what and whom caries which business card. The form the organization takes can be defined simply as the sum total of the ways in which it divides its labor into distinct tasks and then achieves coordination among them (Mintzberg, 1980). Combining Barnard's view of organizations, and the idea of contracts informed by stakeholder theory, we can think about "the firm" as: A system of consciously coordinated activities of two or more people who voluntarily cooperate, with the recognition of mutual dependence and mutual benefit. Freeman and his colleagues (2010) described business as "people creating value and trading with each other." Saxegaard refers to business as, "[Applying] your business energy ethically and responsibly with the purpose of creating economic value that also creates value for society." But until we revise our practice of defining "the firm" as a distinct entity, these visions of business will likely remain parts of the alternative narrative. If we discard the vision of "the firm" or "the organization" as something that refers to a specific corporation, we free our minds to accept a vision like that articulated by Mr. Saxegaard, in which the border between business and society does not exist.

REFERENCES

Alchian, A. A., & Demsetz, H. 1972. *Production, Information Costs, and Economic Organization.* The American Economic Review, 62(5): 777-795.

Barnard, C. I. 1936. *The Functions of the Executive.* Cambridge, MA: Harvard University Press.

Boatright, J. R. 2002. *Contractors as stakeholders: Reconciling stakeholder theory with the nexus-of-contracts firm.* Journal of Banking & Finance, 26(9): 1837-1852.

Cooper, W. W. 1951. *A Proposal For Extending The Theory of the Firm.* The Quarterly Journal of Economics, 65(1): 87.

Cyert, R., & March, J. G. 1963. *A Behavioral Theory of the Firm.* Englewood Cliffs, NJ: Prentice-Hall.

Dewey, J. 1927. *The Public and Its Problems.* New York: Holt.

Fama, E. F., & Jensen, M. C. 1983. *Separation of Ownership and Control.* Journal of Law and Economics: 301-325.

Ferraro, F., Pfeffer, J., & Sutton, R. I. 2005. *Economics Language and Assumptions: How Theories Can Become Self-Fulfilling.* Academy of Management Review, 30(1): 8-24.

Freeman, R. E. 1994. *The Politics of Stakeholder Theory: Some Future Directions.* Business Ethics Quarterly: 409-421.

Freeman, R. E., Harrison, J. S., Wicks, A. C., Parmar, B. L., & de Colle, S. 2010. *Stakeholder Theory: The State of the Art.* Cambridge: Cambridge University Press.

Freeman, R. E., Keevil, A., & Purnell, L. 2011. *Poor People and the Politics of Capitalism.* Business and Professional Ethics Journal, 30(3/4).

Jacobe, D. 2011. "Americans Trust Governors, Business Leaders Most on Economy." Gallup: April 14.

Jensen, M. C., & Meckling, W. H. 1976. *Theory of the Firm: Managerial Behavior, Agency Costs and Ownership Structure.* Journal of Financial Economics, 3(4): 305-360.

Klein, B., Crawford, R. G., & Alchian, A. A. 1978. *Vertical Integration, Appropriable Rents, and the Competitive Contracting Process.* Journal of Law and Economics, 21: 297.

Krugman, P. 2009. *How Did Economists Get It So Wrong?* New York Times Magazine: September 2: 36.

Mintzberg, H. 1980. *Structure In 5'S: A Synthesis of the Research on Organization Design.* Management science: 322-341.

Norman, W. 2011. *Current and Future Trends In Business Ethics Scholarship.* Society for Business Ethics Annual Meeting Awards Luncheon Panel Discussion

Olson, R. 2009. *Don't Be Such A Scientist: Talking Substance In An Age of Style.* Washington, DC: Island Press.

Phillips, R. 2003. *Stakeholder Theory and Organizational Ethics.* San Francisco: Berrett-Koehler.

Putnam, H. 2002. *The Collapse of the Fact/Value Dichotomy and Other Essays.* Cambridge, Ma: Harvard University Press.

Rorty, R. 1999. *Philosophy and Social Hope.* London: Penguin.

Sen, A. 2005. *on Ethics and Economics.* Malden, MA: Blackwell.

Sen, A. 2009. *The idea of justice.* Cambridge, MA: Harvard University Press.

Simon, H. A. 1947. *Administrative Behavior: A Study of Decision-Making Processes In Administrative Organizations.* New York: The Free Press.

Smith, A. 1937. *Wealth of Nations* (1776). New York: Modern Library.

Smith, A. 2009. *Theory of Moral Sentiments* (1759). London: Penguin.

Stokes, D. E. 1997. *Pasteur's Quadrant: Basic Science and Technological Innovation.* Washington, DC: Brookings Institution Press.

Sunder, S. 2002. *Management Control, Expectations, Common Knowledge, and Culture.* Journal of Management Accounting Research, 14: 173-187.

Trachtenberg, A. 2007. *The Incorporation of America: Culture and Society In The Gilded Age* (25th anniversary edition). New York: Hill & Wang.

Werhane, P. H. 2008. *Mental Models, Moral Imagination and System Thinking In The Age of Globalization.* Journal of Business Ethics, 78(3): 463-474.

Werhane, P. H. 1991. *Adam Smith and His Legacy For Modern Capitalism.* New York: Oxford University Press, USA.

Wicks, A., Keevil, A., and Parmar, B. 2011. *Normative Theories of the Firm and Sustainable Business Development: A System Mindset Approach.* Submitted for review to Business Ethics Quarterly

Williamson, O. E. 1979. *Transaction-Cost Economics: The Governance of Contractual Relations.* Journal of Law and Economics, 22: 233.

Practical Considerations of Corporate Governance

Dr. Jack London, Chair of the Board, CACI

'll quickly say that from the standpoint of ethical considerations, perspectives, ethics within the firm, as a dimension element of the firm, I couldn't agree more with Per. On the other hand, I think I'm going to talk to the aspect of the firm, the organization, primarily the corporate organization, public corporate organization. And like every coin, there are two sides. I think Per's provided you the one side which has to do with the notions of aspiration and what would be good and worthy philosophical objectives and considerations. I'm perhaps going to be a little bit of a contrarian here and talk to more of what is the real world and what can be done in the real world without simply statements and aspirations.

Implementation is crucial in the business environment and I want to ground you a little bit in that and the realities of some of the things that need to be done as we move forward. But I do want to emphasize even before I begin my talk that the notion of corporate ethics and business ethics is fundamental to the success not only of the business enterprise, but also to our economy and perhaps even on broader scale, to the success of our nation. So within that context, let me reinforce as much as possible and getting your attention on that value element as such.

Along that line, I'd like to know who I'm talking to and I would be most interested to have some show of hands up. How many individuals here have had experience working in public corporations, like a show of hands, engaged in public corporations? How many have managed a business on their own at some fashion? How many have managed a profit/loss center either in their own business or have managed a P&L center in a public corporation or in any business for that matter? I was going to ask how many have had the challenge of making payroll but that's perhaps a little beyond where we are today.

We're talking about some philosophical issues and perspectives and the importance of a business enterprise in our national economy and where we're headed with it, the contributions that they may or may not be able to make and I intend to address those.

CACI is a $3 billion enterprise. We have close to 13,000 people working around the world for the United States federal government. In most instances, we are a government contracting organization. We've been in business since 1962. We've been a public corporation since 1968. We've been a Delaware corporation since the mid-'80s and a New York Stock Exchange company since the early part of the century.

I joined the company in 1972 and my employee number was 33 so I guess I lasted the longest. I am now in my 39th year I think; soon to be 40 years with the current firm. In this time our industry has grown significantly. The information technology field per se is a world enterprise that you're all familiar with, perhaps in some ways more than I. Technology, business processes and skills keep evolving and we've seen a number of changes in governance, haven't we? The standards we're expected to meet and the new laws and regulations we're obligated to comply with. And we have more recognition of the importance of best practices and I certainly think that many ways of what Per presented to you and for you.

So with all these changes, it seems reasonable to me to want to examine what a company should be and that indeed is the thesis, if you will, for the organizational debates here these two days. But perhaps we should go back to the basics to answer the question, what is a company? What really is a company? Again, my comments are related to the larger public corporations and all kinds of business enterprises, from a one-man/one-woman consulting organization all the way up to the largest corporations in this country or in this world actually.

As the saying goes, the more things change, the more things stay the same. The basics of business I contend have been the same for certain decades if not centuries. While there are businesses of all shapes and sizes, again, we're going to talk a little bit about the larger companies. The management consultant and guru, who probably some of you had the distinct pleasure of reading about, saw his theory and commentary, Peter Drucker once said that "a business exists to create a customer". That's the purpose of business.

But I'll add one stipulation that's crucially important. I would add it's a customer who will want to buy what you have to sell. I want us all to bear that in mind. And you have to continuously offer competitively a quality product or service, again that offers real value to the marketplace. If you don't, someone else will. It's just that simple, especially in the highly competitive industry that I find myself. Without a customer there's no business. As Thomas Watson once said, the founder of IBM, and maybe you've heard this rather famous quotation, "There is nothing that happens in any business until after a sale is made." Think about that.

So first, the defining characteristic of a company is providing a product or service that meets an economic need in the market space. If you don't do that, you won't survive. You will go out of business, notwithstanding any goals that you may have, any ethics you may want to convey or subscribe to.

Second, companies exist to create value for their shareholders and owners. In the case of public companies, the owners are shareholders. Shareholders, be they employees, pension funds—and I suspect many of you are now engaged in the creation of your retirement funds, your 401(k)s, your IRAs and so on, putting a bit of money away for a nest egg. So you're probably in some ways investing in corporate organizations around the world; certainly if you're in mutual funds, or in the case even individual investors.

They're looking for the best financial returns they can make. That is the operating criteria and it is *sine qua non* for success in business. If you can't make a profit, you're not successful, period. How you go about it is yet the more important issue that Per raises and I would subscribe to his thesis. Investing in public companies then gives the intent of investors and the objective is to really maximize the return and shareholder wealth creation.

I think we also need to consider what a company is not. I don't believe, perhaps it's just my opinion, companies are not activists or shouldn't be activists. Nor are they social institutions. With so many companies, perhaps, these days taking up some of these causes, it may be that people are forgetting that it is not their role to engage in the development or implementation of social policies. I might have gone on a little bit there, so I'll quickly say corporations that engage in social causes do so because they see value, they see purpose, and they see the creation of a reputation or image and an acceptance among their peers as being credible to do business with.

So there is an underlying business motivation, even to support in my view the thesis that Per has laid out. It could be for marketing purposes as I said, image creation, reputation, be part of business development strategies. But I submit it's not why companies exist—not on the fundamental basic level.

Larry Ellison, co-founder and CEO of Oracle Corporation, a rather successful enterprise, pointed out that "a corporation's primary goal is to make money. Government's primary role is to take a big chunk of that money and give it to others."

In any case, Larry does have a point, but obviously, and I'm sure you would share there's more to it, and that is, along the many things it does, government creates policies which corporations must comply with, regulations and laws. For example, it establishes minimum wage and employment standards, and that's good. Government sets safety standards and creates environmental regulations to which companies must adhere, and that's good. For example, OSHA, that's the Occupational Safety and Health Administration, issues and enforces rules and standards for workplace safety and health, and again that's good. The FDA is responsible for regulating and supervising the production and safety of foods, medications, medical devices and much more. I even have a daughter-in-law that's a lawyer that works with the FDA, so I have a little insight there as well.

By adhering to policies and regulations developed by the government, companies may help and assist and support getting to these larger public goals. That's a very viable and realistic and proper role in my book. Government also has a responsibility to create, maintain and monitor a workplace framework environment in which companies can operate and compete on fair and level playing field.

Government creates that level playing field and should do so, and empower markets, empower corporations to be productive, successful and to thrive. Government and business are not mutually exclusive therefore, but each has its own purpose and place in all this. It's easy to talk about these kinds of basics in the classroom. In the real world, there are many practical challenges that arise as the corporate environment evolves.

One of the big business issues and challenges that I have discovered in my career is regulation. But why, you say. Well, I'll tell you why. In my observation—careful observation—is that regulation tends to be reactionary. Typically governments, government organizations, when confronted with crisis problems—and some of them have already been mentioned—immediately proceed with hearings and the writing of regulations and new laws that's usually for political purposes. What do you mean by that, Jack?

Well, I simply mean that it's assessing the public outrage. Politicians want to appear tough in combating and confronting and bringing to justice, if you will, in some fashion, the perpetrators. I might quickly add that, in my opinion, both political parties, if you will, or advocates of different perspectives, have been guilty in this area. Too often the result is regulation that exceeds what's necessary. Politicians probably don't realize it. More and more, there are less and less businessmen in Congress here in United States; more lawyers, less business people.

They had good intentions for sure, but what happens is, akin to holding up a pair of pants with two pairs of suspenders and two belts, but maybe all you need is a new button. Overkill. The consequence is that you wind up hurting business more than restoring credibility. Not so, you say. Corporations; there are a lot of bad guys and bad companies out there. Well, I'll challenge that to begin with. First, you penalize companies by this process that did not create the problem. You punish and penalize in some fashion with more burdens of regulation those companies that had clean records and had been viable and productive in the economic market.

More laws, regulations and constraints push down the whole lot, not just the violators. I firmly believe that bad apples should be prosecuted appropriately under applicable statutes. Why should the whole bushel of companies be punished for one or a few or a handful of companies that have committed wrongdoing? If you stop and think about it, it's grossly inappropriate. For example, my favorite, Sarbanes-Oxley, in my opinion, was an overreaction, gross in some ways, designed to address dishonesty in public disclosures and other frauds, truly violations, no question about that.

However, it's simply not possible to regulate honesty. By the way, that's what the definition of crook is—somebody who breaks the law. You write a law, and for some people, the law is for breaking. You cannot regulate honesty and you cannot regulate ethics. As a reaction to the wrongdoings of Enron and Worldcom and others that you're familiar with, Sarbanes-Oxley required enormous, disproportionate and expensive amount of accounting and financial work within public companies. And it was a bonanza for the outside audit firms as well.

Think of it this way, if you will: All of a sudden, your $200 million-company had the same burdensome, excruciating set of regulatory compliance issues and challenges to meet as did the multi-billion dollar corporations. It also bothered me on a personal level. When Sarbanes-Oxley was enacted in 2002, a good part of the legislation focused on the consequences of filing fraudulent and misleading reports. And it should. When first briefed on Sarbanes-Oxley by my legal and accounting advisers, I was told we had to take these new requirements seriously.

My God, we got to take it seriously? Boy, did my blood boil! I'd always thought that my financial signoffs were serious business. I had been taking this responsibility seriously for over 20 years, for SEC filings and more each year, well over 100 filings with my name on them and now they were telling me I'd better be serious about it. There's an irony there. To me each time I had signed, I pondered and thought about it, had conversations with my attorneys, my outside accountants and chief financial officers to make sure I personally felt that we had complied with the law and publicly disclosed proper data about our performance, with not one scrap permissible to be inappropriate.

I'd always felt that every time I signed the SEC documents that both CACI and my personal integrity and ethics were involved. Frankly, I'll share with you, ladies and gentlemen, in my opinion, it was insulting that Sarbanes-Oxley was trying to enforce honesty on me. As I saw it, Sarbanes-Oxley was enacted all because a few crooks broke the law and got caught. But the government's reaction in effect was to punish, literally, and I use that word appropriately, punish all public companies with the burden of excessive regulation. And I'm not alone on that opinion. There are many that share that with me.

Let me be clear, however, there cannot be any compromise, any fashion with corporate integrity. I believe I have shared that. I have a long career of espousing the importance of business ethics. I think, as Jennifer mentioned, there is a program here in the city, in the greater HR community that has to do with ethics and business and awards and recognition of individuals that excel and are leaders in that espousing those theories and implementing them with their organizations.

Integrity should be the foundation for every corporate culture, and at CACI we have a very strong corporate ethical culture. But it didn't start with Sarbanes-Oxley, I got to tell you. It started many, many years ago. As a company, we began to evolve into a government contracting organization where the highest sense of quality, effort, reliability, dependability and ethical performance was paramount, not just "oh-by-the-way" issue but paramount. Ladies and gentlemen, every company is not Enron.

At CACI, integrity, honesty, fairness and respect are given the same importance as quality client service, shareholder value and career opportunities. In 2008, just a couple of years ago, the independent Ethisphere Institute of New York ranked CACI as having one of the best overall government contractor ethics programs from more than 1,000 contractors reviewed—an independent organization. We make ethics a big deal in our company. It's the cornerstone of our culture. It's how we want to do business. It's how we want to treat each other, with mutual respect and do it the best we possibly can. And I know that we're not alone as an organization, at least in our industry which I can speak for.

There's another regulatory conflict when it comes to transparency. How transparent is too transparent? I have no problem with disclosure. I believe in it, but I am concerned with having to reveal proprietary information that competitors would be able to use and see.

Take the current debate over executive compensation. Salaries and total compensation of a company's top executives has always been public information, at least I believe in essence for the 34 Act and forward.[108] But will aggressive compensation oversight mean disclosing performance metrics and operating algorithms that go into determining compensation? I would submit to even shareholders who have a genuine interest in the relationship of executive compensation to business operations don't focus on such metrics as long as executive compensation is commensurate with, proportional to and appropriate to performance. The point is that you don't want to be so transparent that your competitors have insights to what might be your proprietary management methods and techniques or to how you treat your senior executives.

Second, regulation often neglects the real purpose of regulation, and that is enforcement. We've certainly seen a lot of that in the banking industry here in the last financial mark, haven't we? There are lots of regulations, but I submit to you the notion of the administration of the enforcement aspect was grossly missing in all of that equation and you don't hear any much talk about it, do you? What you hear is we're going to have more regulation.

I think the cart may be out in front of the horse on this. Many think it's perfectly acceptable to regulate big business, place financial bureaucratic burdens on them when they ought to, in my opinion, focus more on the violators and perpetrators of the fraud and whatever is involved. There needs to be more emphasis, in my opinion, on the enforcement of laws rather than the creation of more regulations. The statutory authority must be wielded carefully, in my opinion, or it will undermine corporate viability. I've got a good example.

Many of you may be familiar with Arthur Andersen. In 2002, the former big five accounting firm was found guilty of criminal charges related to the firms handling of Enron audit documents prior to an SEC inquiry. As result of the conviction, Arthur Andersen surrendered its CPA licenses and only 200 of its 28,000 employees were left to close up the shop. But three years later, after the company had ceased operations, the Supreme Court of the United States of America overturned that verdict. They found the conviction was the result of faulty instructions, interpretations and that Arthur Andersen had been convicted without proof that it had deliberately disposed of the documents pursuant to Enron. One observer noted the government gave "the corporation the death sentence and the corporation died." I submit that's where the

---

108 Refers to the Securities Exchange Act of 1934. In order to protect investors, the Act provides governance of securities transactions on the secondary market (after issue) and regulates the exchanges and broker-dealers.

discussion is. The lesson here is that we must guard against egregious overreaction as well as regulatory violation.

There are also been many changes and developments in governance that have been quite good. I think some of the enhanced reporting requirements in the expansion of fiduciary responsibilities have been very important. For example, Regulation Fair Disclosure, some of you may be familiar with Reg FD adapted by the SEC in 2000, provides the disclosure of material nonpublic information to certain entities, like stock market analysts and large shareholders, must be also made public to everyone. You can't have insider pieces of information being pushed out to separate individuals without making sure all your shareholders are aware of those considerations. That's a very powerful regulation and I went through the process of implementing that and I'm very much in support of it. In fact, one might think how can it be any other way.

The SEC and the New York Stock Exchange also made changes to increase the ratio of independent directors on boards, as well as qualifications for members of audit committees and compensations committees for independence purposes and so on, as well as making it necessary to establish the bona fides and credentials of these executives in these positions.

There also have been many non-governance related developments that improved the work environment. Rules from smoking bans to those on equal opportunity and sexual harassment have been excellent in their purpose and intent. Those kinds of things have not only been for the greater good but also have been part of leveling the playing field for all the organizations that are in the public arena.

Speaking of the greater good, according to a recent survey, 72 percent of surveyed executives agreed there would be more demands on businesses to solve societal problems. More disturbing was that over half were confident that businesses will meet those demands. One might ask, how do you know you can meet it if you don't know what it is? But that's something else.

This is also a challenge. I'm sure most corporate executives and employees want a better world for heaven sakes, but it's actually, in my opinion, a mistake to superimpose the expectation of a responsibility of creating better world on companies. Companies may play a part or an important role in this vision, but at best, it would be a supportive role guided by government regulation.

Shareholders expect returns. Customers expect results. Of course, they want to align themselves with companies that operate lawfully and with integrity and have the essence of ethics in their behavior and marketplace activity. But as surprising it is might seem to some of you, shareholders that I know and love are not by and large concerned with the greater good in the sense of how the business is run, not that we don't represent positive things that we discussed.

Herb Karr, one of the co-founders of CACI, once said in a board meeting, "Charity is not a line item on our P&L." It's kind of a harsh statement, but let's stop and think about it. He wasn't saying that corporate philanthropy or the consideration of social issues was bad. He wasn't saying that at all. He meant that there wasn't a way—at least in those days, perhaps even today I would submit—a way to get credit for it as a business enterprise. Charity dollars simply come out of profits and believe me shareholders are always concerned—always concerned—of money spent that could otherwise be profit.

Yet there's a growing trend of expecting companies to both save the world and I have heard about it and read about it. We've seen people talk about it. Even definitions of good corporate governance have started to equate environmental stewardship and community engagement with sustained financial performance. I'm going to have a thought here that it's just the other way around.

I accept the viewpoint that companies may sometimes need to integrate environmental and social factors in analyzing risks, allocating resources, and discovering opportunities for that matter, but they simply do not have the same importance or priority in different companies or in different industries. One size doesn't fit all. Yet you simply cannot have the same expectations for different companies. Shareholders and customers certainly don't. Like, for example, sustainability issues. Shareholders, like those at Exxon likely consider sustainability important factor to that company's development. But it's not always the case.

Even at CACI, for example, in the environmental aspect, we recycle, we repurpose, we properly dispose of everything from trash to old electronics. But nowhere in our bids or our proposals in the system integration business is the environmental issue an issue. And the talk about community good might not work as well because in bids to the government and to the class we deal with, they might even see that as a business distraction in terms of what they want us to perform and do.

At CACI we recognize that there is a social good also from the line of business we perform for the American people. Working with the United States government and in large part the defense establishment and the intelligence community, we believe we have an ethical and social value in representing the American taxpayer and to provide the very best services and solutions we possibly can.

We're also involved in a number of very important initiatives in supporting the many cases, for example, of the men and women of the United States Armed Forces. We're able to do things because we have a strong business enterprise and because we're successful. If business were bad, there will be loss of jobs and productivity.

It's important to remember that it's only a successful business that has the resources, financial and skill sets to provide inputs to some of these other activities that we talked about. If your business isn't successful, if you can't make it viable in the marketplace or can't stand on its own merits in terms of competition in the products and services it provides, then all of the rest of it will never happen because then we'll go out to business and have products and services that nobody wants.

So I don't know if there's really a need to redefine the company. I think that if we continue to think of the business organizations and public corporations neither as saints or sinners or saviors or villains but part of our economic environment, we would keep to the idea of their need to create, need to be successful. They are the creators of jobs, they pay taxes, they create innovation, they make our world competitive, and I would submit to you further if you're thinking about the future of the United States and our national economy in world competition, we had better be productive, innovative and able to maneuver very rapidly on the global economic environment. Corporate governance is about accountability, structure, practices and the practices of company. It's one thing to have companies be more aware of environmental issues and social implications, even regulated in that way where appropriate, but we need to guard against the inclination to overdo it.

Finally, there's a need to have a stronger emphasis on global competitiveness. We take sometimes, for example, with Coca Cola and the Apple organization in their world-wide span have been very successful and do some of these things we've been talking about, yet rules of engagement especially in international markets have been changing.

I want to talk about one little example then I'll close. Let's look at an industry driven by environmental sustainability, for example. Which country is at the forefront of the alternative energy industry, anybody know? I'll give you a hint, not the United States.

Male Voice: China.

Jack P. London: Five years ago, China essentially had no presence in wind or solar manufacturing. Today, it is the largest maker and exporter of equipment to generate solar and wind power. The Chinese government is devoting more than $200 billion to clean energy in its economic stimulus package. And they recently announced that China would generate 50 percent of its energy from renewable sources by 2020 and that it tends to become the world's largest exporter of clean energy technologies.

Meanwhile, back at home up on Pennsylvania Avenue what do you see happening? I'm going to be generous and say gridlock. We neither have a policy framework nor national goals to create a presence or marketplace presence in the renewable energy marketplace. China, however, is on top of new technologies driving a global economy while we again are gridlocked and may miss out in this particular instance on clean energy—the clean energy push.

Now, we don't want to, I guess, implement similar governance processes as the Chinese on our enterprises. But the point is, if we want companies to do more, to be more, especially for the public good, that we need to enable them, not hinder them, especially if we expect to compete in the global economy.

So while the business environment changes, what would be the biggest challenge? I submit I think the challenge will simply be to let the company be what it is and does best, and that's create products and services. And then it can, if it's successful, in supporting the greater interesting goals of the nation but it also has to do that—making a dollar. And I have no argument whatsoever with the notion of the permanence of ethics and behavior in enterprise. Those are my thoughts, perhaps a little bit of a different perspective you might want to think about.

Response to Dr. Jack London

Patricia Kanashiro, Assistant Professor of International Business;
Loyola University Maryland

In this review, I provide a response to Dr. Jack London's article "Practical Considerations of Corporate Governance". Based on his forty successful years as an employee and later as a chairman of a large publicly-traded corporation, Dr. London provides a bold and thought-provoking perspective on business ethics and the role of business in society. While being a strong advocate of business ethics, he argues that the primary purpose of the firm is to maximize profits for shareholders. To support his view, I offer a theoretical reasoning on the convergence between shareholder supremacy and business ethics.

Dr. London also believes that businesses should not engage in corporate social responsibility because businesses may support these larger public goals by adhering to regulations developed by the government. I attempt to provide a slightly different perspective and argue that businesses are intertwined in society and actively interact with the public agenda.

Lastly, he asserts that government cannot regulate in all matters of society. According to him, policies attempting to regulate ethics are inefficient because honesty is a matter of personal integrity. While I agree with his remarks, I conclude that regulation is necessary to curb dishonest behavior and to reestablish trust in the market.

On Shareholders Supremacy and Business Ethics

Dr. London has long been a strong advocate of business ethics and his company places ethics as a highest priority. Dr. London is the current chairman and past CEO of CACI, a member of the Fortune 1000 largest companies, which provides services and information technology in the areas of defense, homeland security, and government transformation. CACI has a comprehensive code of ethics that regulates the relationship between the company and its customers, employees, and the government. In Dr. London's words, "ethics is fundamental to the success not only of the business enterprise, but also to our economy and perhaps even or broader scale, to the success of our nation" (103).

Dr. London makes clear to the audience that ethics is very important. Nonetheless, he argues that there is a separation between the business aspirations and what can be done in the real world. According to him, the sole purposes of the corporation are to serve its clients and to maximize shareholders' wealth. Corporations have no business in serving a social purpose: corporations are not social institutions and such social responsibility should be left to the government.

Thus, the question is whether or not it is possible to conduct business ethically by primarily (or exclusively) focusing on shareholders' interests over other stakeholders concerns. I argue that the notion of shareholder supremacy has a foundation on the moral view of the world and therefore is in perfect agreement with business ethics. In this sense, decisions to serve primarily the interests of shareholders and decisions based on ethics do not necessarily lead in opposite directions.

The notion of shareholder supremacy derives from a moral view of the world (Jensen, 1991; Quinn & Jones, 1995; Sen, 1985). This is because a morally better world is represented by a Pareto optimum, in which social welfare is maximized when all firms maximize profits (or maximize shareholders' wealth). When managers do other things besides maximizing profits, a distortion in the investment markets occurs. Resource allocation is optimized when managers try to maximize firm's share prices. Since the best allocation of resources is morally desirable, managers should maximize shareholders' wealth (Quinn & Jones, 1995: 24).

Quinn and Jones (1995) argue that, by attempting to maximize shareholders' wealth, managers are required to comply with at least four moral principles: honor agreements, avoid lying, avoid harm to others, and respect the autonomy of others.

To honor agreements is a necessary condition for the principal-agent contract to hold. In the principal-agent model, principals (shareholders) delegate power to agents (managers) to act on their behalf (Berle & Means, 1932; Fama & Jensen, 1983a, b; Jensen & Meckling, 1976). To avoid lying reduces information asymmetry between market participants. These two moral principle are believed to be a prerequisite for markets to function efficiently (Hausman & McPherson, 1993) and form the foundation of trust between participants in the market. The last two principles—avoid harm and respect the autonomy of others—give rise to the condition of individual liberty, which means the recognition and respect of each individual's freedom (Quinn and Jones, 1995). Liberty is a necessary condition for markets to work efficiently (Friedman, 1962) since liberty allows agents to make contracts freely with each other that are morally binding.

The principal-agent model intrinsically presumes that moral principles are recognized and are antecedents to the obligation of maximizing shareholders' wealth.

For instance, moral principles have priority over agents' promise to maximize wealth since the moral obligation of avoiding harm to others is superior to profit maximization (Quinn & Jones, 1995: 34-35).

A common misconception is to say that agents lack moral reasoning because they are rational economic individuals who seek to maximize self-interest and adopt opportunistic behaviors. Agents behave in self-interest but that does not mean that they are selfish and egocentric. Individuals are assumed to maximize their own utility, which may represent a range of preferences, including altruistic motives and regard to others (Heath, 2009). Opportunistic behavior means that individuals will try to take advantage of circumstances or will act without regard for moral principles. The principal-agent model proposes that agents have a tendency to adopt an opportunistic behavior but does not prescribe that they should behave opportunistically.

Amartya Sen, Nobel Laureate in Economics, contends that self-interest is enough to motivate simple exchanges in an economy but the results of such exchange would not be as good if individuals try to behave opportunistically (Sen, 1993, 1999). Sen explains that exchanges are complex (i.e., involve motivation for exchange, production, and the challenge of distribution) and require that economic institutions operate based on mutual confidence and shared trust.

Sen concludes that business ethics makes economic sense (1993) and therefore such a separation between ethics and profit maximization does not necessarily exist. If economics sense is narrowly defined as the achievement of business profits, than ethics can be justified based on instrumental arguments, in terms of how ethics indirectly contribute to profit. If economics sense means overall good for society, then promoting societal improvements represents a reward in itself, and business ethics is justified as being intrinsically good.

Thus, to reinforce Dr. London's view of shareholders supremacy and the importance of ethics for business, I showed that profit maximization has its foundation on the moral view of the world and it presupposes that managers behave according to fundamental moral principles for markets to function efficiently.

On Ethics vs. CSR

Dr. London makes a clear distinction between ethics and corporate social responsibility. For him, ethics is fundamental to the business operations and should be at the core of the business strategy. However, corporations should not engage in social responsibility since it does not represent a priority for investors. Dr. London's considers that investments in corporate social responsibility need to be aligned with the business' core strategy in order to be justified. Based on stakeholder theory, I explain why business ethics and corporate social responsibility can be integrated to serve both shareholders and stakeholders interests.

The stakeholder theory suggests that managers are constantly engaging with different stakeholders. Such interactions are not limited to shareholders and clients, but also involve transactions with employees, suppliers, government representatives, and the community (Clarkson, 1995; Donaldson & Preston, 1995; Freeman, 1984; Freeman & Philips, 2002). Because these stakeholders affect and are affected by the company's activities, managers should take their interests and concerns into their decision making.

The stakeholder theory prescribes that a relationship based on ethics between the company and its stakeholders creates maximum long-term value for all the stakeholders: if the stakeholders are treated ethically, then stakeholders will respond with commitment, respect, and loyalty (Clarkson, 1995; Donaldson & Preston, 1995; Freeman, 1984; Freeman & Philips, 2002).

Managers are constantly asking themselves ethical decisions that involve tradeoffs between the stakeholders' interests. For example: if I take this decision, for whom am I creating and/or destroying value? Am I violating any rights and if so, what are the consequences? How will I feel after this decision is made (Agle et al., 2008: 164)? When interests between stakeholders conflict, the role of the manager is to make the tradeoffs without resorting to fraud and deception (Agle et al., 2008). Thus, profit maximization is an outcome of a well-managed company, whose executive managers attempt to create as much value to all stakeholders since that's how it is possible to create as much value for shareholders in the long-term (Agle et al., 2008: 166).

There is an understanding that businesses have an implicit and unconditional obligation to both maximize shareholders and to treat stakeholders ethically (Cragg, 2002). Corporations serve a private (shareholders' wealth) as well as a public component (societal welfare) given that their business operations are not only approved by the shareholders but also legally conceded by the government and the local community. For this reason, firms are accountable to their shareholders for meeting their financial expectations as well as accountable for meeting societal expectations of business ethical behavior. Corporate social responsibility derives from the notion that business is embedded in society rather than a distinct and separate entity and therefore it is legitimate to comply with societal expectations of business behavior (Wood, 1991: 695).

In contrast, Dr. London seems to propose that businesses and governments should serve different purposes: businesses create value added to consumers, employees and shareholders while the government should serve a public purpose. He implies that companies may support the larger public goals by adhering to policies and regulations developed by the government.

I contend that such division of roles is not so clear because businesses may serve a public purpose by attempting to influence the government agenda. In fact, businesses engagement with public policy making ranges from active resistance to cooperation with the government (Oliver, 1991; Rivera, 2010; Rivera et al., 2009). At the highest level of resistance, firms try to manipulate results to influence public policies. On the other end, firms may cooperate with governments in the formulation of public policies or may even initiate cooperation at the industry level to reduce regulatory burden. Thus, to the extent that businesses engage in the policy process, businesses may serve a public interest by advocating policies deemed desirable to the business operations that will simultaneously affect societal welfare.

On The Importance of Regulation

As addressed by Dr. London remarks, regulations cannot fairly and efficiently regulate all areas of society. According to him, honesty and ethics cannot be regulated since these are matters of personal integrity. Furthermore, the cost to regulate such matters outweighs its benefits: because of the wrongdoing of few companies, the government imposed regulations that represent a burden to the majority of companies. While I share his understanding that ethics and honesty cannot be regulated, I attempt to explain why regulation is necessary to minimize opportunistic behavior of managers and to reduce spillover of negative externalities.

The cases of corporate frauds in 2000 to 2002 involving Enron, Arthur Andersen, Worldcom, and others, represent the worst case of corporate governance failure in the U.S., resulted from excessive management greed and absence of independent oversight. Following the scandals, the U.S. government increased regulatory oversight with the passage of the Sarbanes-Oxley Act of 2002. The purpose of the legislation was to reestablish investors' confidence in the financial market by reforming the corporate governance structure of the corporation. The Act increased executives' liability and imposed greater disclosure requirements, enforced independent monitoring and auditing, and better risk management systems.

Dr. London's criticism that the Sarbanes-Oxley Act was an overreaction is echoed by many other business people who similarly argue that the costs of the legislation outweigh its benefits. Nonetheless, it is empirically challenging to verify the effects of the legislation since it was enacted during a period of economic and political turbulence. Despite criticisms, most studies have been indicative that the Sarbanes-Oxley was beneficial (Coates IV, 2007): there has been a reduction in the incidence of frauds (Dyck, Adair, & Zingales, 2006) and investors' confidence was—at least partially—restored (Verschoor, 2009).

One of the reasons why regulations and codes of ethics may be efficient to curb dishonest behavior is that individuals are less willing to engage in dishonest or illicit behavior when they are made aware of ethical standards (Shu, Gino, & Bazerman, 2009). Reinforcing rules and making them explicit increase the chances that they will adhere to greater ethical behavior because individuals are more aware of the sanctions associated with non-compliance.

Government regulation is especially crucial in reestablishing confidence in periods of crisis (Verschoor, 2009). Even though the financial frauds represent isolated causes, the corporate scandals caused significant negative externalities. Externalities are defined as those situations in which the agents engaging in a transaction do not bear full responsibility for their actions. In this case, managers of few companies reported misleading financial statements to maximize their short term gain. The consequence of their acts were not limited to the companies they worked for but spilled over to the entire economy causing an increase in systemic financial risk. The fraudulent companies damaged the other companies by significantly decreasing investors' confidence on financial reporting (Macey, 2004). In this case, Sarbanes-Oxley was necessary to restore investors' confidence in the market.

The corporate scandals and the recent financial crisis have changed societal view of business' legitimacy. Shareholders and the public at large demand increasing monitoring and punishment for unethical conduct. While some critics believe that such level of disclosure can harm the competitiveness of the firms, the majority seems to believe that firms should be made accountable for their actions and expenses (Verschoor, 2009).

To sum up, economics theory contends that the well functioning of the market is based on the realization of moral principles of shared-trust and liberty. To correct market imperfections, the government plays a central role in reducing externalities by imposing regulations, taxations, and civil liability (Arrow, 1973). Therefore, government regulations as well as corporate governance mechanisms change incentives faced by managers in such a way that the interests of shareholders, management, and society are aligned (Quinn & Jones, 1995).

Concluding Remarks

In this response paper to Dr. London's remarks, I have attempted to provide theoretical evidences to provide a more nuanced perspective on business ethics and the relationship between business and society. I have tried to provide support to Dr. London's view of the alignment between shareholders supremacy and business ethics by arguing that the shareholders supremacy requires an efficient market governed by moral principles. I have also mentioned that managers are moral agents and constantly use ethical reasoning when making their daily decisions. Finally, even though I share Dr. London's argument that ethics cannot be regulated, I conclude that regulation is necessary to curb dishonest behavior and to reestablish confidence in the market.

REFERENCES

Agle, B. R., Donaldson, T., Freeman, R. E., Jensen, M. C., Mitchell, R. K., & Wood, D. 2008. *Dialogue: Toward Superior Stakeholder Theory.* Business Ethics Quarterly, 18(2): 153-190.

Arrow, K. 1973. *Social Responsibility And Economic Efficiency.* Public Policy, 21: 303-317.

Berle, A., & Means, G. 1932. *The Modern Corporation and Private Property.* New York: MacMillan.

Clarkson, M. B. E. 1995. *A Stakeholder Framework for Analyzing and Evaluating Corporate Social Performance.* Academy of Management Review, 20(1): 92-117.

Coates IV, J. C. 2007. *The Goals and Promise of the Sarbanes-Oxley Act.* The Journal of Economic Perspectives, 21(1): 91-116.

Cohen, D., Dey, A., & Lys, T. 2007. *Real And Accrual-Based Earnings Management In The Pre- and Post- Sarbanes-Oxley Periods.*

Cragg, W. 2002. *Business Ethics and Stakeholder Theory.* Business Ethics Quarterly, 12(2): 113-142.

Donaldson, T., & Preston, L. E. 1995. *The Stakeholder Theory of the Corporation: Concepts, Evidence, And Implications.* Academy of Management Review, 20(Journal Article).

Dyck, A., Adair, M., & Zingales, L. 2006. *Who Blows The Whistle On Corporate Governance?*, Vol. 618 University of Chicago: Working Paper.

Eisenhardt, K. M. 1989. *Agency Theory: An Assessment And Review.* Academy Of Management Review, 14(1): 57-74.

Fama, E. F., & Jensen, M. C. 1983a. *Agency Problems And Residual Claims. Journal Of Law And Economics,* 26(2, Corporations and Private Property: A Conference Sponsored by the Hoover Institution): 327-349.

Fama, E. F., & Jensen, M. C. 1983b. *Separation of Ownership and Control. Journal of Law and Economics,* 26 (2, Corporations and Private Property: A Conference Sponsored by the Hoover Institution): 301-325.

Freeman, R. E. 1984. Boston: Pitman.

Freeman, R. E., & Philips, R. A. 2002. *Stakeholder Theory: A Libertarian Defense.* Business Ethics Quarterly, 12(3): 331-349.

Friedman, M. 1962. *Capitalism and Freedom.* Chicago: University of Chicago Press.

Hoffman, A. J. 1999. *Institutional Evolution and Change: Environmentalism and the U.S. Chemical Industry.* Academy of Management Journal, 42(4): 351-373.

Jensen, M. C. 1991. *Corporate Control And The Politics Of Finance.* Journal of Applied Corporate Finance, 4(2): 13-33.

Jensen, M. C., & Meckling, W. H. 1976. *Theory of the Firm: Managerial Behavior, Agency Costs and Ownership Structure. Journal of Financial Economics,* 3(4): 305-360.

Macey, J. R. 2004. *Efficient Capital Markets, Corporate Disclosure and Enron.* Cornell Law Review, 89: 394-422.

Oliver, C. 1991. *Strategic Responses to Institutional Processes.* Academy of Management Review, 16(1): 145-179.

Quinn, D. P., & Jones, T. M. 1995. *An Agent Morality View of the Business Policy.* Academy of Management Review, 20(1): 22-42.

Rivera, J. 2010. *Business And Public Policy: Responses To Environmental & Social Protection Processes.* Cambridge, UK: Cambridge University Press.

Rivera, J., Oetzel, J., deLeon, P., & Starik, M. 2009. *Business Responses To Environmental And Social Protection Policies: Toward A Framework For Analysis.* Policy Sciences, 42(1): 3-32.

Sen, A. 1985. *The Moral Standing Of The Markets.* Social Philosophy And Policy, 2: 1-19.

Sen, A. 1993. *Does Business Ethics Make Economic Sense?* Business Ethics Quarterly, 3(1): 45-54.

Sen, A. 1999. Economics, *Business Principles and Moral Sentiments.* Business Ethics Quarterly, 7(3): 5-15.

Shaffer, B. 1995. *Firm-level Responses to Government Regulation: Theoretical and Research Approaches.* Journal of Management, 21(3): 495-514.

Shu, L. L., Gino, F., & Bazerman, M. H. 2009. *Dishonest Deed, Clear Conscience: Self-Preservation through Moral Disengagement and Motivated Forgetting,* Vol. 09-078: Harvard Business School.

Smith, A. 1776. *An Inquiry into the Nature and Causes of the Wealth of Nations.* London: Dent.

Tosi, H. L., & Gomez-Mejia, L. R. 1989. *The Decoupling Of CEO Pay And Performance: An Agency Theory Perspective.* Administrative Science Quarterly, 34: 169-189.

Verschoor, C. C. 2009. *Can Government Manage More Ethically Than Capitalism?* Strategic Finance, 91(4): 14-63.

Hausman, D., & McPherson, M. S. 1993. *Taking Ethics Seriously: Economics And Contemporary Moral Philosophy.* Journal Of Economic Literature, 31: 671-731.

Shu, L. L., Gino, F., & Bazerman, M. H. 2009. *Dishonest Deed, Clear Conscience: Self-Preservation through Moral Disengagement and Motivated Forgetting,* Vol. 09-078: Harvard Business School.

Verschoor, C. C. 2009. *Can Government Manage More Ethically Than Capitalism?* Strategic Finance, 91(4): 14-63.

Wood, D. J. 1991. *Corporate Social Performance Revisited.* The Academy of Management Review, 16(4): 691-718.

The Paradox of Pharmaceutical CSR: The Sincerity Nexus

Alexandra Countess of Frederiksborg[1] & Timothy L. Fort[2]
57 Business Horizons (2014)

I F A BOARD OF DIRECTORS sought to improve a given corporate function–strategy, marketing, human resources, etc.—how would it begin? A common starting point would be to benchmark what the company does against a set of "best practices."[109]

But what if "best practices" aren't good enough?

This problem lies at the core of corporate ethics. Practitioners and scholars alike differentiate between CSR, compliance, ethics, citizenship and a host of other names for companies' efforts to adhere to obligations other than maximizing short-term profit. When people tire of the criticisms of one name, they adopt another term to shed the baggage of the first. But whether the effort is contributing money to feed the poor or instituting a values-based model of human resource management, we use terms such as CSR and ethics interchangeably, knowing that a full defense of this conflation of terms requires a larger justification than we can provide here. Whether characterized as corporate social responsibility ("CSR"), business ethics, or some other name, however, best practices in a given industry often fall short, thus causing efforts of companies seeking to improve their own CSR practices to fall short as well.

A typical CSR model uses philanthropic donations to demonstrate the company's commitment to social welfare. Even a strategic version of CSR falls short of what it could achieve. To be sure, these can be important efforts worth celebrating, but we seek to raise the bar higher. Our case study focuses on the pharmaceutical industry because of our experience working in and studying that industry, though one could select any industry. This article has three parts. In Part I, we identify the typical CSR efforts of pharmaceutical companies. Dissatisfied with the scope of current efforts, Part II switches from an inductive approach to a deductive one in which we rely on scholarly literature and some exemplary benchmarks to propose a stronger model of corporate ethics. At the heart of this model is the claim that optimum instrumental benefits accrue to corporate CSR actions when they are undertaken for sincere aims rather than for instrumental ones. Part III explains how this framework provides a way for pharmaceutical companies to embrace a more robust model of corporate responsibility that could be extended to other industries as well. Although some scholars caution that CSR analysis should be done on an industry-by-industry basis because of differences in how industries interface with society (Griffin & Weber, 2006), we argue

---

109 The authors would like to acknowledge the assistance of several research assistants in preparing this article: Jason Allen, Mengxing Li, Chenxi Li, Christopher Oman, and Arturs Oganesjans.

that our proposed framework can be extended across industries by taking into account the uniqueness of specific industries.

1. Best Practices Incomplete

Do corporations manage solely for the benefit of profit or should they consider the well-being of other stakeholders? While vast amounts of ink have been spilt arguing about the best response to this question, pharmaceutical leaders and companies provide the answer to the question themselves even when their own businesses have been subject to significant criticism and litigation. Hank McKinnel, former CEO of Pfizer, which has been hit with significant fines and other legal action over the past few years, captured the essence of the pharmaceutical response when he said: "Because we have the ability to help in so many ways, we have a moral imperative to do so" (Nussbaum, 2009, p. 67). It is hard to see how they could not. Their very business is about making people's bodies, minds, and lives as a whole function better in a very real, concrete way. Nor is McKinnel's comment inconsistent with other companies in the industry, which through statements or policies extend the commitment of companies even beyond personal, consumer well-being. Johnson & Johnson, GlaxoSmithKlein, Norvartis, Abbot Laboratories and others have made similar commitments to the good of environmental responsibility (Nussbaum, 2009, p. 25).

Actions seem to follow these pronouncements. Pharmaceutical companies frequently find a place in examples of exemplary conduct, none being more famous than Johnson & Johnson's handling of the 1982 Tylenol Crisis. Tylenol was the leading brand of painkiller in the United Sates in the 1980s. In October of 1982, seven people died after taking extra-strength Tylenol capsules. It was reported that 65 milligrams of deadly cyanide were put into Tylenol capsules. Johnson & Johnson recalled all the Tylenol in the market in the U.S., which cost the company roughly US $100 million (1982) dollars. Advertisements for the product were removed at the same time. When asked why the company took such a strong action, even though company practices themselves were not implicated, CEO James Burke responded that to do otherwise would cause the company to fail to live up to its famous Corporate Credo, which placed customer well-being as the most important responsibility for the company (Knowledge@Wharton, 2012).

In another action, Johnson & Johnson created the "Children Without Worms Program" and the "Task Force For Child Survival and Development," which aim to treat up to 25 million children a year with the drug Mebendazole, donated by the company. Both programs include education and sanitation facilities (Johnson & Johnson, 2013).

Johnson & Johnson's commitment to its Credo stemmed from the belief that if the company first served customers, employees, suppliers, and the community, profits would follow. This was deeply embedded in the company's culture, so much so that when the company began to stumble with recalls, shutdowns of manufacturing facilities, and legal disputes, shareholders recently took things into their own hands to put the company back on its traditional path (McGrath, 2011). After the company was hit with several lawsuits and investigations, the company's shareholders filed a derivative suit against the Board of Directors for failing to maintain the company's commitment to legal and ethical behavior. The fact that the shareholders themselves saw this as a problem indicates that there was a corporate authenticity—indeed, a corporate sincerity at stake—that had been undermined. Without admitting any wrongdoing, the board and the shareholders reached an agreement whereby the company would undertake efforts to restore its admired identity (Robinson & Oakes, 2012).

The Johnson & Johnson example lays bare one of our central concerns and points to where pharmaceutical companies could better aim. Which is more compelling, a philanthropic program or a commitment to the integrity of a company? Lest we be misunderstood, we believe that philanthropic programs are very important and admirable. The difficulty with them, however, is that they tend to be out of context. Numbers—the number of people helped and the number of dollars spent—are presented as proof of social commitment, but it is difficult to know how to assess the company's true level of social commitment without context of the number of people affected and the number of dollars earned. It is not that the philanthropic program is bad; it is merely difficult to put into a measurable context. These are often stand-alone cases and because of that, companies can present such actions as evidence of how much they care while at the same time having such actions dismissed as window dressing by critics.

Conversely, Johnson & Johnson's commitment to protect its stakeholders against any danger from Tylenol has been universally recognized as an ethical action, exactly because so much of the company's financial well-being was at risk. In the face of that risk, the company still stood by a central tenet of its Credo. To be sure, Johnson & Johnson had good public relations experts working with them in 1982, but institutional, operational actions tend to reflect identity and sincerity in ways just as profound as philanthropy.

Examples of philanthropic activities proliferate in the industry. Eli Lilly has been a major funder of "Diabetes Camps" in which children with Type 1 diabetes are able to participate in traditional camp activities under the supervision of personnel equipped to deal with issues of children with the condition. According to its February 13, 2013 press release, Lilly has donated more than US $20 million to these camps over the past ten years. Much good has undoubtedly resulted from this philanthropy and it should be recognized as good CSR, but to put this in context, it is also worth noting that Lilly's 2011 revenues totaled nearly US $25 billion (Eli Lilly, 2011).

Likewise, Bayer's 2012 revenues exceeded US $52 billion (Bayer, 2013). It chose to support drug donations such as the "Medicines for Malaria Venture," an organization created by the World Health Organization and financed by the World Bank (Medicines for Malaria, 2013) and the United Nations Environment Programme to organize environmental projects every year for young people (UNEP, 2011). Its subsidiary, Bayer

Cropscience, focuses on sustainable agriculture, and has a program addressing African Sleeping Sickness (Bayer, 2013).

Following the same pattern, Pfizer's 2012 revenues of US $59 billion provide ample cash to fund its "Diflucan Donation Program" (donating anti-fungal medication in 63 countries) and other programs (Pfizer, 2013). The Lilly, Bayer, and Pfizer examples can be replicated. GlaxoSmithKline donates Albendazole as part of the company's effort to combat the tropical disease Lymphatic filariasis, a leading cause of permanent disability and disfigurement (GlaxoSmithKline, 2012). Novartis donates multi-drug therapy to all leprosy patients in the world through the World Health Organization, totaling more than 48 million packs valued at US $77 million to help cure more than 5 million patients to date (Novartis, 2012). AstraZeneca participates in a program focused on hygiene, infection, and reproductive health in Delhi (AstraZeneca, 2013). Boehringer Ingelheim provides free doses of a drug named Nevirapine to treat mother-to-child transmission of AIDS (Boehringer Ingelheim, 2013). Bristol-Myers Squibb launched a five-year, US $100 million program in 2010 to fight Type 2 diabetes in the United States, and pledged an additional US $15 million in 2012 to expand the program to China and India (Bristol-Myers Squibb, 2013). Genzyme sponsors the Gaucher Initiative, a partnership with Project HOPE that provides the drug Cerezyme to patients with Gaucher disease who live in developing countries (Genzyme, 2013). Abbott formed a public-private partnership with the government of Tanzania to strengthen the country's health care system and address critical areas of need, funding the program with more than $100 million (Abbott Fund, 2013). In perhaps the most famous public-private partnership, Merck has donated millions of dollars worth of Mectizan to fight against and prevent Onchocerciasis, also known as river blindness (Merck, 2012). Each donation may earn a press release touting the company's commitment to society, but does each press release carry the same weight? In other words, how can these programs be compared to, and measured against, each other?

In addition to the difficulty of comparing numbers helped and dollars spent to revenues earned, CSR-as-philanthropy also makes doing good dependent on pre-existing profit. This is an old criticism of CSR: A company can only help after it has first been profitable. Thus, profits come first and responsibility later. What does that do to responsibility during hard times? Does it go out the window? Does such a model have any analytical basis to critique how profits have been made? If there is no model critiquing how profits are made, could that then validate the claim that CSR-as-philanthropy really is just window dressing? These questions demonstrate that any kind of robust and sincere CSR must go deeper than philanthropy, though philanthropy may be part of a robust strategy.

One constructive response to these concerns has been building in the academic literature and in business itself over the past few years. This response looks at CSR as a strategy rather than an after-the-profits-are-made donation. With a strategic approach to CSR, a company seeks alignment between its social outreach and its core business products. To digress from the pharmaceutical industry to the financial industry for a moment, Barclays has developed programs for the "unbanked" that address the needs of low-income earners, and it sponsors a trade association that helps credit unions introduce lending for people who are unemployed or who have poor credit history (Barclays, 2009). This strategy helps meet the needs of those who often go without banking services; it also helps build business for Barclays. Similarly, in 2012, JP Morgan Chase committed more than US $1 million to launch a catalyst program to help small businesses in South Africa. The program provides small- and medium-sized businesses with access to hard-to-obtain business development services (Dalberg & Chase, 2012).

While Barclays and JP Morgan Chase have programs to build revenues by reaching out to underserved populations, HSBC looks for bottom-line benefits through environmental savings. It operates a Global Environmental Efficiency Program aimed at improving the company's existing and future environmental reduction targets and providing opportunities for showcasing environmental innovation (HSBC, Environmental Efficiency, 2013). The program encourages employees to submit proposals and projects with clear business plans, which may then be implemented. The program has already enabled the company to reduce energy waste, water pollution and carbon dioxide emissions (HSBC, Sustainability Report, 2013). Here again, the company is creatively identifying a social concern of interest to its stakeholders; by engaging them, HSBC also produces savings that will help the company's bottom line. Similarly, JP Morgan Chase has an environmental sustainability program focusing on the use of "green" chemicals and technology and a culture of philanthropic employee volunteerism (JPMorgan Chase, 2013).

As with the pharmaceutical industry, examples can be found in the financial industry as well. Citi works with African-based NGOs to implement mobile payment technology (Citi, 2013). Goldman Sachs' 10,000 Women program provides business and management education to underserved female entrepreneurs in developing and emerging markets to improve local economies and create greater shared prosperity and social change (Goldman Sachs, 2013). Credit Suisse partners with Habitat for Humanity, operates a microfinance program in Southeast Africa, and runs a book donation program—"Room to Read"—that stretches around the world (Credit Suisse, 2013). The UBS Social Entrepreneurship Award, created in partnership with Ashoka in 2004, brings recognition and added impetus to leading Mexico-based social entrepreneurs who use innovative and groundbreaking ideas to solve social problems (UBS, 2013).

These examples begin to raise paradoxes. Philanthropic donations carry with them a sense of altruism because of the good—helping children affected with worms, for example—that is appealing, but such donations are also vulnerable to the charge of window dressing because their impact is presented without context of dollars spent, revenues earned and people helped. It is also sustainable only as long as the companies earn profits. Strategic CSR more deeply embeds practices that can address social issues—financial literacy and empowering unbanked women, for example—more sustainably exactly because the facing of the social issue is framed to help the company's self-interest. Yet, that seems to make ethics into just another business strategy on par with a money-back guarantee. Shouldn't ethics exist on a higher moral level? We seek to maintain the vibrancy of both philanthropic CSR and strategic CSR by articulating another paradox.

2. Beyond Best Practices

Why do firms engage in these activities? Marketing experts Kotler and Lee offer four reasons: It enhances corporate image; it feels good (which helps employee recruitment, motivation, and retention); it does good (increased market share or sales); and it lasts longer (increased appeal to investors and analysts) (Nussbaum, 2009, p. 69). Companies may not engage in these kinds of activities for all four of these reasons; a firm may simply see benefits from just one or two of them. Yet, the four reasons raise two important questions.

First, do the benefits cited by Kotler and Lee come from these philanthropic engagements or do they result from a more systemic corporate approach to responsibility? Corporate support of efforts to alleviate disease and improve sanitation should, one would think, help a corporate image. A boost in reputation may also impact some of the other factors identified by Kotler and Lee, such as employee recruitment and increased market share and sales. But would such engagements really help in, for example, employee retention? We suggest that it would do so only if combined with other corporate actions that appeal to everyday concerns of employees, such as how they are treated and how they are empowered in their work.

Second, Kotler and Lee's four reasons beg the perennial question: Are these firms sincere in their efforts or are their philanthropic efforts simply an instrumental, public relations maneuver? That is not to demean good public relations, which are important to a company, or to suggest that companies must be wholly altruistic in their actions.

Some degree of self-interest, of course, can be construed in any action. We are not suggesting that an ethical action is only ethical if it shuns self-interest, but we do want to suggest that the more a company and the individuals in it are sincere about a commitment to doing good, the more their actions become trustworthy and beneficial to the company's instrumental consequences. Three examples explain this.

The first comes from Nobel Prize-winning economist F.A. Hayek. Hayek argued that trade is fostered by individuals adhering to some basic integrity-based virtues such as truth-telling, promise-keeping, and production of high-quality goods and services (Hayek, 1988) Adherence to such virtues reduces the policing costs of ensuring that trading partners deliver. Trade occurs more efficiently if businesses can trust their trading partners, but that trust is based on practicing these virtues. Hayek does not provide a philosophical justification for the "good" of honesty, promise-keeping, etc.; their good arises from the fact that practicing them generates more trade and wealth.

While we would prefer to advocate for a nobler justification of these virtues, Hayek acknowledges that one can understand the instrumental benefits of these virtues and therefore have a reason to practice them (Hayek, 1988) But it is more efficient if institutions such as religion, education, and other normatively oriented organizations teach the virtues as inherently good. In other words, trade flourishes more if traders sincerely believe in the inherent good of these virtues than if they practice the virtues simply for instrumental benefits.

This is crucial and at the same time paradoxical. If businesses practice philanthropic CSR or strategic CSR simply for their economic benefits, they short-sell the opportunities for ethics to benefit business.

The intuitive sensibility of Hayek's insight can be seen in a second, interpersonal hypothetical. Two people may begin to work together knowing that each brings something to a project they both wish to complete. There is an instrumental trusting of the other because there is a readily apparent self-interest in treating the partner decently in order to achieve the agreed-upon objective. If one of them becomes ill, the other might care for the sick one simply because a healthy partner is more likely to be able to make the necessary contributions to the project. However, there is a higher level of trust if the parties are authentically concerned about each other's well-being, even beyond the instrumental goal of the particular project. That might make the healthy partner care for the sick one irrespective of the project. Again, the paradox is that the instrumental value of practicing virtues is at its highest when those virtues are practiced for non-instrumental reasons.

Stakeholders sense this as well. A company that engages in CSR activities as a slick PR move will not elicit as much value from those activities as if it is perceived as being sincerely interested in the activities. This is the fundamental, paradoxical complexity of CSR. There is more economic value when the economics are secondary to something more primary. Ultimately, then, a core question of any corporate social responsibility effort is whether or not the company cares. How does an artificial entity —such as a corporation—"care"? It does so by having a critical mass of individuals, especially at certain levels of the company, make it part of their personal identity and something that becomes part of the institution's identity.

This argument is not as far from business reality as one might think. In a conversation with a high-ranking manager of the human rights/supply chain division of a Fortune 50 company, one of the authors asked what academics can do to help the manager in his work. The author assumed that the manager would want more empirical studies of how an action had more business payoff. He was surprised to hear the manager say instead that he needed good stories of how a company can help people. "Anyone who opposes what I suggest can come up with a different number," he said. "But people still react to how company actions can impact other people" (D.B., personal communication, 2003).

Consider Whole Foods CEO John Mackey. In his articulation on "Conscious Capitalism," Mackey argues that every entrepreneur starts a business for at least two reasons (Mackey & Sisodia, 2013). One of those reasons will be economic, even if the monetary rationale is to break even. But some other reason motivates the entrepreneur. It may be that the entrepreneur needs to start his own business because he has authority issues and cannot work for anyone. It could be that the entrepreneur wants to show her father than she can run a business just as well as her brother can. Mackey argues that each employee has the same motivation: They want to achieve some good other than a paycheck. Mackey's quest is to find a way to harness those motivations and focus them on work experience. We agree with Mackey, and propose that companies work through short-term pressures by emphasizing the importance of empowerment, trust, and other normative values that ultimately lead to the consequential benefits that reputation and goodwill provide.

Harvard Professor Lynn Sharp Paine synthesizes these insights well in her book Value Shift (2003), in which she argues that companies do not get the full value of ethical behavior unless stakeholders believe that the company acted for sincere reasons. For example, Paine argues that the sincerity behind Johnson & Johnson's actions during the 1982 Tylenol crisis gave it a halo effect (Paine, 2003) In a video that accompanied the Harvard Business School case on Johnson & Johnson, former CEO James Burke talked very explicitly about this sincerity factor (Aguilar, 1984).

A numbers-driven orientation can undermine the instrumental benefit that a company would achieve by leaving out what counts for a lot: The perception that the company is sincere. Soft as that may sound, it may just be the hardest to demonstrate and have the most concrete normative and business results.

3. Our Proposed Approach

If the paradox we described is accurate, the question becomes how companies implement such a model. A starting point is to reposition slightly what companies seek from CSR specifically or their business models in general, which may have an economic payoff because constituents repose trust in the company. Consumers are willing to purchase a company's product or service because they trust the company's reputation. Trust is what makes reputation actionable. By phrasing it in this way, we can see three types of trust that companies can use to create relationship that make a bottom-line difference: Hard trust, Real Trust, and Good Trust (Fort, 2011).

3.1 Hard Trust

The first type of trust we call Hard Trust. Constituents may trust a company because a powerful third party makes it behave. That third party might be the government through its laws, or it may be public opinion. This is a key battleground for many pharmaceutical companies. Class action lawsuits, regulatory recalls of products, and other legal actions undermine stakeholders' trust in the company. There is a long list of stakeholders whose trust in a company might be undermined in a situation like Merck's Vioxx scandal, extending from consumers and regulators to employees and the general public, thus triggering the other kind of Hard Trust: Public opinion. The first step for companies to protect their reputation is to attend to legal compliance and negative public opinion.

Pharmaceutical companies have been charged with exploiting local populations by conducting drug trials where the regulatory apparatus is not as stringent as in the company's home country. They have been criticized for using direct advertising to consumers (as opposed to using care providers as the sole provider of information to patients), and for advertising that their drugs will address needs that they simply do not. For example, Bristol Myers Squibb paid US $515 million in fines after it was discovered that the company marketed its antipsychotic drug, Abilify, to treat conditions the drug is not approved to treat (U.S. Department of Justice, 2007). Similarly, in the largest settlement involving a pharmaceutical company, the British drugmaker GlaxoSmithKline agreed to plead guilty to criminal charges and pay US $3 billion in fines for promoting its best-selling antidepressants for unapproved uses and failing to report safety data about a top diabetes drug (Schmidt & Thomas, 2012).

Another charge made against some pharmaceutical companies is that they essentially bribe care providers. In June 2007, The *New York Times* reported that psychiatrists in Vermont and Minnesota topped the list of doctors receiving pharmaceutical company gifts and that this financial relationship corresponds to the "growing use of atypicals [new antipsychotics] in children." From 2000 to 2005, drug maker payments to Minnesota psychiatrists rose more than six-fold to US $1.6 million. During those same years, prescriptions of antipsychotics for children under the state's insurance program rose more than nine-fold (Harris, 2007).

Companies tend to understand fairly well the need to avoid lawsuits and bad public relations, though they are not always successful in staying out of trouble. Especially in the aftermath of the enactment of the Federal Sentencing Guidelines and Sarbanes-Oxley in the U.S., companies have been required to intensify their board oversight of compliance issues on a variety of fronts.

One might think that corporate codes of conduct would be the elixir that prevents many of these problematic actions from occurring. But every major pharmaceutical company has a corporate code of conduct just like nearly every other major company (and a lot of not-so-major companies) today. Codes of conduct do little, if anything, to actually prevent illegal or unethical behavior unless there is some authentic, sincere commitment to conduct business in an exemplary way. Rhetorical odes to ethical conduct may even create a more cynical view of corporate responsibility if sincerity and actions fail to match politically correct verbiage. Hard Trust works—codes of conduct work—when there is an aspiration motivating a quest for excellence (what we refer to below as Good Trust).

3.2 Real Trust

Companies also might be trusted because good ethics can be good business, especially if measured over the long term. Many empirical studies show exactly that (Margolis & Walsh, 2001; Orlitzsky et al., 2003). This is Real Trust and it occurs when a company takes care of its employees and customers, where it is honest, keeps its promises, and produces high quality goods and services. This is an instrumental view of trust and it is what tends to dominate in the business world and in business schools.

Real Trust shares much in common with Values-Based Management approaches that have been around for a long time in Human Resources circles, and that one of the author's has elaborated on in the pharmaceutical industry (Christina, 2012). Many companies invest hugely in getting their managers to also be good people managers, who listen to their employees and help them maximize potential. There will always be situations that are not described in the company manual; therefore, it is preferable that management generates the company's values for employees, and that employees take these values into careful consideration in the way they conduct themselves and their work on a day-to-day basis. This is an "empowering-of-managers" approach that corresponds to placing greater responsibilities on individuals and tapping into employee motivation and interest for learning.

Values-based training does not happen in a vacuum. If one seeks to integrate a values-based approach throughout a company, logic dictates that the most powerful elements of the company must be involved. To be sure, that means CEO involvement. The old adage that ethics starts at the top is true, but if a values-based approach is going to be institutionalized, it cannot depend solely on the views of any one person. This means that an integrated approach must involve the Board of Directors. Just as compliance issues must have direct oversight by a Board Committee, so too should a values-based approach.

During one of the author's service on the Board of Directors of Ferring Pharmaceutical, senior management at Ferring appointed an independent global ethics officer to take overall responsibility for ensuring that the philosophy and the principles behind it are known and applied actively in all Ferring divisions. This work is organized in an ethics committee, which refers directly to the board of directors. The day-to-day work is carried out from the ethics office, and its remit is to disseminate awareness of these principles and values throughout the organization, and to train and underpin each individual employee's integrity.

In many companies, work with ethical guidelines and compliance are consolidated into a single function and the company implements a common and coordinated effort. In such cases, the compliance function often has the greatest influence because it is easier to comply with something devised by a regulatory authority. Ferring separates the two functions of ethics and compliance so that both disciplines are worked on in parallel. By separating these functions organizationally but reporting the two together to a board committee, Ferring aims to place intense focus on the ethical component in its own right. It is important at Ferring that individuals are trained and supported making the right decision in difficult situations.

To be sure, the reputational advantages of a halo effect are beneficial for a company. For example, the halo effect may have helped Merck after the FDA found that Vioxx put patients at a significantly greater risk for heart attack and stroke. Merck recalled its popular pain reliever, set aside US $4.85 billion in court judgments along with an additional US $1.9 billion for legal costs (Randall & Voreacos, 2010). But this was no more than a short-term hit to the company. Merck recovered financially, reporting US $47 billion in gross revenues by 2012 (Merck, 2013). Focusing on reputation, however, may not be as advantageous as focusing on the good that results from sincerely taking people's lives seriously. Like any business, pharmaceuticals regularly deal with pressures to increase sales and reduce costs. Those pressures are especially pressing in the short-term, particularly at a time when long-term economic benefits (like reputation) are difficult to quantify. If a company seeks to establish a good, long-term reputation, some other value needs to be present to get companies through short-term pressures and to keep it trustworthy.

3.3 Good Trust

That leads us to the final kind of trust: Good Trust. This exists where there is an authentic concern for others. This sincerity recognizes business realities, but it also recognizes that there are many things that motivate people. Good Trust taps into a part of human nature that makes people want to be proud of what they do.

One key way is through the values-based empowerment methods described above in Real Trust. This demonstrates the point we have been making throughout this article. If a senior manager seeks to empower someone lower on the corporate ladder, he or she needs to convey an authentic belief in the capabilities of that person or else the empowerment may fail. Sincerely believing in another person complements the message of empowerment.

This is a crucial point. For ethics to be practiced and embedded in a company, there must be an important core of sincerity. Stated differently, Real Trust—like Hard Trust—requires a degree of sincerity to be effective.

There are other ways to unleash this positive spirit within a company. The most natural way for people to talk about ethics is by presenting real cases in the form of storytelling. While legal rules, philosophical principles, and corporate edicts have a place, human beings have always told stories to communicate moral values. This suggests that there is a place for corporate stories that narrate a positive corporate identity. This explains why shareholders of Johnson & Johnson held its leadership to the fire; the company's recalls and other difficulties were inconsistent with its narrative identity.

Storytelling can also play into the values-based approach insofar as there are times and places in an organization where individuals are able to tell their stories. Indeed, in several consulting experiences, one of the authors has used this tactic to resolve cultural issues in the company. After everyone in the relevant management group had a chance to articulate what was important to them, members were able to then see how to integrate their collective values in a positive way (Fort, 2011).

The size of an organization matters as well. Research has shown that human beings are most "at-home" in fairly small sizes of groups. Our neurobiology has increasing difficulty communicating and understanding the consequences of individual actions at breaking points of six, 50, and 150 (Fort, 2001). Beyond those numbers, it becomes difficult for a person to understand that their actions impact others and so, logically, it becomes harder to foster ongoing ethical actions if one's actions do not "matter." Contemporary pharmaceutical companies are much larger than 150 people, but the point is that companies can design the sizes of work-groups, teams, and other corporate components if they keep these group sizes in mind.

A final way to tap into this positive nature of human beings is to show that the combined actions of those in the company can have a significant impact on important issues in the world. This is at the heart of sustainability efforts. Any individual's effort to recycle amounts to a drop in the bucket of sustainability issues in the world. But the message that each person's effort makes a difference can motivate a person to conscientiously recycle.

These Good Trust actions matter. We fully understand that further empirical research is necessary to elaborate upon the relationship of sincerity to profitable CSR. Indeed, we call upon researchers to look at this relationship.

4. Conclusion

The good news about corporate responsibility is that it has become far more mainstream than was the case 20 or 30 years ago. Our critique of corporate actions results from the fact that companies do see the importance of ethics and CSR. But we do want to question if these practices are good enough. Can we do better when companies really commit to the good of ethical actions, which paradoxically will have even greater trust-building impact? We recognize that many of our assertions require additional, refined empirical testing, but there are concrete examples of how this model does work, and a strong theoretical justification for why the model can help many companies to do better than their current best.

REFERENCES

Abbot Fund. (2013). *Public-Private Partnership For Health Care In Tanzania.* Retrieved from http://www.abbottfund.org/project/17/67/Modernizing-Regional-Level-Labs-in-Tanzania

Aguilar, F. A. (Director) (1984). *Johnson & Johnson: Philosophy & culture* [DVD].

AstraZeneca. (2013). *Astrazeneca Young Health Programme (India) Annual Report.* Retrieved September 16, 2013, from http://www.younghealthprogrammeyhp.com/_mshost2669695/content/pdf/india-report-2013.doc.

Barclays. (2009). *Banking on Change: Breaking the Barriers To Financial Inclusion.* Retrieved September 16, 2013, from http://group.barclays.com/Satellite?blobcol=urldata&blobheader=application%2Fpdf&blobheadername1=Content-Disposition&blobheadername2=MDT-Type&blobheadervalue1=inline%3B+filename%3DRead-the-Report-PDF-1MB.pdf&blobheadervalue2=abinary%3B+charset%3DUTF-8&blobkey=id&blobtable=MungoBlobs&blobwhere=1330698046959&ssbinary=true

Bayer. (2013). *Annual Report 2012.* Retrieved from http://www.bayer.com/en/annual-reports.aspx

Boehringer Ingelheim. (2013). *Combating HIV/AIDS.* Retrieved from http://corporateresponsibility.boehringer-ingelheim.com/corporate_citizenship/combating_hiv_aids.html

Bristol-Myers Squibb Foundation & National Network of Public Health Institutes. (2013). *2013 Together on Diabetes U.S. Grantee Summit.* Retrieved from http://www.bms.com/documents/together_on_diabetes/2013-Summit-pdfs/ToD-Program.pdf

Christina, A. (2012). *the Essence of Trust In Business Today.* Speech presented at the 2012 Business for Peace Summit, Oslo, Norway.

Citi. (2013). *Ngos In Africa Embrace Mobile Payments.* Retrieved from http://www.citigroup.com/citi/citiforcities/regeneration_development/n_ngos_in_africa.htm

Credit Suisse. (2013). *Corporate Responsibility Report 2012.* Retrieved from https://www.credit-suisse.com/publications/annualreporting/doc/2012/csg_crr_2012_en.pdf

Dalberg Global Development Advisors & JPMorgan Chase. (2012). the *small and medium enterprise (SME) scector—catalyst for growth in South Africa.* Retrieved from http://www.jpmorgan.com/cm/BlobServer/JPM_Dalberg_SME-Catalyst-for-Growth.pdf?blobkey=id&blobwhere=1320545178691&blobheader=application%2Fpdf&blobheadername1=Cache-Control&blobheadervalue1=private&blobcol=urldata&blobtable=MungoBlobs.

U.S. Department of Justice. (2007). *Bristol-Myers Squibb To Pay More Than $515 Million To Resolve Allegations of Illegal Drug Marketing and Pricing* (07-782). Washington, DC: U.S. Government Printing office. Retrieved September 17, 2013 from http://www.justice.gov/opa/pr/2007/September/07_civ_782.html.

Eli Lilly & Company. (2012). *2011 Annual Report.* Retrieved from http://investor.lilly.com/common/download/download.cfm?companyid=LLY&fileid=548541&filekey=E8FFDA89-5EC1-4D08-AB37-CD85F4C0863D&filename=English.PDF

Fort, T. L. (2011). *Business, Integrity, and Peace: Beyond Geopolitical and Disciplinary Boundaries (Business, Value Creation, and Society).* Cambridge University Press.

Fort, T. L. (2001). *Ethics and Governance: Business as Mediating Institution.* Oxford: Oxford University Press, USA.

Genzyme. (2013). *Free Drug Programs*. Retrieved from http://www.genzyme.com/Responsibility/Patient-Access-to-Treatment/Free-Drug-Programs.aspx

Glaxosmithkline. (2012). *Gsk Joins New Global Partnership To Help Defeat Ten Neglected Tropical Diseases By 2020*. Retrieved from http://us.gsk.com/html/media-news/pressreleases/2012/2012-pressrelease-875501.htm

Goldman Sachs. (2013). *2012 Annual Report*. Retrieved from http://www.goldmansachs.com/investor-relations/financials/current/annual-reports/2012-annual-report-files/annual-report-2012.pdf

Griffin, J., & Weber, J. (2006). *Industry Social Analysis: Examining the Beer Industry*. Business & Society, *45*(4), 413-440. doi: 10.1177/0007650306289399

Harris, G. (2007). *Psychiatrists Top List In Drug Maker Gifts. the New York Times*. Retrieved from http://www.nytimes.com/2007/06/27/health/psychology/27doctors.html?_r=0

Hayek, F.A. (1988). *the Fatal Conceit; the Errors of Socialism*. University of Chicago Press.

HSBC. (2013). *Environmental Efficiency*. Retrieved from http://www.hsbc.com/citizenship/sustainability/environmental-efficiency

HSBC. (2013). *Sustainability Report 2012*. Retrieved from http://www.hsbc.com/~/media/HSBC-com/citizenship/sustainability/pdf/130521-hsbc-susreport-2012-online-ready-version.ashx

Johnson & Johnson. (2013). *Our Global Giving*. Retrieved from http://www.jnj.com/sites/default/files/pdf/2012-Johnson-Johnson-Contributions-Report.pdf

JPMorgan Chase. (2013). *J.P. Morgan Corporate Responsibility Report*. Retrieved from http://www.jpmorganchase.com/corporate/Corporate-Responsibility/document/jpm_corpresp091912_hires.pdf

Knowledge@Wharton. (2012). *Patients Versus Profits At Johnson & Johnson: Has the Company Lost Its Way?* Retrieved from http://knowledge.wharton.upenn.edu/article.cfm?articleid=2943

Mackey, J., & Sisodia, R. (2013). *Conscious Capitalism: Liberating the Heroic Spirit of Business*. Boston, MA: Harvard Business Review Press.

Margolis, J. D., & Walsh, J. P. (2001). *People and Profits? the Search For A Link Between A Company's Social and Financial Performance*. Mahwah, N.J.: Psychology Press.

McGrath, W. (2011). [Web log message]. Retrieved from http://www.fedseclaw.com/2011/05/articles/foreign-corrupt-practices-act-1/shareholders-derivative-complaint-filed-against- johnson-johnson-for-fcpa-violations/

Medicines for Malaria Venture. (2013). *About Us*. Retrieved from http://www.mmv.org/about-us

Merck. (2012). *Annual Highlights 2011 Celebrating 25 Years of the Mectizan Donation Program In 2012*. Retrieved from http://www.mectizan.org/sites/www.mectizan.org/files/attachments/resources/Annual%20Highlights%202011%20English.pdf

Merck. (2013). Form 10-K *Annual Report*. Retrieved from http://www.merck.com/investors/financials/annual-reports/

Novartis. (2012). *Q&a about the Novartis MDT leprosy donation*. Retrieved from http://www.novartisfoundation.org/page/content/index.asp?MenuID=364&ID=1010&Menu=3&Item=43.2.4

Nussbaum, A. K. (2009). *Ethical Corporate Social Responsibility (Csr) and the Pharmaceutical Industry: A Happy Couple?* Journal of Medical Marketing, *9*(1), 67-76. doi:10.1057/jmm.2008.33

Orlitzky, M., Schmidt, F., & Rynes, S. (2003). *Corporate social and financial performance: A meta-analysis*. Organization Studies, *24*(3), 403-441. doi: 10.1177/0170840603024003910

Paine, L. S. (2003). *Value Shift: Why Companies Must Merge Social and Financial Imperatives to Achieve Superior Performance*. New York: McGraw-Hill.

Pfizer. (2013). *Diflucan Partnership*. Retrieved from http://www.pfizer.com/responsibility/global_health/diflucan_partnership_program

Randall, T & Vereacos, D. (2010) *Merck Legal Costs for Vioxx Reduce Profit Six Years After Recall* Retrieved from http://www.bloomberg.com/news/2010-10-29/merck-legal-costs-for-vioxx-reduce-profit-6-years-after-recall.html

Robinson, F., & Oakes, M. (2012). *Johnson and Johnson Settles Derivative Litigation Through Corporate Governance and Compliance Reforms*. Retrieved from http://www.nortonrosefulbright.com/knowledge/publications/93618/johnson-and-johnson-settles-derivative-litigation-through-corporate-governance-and-compliance-reforms

Schmidt, M., & Thomas, K. (2012). *Glaxo Agrees To Pay $3 Billion In Fraud Settlement.* the New York Times. Retrieved from http://www.nytimes.com/2012/07/03/business/glaxosmithkline-agrees-to-pay-3-billion-in-fraud-settlement.html?pagewanted=all

UBS. (2013). *the UBS Visionaris Social Entrepreneurship Award*. Retrieved from http://www.ubs.com/global/en/about_ubs/corporate_responsibility/community/visionaris.html

UNEP. (2011). *Partners For Youth and the Environment*. Retrieved from http://www.unep.bayer.com/en/about-partnership.aspx

Building on Collaboration and Trust for Innovation: Ford as a Mobility Company

David Berdish, Social Sustainability Manager,
The Ford Motor Company

Meghan Chapple-Brown, Director, Office of Sustainability,
The George Washington University

Abstract

INNOVATION REFERS *to the ability of the firm to be creative enough to identify, experiment with, and implement changes that position the company for the future. Truly innovative companies monitor market and societal trends, and position themselves to respond to those trends with services and profit models that generate genuine value for customers and investors. Companies can transition more deftly from the current state to future innovation when they are operating in an environment of transparency and trust. One can argue that constructive dialogue and meaningful relationships with stakeholders help a company understand market needs, and in a reciprocal manner, allow market players to believe in the firm's new offerings.*

Ford Motor Company is in the midst of such an innovation transition that stands on decades of trust building. Henry Ford created a company that provided vehicles for personal transportation, and simultaneously contributed to the creation of a middle class of American workers who could afford to buy the product. Since then, Ford has revitalized its legacy of fair labor by leading the industry in human rights commitments and practice. Ford has built on these strong relationships with stakeholder groups and partners around the world to develop innovative business ideas to address the need for new mobility solutions in megacities such that underserved people can get access to jobs, education, and health care.

Ford is positioning to respond to demand with a unique offering called Sustainable Urban Mobility with Unrestricted Rural Reach (SUMURR). This form of New Mobility grew out of an extensive global stakeholder coalition focused on multi-modal transportation to connect Ford vehicles and every other mode of transportation imaginable. SUMURR uses Ford's vehicles and its technology platforms to bridge the mobility gap for isolated, rural communities by providing them with sustainable access to key services such as healthcare, clean water, and education. SUMURR is enabled by a sophisticated, on-the-ground ecosystem of universities, non-governmental organizations, social entrepreneurs, government, and global corporations specific to each rural region. . By "co-inventing" SUMURR, Ford has created a process for sustainable innovation utilizing stakeholder engagement, systems thinking, and trusted partnerships.

Introduction

Business today is navigating trends ranging from globalization of financial markets and unprecedented electronic availability of information, to isolation of disenfranchised cultures, growing young populations in developing countries, and increasing rates of chronic and communicable disease. There is increasing pressure on natural resources such as fresh water and biodiversity as well as the imminent impacts of climate change. Innovative companies monitor and adapt to such macro-trends. Riding the wave of these challenges, companies with an eye towards sustainable development build on collaboration and trust with stakeholders to find innovative ways to generate value for customers, investors, and society at large.

However, the process for transitioning from a current business model to a sustainable business model that generates long-term value is not well understood. Contemporary cases provide a lens into real time efforts, and are the best resources for business leaders to learn about, and for academics to reflect on the transition to sustainable innovation. Ford Motor Company is demonstrating how stakeholder engagement, voluntary compliance, and humility can lead to trusted partnerships and sustainable innovation. Here we explore how a company can transition more deftly through such a complex web of social, environmental, and economic systems when it is operating in an atmosphere of transparency and trust.

A Vision for Collaboration

Engaging local stakeholders can be a useful tool for companies to understand the needs of the communities in and around which they operate—especially in emerging economies—and to integrate these considerations into their future business offerings. Ford is developing a more integrated approach to its local community engagement and human rights efforts, and linking them to the development of new products and services that meet the unique needs of the communities in emerging markets.

One component of Ford's strategy for stakeholder engagement is to look for collaborations in unlikely places. In particular, the company has begun to explore the viability of partnering with governments at the local, national, and international level as they relate to particular markets or areas of social need. Globalization has shrunk the perceived space between geographically distant parts of the world; but simultaneously those advancements have expanded every community's sphere of vulnerability from including itself and its neighbors, to encompassing the trials faced by communities on the other side of the world. To address global problems, global solutions are necessary, including public-private partnerships that synthesize skills and resources to overcome these challenges.

This case explores how Ford is forming partnerships to uncover market solutions for one issue area in particular—maternal and fetal health in rural India. With more transparency into the lives of people in developing countries comes greater understanding of how to empower those individuals. It has been determined that access to basic health services can significantly impact the quality of life for women and children in developing countries, and the widespread accessibility of mobile technology presents a unique opportunity to efficiently address a manageable barrier to empowerment.

A Foundation of Trust

Ford Motor Company is drawing on decades of deep engagement with stakeholder groups and local businesses in mega-cities around the world, like Salvador, to explore new relationships that take the market system to a higher and more harmonious level. Ford has found that the energy from embracing complexity, systems thinking, and stakeholder engagement builds trust and uncovers pathways for innovative solutions. The company's first step in building trust with potential partners, and eventually in creating sustainable innovation, is to learn from stakeholders. Stakeholder dialogue provides the proper forum to balance inquiry into issues and advocacy of viewpoint, and to engage in the conversation and the learning.

In the summer of 2000, shortly after William Clay Ford, Jr. was named Chairman of the Board at Ford Motor Company, several members of the Ford executive team met with environmental and human rights non-government organizations and activists, socially responsible investment funds, and sustainability thought leaders. This is when stakeholder engagement became a key part of the Ford sustainability strategy, and is a core competency a decade later. Over the years, Ford has maintained open dialogue and inquiry with groups such as the Coalition for Environmentally Responsible Economies (CERES), Interfaith Center on Human Rights, the Union of Concerned Scientists, and the Rainforest Action Network. The company has looked to some of these groups as trusted advisors when faced with difficult ethical decisions such as management of a labor issue in the supply chain. And the company strives to humbly provide honest feedback to these groups on the complexities and current limits the company faces on its journey to sustainable innovation, whether related to vehicle technology or financial markets. Ford has been planting and nurturing seeds of transparency and trust that continue to sprout into better ways of doing business and new ways of delivering value in the future.

For example, an outgrowth of Ford's involvement with human rights groups was the confidence and evidence that it could make a commitment to the issue. At the Centennial Shareholders meeting in May, 2003, the Company announced the development of its Code of Basic Working Conditions. The plan was to make Ford a leader in human rights practices and to differentiate the company on social issues for potential business benefits. The code development was supported and reviewed by leading human rights experts including the Interfaith Center for Corporate Responsibility and the Lawyers Committee for Human Rights (now Human Rights First!). According to publicly available information, Ford is the first company in the automotive industry to develop its own code. And, the company has the infrastructure to enact the code; Ford is the only company in its industry to train, assess, audit and remediate among its first tier supply base. Ford has taken strong actions to enforce its code, which is stronger than international standards.

Like most US-based global companies, there are challenges when entering new markets, especially as there is an increasing reliance on emerging market sourcing for export and domestic production. There is wide variation in working conditions and labor laws in emerging markets, and differing levels of safety and security. Positive reputation in the international community is essential to gain trust, understanding, and to navigate the complexity. As a result of implementation of the human rights code and broad stakeholder engagement, Ford is earning trust with global stakeholders as it operates in low cost markets. Implementation of the code has also enhanced the company's ability to better understand legal and regulatory liability, shareholder resolutions, and collaborative efforts with human rights groups to ensure resolution of potential company-related issues, such as risk of unethical labor practices in its supply chain.

However, implementing human rights in worldwide operations and building stakeholder dialogue is more than just risk management. Ford Motor Company is recognized as a leader in human rights[110], and its business practices ensure a differentiation from its international competition. This differentiation enables more business opportunities and access to new markets around the world.

Uncovering Pathways to Partnership and Innovation: Ford is learning the various perspectives that allow the company to find connections among the aforementioned macro-trends such as financial globalization, connectivity, cultural isolation, population changes, disease patterns, and natural resource constraints. The company is also partnering with stakeholders to pilot innovative business models. Ford is exploring what it takes to make jobs, healthcare, and knowledge accessible through transportation and information technology that is affordable and environmentally sustainable in and around large, crowded urban areas internationally. In embarking on the journey of sustainable innovation, Ford Motor Company has partnered with stakeholders like various national governments, local city transport leaders, NGOs at all levels, and academics like the University of Michigan Sustainable Mobility and Accessibility Research Transformation center, the Georgia Institute of Technology, and the George Washington University.

Through these engagements, Ford has found that shifting demographics and social inequality will lead to increasingly diverse and fragmented markets. And, increasing resource costs, urbanization, and congestion on roadways will cause the company's

---

110   Ford was ranked number one in the world in for human rights in the "Corporate Responsibility Officer (CRO) Magazine" *2010 Best 100 Corporate Citizens List.* Ford received a perfect 100 on the Human Rights Campaign 2008 Corporate Equality Index. On International Human Rights Day 2010 change.org and ICCR commended Ford as 1 of 5 companies for their work to improve human rights performance.

customers to change purchasing behavior and explore other means of transportation and access.

The company has learned that connectivity and information technology show promise for overcoming barriers to integrated urban mobility systems that rely on multiple modes of transportation seamlessly tied together. As the company strategically plans for the changing demand for personal mobility and as Ford leads in the design of the "next billion" cars, Ford's governance, marketing, product development, and research divisions have taken inputs from and co-created with trusted stakeholders a vision for how their company will address these trends.

Launching An Innovative Business Model: SUMURR

SUMURR uses Ford vehicles and Ford technology platforms to bridge the mobility gap for isolated, rural communities by providing them with sustainable access to key services such as healthcare, clean water, and education. Simply, SUMURR is a combination of Ford's "wheels on the ground and apps in the cloud" to empower underserved communities. A Ford vehicle delivers services to remote rural areas, while connecting communities with data and expertise via the cloud through the use of applications and Ford's OpenXC platform.

OpenXC is an open-source research platform that will enable developers to create custom-specific applications to advance in-car connectivity innovation. OpenXC transforms the car into a 'plug-and-play' platform where a combination of interchangeable open-source hardware and software modules can be quickly and easily customized to create unique applications.

SUMURR is facilitated by a public-private partnership between the Ford Motor Company, the U.S. Department of State, and George Washington University. The partnership objective is to leverage Ford Motor Company's SYNC technology and the IT "cloud", the diplomatic and policy relationships of State, and the private-public partnership expertise of GW's Institute of Corporate Responsibility to launch a pilot project in 2013 providing access to health care services to women in the rural areas outside of Chennai, India. The partners' contributions in technology, research, and on the ground expertise position SUMURR for success.

The SUMURR pilot will be deemed a success when sustainable access to healthcare services is available to women in rural areas outside of Chennai, thereby inching closed the omnipresent social equity gap. Ford has developed innovative technologies that capitalize on open architecture and open networks to make available unprecedented connectivity. Ford has developed "apps for society" based on open-source application programming interfaces (APIs) that will allow health service providers to travel to rural communities with few medical resources and teleconnect back to Chennai via the "cloud". Support, maintenance, and further development of those existing and new apps will be provided on the ground by the India Institute of Technology Madras.

SUMURR responds to emergent phenomena whereby personal mobility may be designed by the mash-ups of data coming from a world that is rich in digitally networked sensors and vibrant with social communities. Key enabling technologies and major research endeavors have stimulated an open dialogue about the might, delight, and potential fright of collectively programming cars and communities. SUMURR is an innovation that is creating social value and positioning the company for the future. It can provide access to natural resources, financing, education, health information, even jobs, while it reduces congestion, fuel consumption, pollution and carbon emissions.

Ford's Core Competencies and Contributions

Ford is striving to understand the long-term outlook for transportation, mobility, and access. The company has leveraged its experience in environmental, economic and social sustainability to inform its plans for long-term growth in providing transportation. Understanding mobility challenges is also consistent with Ford Motor Company's legacy—the Company that transformed personal mobility in the 20th century wants to influence how it will be made available in the 21st century. And Ford's experience with transportation, vehicle manufacturing, logistics planning, IT and global infrastructure challenges makes it uniquely qualified to play a leadership role in the development of urban transportation solutions.

This thinking is reflected by the company's leadership. Bill Ford has "told my people many times, 'Don't assume we're always going to be in the car business. We're going to be in the transportation business, and it's going to look very different 20, 30, or 50 years from now.' The notion is you don't have to have ownership of a vehicle; you just want to get from point A to point B. You may have a car, a bicycle, a moped, and we at Ford and others are going to help you do that."

SUMURR is one manifestation of Ford's exploration of the future of mobility, access, and transportation, one which connects urban and rural areas. Additionally, Ford is well-positioned to create an integrated urban mobility consultancy supplying best of breed global public transportation solutions. As convener, Ford can help to augment the viability of SUMURR as the company brings together thought leaders and local partners to assess megacity metro-areas. The company is poised to collaborate on systemic transportation solutions, including providing cities with tailored plans and logistical support to address mobility challenges and establish proprietary routing integration and ticketing system that can be reproduced and implemented across metro-areas. Ford's award-winning SYNC® system, powered by Microsoft® to connect drivers with information technology, is a key component for connecting the company's vehicles with the transportation system.

Ford is acting as an agent of change for a better world by forging innovative public-private partnerships with government, academic institutions, nonprofit stakeholders and company resources to support positive social advancement. Projects similar to

SUMURR are already being considered for other regions around the globe, including other parts of rural India, one in the state of Gujarat, India—where Ford has a manufacturing plant—and also in China and Brazil. Ford Motor Company is not in the business of telemedicine, but between the vehicle and the technology it provides, it can make it better.

The SUMURR pilot program began in June 2012 and concluded in February 2013. In addition to facilitating safe childbirth for the women with high-risk pregnancies, the program led to 27 temporary pediatric and gynecology camps being set up in remote villages. Such visits enabled about 1,600 women and children to receive much needed healthcare, including screenings for basic illnesses and immunization coverage. SUMURR reached another 3,100 people with its partners as the program traveled to 54 villages to facilitate community awareness programs on maternal and child health issues.

"Leveraging our strengths in building vehicles and in democratizing technology, we have pioneered a unique effort to remove all hurdles to mobility for these women and have made safe childbirths possible for them," said Joginder Singh, president and managing director, Ford of India. "SUMURR truly embodies Ford's DNA of utilizing smart technologies for a better world."

Planning for a new form of transportation, the cutting-edge vision for the SUMURR business model gives Ford a strategic competitive business advantage and allows Ford to serve a social purpose, locally, everywhere. There are significant business opportunities in the emerging markets, coupled with population growth, pollution, and congestion. Ford is leveraging its positive reputation and stakeholder relationships in the international community, global reach, and convening power with governments, business, civil society and other stakeholders to address the trends and provide innovation, reliability, and accessibility.

The Ford Methodology for Trust and Innovation

By "co-inventing" SUMURR, Ford has created a process for sustainable innovation. The company embarked on this journey by building a platform of trust through stakeholder engagement. This led to credibility and opportunity for co-creation of ground-breaking solutions. With inputs and contributions from global experts, Ford and its partners have provided a clear focus on the social goal and value-added of SUMURR, and a vision for future market opportunities. The network of regional partners (companies, entrepreneurs, governments, utilities, transportation planners, NGOs, etc.) enables exploration and pilots of SUMURR in regions around the world.

A key component to the trust and innovation process at Ford is systems thinking. The company made a strategic commitment to understand its stakeholders and the system in which the company operates. The company found the ability to identify new opportunities by embracing complexity. By integrating social sustainability, systems thinking exercises, and stakeholder engagement into its management processes, Ford managers found they were able to build trust, collaboration, and solutions.

Ford identifies the first step to building trust as admitting shortcomings. Stakeholder engagement provides the proper forum to balance inquiry into issues and advocacy of viewpoint, and to engage in the conversation and the learning. Reflection produces strategy. Trust builds partners, customers, and opportunities. When Ford works with new mental models presented by others like NGOs, managers in the company step into a place of humility, openness, and vulnerability. They use tools from Peter Senge's The Fifth Discipline to work with mental models and the assumptions behind them. For example, the "ladder of inference" provides a process that describes how data is observed and filtered; and how past experiences and predisposed conclusions cause action and decision. Another tool, "systems archetypes" are stories of recurring patterns ("fixes that fail", "shifting the burden", and "tragedy of the commons") told through causal loop diagrams. Reflection and use of the tools have provided insights into stakeholder dialogue at Ford.

Ford has found that reflecting on its role, strengths, and weaknesses, while understanding human relationships within the system allow people in and outside the company to talk, empathize with one another's perspectives and assumptions, and work together towards a compelling vision. By carefully building mutual trust, the company has created a community of people and a network of solutions.

Conclusion

In striving to be a trusted partner, Ford first utilizes the elements of existing research and advocacy within the issues. Then they gain familiarity of public policy at global, national, and local levels, including communities' infrastructure and collective actions with intergovernmental bodies, civil society and multi-stakeholders. At the George Washington University, Professor John Forrer states, "The concept of a 'trusted partner' puts firms in a pro-active position, addressing issues and concerns alongside external stakeholders, and making decisions that take into account the interests of the communities in which they operate." The Ford case is aligned with Forrer's perspective. The company's work in stakeholder engagement and social sustainability is evidence that trusted partnerships influence the global economy; positively impact the societies in which the company operates; and establish new markets. The Ford record on human rights, along with subject matter expertise in urban mobility is building a strong reputation within the emerging marketplace—in the municipalities, for fleet buyers and for citizens who may see Ford as the premiere provider of sustainable mobility solutions.

Since 1903, Ford Motor Company has been providing transportation to people. The $5 a day work wage and the mass production of the Model T resulted in the "democratization of the automobile". The placement of Sync applications in the Focus represents the "democratization of technology". New Mobility will enable more rapid evolution of the technology and its uses within an open architecture and open network. As a partner that helps to create a robust communication platform, Ford can support the "democratization of innovation".

The case of Ford Motor Company co-creating a vision and piloting SUMMUR shows how important iterative, yet strategic, actions are. Conversations with new stakeholders can earn trust and overcome mental models. Co-creation of a vision with partners can unleash creativity. And, collaborative implementation of pilot projects can act as seeds that will sprout into innovation. With each new bond of trust, there is more harmony and greater resiliency of the system.

From Knowledge to Action:
Social Movement Insights for a New Vision of the Firm

Marc Lavine, University of Massachusetts—Boston

Introduction

RECASTING THE THEORY of the firm and its governance is, of course, no small matter. This goal may extend beyond the realm of the ambitious into the nether-regions of the audacious and, some might argue, hare-brained, naïve, or simply impossible. There are, perhaps, three central notions that might fortify us as we contemplate such a daunting or perilous endeavor. First, we take comfort in the knowledge that the nature of the firm has, in fact, shifted over the last century. We need look no further than the work of another contributor to this book, Ed Freeman, to cite stakeholder theory and stakeholder management practices as a fundamental shift from a firm existing to serve owners to one that operates because of a range of stakeholders and for those stakeholders. Corporate social responsibility efforts also represent a shift in the axis of societal expectations of the firm though historians might contend that this returns the corporation closer to its roots where are articulation of the social good that would be created by providing goods and services was perhaps more clearly understood as the basis for creating the corporation. Presently, we see a range of social experiments that all represent some rethinking of the theory of the firm and its governance practices. Social entrepreneurship and the rise of so-called hybrid organizations while not dissimilar from the dual social-financial mission that hospitals, newspapers and other organizations have attended to historically, represents an even more overt example of firms existing to enact social benefit.

This is not to suggest that all changes to the firm or its governance trend toward the socially beneficial. Indeed much of the rise of society rethinking the expectations of firms may be driven by the unbridled growth of many corporations and the multinational firm eclipsing the State in many cases in its strength as a social actor. Therefore the same forces enable firms to play an increasing social role and contribute to societal rethinking of what the firm means and provides, also create the potential for greater malfeasance on the part of the firm. The recent decision by the U.S. Supreme Court to allow firms to play more of a direct financial role in elections underscores the possible peril of the seemingly ever-gathering strength. Beyond influence on civil society an increasing number of firms deemed "too big to fail" remind us that our fate and that of corporate firms is ever more linked.

Yet, each of these developments—whether terrible or terrific- support the notion that the firm can indeed change in profound ways. So, our first realization must be that the theory of the firm and some aspects of governance have changed in our lifetimes. Therefore, the seemingly lofty ambitions of this text may be more reasonable than we initially may think.

This brings us to the second idea that might inspire us as we undertake a reconsideration of the firm and its governance. In the words of President Kennedy, "no problem of human destiny is beyond human beings." Some would contend that this is misplaced optimism or excessive belief in technological innovation and the capacity of human ingenuity. We might contrast Kennedy's words with Mark Twain's seemingly timeless truism that "those of you inclined to worry have the largest selection in history." I am not advocating blind optimism in the face of global climate change and rampant, catastrophic, injustice. Rather, my aim is to remind us of the highly malleable, socially constructed nature of our institutions. Despite plenty of cause for fear and cynicism, we must also recognize that profound change and innovation is possible.

The possibility of change is one thing; instigating and organizing it in any kind of planned way is quite another. Social movement literature is a potentially profound source of insight and practical knowledge for the work of advancing a new theory of the firm and new governance practices. While well-considered, potent theories of the firm must animate change, we need equally wise theories of change to realize the new forms we envision. Simply put, it would be a great shame if these ideas stayed only in the realm of lofty ideals. While new theory is an essential part of the equation, the challenges that necessitate it are too dire to neglect implementation in addition to theory.

Social movement literature provides us with a series of insights that can help us consider how we realize a reconceptualization of the firm and its attendant governance practices. Noted social movement scholars, Rao, Morrill, and Zald define social movements as "organized collective endeavors to solve social problems" (2000). This is precisely the effort it seems we are, or must be, engaged in. All too often we overlook pre-existing scholarly streams, outside our own, that can inform and strengthen our endeavors. Employing social movement theory as a lens has the potential to guide our efforts. by showing what aspects of a nascent movement should be attended to in order for a movement to grow with strength. Additionally, many have noted that over the last half century social movement scholars have done far more to make use of organizational theory and management concepts than organizational scholars have made use of social movement research. Senior social movement scholars note that "the learning to date however, has been largely uni-directional. Social movement scholars have been able to productively borrow and adapt organizational ideas to their own uses; organizational scholars have been far less opportunistic in taking advantage of movement ideas" (McAdam and Scott, 2005, p. 5). This essay represents one small effort to correct this imbalance by using social movement concepts to inform organizational theory.

Yet, because rethinking the firm and its governance is a broad topic, I use a case-based approach here where I explore one specific example of fundamental change to the theory of the firm and examine the social movement considerations for moving this idea from theory to action. This tactic is what Stephen Jay Gould used to refer to as "using specifics to sneak up on generalities" (Gould, 1981, p. 7). Considering action from a place of high abstraction would likely do us little good. Therefore my intent in using a case example is not to constrain, but to provide more nuance by considering the specific challenges and opportunities of igniting a social movement to re-imagine the firm and its governance.

I use Peace through Commerce (PTC) as my case example. PTC is, ultimately, an effort to have re-envision the role of the firm as having a hyper-goal of creating and sustaining peace. I provide detailed background about PTC later in this chapter but, before I do so, let me note that the choice of a case example is not so important. The remainder of this chapter would provide utility even if you were to substitute another "firm- or governance-transforming" example. could have as easily used corporate CSR efforts, shareholder activism and socially responsible investment funds, or the efforts of the social entrepreneurship community just to name a few. It is a worthwhile exercise to read the paper thinking about what the lessons would be for these other allied movements.

The PTC example exemplifies an effort that began in academia and blossomed to take on greater social movement dimensions. In that sense it is a particularly useful choice as our undertaking here has similar origins. The remainder of this chapter is comprised of work that appeared, in largely similar form, as an article in the Journal of Business Ethics entitled "From Scholarly Dialogue to Social Movement: Considerations and Implications for Peace through Commerce" (Lavine, 2010).

Asking whether PTC could reasonably be considered a social movement is an important, albeit rudimentary, starting point. It is important to consider whether the minimum conditions are necessary to make such an assertion reasonable. Movements are inherently permeable and the boundaries often contested, and thus not necessarily agreed upon or understood by all actors involved or by other outsiders. Rather than seeking to establish some type of standard against which we might precisely assess whether something should or should not be considered a bona fide social movement, a much more important, generative, and perhaps skeptical question is "what is gained by conceptualizing PTC as a social movement?" Considering PTC through the lens of social movement theory has the potential to make two contributions which serve as the essential aims of this essay.

Like the agenda of PTC itself, a social movement perspective allows us to consider what might enable or constrain the growth and development of PTC and, more broadly, efforts to change our core understanding of the purpose firm and its governance. In a manner akin to the normative aims of PTC, a social movement perspective increases the potential for the movement to develop with strength and quality by fostering more deliberation about the development of the movement. While a social movement of any substance would ideally become robust enough that it would become resistant to rational planning, thinking through major issues of the movement from a social movement perspective has the potential to improve PTC and broader efforts reconsider the theory of the firm and the manner in which it is governed.

This brings us to the second contribution of this essay: to use social movement scholarship as a resource and framework to organize thoughts and recommendations intended to strengthen PTC. While this is an applied aim, it could well be that thinking carefully through specific challenges and opportunities for PTC, through the lens of social movements, could generate relevant insights for other thought movements and change efforts beyond PTC. Thought movement and academic settings are under-theorized terrain for social movements (Croteau et al., 2005; Hambrick and Chen, 2008) so, at best, this writing can shed further light on the development of a thought movement into a social movement. While the approach I take in this essay is aimed at PTC, my hope is that this writing could aid future theory development beyond PTC by increasing clarity about the relationship between academic dialogue and social movements.

The remainder of this essay is organized as follows: I will first introduce social movement theory as a lens, briefly characterize PTC, and then use three key dimensions of social movement theory—message framing, political opportunity, and resource mobilization—as a framework to analyze PTC. I will offer thoughts and recommendations on how PTC might attend to each of these areas that social movement scholars have deemed critically important to social movements.

Social Movement Theory

Social movement theory explores the ability of collective interests to achieve social change. Social movements are commonly framed as preference structures, held among members of a population, that favor specific social change (Zald and McCarthy, 1987). SM scholars drew from earlier work on an array of related theoretical topics, such as those of group action, collective behavior, mass society (Davis et al., 1996) and on empirical work pertaining to "more evanescent forms of collective behavior" (Rao et al., 2000, p. 238) such as crowds, mobs, and riots. SM scholars "reframed the view of protest and reform activities from one of irrational behavior—a flailing out against an unjust universe—to one involving instrumental action" (McAdam and Scott, 2005, p. 6). SM scholars also shifted the axis of attention from the nature, or cause, of the social grievance that animated group behavior to an emphasis on the methods of mobilization used to attain social change.

Part of this increased attention to the processes and mechanisms of social change helped scholars to recognize that while social movements require shared belief, or collective sentiment among individuals, they largely become visible in the context of collective action carried out by organizations. Thus, social movement scholars offer the crucial distinction between social movements and social movement organizations (SMOs). An SMO is "a complex or formal organization that identifies its goals with the preferences of a social movement...and attempts to implement those goals (Zald and McCarthy, 1987, p. 20)." SM scholars remind us that social movement organizations need not be created "de novo," but can take place within, and make use of, current social structures and organizations. Zald and McCarthy note: "social movements are not created outside of the traditions and institutional bases of the larger society in which they are nested. Instead, the cadre and networks of adherents and activists grow out of, build upon, and use the repertoires of action, the institutional forms and physical facilities, of the larger society" (Zald and McCarthy, 1987, p. 20).

Yet, just as social movements can exist within current organizational forms, they can also give rise to new organizational forms. Rao et al. (2000) describe the role that social movements play in creating new organizational forms, noting that social movements are a source of cultural innovation. The authors cite organizational forms as diverse as micro-breweries, healthcare management organizations (HMOs), and the Total Quality Management (TQM) movement as examples of social movements that gave rise to new organizational forms. These examples also broaden common conceptions of social change to include all collective action that changes social life, not just social change with a social justice orientation. Given this potentially broad interpretation of social movements, scholars have increasingly viewed social movements as a lens for understanding many types of organizational change (Strang and Il-Jung, 2005).

Recent work by Hambrick and Chen (2008) considers the rise of academic thought movements into new scholarly fields from a social movement perspective. The authors offer a theoretical model to explain why some thought movements may grow into free-standing academic fields. While their model does not lend itself to an analysis of PTC because PTC shows no signs of trying to be an autonomous scholarly field, their work adds legitimacy to the notion that an academic thought movement might become a social movement. Recent work by Waddock (2009) considers the development of corporate social responsibility (CSR) as a social movement terms. This movement may be more analogous to PTC in that it has involved practitioners and scholars from an early point of its development.

I follow these authors in using the framework of social movement analysis to organize my thinking. I ask what might be gained by casting a thought movement as a social movement and what social movement scholarship might have to teach a burgeoning thought movement.

Therefore, this article is organized around what SM scholars treat as the key considerations for analyzing and characterizing socialmovements: message framing, political opportunity, and resource mobilization. Notably, Hambrick and Chen give little attention to one of the dynamics that is routinely considered a key dimension of social movement analysis, that of message framing. Based in part on this deficit, I devote considerable attention to this topic. Furthermore, while SM message framing has received considerable attention in the last decade, this topic has historically received less attention than other SM dynamics such as resource mobilization and political opportunity (Zald et al., 2005). Therefore added attention to framing dynamics is even more warranted. Before using a social movement framework to analyze and offer recommendations for PTC's development, I will briefly characterize the PTC movement.

Background on PTC

Peace through Commerce (PTC) started as a scholarly dialogue among a small group of business ethicists and legal scholars. Over the last decade, it has broadened and grown into an increasingly robust movement that includes scholars from several different fields: practitioners from industry, representatives from government, actors from the social sectors, and participants from multilateral organizations. PTC has the aim of understanding how business activity may foster lasting peace and identifying constraints that limit the potential for sustainable peace. PTC grapples with the tension between peace and commerce, acknowledging that business forces have often played a role in inhibiting or undermining conditions favorable to peace, just as some forms of trade and economic opportunity may support peace. As the phrase "Peace through Commerce" suggests, this discussion has the normative aim of producing knowledge and contributing to practice that harnesses the mechanisms of commerce to achieve greater peace. Thus, PTC has an aim of realizing some measure of social change through knowledge development and practice that furthers the goal of enduring peace.

These broad social change ambitions are among the many reasons that it is appropriate to consider Peace through Commerce a social movement. The most basic definitions of social movements describe them as collective interests that align in pursuit of social change (Rao et al., 2000). This certainly fits the intent of Peace through Commerce. Moreover, the peace movement is considered a social movement unto itself (Marullo and Meyer, 2004) and corporate social responsibility–another example of using commerce to achieve greater positive social change–has also been characterized as a social movement (Jonker and De Witte, 2006; Sahlin-Andersson, 2006; Waddock, 2009). PTC can be understood as an off-shoot of these more established movements. Additionally, the sheer growth of PTC, which has now held numerous conferences and produced books, journal articles, and journal special issues, demonstrates that PTC has become an increasingly robust movement. Importantly, beyond growing its scholarly dialogue, PTC movement actors have extended the reach of PTC by influencing other entities, such as the largest and most respected business school accrediting body—the AACSB—to offer PTC-themed initiatives (see the AACSB's Peace through Commerce Resource Center). The PTC participant base has become steadily more diverse and now includes scholars from a rich array of disciplines and fields within and outside of academia. Actors from industry as well as the academy now act in coalition to advance the Peace through Commerce agenda. This is important as two groups previously unaware of one another's existence—in one case scholars and in another social entrepreneurs—discovered that the they were both engaged in efforts that they each were calling PTC. Beyond serendipity, this convergence provides some indication that the PTC concept may have broader social salience in that multiple interests have coalesced around this topic. PTC has grown in size, complexity, and momentum. Instead of isolated activities organized by a small number of actors there is now sustained attention to issues of Peace through Commerce promoted by a number of entities.

Timothy Fort and Cindy Schipani are widely credited with instigating the scholarly Peace through Commerce dialogue with academic conferences that began in 2001 though Carolyn Woo, Dean of The Mendoza School of Business at Notre Dame, is credited with coining the term Peace through Commerce. Fort notes that what was perhaps considered a quixotic pursuit by many quickly took on far greater sobriety and sense of purpose when the first PTC conference was held just weeks after the events of September 11th, 2001.

What primarily began as a core group of ethics and legal scholars has broadened to include those from other management disciplines such as marketing, organizational behavior, and strategic management. Increasingly, PTC activity has expanded to include actors from civil society organizations, NGOs, the nonprofit sector, social entrepreneurs, economic development and peace keeping interests within government, members of multilateral organizations, and representatives from industry. In addition to conferences, Peace through Commerce has given rise to books, journal articles, journal special issues, and sessions at the annual conferences of the Academy of Management, The International Association for Business and Society and The Society for Business Ethics. PTC has formed alliances around the concept with the accrediting body of business schools, the AACSB, as well as the Aspen Institute Business and Society Program and the UN Global Compact.

Unbeknownst to the academic PTC community, a somewhat parallel effort was emerging among industry interests. The private sector effort was largely galvanized by a group co-created by the CEO and co-founder of the Whole Foods markets grocery chain, John Mackey. Whole Foods is the largest purveyor of organic and natural foods in the world and is routinely recognized for its commitments to social responsibility and environmental sustainability. In addition to a commitment to social responsibility, Mackey has been well known for his libertarian political stance and strong belief in the potential for markets to serve as forces for social good. Mackey helped catalyze an organization called FLOW (for "Freedom Lights our World"), that sponsors a series of social initiatives including one on Peace through Commerce, in addition to efforts promoting women and entrepreneurship, and a social responsibility-focused effort termed conscious capitalism. These social efforts were largely carried out by the two staff members and leaders of FLOW—Michael Strong, the organization's CEO and co-founder, and Jeff Klein, the Executive Director of the group. Presently Philomena Blees runs these efforts. Given this shared interest in questions about the relationship of peace to commerce, the FLOW leadership joined forces with the academic PTC community and held a joint conference in 2008. Since then the two groups have partnered with the on-line forum Business Fights Poverty to use previous conference as a platform for further global dialogue. The PTC community also collaborated in an on-going on-line forum.

With this background about social movement scholarship generally, and Peace through Commerce specifically, I will now provide some characterization and analysis of PTC. I organize this section around a framework of topics that social movement scholars show to be crucial dimensions of social movements (Davis et al., 1996; McAdam and Scott, 2005) namely: message framing, political opportunity, and mobilization structures.

Peace through Commerce as a Social Movement

Message Framing

A significant strand of social movement scholarship considers the ways in which social movements craft messages to appeal to current or potential adherents. The goals of framing choices are to create a compelling vision that motivates people to participate and move in accordance with the movement or to demobilize those who would hinder the movement's efforts.

Framing is the "signifying work" or "meaning construction" (Benford and Snow, 2000) of social movement actors. The framing activities of social movement organizations and social movement entrepreneurs are referred to as "collective action frames" which are "sets of beliefs and meaning that inspire and legitimate the activities of social movement organizations (SMOs)" (Benford and Snow, 2000, p.614).

Collective action framing differs, in important ways, from the institutional theory notion of institutional logics or the psychological conception of frames as schema. Institutional logics connote a connection not just to understanding but also to action. This is why Scott, quoting Friedland and Alford, defines institutional logics as "practices and symbolic constructions which constitute (a field's) organizing principles and which are available for organizations and individuals to elaborate (Scott, 2003, p. 224)." While it is hoped that social movement framing inspires collective action, framing itself is represented as meaning-making and does not carry an inherent connection to action. Snow and Benford (1988) note that schema are less of a collective construct and more fundamental in their role as mechanisms to allow for interpretation of the world. Collective action frames imply a broader sense of "what is or should be going on." It is assumed, for example, that one's schema of what constitutes a truck is essentially stable or fixed, but a collective action frame might (convincingly or unconvincingly) construe trucks as symbolic of pollution.

Referring to PTC as a social movement is, by way of example, itself a specific framing choice, distinct from calling PTC a scholarly dialogue, a conversation, a community, or an interest group. The choice of framing PTC as a movement has the potential to convey a comparatively more agentic and powerful image of PTC which might attract more adherents, greater strength and support. This is not to suggest that framing alone makes something a social movement, but given that the boundaries of movements are permeable and that social movements embody collective will, the choice to consider something a movement can itself create momentum in this effort. At an even more basic level, communicative acts are social, persuasive processes. Persuasion neither connotes nor justifies dishonesty but a message's recipient will engage in an interpretive process to understanding the message in a frame and social movement organizations can have an ability to influence the resonance of a frame by choices about how a frame is developed and communicated. A common trap for worthy, socially important, causes is to neglect skillful framing based on a belief that if the goals of an endeavor are inherently noble, the goals themselves will carry the day. This is reminiscent of what social researchers Michael Shellenberger and Ted Nordhaus term "literal-sclerosis" (2004) when referring to a tendency of some environmentalists to believe that if people simply had the facts they would act as we would want them to, rather than realizing that how a message is crafted is itself extremely important. Each of the considerations highlighted below should help PTC, and other social movements, more actively consider issues inherent in framing resonant messages.

Multiple Audiences

Certainly any robust movement is likely to have multiple audiences and constituencies. A key consideration for any social movement's framing choices is understanding multiple audiences and crafting messages that are sufficiently resonant to different constituencies, but that also remain faithful enough to a core representation of the movement so as not to seem disingenuous. This is closely akin to the logic of customer segmentation used by marketing scholars. For example, if the architects of PTC came to learn that the social movement frame was appealing to some audiences, such as students and multilateral actors, but more off-putting to other target groups, such as governmental actors or scholars, PTC might invoke a frame of "community" rather than "movement" if such framing choices made PTC more resonant or palatable to a specific audience. These distinctions would need to be handled deftly in order to maintain sufficient common ground among multiple audiences and so as not to appear disingenuous.

Framing implies not just a consideration of whether to enact a given frame, such as that of a social movement, but how to do so. PTC faces several framing "choice points" as does every social movement. PTC has gained considerable traction in bringing together multiple professional audiences, not just academics from a narrow range of scholarly fields. The increased diversity of the participating audience also creates a need to carefully frame the proceedings in ways that are relevant and resonant to an increasingly varied and specialized audience. This not only implies the need to strike some balance between knowledge development and practical application, but also highlights the need for enduring thematic foci within PTC. The most recent PTC conference employed themes such as economic development/poverty alleviation, working in zones of conflict, legal considerations in promoting peace, and matters of certification and measurement. Certainly, finding enduring themes could enable PTC to make an ongoing contribution and develop expertise, action and dialogue among established streams.

Framing Peace

In the case of PTC, many framing choices relate to how peace is represented. An important divide exists among peace studies scholars about negative versus positive conceptions of peace, or peace as the absence of war/conflict versus peace as the presence of certain positive conditions such as supportive relationships, active non-violence, environmental sustainability, etc. (see Galtung, 1996). While we often assume that positive messages have greater capacity to inspire, peace as the absence of conflict and war lends is more easily assessed or measured.

Peace through Commerce might be wise to borrow a page from the tactics of The Institute for Economics and Peace, creators of The Peace Index, which assesses societal levels of peace in 140 countries worldwide using a standardized set of metrics. The Peace Index acknowledges that peace is comprised of positive conditions but also notes that its measures all have to do with the absence of conflict and war. Thus, it measures peace through a "negative" absence of conflict frame, using metrics related to societal safety, security, and militarization, while acknowledging that it should move towards more asset-based "positive" measures over time. Certainly a case could be made that PTC, unlike a project devoted solely to measurement, is the perfect forum for theorizing about positive peace. That may well be the case. The crucial matter is for PTC to see this as a critical choice point or matter worth deciding.

A final critical framing choice is simply how to refer to peace. Peace as a concept often seems more accessible when modified by various verbs. Thus, frames of peace-making, peace-building, and peacekeeping, may prove more tractable than the broader overarching frame of sustainable peace. Clarity about a broad vision of peace is essential, but these more active "doing" terms might provide a means to concretize the PTC agenda. Peace through Commerce also implies a specific directionality and relationship between concepts: that commerce leads to, or yields, peace. While that is certainly a faithful description of much of the movement, it could well be that exploring "Commerce through Peace" would be a useful undertaking to understand what pre-existing peace is necessary to allow for, or foster, commerce. This understanding might be a means to direct social policy and business investment into peace-promoting activity, recognizing that it is often a necessary precursor for stable commerce.

Clarifying Levels Of Analysis

This schism between positive and negative conceptions of peace reminds us that while peace has broad social appeal, clarity about what constitutes peace is much harder to establish. Again, this speaks to the value of PTC clarifying its vision of peace. A related framing choice for PTC pertains to the levels of analysis at which peace is most commonly analyzed within the movement. Peacemaking activities happen at the societal, organizational, interpersonal, and individual levels (Boulding, 1990; Cox, 1986). While a robust social movement might want some requisite variety, exploring peace-building questions at multiple and varied levels of analysis, it would likely be worthwhile to clarify the level at which PTC most commonly explores peace. To date, those in the PTC movement have largely considered peace at societal and organizational levels of analysis. Micro level considerations of peace itself and/or of processes that might support peace, such as interpersonal trust dynamics (Roussin, 2008), have received little attention thus far. It seems intuitively logical that, like Russian dolls nested inside one another, more micro-level, peace-related processes must be imbedded within organizational and societal peace. Yet it would likely be useful for the movement to clarify where it hopes to make its primary contribution such that would-be adherents can better assess the appeal and fit of the PTC undertaking. Alternately, as PTC grows as a movement, it may want to create somewhat distinct opportunities for dialogue based on differing levels of analysis.

Open Source Versus Proprietary Control of the Term "Peace Through Commerce"

Recently, the scholarly PTC movement engaged with a group of private sector interests who had also been thinking about PTC (as was described earlier under PTC background). There has been substantive collaboration between the two groups. This collaboration offers great synergistic potential given the shared interests off all involved in matters of exploring how business and the activity of commerce can foster greater peace. The resources, talents and insights to create a movement are exponentially expanded by this cooperation.

Working in coalition also creates added complexity when it comes to message framing in that the private sector organization, FLOW, has trademarked the term Peace through Commerce. Type "Peace through Commerce" into any internet search engine and the first resource that appears will read "Peace through Commerce®" with the "®," all rights reserved symbol. This creates important framing questions about the value of open source strategies versus those of proprietary control.

The leaders of FLOW have been clear that their intent in protecting the term through trademark is not to narrowly control its meaning but to guard against misuse and to avoid the term becoming anything anyone wants it to mean. Yet, considering PTC as an "owned term" creates a whole series of framing questions and challenges. A potential, or would-be, adherent of PTC would be likely to ask "who owns this term and why" which leads directly to questions about what the agenda of the ownership firm is, what their politics are etc. Not only does this require some due diligence, if an individual is persistent and tries to ascertain the meaning of trademark ownership, their discernment process might go something like this: "is an organization called Freedom Lights our Way a right-wing group? But they fund peace and women's empowerment…so they must be progressive. Oh, they're connected to Whole Foods, that's a socially responsible company, but isn't the CEO of that company a libertarian? Didn't he come out against healthcare reform?" In short, the possible complexity that an adherent might have to navigate if FLOW "owns" PTC seems far greater than if PTC is simply a jointly used umbrella concept that FLOW has jumped on or is helping to lead. FLOW is also affiliated with John Mackey's "conscious capitalism movement," which also uses trademark protection. This seems more justified (though it still may constrain growth but also ensure greater control for the trademark owners) because this effort coined a new term and developed a specific and somewhat propriety concept about what the term means.

Certainly, these are questions that people routinely ask of non-trademarked terms as well. Astute people will try to ascertain what the politics, agendas, and language choices of individuals and groups they encounter are intended to signal. While trademark ownership heightens considerations of proprietary versus open access, all movements face framing contests to varying degrees. Clearly, what delineates the peace movement, the environmental movement, and the women's rights movement, is not uniformly agreed upon, nor do actors in such movements operate in complete consensus or coordination. Thus, one of the challenges of trademark control of the Peace through Commerce term is simply that it invokes whatever meaning we ascribe to the term/concept of "all rights reserved." Not only does this add to the cognitive complexity of what a potential adherent needs to make sense of, it adds to the meaning of PTC whatever is invoked by the concept of "®." While it is possible that the idea of a trademark is value-neutral, or of limited meaning to some, or perhaps conveys a positive sense of careful and deliberate stewardship to others, I suspect that trademark protection has the real potential to make people wary and undermine trust in this context.

The deliberate crafting of framing messages is, of course, inherently somewhat manipulative in that any communication that is crafted with premeditation and strong consideration of audience is designed to provoke certain outcomes. The concern is not that a trademarked term connotes intent to manipulate. Rather, the risk is that the frame that is evoked by the trademark concept/symbol itself will cause people to view PTC with less trust and diminished support. Based on conversations with those who made the decision to trademark the term, I suspect they would say that critically minded people should always exercise caution about placing their trust in ideas and organizations. They might contend that the trademark protection of PTC serves as a reminder that people should carefully consider the meaning, agenda, background of any movement, company, product, or service. If the trademark sets the bar higher, so be it. Yet, this presumes that people will go onto make an assessment of PTC rather than simply dismiss it because it is commercially owned.

While the road not taken is hard to analyze, interested parties could undertake more empirical means to understand how adherents and would-be adherents make sense of, and respond to, the trademark of this term. Emerging norms of communication seem to indicate that fewer and fewer messages can be tightly controlled. Peer-to-peer and consumer-to-consumer communication, blogs, etc. all seem to tilt the balance of message control away from those who might be officially responsible for managing the message or the brand. In many cases firms seem willing and eager to cede some control over the meaning of terms and brands in exchange for greater ownership on the part of consumers. Allowing consumers to create advertising content is one such example.

Therefore I suspect that control of the definition, or meaning, of ideas must largely be won in open source terms. In other words, it would likely be more successful for stewards of a concept to remain vigilant to the concept's wise use, and aim to control its meaning through both the quantity and quality of their use of a term, than to use the channels of regulatory control or ownership. Because the goal is to inspire people to engage and promote peace through commerce at many levels—from the scholar, to the multinational actor, to the entrepreneur—trademark protection carries the risk that PTC will be seen as something owned by one party. While it is possible that trademark protection could result in better stewardship of PTC ideals, it seems more like that this action would make it harder for the broad range of people that the movement hopes to attract to easily identify with the movement if they feel it belongs to others.

Framing choices for an insider movement: While social movement literature tells us that social movements are not the sole dominion of any specific social group, it may be helpful to note that PTC is "an insider movement." On the scholarly side, the primary actors are well known and respected in their fields. The major private sector actor supporting this movement is affiliated with a large, well known, and respected firm in its industry. This basic characterization supports the informal proposition that insider movements are more likely to choose kinder, gentler, framing messages. Outsider movements would be expected to support comparatively radical transformation and dialectical conflict to achieve social change.

While strong social movements often involve alliances of insider and outsider interests, it is worth considering the dominant status of the overall movement in order to invoke frames that are likely to be received as genuine and resonant to would-be adherents. In 1964, the Berkeley Free Speech movement organized a now famous sit-in on the campus of the University of California at Berkeley. Mario Savio, one of the movement's leaders, gave an impassioned speech that has been quoted ever since. He used the imagery of "putting one's body on the gears of the machine" to prevent it from working. The framing choices in Savio's speech contributed to the resonance of that message and the lasting impact of that speech and of the movement from which it emerged and propelled. This speech has come to typify the image of outsider activists rallying at the gates. It stands to reason, however, that framing choices of those with insider status would need to use a different governing logic to be seen as credible, regardless of the change agenda of the movement in question. Thus, while we might associate social movements with fiery rhetoric, because of PTC's insider status and involvement with industry, one would expect resonant framing to adopt a comparatively more subdued tone even if the aims of the movement are profound and far-reaching.

Political Opportunities

Social movement scholar's consideration of political opportunities acknowledges that movements do not operate in isolation from broader social forces. The wider political landscape affects the ability of a social movement to gain momentum or to fail to do so.

As I note in the section entitled "Background on PTC," because PTC efforts coalesced in the wake of the tragic events of Sept. 11th, PTC reminded many management scholars of the imperative of peace, the need to better understand the dynamics of peace, and the importance of doing research that can support positive real-world social change.

Looked at from a similar light, the current economic crisis may be a means to underscore the importance of the PTC agenda. The global recession could help rather than hinder PTC. Such a dramatic economic downturn reminds people far and wide of the importance of economic prosperity and the role of commerce and job creation in society. Even those who have thoughtful critiques of current forms of transnational capitalism acknowledge that the engines of commerce have a critical role to play in social wellbeing for all. Thus, economic crises may have the somewhat counter-intuitive potential to increase social receptivity to the idea of PTC, or perhaps of the necessity of "C" in making "P" possible.

Other global crises may create a dimension of political opportunity for PTC. Despite the devastating tragedies already faced by global warming, with intensified risk pending there is an opportunity for PTC to gain greater recognition and relevance. Issues that have historically been understood as purely environmental concerns are increasingly being understood as security issues as well. PTC might be able to form a bridge to dialogue about matters of sustainability and the environment as they relate to issues of global security and peace.

Just as we have seen how interdependent the world is financially, a new Presidential administration in the United States, that has stated goals of rebuilding relationships and image in the global community, represents an example of a political opportunity that PTC might be able to capitalize upon as an agenda for increased peace and economic prosperity. With a setting President who is a Nobel Peace Prize winner, it is clear that the global community has great peace-making expectations for this President. The award may carry an increased mandate to make good on a peace-promoting agenda.

It is also possible that, during times of economic downturn, vital social supports fray under the dual pressures of increasing need and decreasing resources. In these times socially beneficial activity that also has the potential for economic benefit might serve as a means to bridge these concerns. Infrastructure projects that also have a social dimension might be one such example, such as current government initiatives to create jobs by building playgrounds, or dam and bridge projects that stave off environmental degradation and increased pressure on natural resources. Successful social enterprises that combine a social mission with a commerce agenda, such as businesses that operate with the specific aim of employing the socially disenfranchised, are another example of how socially progressive efforts that include a job creation element might be the key for many to support increased public service activity in dire economic times.

Mobilization Structures

Substantial social movement scholarship has been devoted to the processes, practices, and structures that support movement mobilization. To date, PTC has employed conferences and the publication of academic articles and scholarly books as key means to build the movement and mobilize people who come into contact with these materials. A 2006 conference on PTC at Notre Dame University lead to the publication of an edited collection of on PTC (Williams, 2008), journal special issues on PTC in the American Business Law Journal, The Journal of

Corporate Citizenship, The Vanderbilt Transnational Law Review, a 2010 special issue of the Journal of Business Ethics, all serve as examples that PTC is able to make use of the communication and legitimacy-granting resources of scholarly journals. PTC has proven quite adept at multi-sectoral alliance- building, expanding the resource base of the endeavor by forging partnerships and alliances with allied groups such as the Aspen

Institute Initiative for Social Innovation through Business, The FLOW initiative, The International Institute of Peace through Tourism, the UN Global Compact and the like. The size and scope of conferences and events are growing, showing that these efforts are gathering both increased resources and adherents.

Other efforts PTC might consider, in order to enhance mobilization, would include the following: PTC should consider the establishment of a set of "galvanizing principles," that could attract and focus resources as greater clarity is provided for the direction and aims of the movement. Agreement on vision need not restrict the organization excessively nor limit the organization from expanding with flexibility in the face of new opportunities and challenges. Such principles could be amended over time to factor in political opportunities, in addition to the needs and priorities of those participating in the movement.

The production of scholarly research would also be complemented by more efforts to produce practitioner-focused articles in order to broaden the influence of the move-ment and draw greater support from interested actors outside of academe. Authors David Croteau, William Hoynes, and Charlotte Ryan, contributors to, and editors for, a text on the interaction between academics and social activists (2005) note that while academic social movement actors and social activists would ideally be sources of sup-port and insight to one another, all too often this interaction is characterized by lost potential. Fort and Schipani (2007) also make this case for the need for interaction in detail. While PTC is fortunate to have attracted considerable interest and involvement from practitioners, the majority of emphasis thus far has been on scholarly knowledge production. More industry-focused effort can ensure relevance to practice as can alli-ance-building with historic peace interests. There is also a real potential to mobilize resources by deepening ties and dialogue underway in the corporate social responsibil-ity community. One tangible outcome of this effort might be to see an articulation of peace-promotion as part of social reporting efforts. This can be seen as a mechanism with the long-range aim of causing businesses to construe peace-making as a "hyper-goal" of commerce (see Fort and Schipani, 2004). PTC has begun experimenting with efforts focused on specifics industries, such as tourism. This targeted approach might be another means to mobilize resources by specializing dialogues to appeal to specific scholarly and professional communities.

Legitimacy-Building

Thus far, PTC has fostered partnerships, held repeated conferences and engaged in scholarly writing. The alliances that the movement has built with other respected entities, such as the AACSB or Aspen Institute, further the movement's reach and its legitimacy. The involvement of esteemed and visible scholars, members of industry, gov-ernment and the social sectors all serve to increase legitimacy because of the diverse coalition that comprises the movement and the reputation of those at the forefront of the movement. All of these practices have helped to ensure the continued availability of resources largely through building legitimacy for the movement. Legitimacy-building and resource mobilization can rightly be thought of as mutually reinforcing dynamics.

PTC could now focus on matters of depth and breadth. It could both broaden and deepen the alliances it has. It should also deepen its foundation through more empirical scholarship. Continued learning, to upgrade the quality of understanding about how to foster peace and what role commerce can play, is the fundamental means to gain legitimacy and mobilize resources. A movement cannot stand on the quality of its insights alone. Yet, without high quality, empirically grounded, theoretically robust, understanding little else matters.

Conclusion

In this essay I consider the burgeoning PTC movement in light of key social movement dimensions of message framing, political opportunity, and resource mobilization to increase the likelihood that those involved in PTC devote greater attention to such matters and that other academic social movements or movements that interact with academia consider these important dimensions. These key areas of social movement scholarship provide considerations that any nascent movement ought to attend to.

Throughout this writing I have concentrated almost exclusively on movement dynamics, but in closing I want to devote a bit more thought to the "social" in social movement. It is my hope that making the case to consider PTC as a social movement will remind us that social movements are indeed inherently social processes. In addition to PTC as a "movement of ideas," like any movement, it is a highly relational process. Attention to the relational aspects of movement building would, ideally, not be seen as a distraction, or secondary part of the agenda, but as integral to the success of PTC. An easy illustration of this idea is evident in conference design. Providing adequate time for social interaction and relationship building ceases to be a matter of secondary importance—with content-knowledge as the primary agenda—when one thinks in movement terms. Attending to the relational elements of movement building need not come at the expense of PTC content. Indeed, one of the aims of PTC could easily be to consistently upgrade our theories and ideas about change and commerce-based means to foster peace. This shared organizational learning can improve the quality of analyses and practices while simultaneously serving as a means to strengthen ties among adherents.

In the eighth and most recent Peace through Commerce conference, a session was held "in the round" for all participants to address the core principles of PTC and to discuss the interests, actions, and methods to advance the PTC agenda. This was a clear example of group learning combined with community building. It would certainly strengthen the movement to continue such practices.

My hope is that this essay will provoke dialogue among PTC actors that contributes to the vitality and success of PTC. This writing can also benefit readers who are engaged in social change efforts other than PTC by causing them to consider analogous issues in their endeavors. For those engaged in social movement scholarship, this work may provide case specifics that will prove useful to you or inspire you to consider academic settings as contexts for developing or testing theory about social movements.

REFERENCES

Benford, D. and D. Snow: 2000, 'Framing Processes and Social Movements: An Overview and Assessment', Annual Review of Sociology 26, 611–639.

Boulding, E.: 1990, Building a Global Civic Culture (Syracuse University Press, Sycracuse, New York).

Cox, G.: 1986, *The Ways of Peace: A Philosophy of Peace as Action* (Paulist Press, Mahway, New Jersey). Croteau, D., W. Hoynes and C. Ryan (eds.): 2005, Rhyming Hope and History: Activists, Academics and Social Movement Scholarship (University of Minnesota Press, Minneapolis, Minnesota).

Davis, G., D. McAdam, J. McCarthy and M. Zald (eds.): 1996, *Comparative Perspectives on Social Movements: Political Opportunities, Mobilizing Structures, and Cultural Framings* (Cambridge University Press, Cambridge).

Fort, T. and C. Schipani: 2004, *The Role of Businesses in Fostering Peaceful Societies* (Cambridge University Press, Cambridge, United Kingdom).

Fort, T. and C. Schipani: 2007, 'The Role of Business in Fostering Peaceful Societies: An Action Plan', American Business Law Journal 44, 359–377.

Galtung, J.: 1996, *Peace by Peaceful Means: Peace and Conflict, Development and Civilization* (Sage Publications, Thousand Oaks, California).

Gould, S. J.: 1981, *The Mismeasure of Man* (W.W. Norton and Company, New York, NY).

Hambrick, D. and M.J. Chen: 2008, 'New Academic Fields as Admittance-Seeking Social Movements: The Case of Strategic Management', Academy of Management Review 33(1), 32–54.

Lavine, M.: 2010, 'From Scholarly Dialogue to Social Movement: Considerations and Implications for Peace through Commerce', Journal of Business Ethics 89(4), 603–614.

Marullo, S. and D. Meyer: 2004, 'Antiwar and Peace Movements', in D. Snow, S. Soule and K Hanspeter (eds.), The Blackwell Companion to Social Movements (Blackwell Publishing, Malden, Massachusetts).

McAdam, D. and W.R. Scott: 2005, 'Organizations and Movements', in G. Davis, D. McAdam, W.R. Scott and M. Zald (eds.), In Social Movements and OrganizationalTheory (Cambridge University Press, Cambridge), pp. 4–40.

Rao, H., C. Morrill and M. Zald: 2000, 'Power Plays: How Social Movements and Collective Action Create New Organizational Forms', Research in Organizational Behaviour. 22, 237–281.

Roussin, C.: 2008, 'Increasing Trust, Psychological Safety, and Team Performance Through Dyadic Leadership Discovery', Small Group Research 39(2), 224–248.

Sahlin-Andersson, K.: 2006, 'Corporate Social Responsibility: A Trend and a Movement, but of What and for What?', Corporate Governance 6(5), 595–608.

Scott, W.R.: 2003, *Organizations: Rational, Natural, and Open Systems*, 5th Edition (Prentice Hall, Upper Saddle River, New Jersey).

Shellenberger, M. and T. Nordhaus: 2004, *The Death of Environmentalism: Global Warming in a Post Environmental World* (Copyright of the Authors 2004).

Snow, D. and D. Benford: 1988, 'Ideology, Frame Resonance, and Participant Mobilization', International Social Movement Research 1, 197–217.

Strang, D. and D. Il-Jung: 2005, 'Organizational Change as an Orchestrated Social Movement: Recruitment to a Corporate Quality Initiative', in G. Davis, D. McAdam,

W. R. Scott and M. Zald (eds.), *In Social Movements and Organizational Theory* (Cambridge University Press, Cambridge).

Waddock, S.: 2009, 'Making a Difference? Corporate Responsibility as a Social Movement', The Journal of Corporate Citizenship 33, 35–46.

Williams, O. (ed.): 2008, *Peace through Commerce: Responsible Corporate Citizenship and the Ideals of the United Nations Global Compact* (Notre Dame University Press, South Bend, Indiana).

Zald, M. and J.D. McCarthy: 1987, *Social Movements in an Organizational Society* (Transaction Books, New Brunswick, New Jersey).

Zald, M.N., C. Morrill and H. Rao: 2005, 'The Impact of Social Movements on Organizations: Environment and Responses', in G. Davis, D. McAdam, W.R. Scott and M. Zald (eds.), *In Social Movements and Organizational Theory* (Cambridge University Press, Cambridge), pp. 25

Appendix

THIS APPENDIX provides four excellent student papers to demonstrate the application of the decision-making process and culture-building dimensions discussed throughout the text. I am grateful to my former students for their permission in allowing these to be reprinted. You will notice that you have seen a few of them, either in paper excerpts or as modified case studies in the text.

These papers are meant to illustrate a well-constructed research paper from materials publicly available rather than making a definitive assessment of the situation.

SCHOOL OF BUSINESS MBAD 6281—BUSINESS ETHICS
Ethics in Business: The Nestlé Boycott

Gregory A. Harold, Mary Anne Fombu, Sumon Roy

May 20, 2013

Introduction and Background

The innocence of a baby represents an idealistic goodness in our world. There is so little known about the true development of babies' minds, what they may understand, or what they may be trying to communicate. Nonetheless, this does not discourage adults— we still find significant happiness as we try to identify various characteristics in a baby, including their imaginative curiosity, the purity of their emotions, and an enviable freedom to lead a carefree life. Perhaps one of the most earnest wishes is to welcome a fully healthy newborn into the family. Hardship upon children is difficult to fathom, and parents strive to take every measure possible to protect their young ones and preserve their innocence. The most unfortunate individuals who have experienced the extreme, incomprehensible grief of losing a child acknowledge unconditionally there is nothing more devastating. The grievous tragedy of Newtown, Connecticut, comes to mind. We live with the hope that mankind represents a certain decency, where we would not wish such pain upon even our worst enemies. Therefore, when an issue arises concerning the health of infants and children, whether it is domestic violence, the right to bear arms, or products that may be dangerous, we hope the best decisions are made to protect our children.

The 1970s saw one such issue sparked by several articles explode into a global boycott that has now spanned 40 years and counting. In 1973, a British reporter interviewed two tropical medicine experts who believed that the aggressive marketing of infant formula was contributing to infant health issues, particularly related to gastroenteritis and diarrheal disease (UNICEF, 2012). Perhaps more incriminating than the article itself was the magazine cover (Figure 1), which showed a tin of milk powder and a feeding bottle above a baby's grave (Internationalist, 1973). The caption read, "A tin of milk powder and a feeding bottle lie on a baby's grave in Zambia —placed there by the mother as symbols of her child's short life. In fact, the use of these items was one of the main causes of the child's death. The Baby Food Tragedy." The war against infant formula was just beginning. Less than a year later in 1974, a South African journalist published an article entitled "War on Want —The Baby Killer" (Figure 2) (Want, 1974). The author notes that the "object of this report is not to prove that baby milks kill babies," and that "in optimum conditions, with proper preparation and hygiene, they can be a perfectly adequate infant food." However, extremely damaging comments are littered throughout the article such as, "Third World babies are dying because their mothers bottle feed them with western style infant milk." The author continues, "In the squalor and poverty of the new cities of Africa, Asia and Latin America the decision [to switch to infant formula rather than breast milk] is often fatal" (Want, 1974).

It was only a matter of time before the general distaste became personal. In the same year "The Baby Killer" was published, another article was released entitled "Nestlé Kills Babies" (Moorhead, 2007). It was not entirely surprising to target Nestlé, since the corporate giant then accounted for nearly half of the $1 billion market in infant formula. They were prepared for legal warfare, promptly suing the authors on the grounds of libel. While the legal battle ensued, in 1975, an anti-Nestlé movie was produced, "Bottle Babies," which slammed Nestlé as a corporation manipulating their aggressive marketing strategies into less developed countries simply to maximize sales, without any consideration for the society (Lorber, 1982). In fact, the film presented Nestlé as the primary cause of infant malnutrition and even mortality. Even through such negative publicity, Nestlé managed to win the case against the authors of "Nestlé Kills Babies" in 1976 (Sethi, 1994). However, the judge strongly encouraged Nestlé to highly consider revising their marketing strategies if they wished to avoid accusations of unethical practices. These warnings were viewed as a victory for the anti-Nestlé campaign (TIME, 1976).

The following year witnessed the official initiation of the Nestlé boycott, based in the United States, on the premise of Nestlé's controversial marketing of infant formula, which allegedly contributed to the deteriorated health of infants and caused fatalities. In June of 1977, the Infant Formula Action Coalition (INFACT) was founded, headquartered at the University of Minnesota (Winsted, n.d.). The fundamental concepts underlying the boycott are both practical and medical (IBFAN, n.d.). Among the primary concerns is the availability of clean water, which is necessary to properly mix the formula before feeding. In third world countries, clean water is often difficult to obtain. Contaminated water significantly increases the likelihood of disease in infants, who are not yet in possession of a fully matured immune system. In addition, several allegations have been made that numerous Nestlé products have not been marketed in languages that are comprehensible to the local community. This includes infant formula containers, which contain essential information such as the importance of hygiene. In other cases, even if mothers are able to understand the instructions, they may not have the means to implement the sanitary standards necessary. Due to financial hardship, some mothers use less than the proper proportion of formula powder than recommended to obtain more feedings from a given container. This understandably, and sadly, contributes to notable malnutrition in infants.

Medical recommendations in the 1970s to current day tout the importance of breast milk as the only source of nutrition for at least the first six months, as supported by the World Health Organization (WHO, 2013) and the American Medical Association (Nemours, 2013). A lengthy discussion of the medical benefits of breast milk over infant formula is beyond the scope of this report; however, it is important to note that several nutrients, vitamins, and antibodies are able to cross from mother to child through breast milk that are not components of infant formula. These essential biological factors provide the infant with sufficient and appropriate nutrition while also expediting the development of the immune system for protection against various diseases.

The allegations against Nestlé enter murkier waters, as multiple anti-Nestlé campaign groups have leveled accusations of unethical marketing. This includes promoting infant formula as a better alternative than breast milk, which is questionable at best. Further damaging accusations included bribing medical professionals to encourage infant formula usage, providing free samples to mothers that are no longer free after leaving the hospital, and employing advertising techniques implying their products are endorsed by the health care system (IBFAN, n.d.). Although Nestlé has denied most of these allegations, the Nestlé boycott has now spanned over four decades, and stands strong still today. Since the initiation in the 1970s, the 1980s saw significant progress with the introduction of the International Code of Marketing of Breast-milk Substitutes (henceforth, the Code), which banned promotion of breast milk substitutes. The 1990s witnessed Nestlé losing a case due to their inability to support their own claim of marketing infant formula ethically and responsibly. The turn of the century has seen the boycott gain strength, even though Nestlé currently claims complete compliance with the Code. Today, over 60 countries now have laws implementing the Code. In Europe, Nestlé's home continent, hundreds of universities, colleges, schools, businesses, faith groups, health groups, trade unions, and celebrities support the Nestlé boycott (IBFAN, n.d.). Nestlé currently claims to carry out annual performance evaluations and inspections to maintain the standards of the Code. The corporation also continues to claim many of the original allegations against them are unsubstantiated.

The welfare of innocent children is paramount to the success of the human race. The Nestlé boycott raises significant concerns about infant health. The ensuing discussion addresses this complex moral issue, and whether Nestlé has handled it well. Hosmer's six-step moral reasoning process will be applied to define the moral issues, identify additional facts that would be helpful to analyze the case, propose alternative approaches to handling the case, assess the personal impacts on the decision makers themselves, analyze the issues using the three ethical frameworks, and conclude with our own moral perspectives.

The Moral Dilemma

The Nestlé Company is a household name by any standard. Producing products that impact and ease our daily lives is synonymous with the multitude of products with the Nestlé brand since its inception in 1866. For the last 150 years, Nestlé has indeed performed with a strong recipe for success. Producing scores of consumables with individual sales in excess of $1 billion is a testament to the company's impact and reach into our society. Ordinary items such as ice cream, pet food, cosmetics, frozen meals, coffee, and candy bars are seemingly harmless products, but one calculated misstep by Nestlé proved to be the formula for disaster for an entire continent while also negatively impacting Nestlé worldwide.

Nestlé began its campaign of self-tarnish when it decided to aggressively market ready to mix infant formula on the African continent. The casual observer may ponder why marketing and providing a nutritious breast milk supplement is unethical. In this case, Nestlé appeared to be providing a means for new and working mothers to enhance the nourishment they give to their newborns in a healthy and supposedly cost effective manner. Furthermore, the intent was to decrease the impact of disease and sickness from the lack of proper nutritious food. To understand the harm and damage that occurred to one of the most vulnerable groups to mankind, infants, one must have a more thorough and complete understanding of the socio-economic factors such as education, income, personal hygiene, access to health care, and the ability to acquire the basic subsistence of food and clean water.

Shortly after Nestlé began to "formulize" developing countries in Africa, a noticeable increase in infant deaths was observed. The cause is believed to be the mixing of baby formula with contaminated drinking water (Sethi, 1994). Infant mortality is a travesty under any circumstance; however, when a "luxury" product is introduced into an impoverished market that potentially stifles a mother's ability to produce breast milk, an ethical and moral problem manifests itself. While the object of infant formula was to combat malnutrition, its introduction effectively created an inverse relationship resulting from the mothers' inability to fully understand usage directions and the tendency to reduce the formula to water mixing ratio due to inadequate monetary means. Essentially, new mothers were inadvertently starving their children of nutrition as a result of discontinuing a breast-feeding regimen in favor of infant formula.

Additional moral and ethical considerations should be evaluated with relation to Nestlé's aggressive marketing tactics upon entry into the marketplace: product placement within maternity hospitals and clinics, subsidizing medical conferences and junkets to physicians with direct access to expectant mothers, the use of commission based "milk nurses" to provide personal sales service, and offering "education" espousing the benefits of ready to mix infant formula. Nestlé's moral and ethical problems were exacerbated as they continued to skirt regulations and standards established by the World Health Organization and The International Code of Marketing of Breast-milk Substitutes.

Additional Facts for Evaluation

It is certainly fair to hypothesize that the inflicted harm was an unintended consequence of Nestlé looking to expand the market for its infant formula. However, the firm negatively impacted the society, perhaps due to a lack of full understanding of the socio-economic factors in this community. To properly evaluate and analyze Nestlé's actions of introducing and aggressively marketing breast milk substitutes, we must try to obtain a clearer picture surrounding the marketing strategy, its implementation, the resulting ramifications, and ultimately the global reaction.

Nestlé is an enormous multinational company. Quite frankly, prior to conducting this research, we were unaware Nestlé operated with such great magnitude. That being said, it is in our estimation that large corporations sometimes fail to recognize the micro impact of their products. The purpose of this section is not to justify and defend the actions of Nestlé, but it seems apparent that Nestlé management did not evaluate the availability and sustainability of a clean water source. While clean drinking water is taken for granted in developed nations, it is a more precious commodity for residents of developing countries. Nestlé, a Swiss company, hailing from a highly developed nation comprised of government structure, laws, social programs and educational institutions, should be aware of the lack of controls and structure when entering into developing countries. In such places, basic necessities may be difficult to obtain, such as treated water, sewage control, reliable electricity, running water, and dependable protections from an established government. Did Nestlé fully understand the marketplace in which they were contemplating entry? Evidently the financial assessments were complete. However, the social and health implications appear to have been focused only on the product that they were introducing. Did Nestlé study factors such as local language? What percent of households has clean water? What is the average number of children per family? What percent of children are breast-fed? What percent of mothers are capable of breast-feeding? What are the infant malnutrition and mortality rates? Have these rates changed over the last few decades? When a corporation is dealing with a country, government, or people that are not bound by laws to reasonably protect and regulate, a company must exhibit a certain level of responsibility. The authors of this paper would also like to understand why this company resisted attempts of outside regulation from Non Governmental Organizations and even failed to self-regulate their marketing content and activities when they were identified as being negligent to the normal and fully accepted conventions of breast feeding.

Additional Alternatives

There are other alternative approaches to addressing the accusations regarding Nestlé's controversial marketing. We must assess the various factors in play that contribute to the risks in this community. These include significant poverty, illiteracy, minimal clean drinking water and malnutrition. These issues, when combined with the misrepresentation of baby formula as a replacement for breast milk only exacerbate the current problems faced by this community. Therefore, the most ethical, non-negligent, and responsible decision as a business that cares about the wellbeing of its customers would be to stop selling the products. This extreme alternative approach involves completely removing corporate operations and marketing in the countries with a vulnerable populace. This is a drastic measure, but would offer long-term benefit to mothers and children in the developing nations.

Another potential alternative response for Nestlé would be to continue its sales of baby formula with limited market presence. While practicing this, there should be strict compliance with the WHO code and all regulations pertaining to marketing infant formula. This policy would require the banning of "milk nurses," an aggressive anti-bribery campaign against hospitals or doctors, a full explanation of the primacy and significance of breast-feeding, and addressing the need of the formula typically in only medically necessary cases or after the recommended breastfeeding period. Perhaps more importantly, continuation in this market should include programs that would assist mothers and their babies. Examples include water filtration projects, bottle replacement programs, poverty reduction efforts and basic literacy classes. By immersing itself in the community as a whole, Nestlé may better understand the true problems that exist. In turn, the vulnerable populace will gain trust in Nestlé operations and products. Either basic literacy classes or translational services would help ensure proper understanding of labels. This provides a sense of confidence and responsibility if the mother chooses to use the formula. Involvement in enhancing the lives of the mothers and their children shows that the sole interest of this business is not profitability alone. Since the issues here involve an array of other factors, it may be in Nestlé's best interest to help resolve the core problems in order to create a community that is more knowledgeable and stable.

Personal Impacts on the Decision Maker

The presented alternatives would both have an impact on the perception of Nestlé as a company. A decision to withdraw completely may have dramatic consequences on Nestlé. It is our recommendation that Nestlé should withdraw completely, but to do so slowly and diligently. In the process of removing itself from the market, Nestlé should start offering educational resources for those that would still require formula due to medical conditions, or for those who voluntarily want to use formula after six months. It would also be defined as a moral decision as it takes into consideration rights of the mothers and seeks to protect them from any potential harm. This action shows adherence to values of Nestlé and in accordance with the duties and responsibilities of a business. Just as Nestlé has a duty to meet the needs of its stakeholders, there is also a responsibility to the community, which is to not misinform or abuse vulnerability.

It is important for a company to identify the significant needs of the community it is serving. As a company withdrawing from a market, there likely may be decreased profits because of its mass presence in Africa. However, such a decision would offer peace and harmony for the decision maker. This will eliminate over 30 years of accusations of Nestlé's role in infant malnutrition and mortality in Africa. Its presence in Africa or in any other vulnerable communities has already received significant negative publicity, and it may reflect better on Nestlé if they were to leave this market. This decision would offer the most ethical route, bringing out the humane aspects of the stakeholders and the decision maker.

Trust Frameworks

Having presented various aspects of the Nestlé boycott, the discussion now turns more analytical, where the trust frameworks will be applied to assess the goodness of Nestlé's actions. The three trust frameworks are Hard Trust, Real Trust, and Good Trust, which are intricately associated with shareholder theory, stakeholder theory, and virtue theory, respectively. As may be expected, these different analytical perspectives do not necessarily agree at all levels.

Shareholder Theory

We begin with shareholder theory, the foundation of which is that the primary focus of managers and corporations is to maximize profit for the shareholders and benefit the organization overall. Importantly, depending on a given initiative, this may entail sacrificing even the good of the general populace. To better understand such circumstances, a historical perspective is presented using the landmark case of Dodge v Ford. In this early 20th century case, Henry Ford appealed to improve performance of his company by increasing the number of production plants and therefore the number of employees, while in turn reducing the overall production cost of his vehicles. Ford noted that his plan would benefit society by reducing unemployment rates and improving the overall economy. The caveat was that he would use much of the profits obtained through his business to execute his plan for expansion. The pressure mounted when he acknowledged that the effects of his plan on the shareholders were not his primary priority. Although Ford himself was the majority shareholder, the others were not pleased about missing out on extra revenue.

The legal decision was a ruling against Ford. It was determined that Ford's primary responsibility was required to be maximizing the profit of his shareholders, over his interests in expanding the company and theoretically improving economy and benefiting society. More specifically, the "Court held that a business corporation is organized primarily for the profit of the stockholders, as opposed to the community or its employees. The discretion of the directors is to be exercised in the choice of means to attain that end, and does not extend to the reduction of profits or the non-distribution of profits among stockholders in order to benefit the public, making the profits of the stockholders incidental thereto" (Wiki, 2013). This fundamental basis of shareholder theory can be applied to support Nestlé's determination in maximizing profit for the corporation. At least superficially, it appears Nestlé is willing to take drastic measures to boost profits for shareholders and benefit their organization overall. Of course, this raises significant concerns about the morality of their advertising techniques, but with respect to shareholder theory alone, Nestlé's actions may appear at least somewhat acceptable. However, it is clear that these marketing strategies do appear to have a specific negative impact on certain communities. In comparison, the ruling in Dodge v. Ford plans did not necessarily adversely affect the community. Opportunities may have been lost, but this is not specific detrimental effect. The courts simply overruled Ford's notion of helping the society because shareholders were losing out. Over the last century, though, it has become better understood that shareholder theory is certainly not restricted to financial obligations. Benefiting society is of course acceptable, and often even expected.

Hard Trust

A deeper understanding of shareholder theory requires exploring lawful directives, which are crucial in defining the essence of Hard Trust. Dr. Timothy Fort, Professor at George Washington University and author of "Business, Integrity, and Peace," emphasizes that the primary purpose of an organization is not simply to maximize profits for shareholders, but more specifically to "carry out the lawful directives of shareholders" (Fort, 2007). Adherence to shareholder theory is generally considered one such directive, and in order to follow appropriately, corporations need to maintain their duties of loyalty and care. Falling short on these expectations can jeopardize the reliability of an organization. For example, Nestlé's alleged actions such as bribery raise significant concern about the organization's adherence to Hard Trust.

Delving deeper into Hard Trust, we understand that a society develops a sense of trustworthiness upon an organization if they improve their reputation by following rules and regulations. A corporation needs to maintain a certain level of integrity by upholding their own standards and "due diligence" through the Sentencing Guidelines. Dr. Fort reminds us that an organization is responsible for any criminal actions of its members with the intention of benefitting the organization itself (Fort, 2007). Initially, the Guidelines were designed to protect against such actions, retain power from individuals believed more susceptible to such actions, and to maintain procedures to handle violations of organizational policies. Within the next 10 years, further modifications were made to the Guidelines, specifically to establish procedures to build the cultural environment within a corporation by developing "compliance and ethics programs."

The primary goal of this new amendment was to identify acceptable ethical corporate culture in addition to adherence to corporate laws.

In the Nestlé case, several accusations have been made that Nestlé violated their ethical obligations. For example, Nestlé has allegedly advertised infant formula through regular items such as calendars and stickers used at hospitals. Patients at the hospital therefore were given a skewed perspective that the hospitals were supporting the infant formula. Nestlé distributed free samples of infant formula to mothers. Accusers note that even trying infant formula disrupts the breast feeding cycle, making mothers more likely to need more infant formula —which would no longer be free. These actions called into question Nestlé's corporate ethics, fueling the boycott's strength as the public started to lose Hard Trust in Nestlé. More severe allegations included hiring nurses to make personal house calls to pregnant women advocating the Nestlé infant formula. When this news was reported in 1997, Nestlé responded by threatening to withdraw their advertising contract from that television station. Hard Trust was further called into question with the multiple allegations of bribery. For example, in 1993, Nestlé organized a promotional "conference" on a cruise liner for Brazilian pediatricians. All of the allegations discussed here would be violations of the aforementioned Code.

The inability to follow lawful directives even outside the company such as the Code creates a tainted public image. In addition, Nestlé executives have appeared aloof regarding most allegations, which raises significant concern about their compliance with corporate ethical programs. These concerns are furthered when considering the primary issue of the case —the allegation that Nestlé's marketing has caused infant fatalities due to their lack of concern regarding the availability of clean water and labeling in appropriate languages. Dr. Fort emphasizes that the primary purpose of Hard Trust is to establish and enforce rules for organizations, and for a given corporation to show responsibility and accountability for their actions (Fort, 2007). Hard Trust allows the public society to develop certain reliability on a corporation. Given Nestlé's allegations, it is therefore not surprising that the boycott still continues to gain strength four decades later.

Stakeholder Theory

With the foundations of Hard Trust in place, we now allow the discussion to continue in a slightly different angle. Having understood the importance of public trust in corporations, we must also address the reliability and necessity of trust itself, which is identified as Real Trust. Most specifically, Dr. Fort defines Real Trust as the essence of trust: "people living up to the promises they made, being honest, producing products and services that are of high enough quality to satisfy customers, and rewarding people for doing the things the company says are important" (Fort, 2007). These important interactions require trust among all parties involved in the company and its products, including the end users. Taken together, these parties are identified as stakeholders, and thus the concepts associated with Real Trust require a discussion of stakeholder theory.

Stakeholder theory is composed of three primary concepts —Individual Rights, Justice and Utilitarianism. First, we introduce an understanding of how a stakeholder is defined. A stakeholder is very broad term used to identify an individual, organization, or community that has an established claim or interest in the output of a particular firm. This claim of interest can, and often does, extend beyond any physical product or service that an industry or organization provides to stakeholders. Financial creditors, suppliers of natural resources, government and non-government organizations, secondary and tertiary support services and even the common employee, their beneficiaries, and the end consumer are defined as stakeholders. Returning now to stakeholder theory, in practice, the Nestlé case presents unique "point and counterpoint" positions on the three elements. We will address each independently.

Individual Rights

This principle of ethics relies upon the foundation that everybody in a society is entitled to certain rights. These rights are classified as either positive or negative. Negative rights ask if there are any laws or restrictions that prevent one from performing a particular task. Conversely, a governing body grants positive rights. Positive rights allow a person or entity to perform a task by virtue of permission. Nestlé's actions are an example of a corporation exercising under the Negative Rights Theory. Prior to Nestlé entering into the seemingly unregulated African infant formula market, there did not appear to be any restrictions or governance on conducting this type of business. Multinational firms such as Nestlé might utilize this theory as a means of justifying their actions in introducing First world products into Third world countries. Although the systems of guaranteeing purity in mixing infant formula were severely lacking, this theory allows for the choice to be made by the end consumer due to the lack of the company operating under a Positive Rights structure. This position might be correct in its purest form; however, when considering an entire organization, it must be held to a different standard especially when dealing with a vulnerable segment of society, which is a significant issue in Third world countries. A company cannot responsibly or ethically enter into a market and introduce a product that could harm society.

Utilitarianism

Utilitarianism offers the ethical concept that we must strive for the greatest good for the largest number of people. Under this ethical standard, certain individual rights are often sacrificed for the protection of the masses. Nestlé's utilitarian position can be justified because from their corporate standpoint, they are attempting to create a "higher good" by introducing a product that offers a more stable and regular means of nourishment to an impoverished and malnourished community. Providing a ready-to-mix formula allows new mothers the opportunity to continue working or support the family via alternative means without the stress and time constraints of a breast-feeding schedule. Initially, a small percentage may suffer via sickness or death as educational systems and instructions are distributed and more widely understood and accepted. Unfortunately, under this guise, the rights of the few that are being compromised are exactly the same individuals who are supposed to benefit from this program in the first place. In this case, this collective group does not have a large enough voice or the means to adequately protect their rights.

Distributive Justice

The ethical principle of distributive justice is likely the most complex and can be the most controversial. This principle states that ethical theories should prescribe actions that are fair to those being impacted. However, extenuating circumstances may be the means to accept a different decision or outcome. In business applications, distributive justice is basically a risk vs. reward theory—the more risk associated with decisions, the higher the potential reward. This is a widely accepted form of inequality. The distributive justice theory is not entirely evident in the Nestlé case. There are extensive risks associated with entering the market of an underdeveloped country, as was seen in this case study, but the reward mechanism as a percentage of company profit was likely less than that observed in more developed nations.

As the three concepts of Stakeholder Theory were explained and discussed in detail, an additional associated concept will now be discussed. Just as Shareholder Theory was linked to the related concept of Hard Trust, Stakeholder theory also presents an element of trust. This trust is aptly called Real Trust. "Real Trust is about people living up to the promises they made, being honest, producing products and services that are of high enough quality to satisfy customers, and rewarding people for doing the things the company says are important" (Fort, 2007). Real Trust is a very important element in the business sense, in that established laws are not always present, or the laws are either inadequate or unfairly interpreted on certain segments of society. In the Nestlé example, Real Trust is violated by both the company's action of improperly marketing a product that was not suitable for the given social and economic environment, and by their inaction of failing to respond properly in the face of adversity. "Real Trust works within the framework of business to make businesses into organizations in which the public can have confidence" (Fort, 2007). Unfortunately, Nestlé failed to deliver, and as such created an environment of mistrust and bad-will, which has contributed significantly to spurring on a decades-long boycott.

Perhaps Nestlé had a well-developed ethics compliance program that could have identified and corrected its actions in a manner to prevent additional harm to many stakeholders, and allow criticism from government and non-government organizations alike. As we have learned, conducting business involves far more thought and consideration than simply introducing a product to a new market. There is a vast amount of interest as it relates to legalities or lack thereof, ensuring that the expansion of individual rights to "choose" will not have unintended consequences, ensuring that the "utility" does not target or unduly impact a vulnerable segment of society, and while elements of distributive justice were not directly present in the Nestlé case, companies must ensure that these practices are fairly and equally exercised.

Virtue Theory

At this juncture, we have now addressed the importance of having trust in an organization, and among one another. However, both of these aspects are somewhat structured by laws, in the case of Hard Trust, and expectations, in the case of Real Trust. This is not to take anything away from these two trust frameworks; in fact, they are essential for successful corporate activity. There is, however, one last critical factor, which significantly helps identify a given organization as trustworthy. This factor is known as Good Trust, which essentially identifies organizations as actually wanting to be trusted, valued, and simply liked. Society is not infatuated with the corporation's financial portfolio; we are typically far more pleased when employees at local businesses recognize and greet us. We feel more involved in these circumstances, and we feel that the corporation actually cares about our collective well being. This Good Trust is based on various virtues, which society seeks (often subconsciously) in a business. A discussion of critical virtues and virtue theory follows.

Virtue theory is an approach that focuses on the core motivation or reasoning behind our actions. Each of us matures in a family and social environment that cultivates certain virtues, which we generally hold throughout our lives and maintain with consistent usage. These actions then become habits that we as individuals should strive to exercise when making all moral decisions (London Oratory, n.d.). Our moral virtues stream from the practice of good habits. Therefore, it is important to maintain our virtues through active participation in everyday actions to instill these values. A virtuous person is one who naturally does good things and consistently pursues the right actions with the appropriate motives or virtues.

Virtue theory originates from the normative foundations. The normative foundations are thoughts or considerations on how one "ought" to act. Aristotle defined virtues as good habits that are learned (London Oratory, n.d.). The sole purpose of virtues is the development of a good character. He expressed that most virtues are an average between two character traits. For instance, for those that find themselves spending excessively, "generosity" would be the mean between wastefulness and stinginess. In this case, generosity would be associated with a good character (Smith, 2011). The virtues practiced by individuals quite naturally influence the choices he or she makes in life.

The rationale supporting decisions made by an agent is characterized by the virtues he or she holds. Virtues are "attitudes, dispositions or character traits that enable us to be, and to act in ways that develop this potential" (London Oratory, n.d.). In business, virtues are the principles that guide our ethical behavior. There are countless virtues that help define today's world. For this discussion, we will limit our analysis to integrity, honesty, accountability, compassion/empathy, open-minded/tolerance and dependability. These virtues are developed through observational learning or life experiences. In developing these characteristics in business, one would seek the development of these virtues in the surrounding environment. But the motivation to want to develop a virtuous community is what actually leads one to take action.

As was stated above, we understand that a society develops a sense of trustworthiness upon an organization if they improve their reputation by following rules and regulations —this is Hard Trust. Additionally, we previously defined Real Trust as the essence of "people living up to the promises they made, being honest, producing products and services that are of high enough quality to satisfy customers, and rewarding people for doing the things the company says are important" (Fort, 2007). Now, in addressing deeper moral and ethical principles, we address the final trust framework, Good Trust.

Good Trust

Dr. Fort defines "Good Trust" as "the motivation to care about doing good" (Fort, 2007). This desire to do good is influenced by the virtues that we already hold and the values appreciated in the community around us. The values held by an individual, if defined as good, would lead to an expressed behavior in accordance with the values held. In essence, our habitual core value is the underlying motivation to want to do good. In order for a business to employ individuals who practice "Good Trust" they would have to strongly define the meaning of "self" and "good" while educating them on the ethical reasoning underlying company policies. It can be reasonably expected that employees may likely possess some degree of self-interest, but "self-interest is dependent on sacrificing some measure of self-interest to the common good" (Fort, 2007). In essence, this means there can (and should) be common ground between the values of a company and that of an employee, which alone can motivate a person to want to do good. This concept may initially seem complex since it requires a fundamental understanding of the different dimensions of human behavior, which is beyond the scope of this report. However, in general, ethical behavior "arises not from a single-minded pursuit of an object, but in the realization of the complexity of goods and evils that exist and in the developing the "company", and the "self" that is able to differentiate between what is helpful and what is corrupting" (Fort, 2007). With this groundwork in place, we analyze the Nestlé case with respect to several critical virtues in society (Figure 3). Surprisingly, this analysis reveals several ethical failures in Nestlé's operations.

Figure 3. Defining and applying virtues to the Nestlé case.

Virtue	Definition*	Application to Nestlé case
Integrity	*Adherence to moral principles; honesty.*	Nestlé compromised their integrity by abusing their marketing strategy even after becoming aware of the potential negative impacts their actions were causing in the vulnerable Third world countries. Examples include not translating the product labels to the official local languages, providing commission to the "milk nurses" and sending incentives to doctors for advocating their products.
Honesty	*Truthfulness, sincerity, or frankness.*	Nestlé employed "milk nurses" to convince mothers they were real nurses with reliable medical advice. In doing this, Nestlé was not being truthful because mothers were being misguided about their choices. Further concerns are raised about Nestlé's honesty as they have continued to deny several allegations over the years.
Accountability	*Liable, or answerable.*	Though Nestlé responded to the attacks on its marketing techniques, they never issued a statement acknowledging any potential risk their products placed on infants. Rather than accepting some level of accountability, they denied several accusations even though there was significant evidence of violations.
Compassion	*A feeling of deep sympathy and sorrow for another who is stricken by misfortune.*	Nestlé did not respond to the accusations with understanding and cooperative efforts. Instead, they denied most of the claims showing no sympathy or compassion for the deadly results of products and marketing strategies.
Empathy	*The intellectual identification with or vicarious experiencing of the feelings thoughts or attitudes of another.*	Nestlé didn't show empathy to its victims. Though Nestlé revised its marketing rules to abide to the WHO code, there continues to be many reports of repeated violations. In addition, Nestlé did not make any official statements expressing empathy regarding the negative impact their products had on some babies. Neither did they express a plan to address the desires of the community. There seems to be a distant relationship between Nestlé and its customers. The aim and focus of Nestlé appears to be making profit and being competitive; serving the needs of its customers is not the priority.

Open-Minded/ Tolerant	*All-embracing and general.*	Nestlé did not express an embracing attitude when faced with all the criticisms. Rather than being open-minded, they became more defensive. Had they been tolerant, the criticisms leveled at Nestlé could have been used to improve their marketing techniques.
Dependability	*Real and genuine.*	It is clear that Nestlé has other intentions in its persistence to stay in developing nations. They may have other responsibilities that they are trying to adhere to, possibly the duty to increase profit to meet the needs of shareholders. Also, customers expect a level of trust between them and a company when money is invested toward purchasing a product. An end user understandably expects the organization has the customer's best interest in mind. Nestlé's marketing tactics have been deemed deceitful, making it seem that the company's intentions were not to develop a dependable, genuine relationship.

Nestlé failed to uphold the principles identified in Virtue Theory, which assesses the moral reasoning behind decisions made by corporations. This moral reasoning has to be in alignment with the virtues held and practiced by the corporation. Nestlé did not fully practice the essential virtues of integrity, honesty, accountability, compassion/empathy, open-minded/tolerance and dependability. Therefore, the reasoning behind their aggressive marketing techniques could have been for profitability and competitiveness. More importantly, without expressing these virtues, it is difficult to develop Good Trust toward this organization. Nestlé's actions do not create the notion they are interested in being trusted, valued, or liked by the community. They have heedlessly pursued their goals of marketing infant formula in Third world countries without much care for the consequences. Good Trust represents the final level of trust, after an organization gains reputation through Hard Trust and builds trust through Real Trust. Good Trust allows an organization to be truly liked and viewed highly in society. A boycott lasting nearly 40 years and continuing strong accurately reflects that Nestlé has failed to establish Good Trust through their controversial actions.

The Total Integrity Management Framework

"Total Integrity Management builds on and is based on trust: Hard Trust, Real Trust, and Good Trust" (Fort, 2007). While there is an alpha-numeric formula for visualizing this concept (not presented in this report), the principle is that "Total Integrity Management is the result of complying with the law (Hard Trust), provided that the law is just, + Real Trust, which assesses how stakeholders are treated in terms of their Rights, + Justice, + Utilitarianism, the sum of which is multiplied by Good Trust, which is human beings' inherent desire to do good" (Fort, 2007).

In our efforts to build a more ethical culture and framework for an industry or a specific company, one should apply all of the discussed previous theories and attempt to implement them in business practice. The lawful directives of Hard Trust are paramount from a legalistic standpoint. If the company is not able to obey simple lawful measures created to protect and or regulate business practice, then the company is likely not in a position to implement further measures. A company should create and enforce a compliance program or department that is independent of oversight of executive management. Internal conflicts of interest need to be eliminated or minimized to prevent unintentional influence within this department. The concept of Real Trust can be implemented by creating goods and services that serve the public's best interests. Honoring individual rights, building or creating without harm for the masses, and applying an equal means of justice to ensure that all parties are treated fairly are paramount. Companies with responsible research and development departments, properly functioning customer service departments, and appropriately applied community outreach all serve to foster Real Trust concerns. These departments are tasked with ensuring that all stakeholders are treated as fairly as possible.

Lastly, Good Trust is developed in companies that operate with a high moral standard. Moral standards cannot always be accounted for through Hard Trust laws and regulations, or through Real Trust actions implemented by a firm. Good Trust and the associated virtue theory capitalize on the notion that people want to do "good." To foster strong ethical behavior, firms need to identify and hire people with strong ethical standards and implement continuing education or training to ensure these standards are driving the firm forward in the appropriate ethical direction. If a firm understands these trust frameworks and effectively implements them within their business operations, mankind as we know it will continue to flourish for the benefit and betterment of all parties involved, shareholders and stakeholders alike. Accusations can have significant negative consequences for a business. In order to prevent tainting of the company image, organizations need to maintain strict policies to ensure employees practice good ethics. In accordance with virtue theory, in order for a business to maintain a culture that habitually makes ethical decisions, they would first need to identify and define the virtues. Then, the virtues should be implemented fairly to all stakeholders and shareholders, which would help establish and sustain Good Trust.

In this instance, Nestlé needed to assign individuals that would be held accountable and responsible with the implementation of their marketing policies and the associated consequences. Nestlé's Total Integrity Framework appears to be corrupt at various levels, which is the primary driving force for the Nestlé boycott. By violating aspects of Hard Trust, Real Trust, and Good Trust, the public opinion of Nestlé has suffered significantly, and the boycott has been an ongoing frustration for Nestlé operations for years.

The Authors' Perspectives

This case study was very informative. We now have a glimpse into the complexities associated with establishing and maintaining trust frameworks within a corporation. The case analysis has convinced all authors that Nestlé's actions are highly controversial at best. We are surprised and disappointed in Nestlé's handling of the case, and how they have essentially persisted with their goals with relatively little regard for the significant issues raised against them. From a Hard Trust standpoint, we do not believe Nestlé is fully cooperative with all rules and regulations associated with their actions, specifically their aggressive marketing. Assessing Real Trust also shows negativity, as we do not believe Nestlé is living up to their standards and being honest. Lastly, and perhaps most significantly in this case, we were very disappointed from the perspective of Good Trust. In analyzing various virtues, Nestlé fails to uphold each of them, which labels the organization as being untrustworthy, dishonest, and carefully negligent. Moreover, we believe Nestlé's actions have been truly immoral and unethical, as the organization has denied most of the allegations associated with increased infant malnutrition and mortality rates. As analysts of this case study, we would expect Nestlé to provide hard data showing that their introduction and marketing of infant formula has indeed not resulted in detrimental effects. This type of data on infant health should not be difficult to obtain. Without it, Nestlé exemplifies an organization with ulterior motives focused primarily on financial gains alone, with a distinct disregard for serious, humane issues. As such, in conclusion, we are in support of the Nestlé boycott, and would strongly recommend Nestlé re-evaluate their marketing strategies and specifically investigate whether their actions are inflicting harm on impoverished communities.

WORKS CITED

Dictionary.com. Retrieved May 12, 2013, from http://dictionary.reference.com/browse/

Fort, T. (2007). *Business, Integrity, and Peace.* New York: Cambridge University Press, New York.

IBFAN. (n.d.). *How Breastfeeding Is Undermined.* Retrieved May 17, 2013, from IBFAN: http://web.archive.org/web/20070415171525/http://www.ibfan.org/english/issue/bfUndermined01.html

Internationalist, T. (1973, August). European Printing Company. Retrieved May 16, 2013, from The Internationalist: http://oliver.friends.tas.edu.au/ni/issue006/contents.htm

London Oratory. (n.d.). *Virtue Theory.* Retrieved May 14, 2013, from London Oratory: http://www.london-oratory.org/philosophy/philosophies/ETHICS/normative/virtue_theory/body_virtue_theory.html

Lorber, H. a. (1982, July 27). *Bottle Babies Grave Markers.* Retrieved May 16, 2013, from Jump Cut: http://www.ejumpcut.org/archive/onlinessays/JC27folder/BottleBabies.html

Moorhead, J. (2007, May 14). *Milking It.* Retrieved May 15, 2013, from The Guardian: http://www.guardian.co.uk/business/2007/may/15/medicineandhealth.lifeandhealth

Nemours. (2013). *Breast or Bottle?* Retrieved May 17, 2013, from KidsHealth: http://kidshealth.org/parent/growth/feeding/breast_bottle_feeding.html

Sethi, S. P. (1994). *Multinational Corporation and the Impact of Public Advocacy on Corporate Strategy.* Journal of International Business Studies , 658-660.

Smith, N. (2011, December 7). *Summary of the Meaning of the Theory of Moral Virtue by Aristotle.* Retrieved May 18, 2013, from Article Myriad: http://www.articlemyriad.com/summary-theory-moral-virtue-aristotle/

TIME. (1976, July 12). *FOOD: The Formula Flap.* Retrieved May 16, 2013, from TIME Magazine: http://www.time.com/time/magazine/article/0,9171,914298,00.html

UNICEF. (2012, May 25). *Infant and Young Child Feeding.* Retrieved May 15, 2013, from UNICEF Nutrition: http://www.unicef.org/nutrition/index_breastfeeding.html

Want, W. o. (1974). *The Baby Killer.* Retrieved May 16, 2013, from Baby Milk: http://www.waronwant.org/past-campaigns/baby-milk

WHO. (2013). *Exclusive Breastfeeding.* Retrieved May 17, 2013, from WHO Nutrition: http://www.who.int/nutrition/topics/exclusive_breastfeeding/en/

Wiki. (2013, January 10). *Dodge v. Ford Motor Company.* Retrieved May 17, 2013, from Wikipedia: http://en.wikipedia.org/wiki/Dodge_v._Ford_Motor_Company

Winsted. (n.d.). *Nestle Infant Formula.* Retrieved May 16, 2013, from Pace University: http://webpage.pace.edu/kwinsted/nestl250.html

---

Crossing the Invisible Line of Ethical Boundaries

Alex Caine & Jorge Rivera

American Apparel is a clothing manufacturer, wholesaler and retailer that was founded by Dov Charney in 1989. It was later incorporated in Delaware in 2005. Their clothing line attracts young, "hipsters" looking for basic knit and cotton pieces that range from t-shirts, cardigans and leggings to vintage shoes and accessories. Currently, the company has slightly fewer than 300 stores in 19 countries worldwide. In 2012, the company made 617 million dollars and has been frequently compared with the GAP.

Sweatshop Free and Environmental Innovations

American Apparel advertises and prides itself on being "sweatshop free" in an industry where sweatshops are rampant. Most retail manufacturing is outsourced and workers are paid below minimum wage while working in very poor conditions. While some of its clothing manufactured is still outsourced, the garments are mostly produced at American Apparel's primary apparel manufacturing plant in Downtown Los Angeles.[1] The company provides their workers with ample benefits and an opportunity to earn

---

1   http://www.americanapparel.net/aboutus/verticalint/factory/

a fair wage. "The average sewer with experience at American Apparel is making about $25,000 per year... almost twice the federal minimum."[2] Benefits of working for the company include affordable health care for the entire family, subsidized meals and transportation, free massages, and a bike-lending program. Seeing as the majority of their workers are immigrants, they also provide free English language classes in their manufacturing plant. The CEO of American Apparel has stated that providing a sweatshop free environment is not an advertising ruse "criticizing other business models"[3] but a way of "taking care of the people who take care of the company."[4] It is also an effective way of stimulating the local economy through their employees' purchasing power and taxes on payroll and property[5]. Not only does the company provide a sweatshop free environment, but they also view their workers as assets and provide a good work environment as a capital ploy. The "sweatshop free" environment is not the only non-advertising ruse that has influenced individuals to shop at American Apparel.

American Apparel has multiple environmental initiatives aimed at minimizing their ecological footprint. The company makes a genuine effort to manufacture their products in an environmentally friendly manner. Their L.A. factory is powered by a "state-of-the-art solar panel... [that] generates 150 kilowatts of clean, renewable power, contributing 15% of"[6] the energy needed for the factory. American Apparel also efficiently recycles and creatively reuses the leftover scraps of fabric. When possible, the scraps are reused for new garments or are donated to Trash for Teaching (T4T), a Los Angeles based non-profit. T4T's goal is to minimize waste by creating projects for students that reuse the trash. American Apparel also uses 100% recycled paper for its catalogues. Probably its biggest environmental innovation is the use of sustainable fabrics such as organic cotton and bamboo in its product line.

American Apparel's sustainable edition is a line that offers select styles in "100% certified organic cotton. The cultivation of organic cotton works with natural systems to help protect the health of people and wildlife while not contaminating the environment."[7] Their use of a low-impact dyeing process reduces the amount of water and chemical waste as well as provides environmental and health benefits relative to dyeing processes used by other clothing companies. Finally, American Apparel is a member of the clean cotton campaign which aims at incorporating cleaner cotton into clothing product lines by providing cotton farmers with "profitable strategies for

---

2   http://www.americanapparel.net/aboutus/verticalint/workers/

3   http://www.americanapparel.net/aboutus/verticalint/workers/

4   Dov Charney (2007). YouTube American Apparel—Don Charney Interview. CBS News.@3:28

5   http://www.americanapparel.net/aboutus/verticalint/usa/

6   http://www.americanapparel.net/aboutus/corpresp/environment/

7   http://www.americanapparel.net/aboutus/corpresp/organic/

reducing chemical use."[8] Relative to the rest of the clothing industry, American Apparels sweatshop free environment and green initiatives are very progressive and innovative. Unfortunately, in the case of the companies advertising ploys, what they consider to be progressive and innovative is seen as provocative.

Provocative Advertising, Provocative Culture, Provocative CEO

American Apparel's advertisements are designed and created in house by the CEO and his associates. Most 21st century clothing advertisements display retouched, tall, thin models with perfectly symmetrical faces. American Apparel takes an entirely different approach; even their selection process differs significantly from other clothing retailers. Many of the models are picked up in stores or off the streets by Charney while some are selected through photographs sent through the website. The advertisements are rarely retouched and display aesthetic imperfections such as blemishes, sweat marks and tan lines. "The ads are also highly suggestive... showcasing underwear or clingy knits. They depict young men and women in bed or the shower; if they are casually lounging on a sofa or sitting on the floor their legs happen to be spread... a couple of the young women appear to be in a heightened state of pleasure."[9] The women in the ads are also frequently over-exposed with their nipples visible under lace body suits. Their advertisements are not only sexually explicit but a specific advertising campaign took advantage of human tragedy to generate sales.

In November of 2012, hurricane Sandy struck the Northeastern United States. It was a category 2 storm that caused billions of dollars in damage, left millions without power and directly caused 147 deaths.[10] American Apparel, realizing the impact the storm would have on in-store sales, decided to use the hurricane as an advertising ploy and issued the ad on the left. The sale was specifically targeted at those affected by the hurricane. Many customers were outraged by the controversial ad and expressed their disappointment via social media websites. Summer Luu posted via twitter "another tasteless marketing campaign by American Apparel. Why am I not surprised."[11] The spokesperson for American Apparel, Ryan Holiday, responded by saying that the company was not trying "to offend anyone or capitalize on a natural disaster"[12], in fact the company is committed to disaster relief per the corporate social responsibility section of their webpage. He also honed on the fact that the brand is the largest US made brand and that business cannot stop because of a storm.

---

8   http://www.americanapparel.net/aboutus/corpresp/organic/

9   http://www.nytimes.com/2006/04/23/magazine/23apparel.html?pagewanted=2

10   http://www.nhc.noaa.gov/data/tcr/AL182012_Sandy.pdf

11   http://abcnews.go.com/blogs/business/2012/10/hurricane-sandy-sales-good-business-or-bad-taste/

12   http://www.huffingtonpost.com/2012/11/01/american-apparel-hurricane-sandy-marketing-dov-charney_n_2056410.html

In March of 2011, five employees filed sexual harassment suits against the CEO of American Apparel. In 2004 he masturbated in front of a reporter, Claudine Ko, who was writing a profile for Jane magazine about American Apparel's founder. Charney has become known for his "belief that sexual relationships in the workplace are appropriate: 'I think it's a First Amendment right to pursue one's affection for another human being.'"[13] He has also been accused of "using crude languages and gestures, conducting job interviews in his underwear, ordering the hiring of women in whom he had sexual interest and giving one of the plaintiffs a vibrator."[14] He believes that in the hipster clothing industry, sex sells but customers, employees and capital markets seem to disagree.

In 2008 Charney called Ken Cieply, the CFO of American Apparel, a complete loser. A few weeks later Cieply resigned and American Apparels stock price plummeted. In 2009 American Apparel just avoided bankruptcy by receiving an $80 million loan. In 2011 the company announced that it might pursue bankruptcy until it was loaned another $80 million. American Apparel has not been profitable since 2010.

The Moral Issue

American Apparel is a company that has long had a disconnect between its' "socially progressive labor policies and uses of significant environmental advances in their manufacturing, mixed with a highly sexualized nature of the companies advertising"[15] The company pushes some ethical boundaries, justifying them by the company's ethical devotion to American nationalism. Considering the financial difficulties of the company, it is relevant to consider whether this disconnect is sustainable or whether the highly sexualized nature of the company and its advertisements should be changed. American Apparel has some alternatives to address their moral dilemma. They can do nothing; maintain their business practices in a highly sexualized culture. They can completely change the culture; use trendy fashion to sell their brand rather than sex. Or they can do something in between. In order to determine the best alternative for American Apparel, it is relevant to consider four basic ethical theories; stakeholder theory, shareholder theory, virtue theory and total integrity management.

Stakeholder Theory

In order to apply stakeholder theory to a company, it is first important to consider the relevant stakeholders. A stakeholder is any individual who has a stake in the company and is affected by the success or failure of the organization. In the case of American Apparel, the relevant stakeholders are the employees, the shareholders, the environment

---

13 http://theweekinethics.wordpress.com/2011/03/13/american-apparel-and-the-ethics-of-a-sexually-charged-workplace/

14 http://hbr.org/product/american-apparel-unwrapping-ethics/an/W12134-HCB-ENG

15 http://hbr.org/product/american-apparel-unwrapping-ethics/an/W12134-HCB-ENG

and the customers. Stakeholder theory is multi-faceted. The first facet considers basic versus non-basic rights. American Apparel does not violate the basic rights to life, water, food, shelter, or health of any of their stakeholders. In fact, by providing subsidized health care and meals, American Apparel enhances the basic rights of their employees. The company also enhances the basic right of health for the environment their innovative tactics. One could argue that sexual assault violates the basic right to freedom from torture. Based on the cases against American Apparel, none of the allegations against Charney appear to be on the level of torture. Thus, the company does not violate any basic rights, although they do violate two competing non-basic rights

In the case of American Apparel, two non-basic rights can include the right to work in an environment free of sexual discrimination and assault and freedom of expression. Both of these non-basic rights are in conflict with each other. Charney creates a culture that allows for freedom of expression, even if the expression it is sexual in nature. The sexual explicitness of the company, as seen through the company's advertisements and Charney's actions, fosters an environment where instances of sexual assault can be underrated. In the case of two conflicting non-basic rights, a compromise between them is essential. The most sensible compromise is to provide a work environment free of sexual assault and allow freedom of expression within limits. Whereby sexual discrimination and harassment are not permitted under freedom of expression.

One could argue in favor of freedom of expression by saying that it is a part of American Apparel's corporate culture and brand but this would raise the question of whether a company can sell sex without promoting instances of sexual assault. Abercrombie and Fitch is a company that has long been criticized for their use of sex in advertising. In 2003, they even had to recall their holiday catalogue in response to negative reactions from advocacy groups claiming the catalogue "promotes sexual promiscuity."[16] Similarly to American Apparel, Abercrombie uses sex to sell their clothing line, and also has lawsuits against them for sexual assault, namely models being forced to masturbate during photo shoots. Thus, it seems that a sex driven corporate culture and sexual assault instances linked and perhaps cannot be separated. In other words, it appears that a company that uses sex in advertising is unable to prevent sexual assault in the work place.

The justice portion of stakeholder theory emphasizes the importance of equity in the workplace. Workers should be compensated equally for equal work. Based on the justice aspect of stakeholder theory, American Apparel offers more than equal treatment to their workers. They offer significantly better treatment to their employees relative to the rest of the industry. Justice is also about protecting the vulnerable. In a similar case, Dornhecker vs Malibu Grand Prix, Mr. Rockefeller has similar conduct to that of Charney. "Rockefeller put his hands on her hips in an airport ticket line and dropped

---

16   http://money.cnn.com/2003/12/09/news/companies/abercrombie/

his pants in front of passengers while waiting to board the airplane. He touched her breasts."[17] While the sexual lawsuits filed against American Apparel were either thrown out or sent to arbitration, and the case against Rockefeller was overturned, it does not make the conduct acceptable. Evidently, Charney's sexual nature, discrimination and acts of assault are taking advantage of the vulnerable. "The irony of sexual freedom in the workplace is that it is about power, not romance. If often ends up exploiting those most vulnerable."[18] Under the justice component of stakeholder theory, it appears that sexually explicit acts in a business setting can be deemed unjust as they take advantage of the weak.

Utilitarianism focuses on providing the greatest amount of utility to the greatest number of stakeholders. Under a utilitarian view, if American Apparel had to choose between their two biggest ethical stances, certainly providing sweatshop free labor would win. It provides 7,500 jobs in Los Angeles at a higher than minimum rate. But, a culture free of sexual assault and sweatshop free labor are not mutually exclusive; that is to say a company does not have to pick one or the other. The greatest utility to the greatest number of stakeholders would be provided if American Apparel kept the sweatshop free labor, progressive environmental habits and stopped using sex as a component of their corporate culture. This would be the most satisfactory outcome for all the employees.

Evidently, American Apparel is a company with competing moral drivers. In some instances they are industry innovators, creating a better environment for their stakeholders, whereas in other instances they are using their corporate culture as an excuse for the promiscuity of their CEO. The major flaw that American Apparels has is the conflict between two non-basic rights: freedom of expression and sexual assault in the workplace. Disregarding any other theories, stakeholder theory would state that the company should stop using sex as a corporate driver continue the labor and environmental practices. Whether the sex driven culture drives profits will be further considered under shareholder theory but considering rights, equality and maximum utility the culture should be changed.

Shareholder Theory

While traditionally shareholder theory is aimed at maximizing shareholder profitability, recently it has been adjusted to include non-economic lawful directives as well as lawful directives. While American Apparel has a duty to maximize profit and distribute the wealth to its investors, it also has a duty to enhance the reputation of the firm and take interest in the public good. Shareholder theory is one of the few theories

---

17 http://federal-circuits.vlex.com/vid/marvelle-dornhecker-malibu-grand-prix-38397076

18 http://business-ethics.com/2011/03/15/0852-american-apparel-and-the-ethics-of-a-sexually-charged-workplace/

in which the sweatshop free factory in Los Angeles can be appeared as a negative. While it is right and just to provide those employees with fair employment, the rest of the industry does not, so why should American Apparel? Those other companies are also earning a higher profit margin enabling them to redistribute more wealth to their shareholders. On the other hand, the sweatshop free factory creates a precedent for American Apparel. Customers appreciate the brand more knowing that the garments are produced in a fair manner. It is still important to consider whether sweatshop free factories provide American Apparel with longevity and a sustainable business plan. Having been close to bankruptcy twice in the past 5 years indicates that perhaps a change in the structure may be necessary. When Nike was accused of using child labor to manufacture their clothing, their sales and stock price dropped significantly. This was only temporary as eventually sales and the price rose back up. Despite a short run plummet in profits, American Apparel may be able to use sweatshops in the long run but doing so would completely defy one of the biggest non-economic lawful directives and branding labels of the company —being sweatshop free. American Apparel's advertising, on the other hand, may seem to have short-term benefits at huge long-term costs.

The ad that American Apparel ran during Hurricane Sandy was considered to be a marketing ploy in order to prevent the loss of an excess of funds due to the storm. "People forget how expensive it is to run a Made in USA brand like American Apparel and if we made a mistake here it came from the good place of trying to keep the machine going —for the sake of our employees and stakeholders."[19] The company's short term thought process on the importance of maintaining a profit seemed to over look the long-term importance of branding and reputation. Many individuals took to twitter offended by the sale and indicating that they were going to boycott American Apparel and never shop there again. While the company claims they were trying to fulfill what can be seen as an economic lawful directive, to generate a profit for stakeholders and maintain jobs for employees, the ad was insensitive to those who lost their homes and extremely insensitive to those who lost their lives. Furthermore, the reaction of the spokesperson and CEO were appalling. Neither showed any remorse for those who were offended by the ad and the CEO said that he would not lose sleep over the Hurricane Sandy ad that the company ran. In the short term, the ad boosted revenue though in the long term it hurt the reputation of the brand and furthered public issue with American Apparel's no shame advertising.

Virtue Theory

Virtue theory focuses on the fact that human beings are social beings and thus by definition have to practice ethics. The first relevant virtue under virtue theory is

---

19 http://www.huffingtonpost.com/2012/11/01/american-apparel-hurricane-sandy-marketing-dov-charney_n_2056410.html

integrity. American Apparel discusses integrity in its credo; "each person owes a duty to the Company to act with integrity. Integrity requires, among other things, being honest, fair and candid. Deceit, dishonestly and subordination of principle are all inconsistent with integrity."[20] American Apparel does not act with sexual integrity despite its importance being clearly stated in their credo. While their definition of integrity is clear, sexual integrity can be defined as being modest and humble when it comes to ones' personal life. This requires some separation of work and sex, something that is not at all present at American Apparel.

Another relevant virtue for American Apparel is innovation. Whether it is their progressive labor or environmental practices, American Apparel is a leader within the industry. They continually innovate to find more environmentally friendly ways of recycling and producing their materials. They are also industry leaders on their sweatshop free labor practices. A third relevant virtue to American Apparel is efficiency-profitability. Taken independently of other virtues, American Apparel does not necessarily value this virtue. Their labor practices make their costs significantly higher than those of other companies in the same industry. Furthermore, there are more efficient locations and processes that the company could use although they would not be as environmentally friendly. Disregarding the profitability of long-term reputation, in raw dollars the company's practices do not transform efficiency into profit.

Total Integrity Management

American Apparel, like every company, is affected by their reputation. The social and environmental initiatives that they have put in effect distinguish them amongst competitors. From the perspective of hard trust, "accountability of obeying the law is the prime virtue."[21] In regards to hard trust, developing a corporate culture that is not driven by sex is imperative to the company. Per the U.S. Equal Employment Opportunity Commission, "it is unlawful to harass a person because of that person's sex. Harassment can include unwelcome sexual advances..."[22] Although the cases against Charney were dismissed, his actions defy the real trust component. It is simply against the law, regardless of the culture the company is trying to create. Furthermore, American Apparel has published many ads that are considered overtly sexual. In 2012, the company was the subject of several rulings by the Advertising Standards Authority for presenting models in exploitative ways and sexualizing children.[23] The sex-driven corporate culture of the company likely drives the use of provocative advertising. In order to comply with hard

---

20 http://files.shareholder.com/downloads/APP/2353247582x0x169419/1a4a6647-1fe0-4570-8a2d- 314af2a955f8/ AA__Code_of_Ethics.pdf

21 http://www.williamcfrederick.com/articles%20archive/TimFort.pdf

22 http://www.eeoc.gov/laws/types/sexual_harassment.cfm

23 http://www.huffingtonpost.com/2013/04/10/american-apparel-asa-banned-ads_n_3051751.html

trust, the company must set standards that obey the law. This likely involves a restructuring of the corporate culture.

The company's initiative to be sweatshop free and environmentally friendly is an example of good trust. They are acting this way simply because it is the right thing to do. As previously mentioned, they view their employees as human capital and do not use their labor practices as an advertising ploy. Furthermore, American Apparel could easily follow the industry norm and outsourced their clothing to a manufacturer with worse conditions. They also do not need to pay above minimum wage and provide the benefits that they do to their employees. Instead, they produce their clothing in America to assure that their laborers are being treated fairly. The company has gone as far as offering their garment workers stock options, so that they could be shareholders.[24] American Apparel is acting in the best interest of their workers and therefore embodying good trust.

Their labor and environment practices are also aligned with real trust. The company translates their moral values into good business practices. The labor practices are mutually beneficial for the employees as well as the company. Where the company fails to institute basic fairness is, as in the issue in all other ethical frameworks, the freedom to work in an environment free of sexual harassment. From a real trust perspective, violating this non-basic rights is not beneficial for the business or society. Establishing guidelines for accountability would improve American Apparel's reputation. People will acknowledge that the company is making an effort to protect non-basic rights of their workers. While this might not increase sales, it would deter third-party enforcement entities from going after the company.

The interplay between hard trust, real trust and good trust all reach the same conclusion. In order for American Apparel to contribute to peace through business, the sex component in their culture and their advertising needs to stop. They must create a work environment that is free of sexual harassment. In doing so, they would strengthen their brand image. This would allow bring to light the integrity of the company. It would also be in line with their mission to "take care of the people that take care of the company." By protecting all of the rights of their employees they would be embodying all the trust components of total integrity management.

Shares, Stakes, Virtues and Integrity

American Apparel is a company that has a significant disconnect between some of its ethical practices, being innovative and avant-garde for the industry, and its advertising ploys that are offensive and create a negative corporate culture. It appears that the ethical and unethical aspects of the company do not go hand in hand, that is one can be let go without harming the other. American Apparel has established a do-good reputation from its labor practices and does not need racy advertising ploys to be a recognized. In fact, according to virtually all the frameworks above, the company can completely remove sex from its corporation. American Apparel ought to stop using sex to sell their clothing and stop creating a sexually explicit corporate culture. The company may be unable to do so under the rule of the current CEO in which case he should be replaced. Nothing is more personal than providing services to people that they cannot provide for themselves. This is exactly what businesses do and in doing so, businesses ought to act in the best interest of the people. American Apparel needs to align their labor employees with their other employees and provide the same environment for both. That would make American Apparel a truly ethical company.

BIBLIOGRAPHY

American Apparel, http://www.americanapparel.net/aboutus/, (April 2013).

American Apparel, Mission Statements, http://files.shareholder.com/downloads/APP/2353247582x0x-169419/1a4a6647-1fe0-4570-8a2d- 314af2a955f8/AA__Code_of_Ethics.pdf, (April 2013).

Bhatnagar, Parija, *Abercrombie Kill Its Racy Catalog*, http://money.cnn.com/2003/12/09/news/companies/abercrombie/, (December 2003).

Blank, Jessica, *Hurricane Sandy Sales: Business or Bad Taste*, http://abcnews.go.com/blogs/business/2012/10/hurricane-sandy-sales-good-business-or-bad-taste/, (October 2012).

CBS News, American Apparel —Dov Charney Interview, (June 2007).

Cotte, June, Hwan, Seug, Schuette, Brittany, *American Apparel: Unwrapping Ethics*, http://hbr.org/product/american-apparel-unwrapping-ethics/an/W12134-HCB-ENG, (April 2013).

Federal Circuits, *Marvelle Dornhecker, Plaintiff-Appelle, v. Malibu Grand Prix Corp, Defendant-Appelant*, http://federal-circuits.vlex.com/vid/marvelle-dornhecker-malibu-grand-prix-38397076, (April 2013).

Frederick, William, *You Should Really Get to Know Tim Fort*, http://www.williamcfrederick.com/articles%20archive/TimFort.pdf, (Accessed April 2013).

Krupnick, Ellie, *American Apparel, ASA On the Outs Again with New Banned Ads*, http://www.huffingtonpost.com/2013/04/10/american-apparel-asa-banned-ads_n_3051751.html, (April 2013).

O'Brien, Gael, *American Apparel and the Ethics of a Sexually Charged Workplace*, http://business-ethics.com/2011/03/15/0852-american-apparel-and-the-ethics-of-a-sexually-charged-workplace/, (March 2011).

Sieczkowski, Cavan, *American Apparel Hurricane Sandy Marketing 'Not a Serious Matter,' CEO Dov Charney Says*, http://www.huffingtonpost.com/2012/11/01/american-apparel-hurricane-sandy-marketing-dov-charney_n_2056410.html, (January 2012).

U.S. Equal Employment Opportunity Commission, Sexual Harassment, http://www.eeoc.gov/laws/types/sexual_harassment.cfm, (Accessed April 2013).

Wolf, Jaime, *And You Thought Abercrombie & Fitch Was Pushing It?* http://www.nytimes.com/2006/04/23/magazine/23apparel.html?pagewanted=1&_r=1, (April 2006).

Blood-Stained Indulgence:
Nestlé's Use of Slave Labor in the Ivory Coast

Brian Reisman
Professor Tim Fort, 4/25/13

Introduction

As Cynthia McMullan maneuvers the crowded aisles of her local superstore, her 7-year-old son whines about the length of his mother's shopping excursion. Much to her own dismay, Cynthia's son has already wreaked havoc during her afternoon grocery run. Upon entering the store, little Johnny McMullan dropped a can of olives from a promotional stand. A few minutes later, he stepped on a box of strawberries and proceeded to leave fruity footprints throughout the produce section.

Cynthia, normally a calm and collected mother, is beginning to lose her patience. After a long day at work, she is too tired to adequately reprimand her son for his inappropriate antics. Johnny is growing equally impatient and begins to sing his favorite cartoon theme song in an infinite loop. By the time little Johnny begins the 9th repetition of the jingle, Cynthia snaps.

"Cut it out, Johnny! Mommy had a very long day at work and needs to finish shopping before Daddy gets home. You're really getting on my nerves and I need you to cool down. I'll make you a deal. Go to the candy aisle and choose something you want. If you behave for the rest of the time we're here, I'll buy it for you when we check out."

Within seconds, Johnny has disappeared from the frozen goods aisle, leaving his mother in a state of newfound calm. Meanwhile, Johnny scans the numerous sweets available to him. After a long period of deliberation, he snatches a Nestlé Crunch Bar and sprints back to his mother's side. He throws the bar into the shopping cart and pretends he's a mute for the remainder of the shopping trip. He wants nothing more than to enjoy a Nestlé Bar.

On the other side of the world, an African boy slightly older than Johnny accidentally slices his hand with a machete he was given to retrieve cocoa beans. He looks for something to wipe the blood off his hand, but finds nothing. He considers walking back to his supervisor to get medical care, but fears returning without a sufficient cocoa yield. He thinks about the dire situation he has been forced into and tears run down his face. The young boy knows he is worse off on his own, and therefore cannot run from the injustice of slavery. He is stuck. The boy sighs and continues to hack at the cocoa plants in front of him. His blood and tears trickle onto the sweet beans he is harvesting.

When Cynthia finally gets home after the long drive from the superstore, Johnny starts acting up and rubs his strawberry-coated sneakers on an antique rug. Cynthia sits him down and disciplines him as she wipes the soles of his shoes with a washcloth. Johnny demands the Crunch Bar he earned be given to him immediately.

Cynthia, defeated from tiredness, caves in. She begrudgingly hands the bar to Johnny and heads to the kitchen to prepare dinner. He could have it so much worse, she thought to herself.

Although this case is fictional in nature, there is nothing fictional about the circumstances that surround it. Once a company thought to be concerned with human rights and the sustainability of its products, Nestlé is still combating allegations regarding slave labor in its supply chains and abuse surrounding workers not forced into slavery. While the ethical dilemma surrounding Nestlé Company is also relevant to other companies within the chocolate and confectionery industry, it is perhaps most relevant to Nestlé due to its market share and reputation within the industry.

As Nestlé continues to work out solutions in respect to this ethical and moral dilemma, consumers are becoming increasingly active in seeking out humane, sustainable practices from their food providers. With many companies making significant efforts to brand their slave-free operations to socially involved consumers, Nestlé must follow trend and adequately address an issue that could serious harm the company's reputation in both the short-term and long-term.

Thus, the intent of this report is to analyze the ethical dilemma surrounding Nestlé, to critique the initiatives the company has already taken to address the problem, and to propose more appropriate or more extensive solutions if applicable. To achieve this, this paper will first provide background on the issue and will then use a number of ethical frameworks to provide appropriate recommendations and evaluation for the Nestlé Company.

The Moral Issue and Relevant Facts : Nestlé and Unfair Labor Practices

As of March of 2013, Nestlé Company was the world's largest food provider by revenue figures. Specializing in everything from snack foods to health supplements, Nestle is a huge multinational company that has branded itself as a healthy and reputable player within the packaged food business.

Within the spectrum of Nestlé's many market offerings exists Nestlé Chocolate, sometimes referred to as Nestlé Confectionery. This division of Nestlé, one that competes with companies such as Cadbury and Mars, is internationally known for products such as the Crunch Bar, the Kit Kat Bar[25], and the Butterfinger Bar.

Although Nestlé Chocolate is not the company's highest grossing food division, it has been a staple of the Nestlé brand for more than 50 years and continues to maintain a large percentage of market share in the United States as well as in parts of Europe, Asia, and Latin America. Thus, it is reasonable to infer that the preservation of the Nestlé

---

25   The Kit Kat Bar is a Nestlé product in all countries except the United States, where it is owned by Hershey Chocolates.

Chocolate image and the continued profitability of the sub-brand are vital to the success of the parent company.

In 1998, private pressure from social activists led to widespread investigation of the cocoa industry. As a result of the investigation, allegations arose suggesting that large chocolate companies were using child labor in production, and moreover, that some child labor was a product of enslavement. These allegations led to further investigation and more bad news for large chocolate companies. By 2000, it had been revealed that many of those enslaved in the cocoa industry were trafficked or coerced into slavery. While the legitimacy of these reports is still largely in question, the breadth and scope of investigation surrounding the chocolate industry led to serious problems for large-scale chocolate manufacturers.

During this time, Nestlé was directly involved with cocoa plantations under investigation. Nestlé, which is responsible for the purchasing of approximately 10 percent of all global cocoa output, obtains more than one third of its cocoa from the Ivory Coast. The investigations surrounding enslavement and child labor within the cocoa industry were specifically targeted at the Ivory Coast, as the country is known for unfair labor practices and lenient trade rules that allow for exploitation of workers. While Nestlé faced little scrutiny during the early 2000s, it was aware of the investigations taking place as well as the potential for reputational damage to the firm.

In 2005, the International Labor Rights Fund filed a lawsuit against Nestle claiming that three children from Mali had been trafficked to the Ivory Coast by the company in order to work at cocoa plantations. Although the lawsuit was dismissed on grounds that a corporation cannot be held accountable for breaches of international law[26], the public attention surrounding the case created a hurdle that the company is still fighting. Whether or not the malpractice was widespread or simply a remote incident, the scandal propelled Nestlé into the spotlight and made it the poster child for corporate use of slave labor within the cocoa industry.

Although Nestlé was aware that its involvement with the Ivory Coast and the labor practices therein could be damaging to the firm, it did not feel the need to take action or to make statement. This was because Nestlé has never owned a plantation in the Ivory Coast. While the company was cognoscente of labor issues in its supply chain, it felt it was protected by international law statutes and therefore did little to combat initial concerns over labor practices connected to Nestlé.

In the late 2000s, Nestlé became the center of the outrage surrounding child labor in the Ivory Coast. Because the company is so prominent within the food industry and imports a substantial amount of cocoa from the Ivory Coast, NGOs and social activists targeted Nestlé utilizing the idea that it is most effective to target an industry's worst

---

26   This decision was made by the US District Court for the Central District of California.

offender. Suddenly, Nestlé Chocolate experienced widespread boycotts of its products and large demonstrations in metropolitan areas. At this point, the company knew it had to react.

In 2009, Nestlé consulted the Fair Labor Association and asked for guidance on the issue of slave labor within the Ivory Coast. The FLA conducted an investigation on Nestlé's involvement and sent a report detailing their objectives for the company. In an effort to form a strategic ally, Nestlé publicized its response to the report and outlined a plan for improvement based on the FLA's findings. Among the changes promised by Nestlé were better definition of employee roles, better communication of labor expectations, and perhaps most importantly, the mapping and monitoring of Nestlé's entire supply chain. In taking on this last measure, Nestlé aimed to form relationships with all suppliers and to track the flow of labor by frequently visiting labor sites to uncover any wrongdoing or injustice. In 2012, Nestlé became a member of the Fair Labor Association, demonstrating a commitment to the practice of fair labor in its operations.

As of late 2012, however, both the Fair Labor Association and critics of Nestlé's continuous use of child labor claimed that Nestlé was still using unfair labor practices. As most of the company's monitoring policies and supply chain models are opaque and made private, some firmly believe the company is creating an image that represents a false reality. And while the company's dedication to the FLA and internal improvement measures may be genuine, they may not be entirely ethical.

Applying Ethical Frameworks

Shareholder Theory:

According to many business theorists, the goal of any successfully run company is to maximize the value of stock prices, and in turn, to maximize the profitability of shareholders. In accordance with this idea, a company that is succeeding in this regard has little else to worry about. In essence, this view of shareholder theory prioritizes financial gain to the shareholder and forgoes anything that might inhibit it.

In the case of Nestlé Chocolate, someone who believes in this version of shareholder theory may state that the moral obligation of management is to implement the solution that causes the least financial loss to shareholders. From this standpoint, one may suggest that Nestlé should calculate the reputational loss associated with consumer concern over child labor and weigh it against the cumulative costs of changing suppliers.

Although the profitability of shareholders is certainly a large part of shareholder theory, there are other components of the theory that must be taken into account. By definition, shareholder theory is the responsibility of management to carry out the lawful directives of shareholders. This means that shareholders ultimately decide the criteria upon which management acts. While profitability is usually one of the criterions set forth by shareholders, there are most always others.

For a company like Nestlé that promises safe, healthy, and reputable food to consumers, shareholders would likely demand that these conditions be reflected in production processes. As Nestlé's mission statement promises to "...positively influence the social environment in which we operate as responsible corporate citizens, with due regard for those environmental standards and societal aspirations which improve quality of life", this idea becomes even more relevant.

From the perspective of a shareholder that seeks wealth in the short-term, Nestlé's best option in regards to its current dilemma is to continue what it is already doing. In complying with the Fair Labor Association and taking on initiatives that theoretically reduce the dependence on child labor, Nestlé can protect itself from financial loss in the short-term. Furthermore, a shareholder valuing this approach would site Hershey and Mars as offenders of the same violations. Both companies have been associated with unfair labor practices and have taken little action to address them. From the perspective of a purely profit-driven shareholder, it is in Nestlé's best interest to be reactive to claims instead of proactive, and to only take on additional expenses to maintain reputation.

Someone who has interest in promoting the long-term profitability of Nestlé, however, would genuinely disagree with the short-term advocate. Because Nestlé is already being accused of falsifying their efforts to reduce unfair labor practices in the Ivory Coast, one could make the argument that Nestlé needs to act with the long-term in mind.

A long-term approach to shareholder theory would likely advocate for significant and apparent changes within Nestlé's supply chains. Changes could include publicizing the flows of labor Nestlé uses as well as the salaries and conditions provided to workers. Furthermore, Nestlé could choose to reduce its dependency on slave labor by shifting its supply chains to cocoa regions that implement fair labor practices. A long-term strategist would see opportunity in the predicament Nestlé is currently facing.

If the mission of Nestlé is truly to promote social and environmental progress through responsible corporate practice, then Nestlé could complement these initiatives with societal investment in the Ivory Coast. The company could choose to invest in schools and nutrition for children in the region, effectively combating child labor and other societal problems at the same time. While these actions would certainly cost the company and shareholders in the short-term, they could certainly create a competitive edge for Nestlé going forward. If Hershey Chocolate and Mars continue to stand idle on the issue of child labor in the cocoa industry, Nestlé could set itself apart as a socially responsible player within the industry. From a strategic standpoint, Nestlé could use its social benevolence as a long-term branding technique.

There is no right or wrong perspective on this issue. Rather, there are two conflicting ideologies that have different outcomes in the short-term and long-term. While taking little initiative may hurt Nestlé's corporate image in the long-term, investing large sums to improve social conditions in the Ivory Coast would harm the firm financially without concrete reason for investment. Therefore, it is important to consider additional ethical perspectives in order to reach a more informed, comprehensive solution.

Stakeholder Theory:

Although the shareholders of a company ultimately decide the course of action for a corporation, decisions made by shareholders and management ultimately affect other factions of society. In Nestlé's case, the importing of cocoa harvested by children and slaves directly impacts a number of different groups. In order to adequately address the stakeholders affected by Nestlé's market actions, it is important to look at stakeholder theory from a few different viewpoints.

Rights Theory:

The rights component of stakeholder theory addresses any violation of basic or non-basic human rights. As a general rule, any corporate practice that compromises the basic rights of any stakeholder should be modified or replaced entirely.

Although Nestlé is not violating statues of international law by importing cocoa harvested by slaves and those considered too young to work, the company is certainly dealing with an issue of basic human rights. As mentioned earlier, Nestlé does not own a plantation in the Ivory Coast, and therefore cannot be held accountable for the dismal labor conditions present in the region. The company does, however, condone the labor practices by continuing to purchase the products created by child labor.

When considering basic principles of supply and demand, Nestlé has a large impact on the rights of workers being exploited in the Ivory Coast. If Nestlé were to take significant action to purchase only from plants that use fair labor practices, demand for child labor would decrease. Similarly, Nestlé could use its market influence to sway other firms to act in the same way. The fact that Nestlé continues to support the use of child labor means that the company does not see wrong in doing so.

Among the rights considered to be basic human rights are access to food, water, shelter, life itself, and freedom from torture. While Nestlé is not directly responsible for the withholding of any of these basic rights, the company is an accomplice in denying child workers one of them. Because it has been alleged that Nestlé permits plantations to use trafficked and under aged workers, it could be reasonably argued that the company denies such people the right to life. As the company is funding plantations that exploit children and deny them freedom, it is inherently detracting from quality of life.

The rights theory component of stakeholder theory becomes even more important when the stakeholders affected are children. As most of the children being exploited by plantation owners in the Ivory Coast are without family guidance, the corporation assumes more responsibility. Additionally, the Ivory Coast does not have anti-trafficking laws, making it easy to import illegal labor into the country. Because Nestlé does not do anything to combat these problems, it can theoretically be held even more responsible for the exploitation of children and slaves in the region.

Justice Theory:

Another factor that must be considered in respect to stakeholder theory is the degree to which Nestlé's operations reflect justice. While this theory generally discusses the extent to which equal treatment is granted for equal work, this report will also analyze the extent to which the children and slaves working in the Ivory Coast consent to their working conditions.

In July of 2012, the Fair Labor Association filed a report against Nestlé Chocolate. Although the two organizations work together to improve the conditions in the Ivory Coast and beyond, the FLA claimed that Nestlé was still in serious violation of human rights, especially in regard to unpaid labor and working conditions for child workers.

The report specifically mentions that child workers on cocoa plantations in the Ivory Coast are often unpaid and unsupervised. Working large portions of the day, children frequently suffer injuries from machetes given to them by distant supervisors. According to the Department of Justice, most cocoa workers receive salaries that place them on the verge of poverty and starvation. In the case of child workers, most are not paid at all.

Nestlé is aware of these trends, yet continues to support organizations that create them. The company is therefore denying workers the compensation they deserve for their work, and moreover, are using an illegal labor supply. This is a violation of the first component of justice theory. Nestlé is buying cocoa from plantations that do not obtain consent from their workers. As there is no contract of labor between slaves and the plantations, there is no perception of justice within that realm of labor. Nestlé is also in violation of not creating an agreeable social contract. Applying the concept of the categorical imperative, Nestlé views child laborers as means rather than ends, and does not respect or care for exploited parties.

A basic principle of justice theory is that the most vulnerable party should be protected from injustice and wrongdoing. Taking this idea a bit further, ethicists suggest that any corporate action that harms a vulnerable party should be eradicated. Looking at Nestlé's dilemma purely from the justice theory perspective, the company should undeniably shift its production away from child labor in the Ivory Coast. This approach would also suggest that Nestlé should take further action to ensure that child workers are no longer wronged.

Utilitarianism:

The final component of stakeholder theory focuses on finding win-win situations that benefit both the firm and stakeholders involved in a particular issue. This theory focuses on finding optimal solutions that are beneficial to every party with a stake in an issue.

After applying the rights and justice components of stakeholder theory, it is apparent that Nestlé's current approach to fixing the issue in the Ivory Coast is not utilitarian in nature. While the firm is succeeding in minimizing its reputation loss associated with the conflict, it is not taking significant measures to reduce the use of child and slave labor in its supply chains. Although the company has promised to reduce its dependence on unfair labor practices through process mapping and publishing of information, it is already being criticized for its failure to achieve these goals.

While it may be difficult for Nestlé to eradicate the use of illegal labor in the Ivory Coast, it can certainly do a better job of reducing it and can improve its brand at the same time. A utilitarian approach may be costly to the company in the short-term, but it can prove beneficial in the long term as the company leverages its benevolence in a concentrated marketing effort.

Virtue Theory:

While businesses theoretically exist solely to make profit and to satisfy customers and shareholders, there is growing pressure on businesses to act virtuously and in the interest of common good. For large organizations that focus less on corporate missions and more on financial figures, this idea can be frightening. Proper adherence to this philosophy, however, does not have to detract from profitability. When a corporation selects virtues to guide its operations, it essentially creates a brand that society can connect to. Conversely, a lack of virtues can also brand a company. In order to properly convey the choice Nestlé has in regard to virtue theory, this section will focus on three virtues relevant to the food industry: honesty, integrity, and efficiency-profitability.

Honesty:

Food consumers generally demand that the companies serving them be honest about their products. In some cases, this may mean that companies should honestly convey the nutritional value of what they are producing and selling. In the case of Nestlé, honesty pertains to the accurate dissemination of information on how the food was created and who was involved in the process.

Nestlé has taken a semi-honest approach to informing its customers. It has publicly acknowledged that slave labor contributed to its products, and has voiced an effort to fix the problem. For many people, this is enough reason to let Nestlé off the hook and to continue to buy its products. Nestlé has not been honest, however, in regards to solving the issue of child labor. Since 2009, the company has made little progress in altering its supply chains. Furthermore, it continues to keep information about slave labor unavailable to the public.

In 2012, Nestlé's vice president of operations, Jose Lopez, promised to work with NGOs to facilitate progress in the Ivory Coast. Additionally, he pledged Nestlé's support in helping Ivorian children enroll in schools. To this point, Nestlé is still relying on the Fair Labor Association to monitor its supply chains and is doing little on its own to meet these promises. Informed consumers may see this as a lack of honesty.

Seeing virtue theory as a potentially profitable strategy, Nestlé's deliverance on these promises would brand the organization as an up-front, honest organization. Achieving this feat would not only keep reputational loss at a minimum, it may also attract socially aware chocolate consumers who do not yet demonstrate a specific brand loyalty. Failure to be honest going forward, however, would certainly harm Nestlé. In conjunction with the idea of virtue theory, the company should invest in creating an honest, transparent brand image.

Integrity:

Although the word integrity takes on a number of different definitions, it will be defined within this report as a lack of corruption and a commitment to moral values. It is defined as such because it is easy to market these values to the public and because such values are generally viewed as good.

Recent evidence suggests that Nestlé is currently a company lacking integrity. While it may be working to fix the problem of unfair labor in the Ivory Coast, it continues to fund the problem at the same time. It can thus be stated that Nestlé is currently more worried about profitability than it is about meaningful social change. It is hard to blame Nestlé for this, as most successful companies follow a similar agenda.

Furthermore, Nestlé is operating in an industry in which integrity is not the most important criteria to consumers. The taste and quality of the product is ultimately the most valued feature that Nestlé can provide, with integrity being much further down on the scale of importance. With this in mind, Nestlé may feel little reason to change its operations to meet a set standard of integrity.

In setting a new standard for integrity throughout production procedures, Nestlé could once again set itself apart. Although children comprise the largest target market for Nestlé products, parents frequently purchase the product for their children. In that sense, adults with children are an equally important sub-segment. If Nestlé were to launch an integrity program and set a number of societal goals that improve the conditions in the Ivory Coast, the company could differentiate itself and drastically improve its reputation. It could make the public aware of any societal change it is making, branding it as a way of ensuring child happiness both domestically and internationally.

If Nestlé is truly changing its supply chains at this point in time and eliminating all ties to child labor, this strategy seems like a perfectly logical complement. Reducing slave and child labor is a moral decision, and Nestlé needs to leverage it in order to capitalize fully on this opportunity. Nestlé is not yet a company subscribing to the virtue of integrity, but it may be in corporate interest to do so.

Efficiency-Profitability:

Much like the profitability aspect of shareholder theory, this virtue views profitability and general efficiency of business as a moral obligation of a company. Ignoring all other moral principles, this virtue says that smart business practices and good management will lead to profitability.

Applying this theory, one may argue that Nestlé is successfully implementing this virtue throughout its production. The company is consistently a top-tier earner within the confectionery industry and has done so by cutting costs associated with labor. While this is not the only factor contributing to Nestlé's success, it has certainly been a prominent one.

Conversely, another side of efficiency-profitability could suggest that Nestlé does not employ this virtue. Because the company is currently undertaking measures that threaten its long-term success, the company may not have the right kind of profitability in mind. This debate conjures up arguments similar to those mentioned in the short-term and long-term approaches to shareholder theory. Because there is no one right answer within this debate, it is necessary to implement this virtue in conjunction with the other two specified. If the company is seeking to take an honest, integrity-driven approach to profitability and efficiency, it should shift its production away from plantations using child labor. If the firm's only desired virtue is profit, it should continue to purchase from plantations that are allegedly exploiting illegal labor.

Creating Ethical Corporate Culture:
Application of Trust and Total Integrity Management

So far, this report has analyzed the moral concern surrounding Nestlé's continuous involvement with plantations that exploit child labor and slaves in the Ivory Coast. It has also been made clear that Nestlé has choices in regards to this dilemma beyond changing suppliers and doing nothing at all. This report also addresses that Nestle is likely acting to preserve its reputation, and in turn, to protect management from additional coercive pressures from society. Ethical frameworks were then provided to analyze Nestlé's options and to highlight the benefits and harms associated with them.

Before a recommendation can be made, I think it important to emphasize the value of an ethical corporate culture. At this point, I fundamentally believe that Nestlé is lacking an ethical culture. In other words, it is my understanding that the company's actions are not reflective of a uniform ethical creed, but rather the desire to make money despite most any cost. Thus, I believe that Nestlé must not only create a new structure of ethical corporate culture, but also must make a sincere effort to incorporate it in all of its processes and to communicate it to the public. Achieving this would reduce Nestlé's likelihood of involvement in future ethical dilemmas and would create trust within the numerous factions of society. This idea of trust is central to total integrity management and the creation of an easily apparent ethical culture.

Hard Trust:

Hard trust refers to the law's ability to coerce corporations into acting in a responsible manner. This concept incorporates the laws that regulate business as well as the shareholders' ability to regulate the management and structure of a corporation. While Nestlé Chocolate has been successful in dodging legal entities and battling lawsuits, it should be seriously concerned about the directives of shareholders moving forward.

Nestlé's corporate stance promotes the well being of all people that are involved in the production and consumption of Nestlé products. Furthermore, the company promises social advancement in the areas in which it operates. The recent breach of this promise would be legitimate reason for shareholders to file a suit against management. Shareholders could demand that the company return to socially responsible practices, namely the immediate termination of child exploitation in the Ivory Coast. This would disastrous for Nestlé for a number of reasons

In 1919, the Dodge brothers filed a lawsuit on behalf of the shareholders of Ford Motor Company against Ford's management. Claiming that the company was not operating to profit its shareholders, the Dodge brothers sued the company to force change upon management and organizational structure. After winning the lawsuit, the Dodge brothers subsequently founded Dodge Motor Company, prompting many analysts to question the true motives behind the lawsuit.

Regardless of their intentions, the Dodge brothers and their collaborators in the suit demonstrated a very important principle that still holds true today —shareholders ultimately carry a large say over business conduct if they can adequately convey a corporate malpractice in a court of law. Although this particular example of a shareholder lawsuit was driven more by financial gain than it was by corporate ethics, it is not unreasonable to think that Nestlé's shareholders have legitimate ground upon which they could sue the parent company.

A lawsuit of this sort would thrust Nestlé into an extremely undesirable spotlight. As powerful as the efforts of NGOs and the government have been to this point, they have been conducted by outside parties. The involvement of Nestlé's shareholders would demonstrate to consumers that this is an issue beyond management's control. From a public relations standpoint, this damage would be much greater than the monetary damages incurred by the result of the lawsuit itself.

Therefore, the implementation of a solution must accompany a return to accountability within Nestlé's operations. Defining the moral issue is just as important as making an effort to fix it. In acknowledging that the company has been acting unethically, management can set a framework for avoiding similar issues in the future. In the case of hard trust, Nestlé may want to inform shareholders of a commitment to fixing this issue and returning to the values that shareholders bought into in the first place.

Real Trust:

Another form of trust that enables a corporation to create a widespread ethical culture is real trust. Real trust stresses that benevolence and corporate social responsibility are inherently good for business. Furthermore, the idea of real trust states that good business practices that are clearly identified result in tangible rewards for the organization implementing them.

Nestlé's lack of real trust has not been detrimental thus far. This is because Nestlé has not been fully exposed to this point. In my opinion, the corporation has made numerous ethical decisions that go against the idea of real trust. Even if Nestlé is acting responsibly at this point, the company has made no effort to publicize it. In contrast, the corporation has privatized its flow of supplies and has taken a quiet stance on the issue of unfair labor practices in the Ivory Coast and beyond. Furthermore, the company has not invested in any measures to combat unfair labor practices.

Much like in the bug-infested cookie vignette recited by Professor Fort, Nestlé Confectionery is currently violating the principles of real trust by evading tight control measures and processes that ensure accountability. In the vignette, the absence of proper accounting rules put a low-level employee in a difficult situation in which she has to decide whether or not to provide low-income consumers with contaminated cookies. Nestlé's lack of communication in regards to its supply of labor in the Ivory Coast may be viewed similarly —because accountability is not guaranteed by corporate procedures, there is no way to ensure that unethical action is not taking place.

I believe that Nestlé has a great opportunity to promote real trust within its organization by changing a few simple practices. If Nestlé is seriously committed to issues on human rights and social advancement of all people, it must vocalize this commitment. Fair trade is a trend that has been and will continue to be commercially successful. If Nestlé publicizes its labor chains and invests in improving the conditions for workers in the Ivory Coast and other similarly impacted areas, the company can create real trust in the eyes of consumers and Nestlé employees.

This strategy is important because Nestlé is currently acting against its stated corporate values. Just as Nestlé can create a culture of ethical behavior by improving its communication and visibility, it can ruin the reputation it still has by continuing to defy its own ethical creed. This idea is fundamental to the concept of real trust. If Nestlé makes conscious changes and incorporates them from this point, it can brand itself as a socially responsible and ethical company. Should the company not choose to do this, it will eventually be branded as an untruthful corporation that evades its promises.

Good Trust:

The last form of trust that pertains to the long-term implementation of corporate ethics is good trust. Unlike the other two forms of trust, good trust largely focuses on appeal to human emotion within the organization and beyond. Good trust states that responsiveness to stakeholders and customers ultimately pays off and that commitment to ethical behavior is something to be proud of.

In 1982, an ill-intentioned man placed poison in Tylenol packages in the Chicago metropolitan area. After the tainted packages killed 7 people, Tylenol recalled most all of its products on shelves and promised to resolve the issue. Although it was later revealed that Tylenol's production processes were not responsible for the deaths, the recall is still heralded by ethicists as a shining example of how to handle an ethical crisis. The recall cost Tylenol millions of dollars, yet helped brand the company as a truly concerned medical provider.

This story's longevity is a testament to the importance of good trust. Because Tylenol in a manner that reflected human interest rather than profit, people still talk about what the recall means to them. Much like folklore with moral implications, a good demonstration of ethics by a corporation gives consumers a tangible trust that is long lasting and durable. In Nestlé's case, a true commitment to ethical action could result in a similar outcome. Tylenol was able to leverage its ethical decision because of how available and well known its products are. Because Nestlé products are just as known to the public, ethical action taken by the company would be similarly received.

It is for this reason that Nestlé must complement an ethical corporate culture with a sense of good trust that people genuinely believe in. If the company takes action that successfully reduces slave labor in the Ivory Coast, the company can be a hero in the fight against unfair labor practices and exploitation of innocent people. With the idea of consumer and corporate trust in mind, I believe Nestlé has only one option in regards to this moral and ethical dilemma.

The Sweet Taste of Victory: Nestlé The Child Saver

When one considers all of the elements of this ethical dilemma, there is one fact that doesn't quite make sense. Nestlé has acknowledged the moral issue of unfair labor practices within its supply chain, has subsequently promised change, and has theoretically implemented some of it. After all of this, however, Nestlé has failed mightily in reassuring consumers that Nestlé Chocolate is as legitimate and as ethical as it was before the scandal. In accordance with a number of ethical perspectives mentioned earlier in this report, Nestlé's most necessary change must be the communication and framing of ethically oriented corporate action.

The first step that Nestlé must take to achieve this is to make its labor processes completely available to the public. In publishing information regarding the labor Nestlé Chocolate uses, the company can show consumers that the moral issue has subsided and that the product is one of integrity. This not only allows the company to act in accordance with virtue theory, it also creates a sense of real trust. These factors visibly contribute to an improved ethical culture within Nestlé Corporation.

This measure would also force Nestlé to do what many people believe it has not yet done: To abandon the child and slave labor that the company may still be using. The costs associated with monitoring the labor factors in Nestlé's operations are minuscule in comparison to the profitability of a slave-free, socially involved branding campaign. Although Nestlé will incur significant costs in making sure that they are not associated with any plantations that use unfair labor practices, the company will undoubtedly make up for them in leveraging its responsible corporate practice. Moreover, this is something that Nestlé should do simply because it is the right thing to do. Children are undeniably suffering due to Nestlé's lack of action. According to numerous components of stakeholder theory, Nestlé should see correction of the issue as a priority because of a moral obligation to do so.

Furthermore, the existence of an ethical corporation and a profitable one are not mutually exclusive. Nestlé can invest in social projects that benefit business and the stakeholders at the same time. For instance, Nestlé can keep its volume of production in the Ivory Coast at a constant if it creates its own plantations and ensures that those working there are treated with the highest level of care. This could include providing free medical care and basic education to young workers. In addition to this, the company could provide its own food products to workers, showing them that the corporation is one worth working for.

These measures would surely be a financial burden to the company in the short-term. In regards to this issue, however, I feel that the long-term approach to shareholder theory is most appropriate. Improving a corporation's reputation and structure may not create wealth for shareholders in the short-term, but it certainly adds value to the company moving forward. This means that wealth is created for shareholders at the same time.

Perhaps most importantly, however, an innovative correction process will create good trust that people remember when they see Nestlé Chocolate in superstore aisles. The company needs to view this dilemma as a business opportunity and not an unfortunate circumstance. Once the company has published its flows of labor, it can cater its advertisements and labels to demonstrate the company's commitment to the happiness and well being of its workers.

If there is anything that I seek to make clear, it is that Nestlé cannot and should not exit the Ivory Coast. Doing so would not only solidify Nestlé's negative impact on the region, it would also drastically change the company's operations. Nestlé obtains too much chocolate from the region to leave. Therefore, it must make sure that it continues to obtain the same yield from the Ivory Coast, just in a different manner.

In making significant but reasonable investment in the Ivory Coast, Nestlé can continue to produce quality products for consumers without compromising its output or costs in the future. While investment in social change and the promotion of fair labor practices will be costly, I fundamentally believe that the company has no other viable option at this point. This investment will not be a problem for the company, however, as it will contribute to the formation of a more wholesome ethical culture and will promote the company if the initiatives are marketed properly to consumers. If Nestlé fully commits to being a visibly good-intentioned company throughout its processes, this issue will be a distant memory and a very profitable business venture going forward.

WORKS CITED

Hawksley, Humphrey. "Nestle 'failing' on Child Labour Abuse, Says FLA Report." BBC News. BBC, 29 June 2012. Web. 28 Mar. 2013.

"Nestlé Advances Child Labor Battle Plan." The CNN Freedom Project Ending Modern Day Slavery RSS. N.p., n.d. Web. 28 Mar. 2013.

"Nestlé Sets out Actions to Address Child Labour in Response to Fair Labor Association Report on the Company's Cocoa Supply Chain." Http://www.nestle.com. N.p., n.d. Web. 28 Mar. 2013.

"Nestlé." Wikipedia. Wikimedia Foundation, 28 Mar. 2013. Web. 28 Mar. 2013.

"Nestle Audit Finds Child Labor Violations in Cocoa Supply." Bloomberg. N.p., n.d. Web. 25 Mar. 2013.

"Nestle's Slave Labor." Nestle's Slave Labor. N.p., n.d. Web. 28 Mar. 2013.

"Slave Chocolate?" Forbes. Forbes Magazine, n.d. Web. 28 Mar. 2013.

"Sweatshops and Post-Industrial Society: Conflicting Contemporary Phenomena." The Socjournal RSS. N.p., n.d. Web. 28 Mar. 2013

Costco: A Commitment To 'Conscious Capitalism'

Benjamin Besse

April 23, 2013

Business Law & Ethics Professor Tim Fort.

Background

When Jim Sinegal and Jeff Brotman opened the first Costco warehouse in 1983, they envisioned a company built upon an unshakable commitment to customers, employees, and shareholders.[27] Since 1983, Costco has grown to be the largest warehouse retailer in the United States, with over 450 locations and just under $100 billion in revenues.[28]

From the day of their founding until the present, Costco has remained true to its core ethical principles, offering employees some of the most coveted salary and benefits packages in the industry and restricting product markups to no more than 14% on goods sold in the warehouse stores.[29] In their 2005 letter to shareholders, Brotman and Sinegal remarked:

We remain committed to running our company and living conscientiously by our Code of Ethics every day: to obey the law; take care of our members; take care of our employees; respect our suppliers; and reward you, our shareholders.[30]

In upholding these standards, Costco has instituted a number of practices that have been heralded by many as the "conscious" capitalist enterprise. For employees, Costco is committed to a fair wage structure, with the average employee taking home $17 per hour, a staggering amount compared to industry standards, which hover just above minimum wage. Employees also enjoy a wide array of generous benefits options and a supportive work environment. Although labor-related costs account for approximately 70% of Costco's operating costs, the company enjoys a very low turnover rate, limited employee theft, high employee satisfaction, low union participation, and, ultimately, an improved customer experience.[31]

Costco also holds itself to impressive ethical standards in regards to their relationship with customers, or as the company refers to them, members. With a value-oriented

---

27 Costco Wholesale Corporation, History

28 Yahoo! Finance, Costco Wholesale Corporation Stock

29 Casico, "Decency Means More than "Always Low Prices": A Comparison of Costco to Wal-Mart's Sam's Club," 31

30 quoted in Casico 28

31 Casico, High Cost of Low Wages

approach to product procurement designed to appeal to a high-income clientele, Costco delivers high quality products for some of the lowest prices in the market. The warehouse club abides by a strict policy of maintaining profit margins on all goods at or below 14%, or 15% on Kirkland-brand items.[32]

Sinegal and other Costco leaders believe that the company's strategy of maintaining high ethical standards and fair business practices is rewarding to shareholders as well. According to Sinegal, shareholders can expect long-term strength and performance by Costco as a result of the goodwill and customer and employee loyalty stemming from the company's practices.[33]

II. Costco Faces Pressure From Wall Street

In 2004 and 2005, in the face of rising costs, Costco faced increased frustration from shareholders and financial analysts, who argued that the public company needed to adjust its policies to realign corporate directives with the interests of shareholders. Bill Dreher of Deutsche Bank argued that at Costco "it's better to an employee or a customer than a shareholder."[34] Analysts at C. Bernstein & Company echoed these concerns, adding, "Whatever goes to employees comes out of the pockets of shareholders."[35] Analysts and shareholders also pointed out that Costco's pricing strategy failed to take advantage of maximum potential for profits.

Costco's response to these criticisms was limited. Company executives made the decision to raise employees' share of health insurance costs from 4% to 8%, compared to the much higher industry standard of 25%. This marked the first increase in employee health premiums in over eight years. Beyond addressing the raising cost of health insurance, Costco made few other changes in response to Wall Street's criticisms.[36]

Sinegal's reaction to the censures of his management style was equally resolute. The CEO rebuffed the criticisms, stating, "On Wall Street, they're in the business of making money between now and next Thursday... we can't take that view. We want to build a company that will still be here 50 and 60 years from now." In defense of his employees and their compensation, Sinegal added, "that's not altruism, that's good business." Costco has not made any notable changes in policy since.[37]

Under the Hosmer framework, the alleged deprivation of shareholders of higher returns constitutes the injury in this morality case. Wall Street analysts and shareholders

---

32 Casico 31

33 Costco Wholesale Corporation, Costco Mission Statement and Code of Ethics

34 Casico 29

35 Neubert, "Wal-Mart Versus Costco: Is Wall Street Ready for Multistream Strategies?" 17

36 Greenhouse, "How Costco Became the Anti-Wal-Mart"

37 Greenhouse, "How Costco Became the Anti-Wal-Mart"

have expressed that the actions of Sinegal and other executives has negatively and unnecessarily impacted shareholder returns.

III. Alternatives

Alternative One: Acquiesce to Shareholder Requests

The first alternative course of action available to Sinegal and Costco management in response to the shareholder and analyst criticisms of the mid-2000's is to carry out the directives of those dissatisfied shareholders, lowering costs on employee compensation, raising product prices, and instituting other changes to realign Costco on a profit-centric course. This alternative would likely involve cutting employee compensation to near-industry-standard levels, in the case of Costco, a near 40% drop and dramatically increasing the employee share of other benefits, such as health insurance. Such an initiative would also likely entail eliminating Costco's commitment to low markups in their warehouse clubs, from the current 14% to over 30%, the industry standard.[38]

Alternative Two: Maintain Current Approach

The second alternative facing Sinegal is to maintain Costco's current approach to management and resource allocation. This is essentially the path Sinegal selected in 2005, when Costco did little more than adjust health insurance premiums for rising costs to address shareholder concerns that labor costs were hurting company performance.

Alternative Three: Compromise

The final alternative available to Costco in this case is to reconcile the interests of concerned shareholders and those of other involved stakeholders, primarily employees and customers. This approach might involve making modest cuts in employee compensation, while maintaining industry-leading status and improving product margins gradually, perhaps in line with rising costs.

IV. Personal Impacts

In the case of Costco, a company that between 2004 and 2005 faced competing interest between value-oriented shareholders, top management, and other firm stakeholders, immediate decision making power laid in the hands of CEO, Jim Sinegal. The decisions that Sinegal made, or could have made, held the potential to have a sizeable impact on his reputation and the perception of his character amongst the several parties involved.

From the perspective of profit-seeking shareholders, Sinegal's image would further deteriorate under Alternative Two, as they would view him as defying corporate compact in favor of lower ranking stakeholders. On the other hand, were Sinegal to adopt

---

38   Casico, High Cost of Low Wages

Alternatives One or Three, he would likely regain a certain level of trust and respect from his value-oriented shareholders and financial analysts.

From the perspective of other stakeholders, most notably employees and customers, however, the potential impact on Sinegal would be much different. Were Sinegal to violate his own credo to please shareholders, he may be viewed as violating the company's code of ethics- near sacrilege for Costco's employees and dedicated members. The impact of such actions would likely be much greater in comparison to shareholder appeasement. In terms of the Newspaper Test, Loved One Test, and Life Story Test, Sinegal would find himself in a compromised position if he were to pursue objectives that are not in line with Costco's corporate culture.

V. Shareholder Theory

Lawful Directives of Costco Shareholders

The lawful directives, as they pertain to this case, of Costco shareholders are well manifested in Costco's Mission Statement and Code of Ethics, both of which are determined by shareholder committees.[39,40] The Mission Statement stipulates that Costco management should act "to continually provide [their] members with quality goods at the lowest possible prices."[41] To achieve this mission, the Nominating and Governance Committee issues a Code of Ethics, which ranks corporate objectives, by importance, as follows: (1) Obey the law, (2) Take care of our members, (3) Take care of our employees, (4) Respect our suppliers, and (5) Reward our shareholders.[42]

The Code of Ethics explicitly states the importance of carrying out Costco's commitments to the law, members, employees, and suppliers before returning profits to their shareholders. This directive stands in direct opposition to the wishes of the shareholder and analyst criticisms of 2004 and 2005. Following these guidelines reveals that Sinegal and other Costco executives are not in fact acting out of personal taste or preference, which Friedman and other proponents of Shareholder Theory have argued amounts to theft. The socially responsible directives of the shareholders, however, violates Hayek's model of shareholder theory, under which he argues socially responsible companies lead to Socialism.

---

39   Costco Wholesale Corporation, Corporate Governance Guidelines of Costco Wholesale Corporation

40   Costco Wholesale Corporation, Nominating and Governance Committee Charter.

41   Costco Wholesale Corporation, Costco Mission Statement and Code of Ethics

42   Costco Wholesale Corporation, Costco Mission Statement and Code of Ethics

Short-Term Perspective

There are two ways to approach the short-term perspective of shareholder theory in the Costco case. The first involves measuring Costco executives' actions against the traditional, more widely accepted iteration of Shareholder Theory—that the legal directives of shareholders often prioritize the maximization of profit. The second, and more meaningful approach is to measure Costco executives' actions against the corporation's actual shareholder directives, as described previously.

Under the traditional interpretation of shareholder theory—shareholders directing management act in a manner that maximizes shareholder wealth, Costco management has fallen short. The company's commitment to lowering customer cost and offering generous employee compensation has eroded the short-term profits of the corporation.

If Costco were to compensate employees in line with market trends, the company would see an immediate cost savings of approximately 20% in cost of operations. If the company also increased margins just two percent, arguably a negligible amount given Costco's cost leadership status in the industry, on all goods sold in their warehouse store, operating income would surge in the short term. The combination of these two hypothetical initiatives would result in an estimated $3.89 billion increase in net income in the immediate short term. This would represent a hypothetical increase in net income for fiscal 2012 of over 225%.[43]

Under Costco's actual shareholder directives, however, management has performed much better following the Shareholder Theory framework. Costco management has taken a steadfast approach to the first provision of the Code of Ethics, as Costco has not experienced any major legal violations through the present. Under directive two, taking care of members, Costco executives have also excelled. Customers are rewarded with the lowest prices in the industry and a commitment to low margins to help members save money. As such, Costco has garnered an extremely loyal following of members. Management has been equally successful in caring for employees, as discussed previously, with excellent compensation and benefits. Under directive four, Costco management is ordered to take care of the company's suppliers. Executives have done acceptably in this area—the company has repeatedly cut ties with suppliers when not offered the lowest prices, but rewards loyal suppliers with extremely large orders.[44],[45]

If the aforementioned objectives are carried out successfully, the Code of Ethics calls for rewarding shareholders by providing them with a return on their money

---

43   Yahoo! Finance, Costco Wholesale Corporation Stock

44   Greenhouse, "How Costco Became the Anti-Wal-Mart"

45   Casico, "Decency Means More than "Always Low Prices": A Comparison of Costco to Wal-Mart's Sam's Club"

invested in the corporation. In the short term, success of this objective can vary for Costco management, as they prioritize other stakeholders at times. Despite these varying trends, Costco has rewarded shareholders very generously in the long term.

Long-Term Perspective

Viewing the shareholder theory from a long-term perspective reveals an equally flattering image of Costco management. They have succeeded at obeying the law and taking care of members, employees, and suppliers, extending the benefits of the short term into the long term. The benefits extended to all three of these stakeholders have been consistent from the opening of Costco's first store until the present.

In terms of rewarding shareholders, Costco has excelled over the long term. Since Costco's initial public offering in 1985, the company's stock has appreciated by nearly 900%. In comparison to Costco's competitors who are more profit-oriented, this is an astounding return. The following chart demonstrates the performance of Costco (COST) stock in comparison to Walmart (WMT), the owner of Sam's Club and one of Costco's largest competitors, over the past ten years. This includes the period of 2004 to 2005, when some Costco shareholders and financial analysts issued criticisms of the company's management.

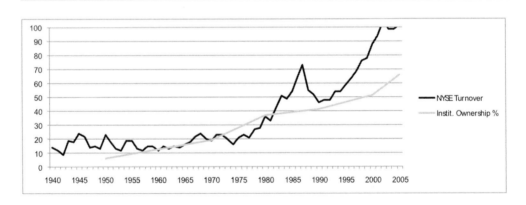

Source: Brancato and Rabimov, Conference Board, "The 2008 Institutional Investment Report"; New York Stock Exchange Fact Book (2006).

The performance of Costco stock over this period clearly demonstrates that Costco has rewarded its shareholders with astounding stock appreciation and dividends over the long term. Furthermore, the comparison to Walmart demonstrates that the profit-driven approach to business advocated by financial analysts and some shareholders, and adamantly opposed by Sinegal, did not serve Walmart well. During the 2004 to 2005 period, Costco stock appreciated nearly 50%, while Walmart stock dropped in value over the same period.

VI. Stakeholder Theory

The primary stakeholders involved in the case of conflict between Costco management and its profit-motivated critics include: shareholders, management (including CEO Jim Sinegal), employees, suppliers, and members.

Rights

Based on the analysis herein, it does not appear that there are any basic rights at stake in the case of Costco and their critical shareholders. While critics called for slashing employee and member benefits, the suggested measures do not interfere with the basic rights of either party. The rights that are being contested in the case are the right of shareholders to the profits (or potential profits) of the corporation and the right of members and employees to fair prices, fair wages, and fair benefits.

The claims by shareholders and analysts that their right to profits is being violated echoes the issues introduced in the case Dodge v. Ford, in which Dodge emerged the victor. This varies in the case of Costco, however, as Costco stock has appreciated significantly, delivering some form of significant shareholder wealth. The claims also relate to those of the Wrigley v. Shlensky case, however. The practices of Costco's competitors have not been proved to be more profitable or equitable to negligence on the part of Costco management, especially in the long run.

The rights of customers and employees to fair prices and wages, respectively, are included in Costco's Code of Ethics and, while not the industry standard, have strong support from Sinegal and other Costco loyalists.

In attempting to minimize harm and the violation of rights in this case, it is concluded that following the directives of Costco critics would result in greater harm overall, as employees would lose highly valued compensation and customers would lose the value and trust they have come to treasure. In return, shareholder may enjoy some heightened profits in the short term, but the long-term feasibility of these objectives is untested and not highly reliable, especially under Sinegal's allegations that Costco's success is founded in these principles.

Justice

The justice interpretation of Stakeholder Theory also favors Costco members and employees. Given the marked returns to shareholders over the disputed period, especially in comparison to industry competitors, the most vulnerable parties appear to be both employees and members. Employees are vulnerable to a shift in their standard of living and dramatic changes in wage were Costco to cut costs in this area. Customers are also vulnerable to an increase in margins if Costco were to abandon their commitment to low markups. The shareholder majority may also be considered a vulnerable part in this case, as they have issued the current directives and Code of Ethics for Costco management and claim that these are the basis of their financial success. Therefore, under the principles of fairness and equality, Costco should act to protect the most vulnerable stakeholders, in this case by continuing on their current course and ignoring the criticisms of profit-driven shareholders.

This is likely also the case under the social justice framework. Under the veil of ignorance, Costco shareholders and management would likely act to protect employee wages and customer prices, as these parties are the most vulnerable to dramatic shifts in policy. Additionally, the potential rewards for shareholders are not proven.

Utilitarianism

For Costco, carrying out the utilitarian outcome of Shareholder Theory mirror the actions to be taken under the long-term context of Shareholder Theory. The greatest good for the greatest number of stakeholders will result when Costco maintains their current policies. This is particularly true upon taking into account the apparent positive impact of Costco's ethical business operations of shareholder wealth in comparison to their competitive rivals. Following such evidence, adopting the suggested practices of critics may actually result in no heightened good for any stakeholders, especially in the long run, thus positioning the company in a utilitarian-inferior position.

VIII. Virtue Theory

The three virtues most closely related to the case of Costco are integrity, efficiency-profitability, and respect. Integrity is relevant to the case as Costco management, particularly Sinegal, argue that in order to operate with integrity, the company must take account of stakeholder interests beyond its shareholders. This ideal is challenged by profit-oriented shareholders and financial analysts in 2004 and 2005, both of whom argue for a more purely capitalistic approach to business that values efficiency and profitability in operations. Improved financial efficiency and profitability, they argue, will result in more sizeable shareholder return. Finally, respect is relevant to the case as Sinegal argues that in order to carry out the company's standards, Costco must maintain a high level of respect for the law, their employees, suppliers, customers, and shareholders.

Integrity

In the context of Costco, integrity is defined as the quality of acting in a manner that is honest to one's moral and ethic values, which themselves are characterized by strength and uprightness. For Costco, this signifies acting in a way that is true to the company's Code of Ethics. As described previously, Costco management under Sinegal has performed extremely well in operating in a fashion that protects customers, employees, suppliers, and shareholders.

Efficiency-Profitability

Efficiency-profitability, as it relates to Costco is defined as acting in a way that maximizes the potential of available resources, resulting in a positive return for shareholders. At Costco, the strength of this virtue is difficult to determine. The company has long been profitable, although some argue that efficiency and profitability could be easily improved. While this may be the case, it is also possible that by improving efficiency and profitability at Costco, the other chosen virtues may be compromised.

Respect

Respect is defined as to hold in a heightened regard for reasons relating to abilities, qualities, or achievements. For Costco, this means respecting all stakeholders, including shareholders. The case surrounding the criticisms of the mid-2000s involves an alleged tradeoff between the corporation's respect for profit-driven shareholders and their interests and the corporation's respect for other stakeholders. According to Sinegal, treating employees, members, and supplier with respect involved rewarding them with fair prices and wages. The CEO adds that strongly believes that by respecting its other stakeholders, Costco is demonstrating great respect for its shareholders.

IX. Total Integrity Management

Hard Trust

Being a United State corporation, Costco is subject to a myriad of complex corporate laws and regulations, including but not limited to the Internal Revenue Code, legal responsibilities of executives and management, such as Sarbanes-Oxley, employment laws, competitiveness and consumer protection regulation, and financial regulatory law. Additionally, Costco must adhere to their corporate mission statement, code of conduct, and various other bylaws established by the shareholders under the direction of the Board of Directors.

In addition to being accountable to the law, a responsibility Costco has explicitly stated in their Code of Ethics (in fact, "Obey the Law" is the first directive in the code), the corporation had also established stringent internal accountability standards.[46] For example, the corporation maintains an audit committee, which reports to the Board of Directors, which must adhere to strict guidelines for monitoring management actions, suggesting changes when appropriate, and facilitating the independent auditing process.[47]

---

46   Costco Wholesale Corporation, Costco Code of Ethics

47   Costco Wholesale Corporation, Audit Committee Charter

Real Trust

Public opinion of Costco, particularly that of its members, reveals that the company exhibits strong Real Trust. The company and its management are committed to a fair working environment for their employees and a fair market for their millions of customers, as discussed in previous sections. Jim Sinegal established a set of integral truths for Costco from its earliest days, and the company is exemplary of a corporation holding itself to its own values over the long run.

Costco's commitment to creating Real Trust is further exhibited by the corporation's involvement in the Conscious Capitalism movement. Conscious Capitalism is defined by four key elements: the existence of a higher purpose, the aligning of stakeholder interests around the higher purpose, conscious leadership, and conscious culture. Costco embodies all of these characteristics.[48]

Good Trust

Costco's commitment to the Conscious Capitalism movement is representative of the company's Real Trust, but also of its Good Trust. Costco and its leadership have succeeded, from early on, in identifying what "moves" their employees, customers, and other stakeholders and have succeeded in rallying them around their core ethical truths. There is limited evidence of mediating institutions and other hard evidence of Good Trust at Costco, but interviews with employees and management often reveal an inherent drive towards ethical and moral excellence—particularly in the case of the founder and former CEO Jim Sinegal. "Stories" play a rather significant role in employees' explanations of Good Trust at Costco and provide evidence for the ethical quests woven into workplace life.

X. Conclusions

Based on the analysis of Costco management's dilemma in regards to the shareholder and analyst criticism of 2004 and 2005 described herein, it is evident that Costco management made the correct, most universally beneficial, and most ethical decision. Under all three ethical frameworks, Alternative Two, or maintaining the company's current approach, results in the superior outcome for Costco.

Costco should continue their stellar efforts to promote Total Integrity Management, from their intransigent accountability to the law and their own codes to their support for ethical quests like Conscious Capitalism. Promoting Hard Trust, Real Trust, and Good Trust in the years to come will continue to prove extremely beneficial for Costco, from both a moral and economic perspective.

---

48   Whitford, "Can compassionate capitalists really win?"

WORKS CITED

Cascio, Wayne F. "Decency Means More than "Always Low Prices": A Comparison of Costco to Wal-Mart's Sam's Club." Academy of Management Perspectives 20.3 (2006): 26-37. JSTOR. Web. 24 Mar. 2013.

Cascio, Wayne. "The High Cost of Low Wages." Harvard Business Review: Web. 24 Mar. 2013.

Costco Wholesale Corporation. Audit Committee Charter. Rep. Issaquah: Costco Wholesale Corporation, 2011.

Costco Wholesale Corporation. Corporate Governance Guidelines of Costco Wholesale

Corporation. Rep. Issaquah: Costco Wholesale Corporation, 2011.

Costco Wholesale Corporation. Costco Mission Statement and Code of Ethics. Rep. Issaquah: Costco Wholesale Corporation, 2010.

Costco Wholesale Corporation. "History." Costco. Web. 24 Mar. 2013.

Costco Wholesale Corporation. Nominating and Governance Committee Charter. Rep. Issaquah: Costco Wholesale Corporation, 2011.

Greenhouse, Steven. "How Costco Became the Anti-Wal-Mart." *New York Times* [New York] 17 July 2005.

Neubert, Mitchell. "Wal-Mart Versus Costco: Is Wall Street Ready for Multistream Strategies?" Management in Practice. By Bruno Dyck. Boston: Houghton Mifflin Harcourt, 2010. 17.

Whitford, David. "Can compassionate capitalists really win?" Fortune. [New York] 30 March 2011.

Yahoo! Finance. "Costco Wholesale Corporation Stock." Yahoo!. Web. 24 Mar. 2013.

INDEX

HOSMER 6's

1. Identify moral Issue
2. Add other Information: Information maker had no Idea about. Things the decision maker had no due about at the time.
3. Available Alternatives: Change in Marketing strategy.
4. Personal Impacts: Name a person and his perspective.
5. Tools: Newspaper, Loved One, Tombstone.